MCAT®

Verbal Reasoning & Writing Review

The Staff of The Princeton Review

Random House, Inc. New York

The Princeton Review

The Princeton Review, Inc.
2315 Broadway
New York, NY 10024
E-mail: editorialsupport@review.com

ISBN: 978-0-375-42796-1
ISSN: 2150-8909

Editor: Laura Braswell
Production Coordinator: Kim Howie
Production Editor: Kristen O'Toole

Printed in China.

10 9 8 7 6 5 4 3 2 1

Editorial

Rob Franek, VP Test Prep Books, Publisher
Seamus Mullarkey, Editorial Director
Laura Braswell, Senior Editor
Rebecca Lessem, Senior Editor
Heather Brady, Editor
Selena Coppock, Editor

Production Services

Scott Harris, Executive Director, Production Services
Kim Howie, Senior Graphic Designer
Ryan Tozzi, Production Manager

Production Editorial

Meave Shelton, Production Editor
Jennifer Graham, Production Editor
Kristen O'Toole, Production Editor

Random House Publishing Team

Tom Russell, Publisher
Nicole Benhabib, Publishing Manager
Ellen L. Reed, Production Manager
Alison Stoltzfus, Associate Managing Editor
Elham Shabahat, Publishing Assistant

CONTRIBUTORS

Jennifer S. Wooddell
>   Senior Author and Editor

Edited for Production by
Judene Wright, M.S., M.A.Ed.
>   National Content Director, MCAT Program, The Princeton Review

Jennifer and Judene would like to thank the following people for their contributions to this book:

Elizabeth Aamot (Fatith), John Bahling, M.D., Gary Bedford, Jessica Burstrem, M.A., Alix Claps, M.A., Cynthia Cowan, B.A., Sara Daniel, B.S., Cory Eicher, B.A., (James) Ben Gill, Jacqueline R. Giordano, Gina Granter, M.A., Corinne Harol, Christopher Hinkle, Th.D., Alison Howard, Paul Kugelmass, Jay Lee, Rohit Madani, B.S., Mike Matera, B.A., Ashleigh Menhadji, Katherine Montgomery, Don Osborne, Rupal Patel, B.S., Vivek Patel, Tyler Peikes, Nadia Reynolds, M.A., Maryam Shambayati, M.S., Angela Song, Kate Speiker, David Stoll, Jonathan Swirsky, Neil Thornton, Laura Tubelle de González, and David Weiskopf, M.A.

VERBAL REASONING CONTENTS

CONTENTS

WRITING SAMPLE CONTENTS

CONTENTS

Chapter 1
Introduction

SO YOU WANT TO BE A DOCTOR

So...you want to be a doctor. If you're like most premeds, you've wanted to be a doctor since you were pretty young. When people asked you what you wanted to be when you grew up, you always answered "a doctor." You had toy medical kits, bandaged up your dog or cat, and played hospital. You probably read your parents' home medical guides for fun.

When you got to high school you took the honors and AP classes. You studied hard, got straight As (or at least really good grades!), and participated in extracurricular activities so you could get into a good college. And you succeeded!

At college you knew exactly what to do. You took your classes seriously, studied hard, and got a great GPA. You talked to your professors and hung out at office hours to get good letters of recommendation. You were a member of the premed society on campus, volunteered at hospitals, and shadowed doctors. All that's left to do now is get a good MCAT score.

Just the MCAT.

Just the most confidence-shattering, most demoralizing, longest, most brutal entrance exam for any graduate program. At 5.5 hours (including breaks), the MCAT tops the list... even the closest runners up, the LSAT and GMAT, are only about 4 hours long. The MCAT tests significant science content knowledge along with the ability to think quickly, reason logically, read comprehensively, and write clearly, all under the pressure of a timed exam.

The path to a good MCAT score is not as easy to see as the path to a good GPA or the path to a good letter of recommendation. The MCAT is less about what you know, and more about how to apply what you know...and how to apply it quickly to new situations. Because the path might not be so clear, you might be worried. That's why you picked up this book.

We promise to demystify the MCAT for you, with clear descriptions of the different sections, how the test is scored, and what the test experience is like. We will help you understand general test-taking techniques as well as provide you with specific techniques for each section. In this book, we'll give you strategies for the Verbal Reasoning and Writing Sample sections, while our other MCAT subject books review the science content. We'll show you the path to a good MCAT score and help you walk that path.

After all...you want to be a doctor. And we want you to succeed.

WHAT IS THE MCAT...REALLY?

You might want to approach the MCAT as though it were a typical college science test, one in which facts and knowledge simply need to be regurgitated in order to do well. You might think you can study for the MCAT the same way you did for college tests, by memorizing facts and details, formulas and equations. You can't!

It's a myth that the MCAT is purely a content-knowledge test. If medical school admission committees want to see what you know, all they have to do is look at your transcripts. What they really want to see, though, is how you *think*. Especially, how you think under pressure. And *that's* what your MCAT score will tell them.

The MCAT is really a test of your ability to apply basic knowledge to different, possibly new, situations. It's a test of your ability to reason out and evaluate arguments. It's a test of your ability to communicate ideas. Do you still need to know your science content? Absolutely. But not at the level that most test-takers think they need to know it. Furthermore, your science knowledge won't help you on the Verbal Reasoning or Writing Sample sections. So how do you study for a test like this?

You study for the science sections by reviewing the basics and then applying them to MCAT practice questions (more information about the specific sciences on the MCAT can be found in their respective *MCAT Review* books).

You study for the Verbal Reasoning section by learning how to adapt your existing reading and analytical skills to the nature of the test. Because Verbal Reasoning does not test content knowledge, it's all about technique: approaching the passages in a way that maximizes your accuracy and efficiency in answering questions. To accomplish this, you need to learn the ways in which passages are organized, the types of questions that appear, how to extract and evaluate information provided in the passage in a way that is appropriate for those question types, and most importantly, how to recognize and eliminate wrong answers. The book you are holding will teach you all of these things.

This book also prepares you for the Writing Sample by teaching you about the question topics; how the questions are structured; and how to write a clear, cohesive, organized, and well-developed essay.

You have well more than a few hundred questions in this book to help you prepare, practice, and refine your approach to the Verbal Reasoning and Writing Sample sections. You also have online access to more practice passages and full-length exams to further hone your skills.

MCAT NUTS AND BOLTS

Overview

The MCAT is a computer based test (CBT) that is *not* adaptive. Adaptive tests base your next question on whether or not you've answered the current question correctly. The MCAT is *linear*, or *fixed-form*, meaning that the questions are in a predetermined order and do not change based on your answers. However, there are many versions of the test, so that on a given test day, different people will see different versions. The following table highlights the features of the MCAT exam.

Registration	Online via www.aamc.org. Begins as early as six months prior to test date; available up until week of test (subject to seat availability).
Testing Centers	Administered at small, secure, climate-controlled computer testing rooms.
Security	Photo ID with signature, electronic fingerprint, electronic signature verification, assigned seat.
Proctoring	None. Test administrator checks examinee in and assigns seat at computer. All testing instructions are given on the computer.
Frequency of Test	28 times per year distributed over January, March, April, May, June, July, August, and September.
Format	Exclusively computer-based. NOT an adaptive test.
Length of Test Day	5.5 hours.
Breaks	Optional 10-minute breaks between sections.
Number of Questions and Timing	52 Physical Sciences (PS), 70 minutes. 40 Verbal Reasoning (VR), 60 minutes. 2 Essays for the Writing Sample (WS), 30 minutes each. 52 Biological Sciences (BS), 70 minutes.
Essay Grading	Two graders, one human and one computer, with a third (human) grader if scores differ.
Scoring	Test is scaled. Several forms per administration. PS, VR, and BS receive scaled scores of 1–15, WS receives scaled score of J–T.
Allowed/Not allowed	No timers/watches. No ear plugs. Noise reduction headphones available. Scratch paper and pencils given at start of test and taken at end of test. Locker or secure area provided for personal items.
Results: Timing and Delivery	Approximately 30 days. Electronic scores only, available online through AAMC login. Examinees can print official score reports.
Maximum Number of Retakes	Can be taken a maximum of three times per year, but an examinee can be registered for only one date at a time.

Registration

Registration for the exam is completed online at www.aamc.org/students/mcat. The AAMC opens registration for a given test date at least two months in advance of the date, often earlier. It's a good idea to register well in advance of your desired test date to make sure that you get a seat.

Sections

There are four sections on the MCAT exam: Physical Sciences (PS), Verbal Reasoning (VR), Writing Sample (WS), and Biological Sciences (BS). The PS, VR, and BS sections consist of multiple-choice questions, while the WS section consists of two essays.

Section	Concepts Tested	Number of Questions and Timing
Physical Sciences	Basic concepts in physics and general chemistry, data analysis, basic non-calculus math, critical reasoning skills.	52 questions, 70 minutes, approximately 50% physics and 50% general chemistry.
Verbal Reasoning	Reading comprehension and critical thinking.	40 questions, 60 minutes.
Writing Sample	Organizational skills and written communication.	2 essay prompts, 30 minutes each.
Biological Sciences	Basic concepts in biology and organic chemistry, data analysis, critical reasoning skills.	52 questions, 70 minutes, approximately 80% biology and 20% organic chemistry.

Most questions on the MCAT (39 out of 52 on the science sections, all 40 in the VR section) are *passage-based*, and each section of the test will have a total of seven passages. A passage consists of a few paragraphs of information on which several following questions are based. In the science sections, passages often include equations or reactions, tables, graphs, figures, and experiments to analyze. Verbal Reasoning passages come from literature in the social sciences, humanities, and natural sciences and do not test content knowledge in any way.

Some questions in the science sections are *freestanding questions* (FSQs). These questions are independent of any passage information. These questions appear in three groups of between three and five questions, and are interspersed throughout the passages. There are 13 freestanding questions in each of the science sections and the remaining 39 questions are passage-based.

Each section on the MCAT is separated by a 10-minute break:

Section	Time
Test Center Check-In	Variable, can take up to 40 minutes if center is busy.
Tutorial	10 minutes
Physical Sciences	70 minutes
Break	10 minutes
Verbal Reasoning	60 minutes
Break	10 minutes
Writing Sample	60 minutes
Break	10 minutes
Biological Sciences	70 minutes
Void Option	5 minutes
Survey	10 minutes

The survey includes questions about your satisfaction with the overall MCAT experience, including registration, check-in, etc., as well as questions about how you prepared for the test.

Scoring

The MCAT is a scaled exam, meaning that your raw score will be converted into a scaled score that takes into account the difficulty of the questions. There is no guessing penalty. The PS, VR, and BS sections are scaled from 1–15 and the WS section is scaled from J–T. Because different versions of the test have varying levels of difficulty, the scale will be different from one exam to the next. Thus, there is no "magic number" of questions to get right in order to get a particular score. Plus, some of the questions on the test are considered "experimental" and do not count toward your score; they are just there to be evaluated for possible future inclusion in a test.

To generate a score for the WS section, each essay is scored twice, and the total raw score is the sum of the four individual scores. The individual scores can range from 1–6. All of the individual numerical scores are then added together and averaged to generate a single alphabetic score ranging from J (lowest) to T (highest).

At the end of the test (after you complete the Biological Science section), you will be asked to choose one of the following two options, "I wish to have my MCAT exam scored" or "I wish to VOID my MCAT exam." You have 5 minutes to make a decision, and if you do not select one of the options in that time, the test will automatically be scored. If you choose the VOID option, your test will not be scored (you will not now, or ever, get a numerical score for this test), medical schools will not know you took the test, and no refunds will be granted. You cannot "unvoid" your scores at a later time.

Even though we can't tell you a specific number of questions to get right in order to receive a particular score, we can tell you the percentile numbers that the scores correspond with. The percentile numbers tell you what percent of examinees scored lower or higher than you. For example, if you are in the 90th percentile, then 90% of examinees scored lower than you did, and 10% scored higher.

Score	Physical Sciences Percentile*	Verbal Reasoning Percentile*	Biological Sciences Percentile*
14–15	100%	100%	100%
13	97%	99%	97%
12	91%	96%	92%
11	82%	91%	80%
10	69%	75%	64%
9	52%	53%	41%
8	37%	35%	23%
7	22%	22%	12%
6	11%	14%	7%
5	4%	7%	4%
4	2%	4%	2%
3	1%	2%	1%
2	0%	1%	0%
1	0%	0%	0%

Avg score 9.3, std dev 2.3   Avg score 9.0, std dev 2.3   Avg score 9.8, std dev 2.1

Total Score	Percentile*	Writing Sample Score	Percentile*
42–45	100	T	100
39	99	S	99
36	95	R	93
33	85	Q	81
30	66	P	60
27	43	O	49
24	25	N	35
21	13	M	25
18	6	L	6
15	3	K	2
12	1	J	0
9	0		
6	0		
3	0		

Avg score 28.1, std dev 5.6

75th percentile = Q
50th percentile = P
25th percentile = M

*Data from *The Official Guide to the MCAT Exam*, 2009 ed., © 2009 Association of American Medical Colleges

So, what's a good score? Most people would agree that since the average total score on the MCAT is around 28, you want to at least hit that number. To be competitive, you really want scores in the low 30s, and for the top-ranked medical schools, you'll want scores in the high 30s to low 40s. If your GPA is on the low side, you'll need higher MCAT scores to compensate, and if you have a strong GPA, you can get away with lower MCAT scores. But the reality is that your chances of acceptance depend on a lot more than just your MCAT scores. It's a combination of your GPA, your MCAT scores, your undergraduate course work, letters of recommendation, experience related to the medical field (such as volunteer work or research), extracurricular activities, your personal statement, etc. Medical schools are looking for a complete package, not just good scores and a good GPA.

GENERAL TEST-TAKING STRATEGIES

CBT Tools

There are a number of tools available on the test, including highlighting, strike-outs, the Mark button, the Review button, the Exhibit button, Writing Sample tools, and of course, scratch paper. The following is a brief description of each tool.

1. **Highlighting:** This is done in passage text only (including table entries and some equations, but excluding figures and molecular structures) by clicking and dragging the cursor over the desired text. To remove the highlighted portion, just click over the highlighted text. Note that highlights DO NOT persist once you leave the passage.
2. **Strike-outs:** This is done on the various answer choices by clicking over the answer choice that you wish to eliminate. As a result, the entire set of text associated with that answer choice is crossed out. The strike-out can be removed by clicking again. Note that you cannot strike-out figures or molecular structures, and strike-outs DO persist after leaving the passage.
3. **Mark button:** This is available for each question and allows you to flag the question as one you would like to review later if time permits. When clicked, the "Mark" button turns red and says "Marked."
4. **Review button:** This button is found near the bottom of the screen, and when clicked, brings up a new screen showing all questions and their status (either "answered," "unanswered," or "marked"). You can then choose one of three options: "review all," "review unanswered," or "review marked." You can only review questions in the section of the MCAT you are currently taking, but this button can be clicked at any time during the allotted time for that section; you do NOT have to wait until the end of the section to click it.
5. **Exhibit button:** Clicking this button will open a periodic table. Note that the periodic table is originally large, covering most of the screen. However, this window can be resized to see the questions and a portion of the periodic table at the same time. The table text will not decrease, but scroll bars will appear on the window so that you can center the section of the table in which you are interested in the resized window.
6. **Writing Sample:** Simple cutting, copying, and pasting will be allowed in this section through the use of buttons on the screen, but no keyboard shortcuts are available. There is no spell-check.
7. **Scratch paper:** You will be given four pages (eight faces) of scratch paper at the start of the test. While you may ask for more at any point during the test, your first set of paper will be collected before you receive fresh paper. Scratch paper is only useful if it is kept organized; do not give in to the tendency to write on the first available open space! Good organization

will be very helpful when/if you wish to review a question. Indicate the passage number in a box near the top of your scratch work, and indicate which question you are working on in a circle to the left of the notes for that question. Draw a line under your scratch work when you change passages to keep the work separate. Do not erase or scribble over any previous work. If you do not think it is correct, draw one line through the work and start again. You may have already done some useful work without realizing it.

Pacing

Since the MCAT is a timed test, you must keep an eye on the timer and adjust your pacing as necessary. It would be terrible to run out of time at the end to discover that the last few questions could have been easily answered in just a few seconds each.

If you complete every question, in the science sections you will have about one minute and 20 seconds (1:20) per question, and in the Verbal Reasoning section you will have about one minute and 30 seconds per question (1:30).

Section	# of Questions in Passage	Approximate time (including reading the passage)
Physical Sciences and Biological Sciences	5	6.5–7 minutes
	6	8 minutes
	7	9–9.5 minutes
Verbal Reasoning	5	7.5 minutes
	6	9 minutes
	7	10.5 minutes

When starting a passage in the science sections, make note of how much time you will allot for it, and the starting time on the timer. Jot down on your scratch paper what the timer should say at the end of the passage. Then just keep an eye on it as you work through the questions. If you are near the end of the time for that passage, guess on any remaining questions, make some notes on your scratch paper (remember that highlighting disappears), Mark the questions, and move on. Come back to those questions if you have time.

For Verbal Reasoning, one important thing to keep in mind is that most people will maximize their score by *not* trying to complete every question, or every passage, in the section. A good strategy for a majority of test takers is to complete six of the seven passages, randomly guessing on one passage. This allows you to have good accuracy on the passages you complete, and to maximize your total percent correct in the section as a whole. To complete six of the passages, you should spend about 8 minutes on a five-question passage, 9 minutes on a six-question passage, and 10 minutes on a seven-question passage. That is, a total of about 3 minutes plus 1 minute for each question ("# of Q + 3").

To help maximize your number of correct answer choices in any section, do the questions and passages within that section in the order *you* want to do them in. Skip over the more difficult questions (guess and Mark them), and answer the questions you feel most comfortable with first.

Process of Elimination

Process of elimination (POE) is probably the most useful technique you have to tackle MCAT questions. Since there is no guessing penalty, POE allows you to increase your probability of choosing the correct answer by eliminating those you are sure are wrong. If you are guessing between a couple of choices, use the CBT tools to your advantage:

1. Strike out any choices that you are sure are incorrect or do not answer the issue addressed in the question.
2. Jot down some notes on your scratch paper to help clarify your thoughts if you return to the question.
3. Use the Mark button to flag the question for review at a later time. (Note, however, that in the Verbal Reasoning section, you generally should not be returning to rethink questions once you have moved on to a new passage.)
4. Do not leave it blank! If you are not sure and you have already spent more than 60 seconds on that question, just pick one of the remaining choices. If you have time to review it at the end, you can always debate the remaining choices based on your previous notes.
5. If three of the four answer choices have been eliminated, the remaining choice must be the correct answer. Don't waste time pondering *why* it is correct, just click it and move on. The MCAT doesn't care if you truly understand why it's the right answer, only that you have the right answer selected.

Guessing

Remember, there is NO guessing penalty on the MCAT. NEVER leave a question blank!

SECTION SPECIFICS

Question Types

In the science sections of the MCAT, the questions fall into one of three main categories.

1. Memory questions: These questions can be answered directly from prior knowledge and represent about 25 percent of the total number of questions.
2. Explicit questions: These questions are those for which the answer is explicitly stated in the passage. To answer them correctly, for example, may just require finding a definition, or reading a graph, or making a simple connection. Explicit questions represent about 35 percent of the total number of questions.
3. Implicit questions: These questions require you to apply knowledge to a new situation; the answer is typically implied by the information in the passage. These questions often start "if...then..." (for example, "if we modify the experiment in the passage like this, then what result would we expect?"). Implicit style questions make up about 40 percent of the total number of questions.

In the Verbal Reasoning section, the questions also fall into three main categories:

1. **Specific** questions: These questions ask you for specific information from the passage, such as a fact (Retrieval question), an Inference ("which of the following is best supported by the passage?"), or a definition (Vocabulary-in-Context question).
2. **General** questions: These questions ask you to summarize themes (Main Idea and Primary Purpose questions) or evaluate an author's opinion (Tone/Attitude questions).
3. **Complex** questions: These are typically more difficult questions that can ask you to do a number of different things. Generally, Complex questions will ask you to do one of the following: consider how the author constructs his/her argument (Structure questions), decide how or how well the author supports his/her argument (Evaluate questions), decide which answer most supports or undermines the author's argument (Strengthen/Weaken questions), evaluate how new facts or scenarios relate to or affect the author's points (New Information questions), or apply the author's argument to a new situation (Analogy questions).

Remember that for all sections, you should do the questions in the order you want to. In the science sections, it's wise to do all the FSQs first since they are often quick memory questions, and then tackle the passages. Start with the subject you feel the most comfortable with, and then come back to the other subject. This helps keep your brain focused on a single subject at a time, instead of jumping, for example, between physics and chemistry randomly. Do the passages within a section in the order that you feel most comfortable with, and within the passages themselves, tackle the easier questions first, leaving the most time consuming ones for last.

In the Verbal Reasoning section, it is best to do the Specific questions within a passage first, then the General questions (after you have learned more about the passage by answering the Specific questions) and to leave the Complex questions (which tend to be more difficult) until the end of the set. For the section as a whole, answer the questions for the easier passages in your first "pass" through the section, and then come back for a second pass, completing some of the more difficult passages.

Verbal Reasoning on the MCAT

The Verbal Reasoning section is the only section of the MCAT that is not content-based. Thus, success in this section requires a solid familiarity with strategy. Here are the six basic strategy steps you should be taking for the Verbal Reasoning section. Each of these steps will be covered in detail in the following chapters.

Verbal Reasoning Passage/Question Strategies

1. **Rank and Order the Passages.** As you encounter each passage, decide if it is an easier passage that you will complete now, or if it is a more difficult passage that you will complete later or randomly guess on. If it is a NOW, go ahead and work it through. If it is a more difficult passage (that is, a LATER or KILLER passage), Mark the first question, note the passage number on the top of your scratch paper, and fill in random guesses for all the questions. If you come back to complete the passage later, it is quick and easy to change your answers.
   Note: Steps 2–5 apply to completing each individual passage.
2. **Preview the Questions Before you Read the Passage.** Look for words and phrases that relate to passage content; don't worry about identifying question types at this stage.
3. **Work the Passage.** The passage should not be read like textbook material, with the intent of learning something from every sentence (science majors especially will be tempted to read this way). Instead, look for the major themes and how they relate to each other. Define the main point of each paragraph, and think about how the paragraphs or chunks of the passage relate to each other.
   As you read, annotate by using your scratch paper to make brief and organized notes defining the main point of each chunk, and by using the highlighting tool. However, highlight sparingly, or you will end up with a passage that is completely covered in yellow! Highlight words and phrases that showed up in the questions, that indicate the author's tone, and that provide information about the logical structure of the passage.
4. **Define the Bottom Line of the Passage as a Whole.** That is, the main point, purpose and tone of the passage text.
5. **Attack the Questions.** Read the question stem word for word at this stage, and define the question task. For questions that include references to particular parts of the passage, go back to the passage text before you read the answer choices. Find the relevant information, paraphrase it, and come up with an answer to the question in your own words. For questions that do not include a specific reference to part of the passage, go directly to the answer choices, but go back to the passage as you evaluate each one.
   As you go through the answer choices, always read all four choices carefully before making a selection. Most importantly, use Process of Elimination (POE) and the strike-out tool actively. Look for what is wrong with three of the choices, rather than just picking the one that "sounds good."
6. **Inspect the Section.** At or around the 5-minute mark, inspect the section for blanks. Go to the Review screen and make sure that you have filled in an answer (including random guesses) for every question.

The Writing Sample on the MCAT

The Writing Sample tests your ability to make an organized, clear, and coherent argument. It can be intimidating at first, in part because the essay prompts come from such a wide range of topics. However, the structure of the questions is very predictable, and by following the steps outlined in this book everyone can learn to write a solid response. But before we get into the details, here are the basics.

Writing Sample Strategies

1. Read the entire question, including the full paragraph underneath the bold-face prompt statement.
2. Spend 5–10 minutes before you begin to write brainstorming ideas and examples and outlining your essay.
3. Be careful to address each task, in the order in which they are given. All Writing Sample questions have three related yet distinct tasks. An essay that leaves out one or more of the tasks will get a low score.
4. Use examples that clearly illustrate your argument in each of the first two tasks. Every question involves a basic contrast; make sure that you explain how your examples illustrate this contrast.
5. Spend at least a few minutes at the end proofreading for coherence and for mechanics. While the essay graders expect a few grammatical or spelling mistakes even in high-scoring essays, clean it up as much as possible.

A NOTE ABOUT FLASHCARDS

Contrary to popular belief, flashcards are NOT the best way to study for the MCAT. For most of the exams you've taken previously, flashcards were probably helpful. This was because those exams mostly required you to regurgitate information, and flashcards are pretty good at helping you memorize facts. Remember, however, that the most challenging aspect of the MCAT is not that it requires you to memorize the fine details of content-knowledge, but that it requires you to apply your basic scientific knowledge to unfamiliar situations. Flashcards won't help you do that.

There is only one situation in which flashcards can be beneficial, and that's if your basic content knowledge is deficient in some area. For example, if you don't know the hormones and their effects in the body, flashcards can help you memorize these facts. Or, maybe you are unsure of some of the organic chemistry functional groups you need to know; flashcards can help you solidify that knowledge. You might find it useful to make flashcards to help you learn and recognize the different question types or the common types of wrong answers for the Verbal Reasoning section. (And remember that part of what makes flashcards useful is the fact that you *make them yourself.* Not only are they then customized for your personal areas of weakness, the very act of writing down infromation on a flahscard helps stick that information in your brain.) But other than straight, basic fact-memorization in your personal weak areas, you are better off doing and analyzing practice passages than carrying around a stack of flashcards.

TEST DAY TIPS

On the day of the test, you'll want to arrive at the test center a half hour prior to the starting time of your test. Examinees will be checked in in the order they arrive at the center. You will be assigned a locker or secure area in which to put your personal items. Textbooks and study notes are not allowed, so there is no need to bring them with you to the test center. Nothing is allowed at the computer station except your photo identification, not even your watch. Your ID will be checked, a digital image of your fingerprint will be taken, and you will be asked to sign in. You will be given scratch paper and a couple of pencils, and the test center administrator will take you to the computer on which you will complete the test. (Note that if there is a white-board and erasable marker is provided, you can specifically request scratch paper at the start of the test.) You may not choose a computer; you must use the computer assigned to you.

If you choose to leave the testing room at the breaks, you will have your fingerprint checked again, and you will have to sign in and out. You are allowed to access the items in your locker except for notes and cell phones. At the end of the test, the test administrator will collect your scratch paper and shred it.

GENERAL TEST DAY TIPS

- Take a trip to the test center a day or two before your actual test date so that you can easily find the building and room on test day. This will also allow you to gauge traffic, and see if you need money for parking or anything like that. Knowing this type of information ahead of time will greatly reduce your stress on the day of your test.
- Don't do any heavy studying the day before the test. Try to get a good amount of sleep during the nights leading up to the test.
- Eat well. Try to avoid excessive caffeine and sugar. Ideally, in the weeks leading up to the actual test you should experiment a little bit with foods and practice tests to see which foods give you the most endurance. Aim for steady blood sugar levels; sports drinks, peanut-butter crackers, trail mix, etc. make good snacks for your breaks.
- Definitely take the breaks! Get up and walk around. It's a good way to clear your head between sections and get the blood (and oxygen!) flowing to your brain.
- Ask for new scratch paper at the breaks if you use it all up.

Chapter 2
Introduction to MCAT
Verbal Reasoning

GOALS

1. To understand the structure and scoring of the MCAT Verbal Reasoning section
2. To learn the fundamentals of Verbal Reasoning strategies

Congratulations on choosing Princeton Review for your MCAT preparation. You are well on your way to significantly raising your MCAT score and getting into your top-choice medical school. We understand that the Verbal Reasoning section presents many challenges to the typical MCAT student. We want our students to have every available tool, so we have devoted ourselves to developing the most rigorous Verbal Reasoning materials possible, based on intensive study of the MCAT itself and of the best strategies that lead to success on this test.

2.1 THE VERBAL REASONING SECTION

Structure

- Verbal Reasoning is the second section of the test.
- It consists of seven passages, which average 500–700 words each.
- Each passage is followed by 5–7 questions (with four answer choices per question), for a total of 40 questions.
- You will have 60 minutes to complete the section. You can do the questions and passages in any order that you choose within the 60-minute limit.
- You will be able to scroll up and down within the set of questions for each individual passage, and click on the Next and Back buttons on the bottom of the screen to go back and forth between the passages within the section. Once the 60 minutes are up, however, you cannot go back to any of the Verbal Reasoning passages or questions.

Scoring

The section is scored on a scale of 1–15. The national average score is typically around a 9. Roughly 25 percent of test takers receive a 10 or above. Every school has its own criteria for admission, but many schools consider the Verbal Reasoning score to be especially important.

Pacing

You do not need to complete all seven passages to get a competitive score. In fact, the test is written so that most people do not have time to read all the passages and answer all of the questions with a reasonable level of accuracy. Most people will maximize their score by randomly guessing on at least one passage and focusing on getting a high percentage of the rest of the questions correct. Also, keep in mind that there is no guessing penalty. Never leave a question blank; always select a random guess for questions that you choose not to complete. You have a 25 percent chance of getting those questions right.

Content

The passages may be on any subject in the humanities, social sciences, or natural sciences. Past passage topics have included philosophy, ethics, ecology, evolution, archeology, astronomy, economics, history, political science, literary theory, psychology, sociology, meteorology, anthropology, art history, and zoology. This range of topics may seem overwhelming. However, unlike the other multiple choice sections of the test, Verbal Reasoning tests no outside knowledge of the subject. In fact, using your own factual knowledge or opinions of the subject can lead you to pick incorrect answers; the questions require you to use only the information provided in the passage. Clearly, you can't prepare for or approach this section of the test in the same way as physics or chemistry!

2.2 DEVELOPING YOUR VERBAL REASONING SKILLS

Many MCAT students struggle at first with Verbal Reasoning because they approach the section using a strategy that has led to success in their science classes: memorizing large amounts of detailed information to answer factual questions. Success in the Verbal section, however, requires a very different approach; most of you will need to fundamentally change how you read the passages and how you go about answering the questions. This section tests your critical reading, analytical, and MCAT-specific test-taking skills. The good news is that these are skills that you can develop and improve through practice and careful self-evaluation. These core skills fall into three basic categories:

Working the Passage
- Reading the passage efficiently: identifying the most important points made by the author while moving quickly through the details
- Following the logical structure of the author's argument: identifying such things as key shifts in direction, comparisons and contrasts, conclusions, and author's tone
- Synthesizing the Bottom Line of the entire passage: identifying the author's Main Point and Attitude

Attacking the Questions
- Correctly identifying and translating the questions: knowing what each question is asking you to do in order to choose the correct answer
- Using the passage (and only the passage) as a resource: quickly locating the relevant passage information for each question
- Translating and paraphrasing the passage: predicting what the correct answer will do before considering the answer choices
- Using Process of Elimination (POE): eliminating down to the "least wrong" choice rather than just picking an answer that "sounds good"

General Test Strategy

- Time management: getting what you need from the passage without getting bogged down in irrelevant facts or spending too much time on one question
- Pacing and accuracy: not going so fast that you miss a high percentage of the questions that you complete, or so slow that you do not get to enough questions to reach your target score
- Stress management: thinking clearly and working efficiently under stressful conditions

2.3 FUNDAMENTALS: THE SIX STEPS

Based on these core skills, here are the six steps to follow when working the Verbal Reasoning section.

■ STEP 1: RANK AND ORDER THE PASSAGES

Ranking

The passages are not necessarily, or even usually, presented in order of difficulty. There is no reason to waste time on the hardest passage or passages, only to skip or rush through an easy passage at the end of the section. So, your first step, as you reach each new passage, is to decide if it is a NOW (or easier) passage, a LATER (or harder) passage, or a KILLER passage (one that you will simply randomly guess on). To assign a rank, skim a few lines of the passage and see if you can easily paraphrase it. If you can, it's most likely an easier passage to understand. Also quickly scroll through the questions; notice if there are lots of long, complex questions and answers or difficult question types. Base your ranking on the combination of the difficulty of the passage text and apparent difficulty of the questions.

Ordering

If a passage is a NOW passage, go ahead and work it through, completing all of the questions. If it is a LATER or KILLER passage, fill in a random guess for each question and use the MARK button to identify it as a passage you have skipped over. Also note the passage number on the top of your scratch paper. Once you have completed the NOW passages in the section, come back through the section and complete the LATER passages, and make sure that you have filled in your random guesses on your KILLER passage or passages. (See Chapter 6 of this book for more information on Ranking and Ordering.)

■ STEP 2: PREVIEW THE QUESTIONS

Knowing what topics show up in the questions will help you work the passage more quickly and effectively. Before working the passage, read through the question stems (not the answer choices), looking for words and phrases that indicate important passage content. Do not worry at this stage about understanding the question or identifying the question type. (See Chapter 3 of this book for more information on Previewing the Questions.)

■ STEP 3: WORK THE PASSAGE

As you read through the passage, use the highlighting function (sparingly) to annotate the most important references in the text. This would include things like: question topics, topic sentences, words that indicate shifts in direction, the author's tone, different points of view, and conclusions. As you read, articulate the Main Point of each chunk of information (usually, each paragraph). Use your scratch paper, especially on difficult passages, to jot down these main points. As you read, think about how these chunks relate to each other; that is, track the logical structure of the author's argument in the passage. (See Chapter 3 of this book for more information on Active Reading and Annotation.)

STEP 4: BOTTOM LINE

After you have read the entire passage, sum up the Bottom Line: the main point and tone of the entire passage. For particularly difficult passages, write this down on your scratch paper to make sure that you have understood the main point and purpose of the passage as a whole. (See Chapter 3 for more information on finding the Bottom Line.)

STEP 5: ATTACK THE QUESTIONS

This is how the question will be formatted on the screen:

> 1. When an argument is inductive, that argument:
>
> A) is necessarily less conclusive than an argument that attempts to use deductive logic.
> B) is based on probability, such that the likelihood that its premises are all true is no greater than the likelihood of the truth of its conclusion.
> C) seeks to find or identify causes or explanations.
> D) when valid, may be based on evaluation of a representative sample of a population.

Do the questions in groups: Specific questions first, then General questions, and finally the Complex questions. As you work each question, follow these steps:

- Read the question word for word and identify the question type.
- Translate the question task into your own words, thinking about what the question is asking you to do with or to the passage.
- When the question stem provides a specific reference to the passage, go back to the passage before reading the answer choices and find the relevant information (reading at least five lines above and below the reference).
- Paraphrase the passage information, and then, with the question type in mind, think about what the correct answer will need to do.
- As you go through the choices, use POE actively. Look for reasons to strike out incorrect choices, and select the "least wrong" of the four. (See Chapters 4 and 5 of this book for more information on identifying and answering different question types.)

Before you move on to the next passage, scroll through the questions from top to bottom, making sure that you have not left any questions blank.

STEP 6: INSPECT THE SECTION

At or before the 5-minute mark, double-check to make sure that you haven't left anything blank. You can use the Review function at this stage. Do NOT rethink questions you have already completed. Your goal in this step is simply to make sure that you have selected an answer for each question.

2.4 GUIDELINES FOR USING YOUR REVIEW MATERIALS

2.4

Focus on Accuracy

Whenever you're acquiring a new skill, you need to learn to do it well before learning to do it quickly. Many students feel that speed is their number one concern. This often leads them to rush through the initial "learning to do it well" phase. Unfortunately, this is entirely counterproductive and will ultimately keep you from scoring as well as you possibly can.

As you begin working practice passages, do the passages untimed; focus on following the techniques and on improving your accuracy. Once you become comfortable with these techniques, set a timer to count *up* as you do each passage (or, note your start and end times with a watch). Record how long it takes you to do a passage, but don't attempt to complete the passage within a set time limit. We will let you know when to begin using set time limits for individual passages or for full Verbal sections.

Build Endurance

At first, work on only a few passages at a time, developing the skills you've learned. Allowing yourself this time to practice slowly but accurately gives you a strong foundation for accurate timed practice. Always do passages at least two at a time to practice ranking and ordering them. After a couple of weeks, try to do a number of practice passages at once, and don't take any breaks between the passages. Build up your endurance over time, so that you can eventually maintain your concentration at its peak over the course of an entire 60-minute section. Set aside a daily time for Verbal work and stick to your schedule. Keep in mind the particular strategies you should be focusing on depending on where you are in the book.

Control Your Environment

Give your full attention to the passages when you practice. That is, don't do homework while watching TV or conversing with friends. However, when you take the actual MCAT, you'll be in a room full of people who are muttering to themselves, sniffling and coughing, typing loudly, standing up and sitting down at different times, and generally behaving in a distracting or annoying manner (unintentionally, we hope!). Therefore, practice working in less than ideal conditions. Go to a reasonably quiet coffeehouse, a room in the library where there are people moving around, or some other location with low-level distractions. Learn how to tune out what is going on around you and to keep your focus on the passages in front of you. (Note: Wearing earplugs is prohibited during the actual MCAT. However, you will be provided with noise-reduction headphones on request.)

Evaluate Your Work

Constant self-evaluation is the key to continued improvement. Don't just answer the questions and tally your score at the end. Use the materials to teach yourself how to improve. What kinds of questions do you consistently miss? What kinds of passages slow you down? What kinds of answer traps do you tend to fall for? Use the charts provided at the end of this chapter to identify patterns in the mistakes you are making. Only by identifying your mistakes can you learn to correct them.

However, don't just think about the questions you got wrong; also analyze how you arrived at the credited response when your answers are correct. Did you avoid a common trap? Are there question types on which you are particularly strong? Did you successfully apply one of our techniques?

2.5 SELF-EVALUATION

Every student has different strengths and weaknesses on the MCAT Verbal Reasoning section. To improve on your weaknesses, you must first recognize them. From now on, keep a log of every passage that you do (sample logs follow).

The time you spend reviewing your work is just as important as the time spent doing the passages. After you do a passage, go through each question and answer choice. Pay particular attention to those questions that you got wrong. In order to increase your score, you'll need to assess and change the way that you think. Often we continue to take the same steps or read in the same way, even when we've seen that this way is not successful. You may not even realize that you're making the same mistake over and over again until you see it logged into your chart several times.

Use the following two logs as you work through the Verbal Reasoning practice materials to diagnose the reasons for your mistakes. Based on the patterns that appear, define the ways in which you need to change how you read and think in order to raise your score.

At the end of each chapter are two Individual Passage Logs to use on the practice passages for that chapter. To use the individual Passage Logs on additional practice material (such as the online practice passages or practice tests), make clean copies of the logs, or follow the same structure on notebook paper.

Individual Passage Log

Key for Passage Log

Passage # and Time spent on passage   Indicate the location of the passage and how long it took you to complete it (once we have instructed you to begin timing the passages).

Q # and Q type   For each question you miss in a passage, indicate the number and the type of question. Refer to the list of question types in Chapter 4.

Attractors   List what was wrong with each incorrect answer choice, including the ones that you did not pick. Refer to the Attractors described and listed in Chapters 4 and 5.

What did you do wrong?   Describe the error that led you down the path to the wrong answer, and how you will avoid making that same mistake in the future. Below is a (non-exhaustive) list of common mistakes. Choose one or more items from this list (there may be more than one misstep involved in picking a wrong answer), or, if none fits, describe the error in your own words. If time after time you cannot figure out why you chose the wrong answer, it is very likely that you are working too quickly and/or too carelessly. Did you:

- misread the question?
- fail to go back to the passage?
- fail to read all four of the answer choices?
- fail to read the entire answer choice?
- over-interpret the passage or the answer choice?
- forget the "Except/Least/Not" in the question?
- pick an answer choice that was:
  - …out of scope or not the issue?
  - …too extreme or absolute?
  - …from the wrong part of the passage?
  - …half right, half wrong?
  - …strengthening when it should have been weakening (or vice versa)?
  - …too narrow on a general question?

Using the Individual Passage Log, take the time to assess how your current thought processes led you to a tempting but wrong answer choice, and how a different way of thinking on the question would have been more successful. The log will help you to see how the test is constructed, and most importantly, how you are responding to it. You can't change the test, but you can change your responses to it. This process will allow you to work through the MCAT Verbal Reasoning section more quickly and with greater accuracy.

Individual Passage Log

Passage # _____

Q#	Q type	Attractors	What did you do wrong?

Revised Strategy _____

Passage # _____

Q#	Q type	Attractors	What did you do wrong?

Revised Strategy _____

Test Assessment Log

Use this worksheet to record and monitor your performance on full seven-passage sections, and to continue the self-evaluation process. In particular, use it to see if you are spending the time you need on the easier passages in order to get most of those questions right. Keep track of how much time you spent (roughly) on the NOW passages and on the LATER passages. If you find that you are spending the bulk of your 60 minutes on the harder passages with a low level of accuracy, you need to reapportion your time. Also evaluate your ranking; are you choosing the right passages?

Time	Psg # NOW	Questions Attempted	Number Correct	Number Incorrect	Question Types	Reasons for Mistakes
Start NOWs _____						
End NOWs _____						

Total NOW Passages _____   Total Q Attempted _____

Total Q Correct _____   Total Q Incorrect _____   % Correct _____

Time	Psg # LATER	Questions Attempted	Number Correct	Number Incorrect	Question Types	Reasons for Mistakes
Start LATERs _____						
End LATERs _____						

Total LATER Passages _____   Total Q Attempted _____

Total Q Correct _____   Total Q Incorrect _____   % Correct _____

KILLER Passages(s) Skipped # _____

Revised Strategy _____

Chapter 2 Summary

Your preparation for the MCAT Verbal Reasoning section should include: familiarization with passage structure, question types, and answer traps, and training in the efficient and effective use of passage information.

In addition to reading practice passages and answering the questions, smart preparation includes a careful, continuing analysis of your performance.

Individual Practice Drills

Do the following two passages untimed. Focus on implementing the six steps you learned in this chapter. After you have checked your answers, fill out an Individual Passage Log for each passage.

Chapter 2 Practice Passage 1

We all start out as animists, as toddlers vaguely uncertain about whether our beloved doll or pull-toy puppy might be a living being. When I was a child, my favorite cartoons were those that played in to that confusion, films in which toasters or teapots or slippers sprouted legs and faces and revealed their true natures as menacing agents of mayhem and chaos.

In time, we learn to distinguish the creature from the object, and, later, consumer society conditions us to detach ourselves from our stuff so effectively that we can dedicate ourselves to the perpetual quest for nicer stuff and embrace the necessity of regularly exchanging older models for newer ones. But some vestige of the child remains, evidenced by the tenacious hold material things have over us, as objects of desire and, more mysteriously, as personal mementos and totems — as clues to our secret selves, and as signposts along the circuitous route that has taken us from the past into the present. Objects survive because we need them, or because we are convinced that we need them. The unreconstructed animist will see a Darwinian triumph in the rapidity with which a crumpled boarding pass evolves into an all-important and indispensable detail in the narrative of some meaningful chapter in our lives.

One such chapter is the subject of *Important Artifacts and Personal Property from the Collection of Lenore Doolan and Harold Morris, Including Books, Street Fashion, and Jewelry*. A series of captioned photographs, Leanne Shapton's ingenious book does a deadpan imitation of the auction catalogues that often accompany the sale of an estate or private collection, catalogues that constitute a peculiar genre in themselves. Typically, the detritus of dead movie stars and the obsessions of rich eccentrics crowd the pages of these paperbound volumes designed to persuade potential bidders that the auction is a purely professional, emotionally neutral transaction, and not, as one might suspect, a thinly disguised memento mori, an indication that something has ended — a life, someone's fiscal solvency, or, in the best case, an acquisitive passion.

Shapton presents and describes the artifacts that once belonged to a couple, now broken up. Someone (one or both of the lovers) is jettisoning everything (or almost everything; some lots have been removed from the sale, for unspecified reasons) that the pair possessed or acquired over a relationship that lasted four years, more or less. There are cake stands, blankets, sports equipment, snapshots, T-shirts, clippings, hand-lettered menus from celebratory dinners for two, unopened bottles of wine — and many of these humble items will turn out to signal a plot turn in the history of a romance.

A slightly charred backgammon set, a souvenir of a summer the lovers spend in the country, precedes a handwritten message from Hal: "I want this to work, but there are sides to you I just can't handle sometimes. Chucking the backgammon board into the fire was the last straw." The phone number of a couples' therapist appears on the back of a business card, and we realize that the crisis has escalated when we see a photo of Morris's white-noise machine, which appears to be smashed by a hammer.

Just as the concept of *Important Artifacts* is amusing in itself, so is its central conceit: Although the bidding estimates assigned to the lots fall well within the range that a provident auction house might term "sensibly" or "reasonably" priced, the fact is that a large percentage of what is being auctioned off is basically crap that no sensible person would want, not even for free. The seriousness beneath the joke is that these scraps of paper, used clothes, and borderline garbage were formerly objects of incalculable worth; indeed, they once meant everything to this fictional couple.

Reading the final pages of *Important Artifacts*, I found myself reflecting that the cartoonists whose work I so loved as a child might have been right about the potentially subversive or maniacal ways that objects would behave, if only they could. It may not be true that the furious teapot is plotting to grab a soup spoon and chase us around the house, but it seems inarguable that the deceptively innocent tea cozy could say far more than we would ever want strangers — or anyone, really — to know about who we are, what we did, what was done to us, and how we felt when it happened.

Material used in this particular passage has been adapted from the following source:
F. Prose, "Love for Sale: Appraising the Relics of a Relationship," *Harper's Magazine*, © 2009.

1. All of the following items are listed in the passage as relics of Doolan and Morris's relationship EXCEPT:

A) a white-noise machine.
B) bottles of wine.
C) a crumpled boarding pass.
D) T-shirts.

2. The author's attitude toward Shapton's book is:

A) predominantly critical but balanced.
B) effusive with praise and superficial.
C) approving and contemplative.
D) disparaging and plaintive.

3. Which of the following statements best summarizes the author's central purpose? _concluding stmt._

A) To express her appreciation of *Important Artifacts* and to explain how it gave her an elevated awareness of the meaning of objects
B) To praise Shapton's defense of animism inherent in the pages of *Important Artifacts*
C) To laugh at the irony that the objects that once meant so much to Doolan and Morris as a couple become, after their break-up, objects of little to no worth
D) To heighten the reader's awareness of everyday objects and those objects' potential to speak for us and tell stories of the events of our lives

4. Why does the author present the example of the backgammon set in paragraph 5?

A) To provide proof of Lenore Doolan's bad temper as the reason for the decline of the couple's relationship
B) As a piece of evidence for her claim that objects photographed for the book signal plot turns in the couple's relationship
C) To support her point that worthless objects acquire sentimental value when people are in relationships and are therefore invaluable
D) To suggest that objects only acquire meaning after they are altered in some form

5. The author most likely believes that:

A) her toaster is plotting grand schemes to reveal her darkest secrets.
B) it was not right of Shapton to expose a couple's private life the way she does in her book.
C) Doolan and Morris' relationship was doomed to failure.
D) we turn certain objects into significant and necessary documents of memorable parts of our lives.

6. According to the author, auction catalogues are generally designed to create what sort of impression for potential bidders?

A) A belief that the lives of movie stars and rich eccentrics are more fascinating than our own
B) An acknowledgement that something has ended—a life, someone's fiscal solvency, or an acquisitive passion
C) A wistful imagining of the stories and secrets those objects can potentially reveal
D) An appearance of impartiality and professionalism

4/6

Chapter 2 Practice Passage 2

People's facility with numbers ranges from the aristocratic to the Ramanujanian, but it's an unfortunate fact that most are on the aristocrats' side of our old Mainer. I'm always amazed and depressed when I encounter students who have no idea what the population of the United States is, or the approximate distance from coast to coast, or roughly what percentage of the world is Chinese. I sometimes ask them as an exercise to estimate how fast human hair grows in miles per hour, or approximately how many people die on earth each day, or how many cigarettes are smoked annually in this country. Despite some initial reluctance (one student maintained that hair just doesn't grow in miles per hour), they have often improved their feel for numbers dramatically.

Without some appreciation of common large numbers, it's impossible to react with the proper skepticism to terrifying reports that more than a million American kids are kidnapped each year, or with the proper sobriety to a warhead carrying a megaton of explosive power — the equivalent of a million tons (or two billion pounds) of TNT.

And if you don't have some feeling for probabilities, automobile accidents might seem like a relatively minor problem of local travel, whereas being killed overseas by terrorists might seem to be a major risk when going overseas. As often observed, however, the 45,000 people killed annually on American roads are approximately equal to all American dead in the Vietnam War. On the other hand, the seventeen Americans killed by terrorists in 1985 were among the 28 million of us who traveled abroad that year — that's one chance in 1.6 million of becoming a victim. Compare that with these annual rates in the United States: one chance in 68,000 of choking to death; one chance in 75,000 of dying in a bicycle crash; one chance in 20,000 of drowning; and one chance in 5,300 of dying in a car crash.

Confronted with these large numbers and with the correspondingly small probabilities associated with them, the innumerate will invariably respond with the non sequitur, "Yes, but what if you're that one," and then nod knowingly, as if they've demolished your argument with their penetrating insight. This tendency to personalize is, as we'll see, a characteristic of many people who suffer from innumeracy. Equally typical is a tendency to equate the risk from obscure and exotic malady with the chances of suffering from heart and circulatory disease, from which about 12,000 Americans die each week.

There's a joke I like that is marginally relevant. An old married couple in their nineties contact a divorce lawyer, who pleads

with them to stay together. "Why get divorced now after seventy years of marriage? Why not last it out? Why now?" The little old lady finally pipes up in a creaky voice: "We wanted to wait until the children were dead."

A feeling for what quantities or time spans are appropriate in various contexts is essential to getting the joke. Slipping between millions and billions or between billions and trillions should in the sense be equally funny, but it isn't, because we too often lack an intuitive feeling for these numbers. Many educated people have little grasp for these numbers and are even unaware that a million is 1,000,000; a billion is 1,000,000,000; and a trillion, 1,000,000,000,000.

A recent study by Drs. Kronlund and Phillips of the University of Washington showed that most doctors' assessments of the risks of various operations, procedures, and medications (even in their own specialties) were way off the mark, often by several orders of magnitude. I once had a conversation with a doctor who, within approximately twenty minutes, stated that a certain procedure he was contemplating (a) had a one-chance-in-a-million risk associated with it; (b) was 99 percent safe; and (c) usually went quite well. Given the fact that so many doctors seem to believe than there must be at least eleven people in the waiting room if they're to avoid being idle, I'm not surprised at this new evidence for their innumeracy.

Material used in this particular passage has been adapted from the following source:

J.A. Paulos, *Innumeracy: Mathematical Illiteracy and its Consequences.* © 1988 by Collins Publishers.

1. Which of the following best describes the author's primary purpose?

A) To explain the causes of innumeracy and provide options on how to prevent it
B) To demonstrate that Americans are, on the whole, undereducated
C) To provide data concerning probabilities of various causes of death
D) To describe innumeracy and some of its consequences

2. It can be inferred that, as used in paragraph 1, the term *aristocratic*:

A) describes individuals with better-than-average mathematical skill.
B) refers to the traditional ruling class.
C) represents people with only a limited facility with numbers.
D) refers to an inability to understand the difference between a million and a billion.

3. The author would most likely agree with which one of the following statements?

A) A megaton describes an unimpressive amount of explosive power.
B) It is unlikely that more than a million American children are kidnapped each year.
C) Driving an automobile is less dangerous than swimming.
D) Numbers such as a billion or a trillion are often amusing.

4. Which of the following, if true, most undermines the author's claims in paragraph 3?

A) When traveling overseas, most mathematicians take extensive precautions to help prevent becoming victims of terrorist attacks.
B) A new study presents evidence that almost twice as many Americans were killed by terrorists in 1985 than the passage claims.
C) Many people consider dying in a bicycle crash to be a major risk of travel.
D) The tendency to personalize is commonly accepted as an ineffective form of argument.

5. Which of the following, according to the passage, may characterize the innumerate?

I. Inability to improve their understanding of numbers.
II. Personalizing improbable, but tragic, outcomes.
III. Inaccurate assessments of the probabilities of possible outcomes of medical procedures.

A) I only
B) II only
C) I and III
D) II and III

6. The author most likely included the joke about the old married couple in order to:

A) provide further evidence of innumeracy in the elderly.
B) argue that couples in their nineties should not seek divorce.
C) illustrate the significance of an understanding of apt quantities based on context.
D) further support a point made in paragraph 3.

7. All of the following are given as evidence of innumeracy among doctors EXCEPT:

A) personal experience in the form of an anecdote.
B) the high rate of death due to heart and circulatory disease among Americans.
C) recent academic research.
D) a humorous exaggeration of a common experience.

Solutions to Chapter 2 Practice Passage 1

1. **C** This is a Retrieval question.
    A: No. This item is mentioned in paragraph 5.
    B: No. This item is mentioned in paragraph 4.
    C: **Yes. While a crumpled boarding pass is mentioned in paragraph 2, this is a hypothetical example and not tied explicitly to the relationship.**
    D: No. This item is mentioned in paragraph 4.

2. **C** This is a Tone/Attitude question.
    A: No. Nowhere in the passage does the author say anything critical about the book.
    B: No. While the author praises Shapton's book at a few points in the course of the passage, "effusive with praise" is too extreme. Also, the opening and closing ruminations on the relationship of objects to people's lives mean the author is not superficial in her treatment of the subject matter.
    C: **Yes. This comes closest to capturing the author's tone. She calls the book "ingenious" in paragraph 3, and in paragraph 6 she calls the book's concept and central concept "amusing." The author clearly enjoys the book and has given its ideas some thought (which supports "contemplative") as evidenced by the first and last paragraphs.**
    D: No. This is overly negative. The author never criticizes or disparages the book. Also, there is no mournfulness about, or lamenting of, anything regarding the book, which invalidates "plaintive."

3. **A** This is a Main Idea/Primary Purpose question.
    A: **Yes. While the author does not mention Shapton's book immediately, her early discussion about objects leads into a discussion and appreciation of *Important Artifacts*; the last paragraph shows the author's elevated understanding of the meaning of objects after reading the book.**
    B: No. While the author mentions animism in paragraph 1, she does not indicate that Shapton's book explicitly deals with this concept.
    C: No. This choice puts too negative a spin on the author's tone. While the author is interested in the difference between the dollar value and the emotional investment in objects (paragraph 6), she is not discussing these things to laugh at Doolan and Morris or their possessions.
    D: No. While this answer contains correct information, it makes no reference to Shapton's book, which is central to the author's understanding and explanation of the relationship between people and objects.

4. **B** This is a Structure question.
    A: No. The author is not interested in analyzing the reasons for the decline of the relationship; she is only interested in how the objects that belonged to the couple tell the story of their romance. Also, the word "proof" is too strong.
    B: **Yes. At the end of paragraph 4, the author suggests that objects signal plot turns in the couple's relationship. The backgammon example immediately following is illustrative, along with Hal's note, of this point, since it is evidence of a negative turn for the couple. This is furthered by the author's assertion that the smashed white-noise machine mentioned in the same paragraph helps "us realize the crisis has escalated."**

C: No. This is a point made in paragraph 6 where the author discusses the central conceit of the book. The example of the backgammon set is given to support a different idea in paragraph 5: the connection between changes in the couple's relationship and these objects.

D: No. The author does not suggest that things must be altered in order to acquire significance.

5. **D** This is an Inference question.

A: No. This takes the reference in paragraph 1 out of context. While the author mentions cartoons she watched as a child in which objects would sprout limbs and move, and in the final paragraph she suggests a tea cozy may have a lot to say about one's personal life, she would not go so far as to believe her toaster capable of plotting schemes. Note in the final paragraph she says "if only they could," referring to the fact that objects are unable to enact or consider plots on their own.

B: No. The author makes no negative judgment about Shapton; besides, the author mentions that the couple is fictional (paragraph 6), so real lives are not actually being exposed.

C: No. The author does not weigh in on whether the relationship had chances of survival or not; she is merely interested in how the objects from that relationship tell its story.

D: **Yes. See the final sentences of paragraph 2. This answer fits well with the author's assertion that objects become "all-important and indispensable" details in the narratives of chapters of our lives.**

6. **D** This is a Retrieval question.

A: No. There is nothing in the passage that contrasts the lives of famous people with those of regular people in terms of fascination.

B: No. This choice directly contradicts the passage. In paragraph 3 the author states that the catalogues are not designed to give "an indication that something has ended."

C: No. See paragraph 3. While the author herself expresses this attitude, she does not suggest that the catalogues do so.

D: **Yes. In paragraph 3 the author says, "Typically, the detritus of dead movie stars and the obsessions of rich eccentrics crowd the pages of these paperbound volumes designed to persuade potential bidders that the auction is a purely professional, emotionally neutral transaction."**

Solutions to Chapter 2 Practice Passage 2

1. **D** This is a Main Idea/Primary Purpose question.

A: No. The author addresses neither the causes of innumeracy, nor any options for preventing it.

B: No. While the passage does suggest that most Americans have a relatively poor understanding of numbers, it does not address the overall level of American education. Lack of education is not described as a cause of innumeracy, nor is innumeracy used as an example for a more general critique of the educational system.

C: No. This choice is too narrow. Although the author does this in paragraphs 3 and 4, it's not the primary purpose of the passage.

D: **Yes. The passage describes innumeracy in the first paragraph and discusses its consequences through the rest of the passage.**

2. **C**   This is a Vocabulary-in-Context question.

   A: No. The passage uses the term "unfortunate" to refer to the aristocrats' side of the spectrum measuring people's facility with numbers (paragraph 1), indicating that their facility with numbers is NOT better-than-average.

   B: No. There is no support for this in the passage. Beware of applying outside knowledge to MCAT questions, especially where vocabulary is concerned, since this is a common trap.

   C: Yes. The author states in paragraph 1 that "it's an unfortunate fact that most [people's facility with numbers is]...on the aristocrats' side," and then goes on to discuss students' lack of understanding of numbers.

   D: No. This answer choice is too specific. This is only one example of innumeracy; while the "aristocrats" might not understand the difference between a million and a billion, the word itself does not refer specifically to the lack of understanding of that difference.

3. **B**   This is an Inference question.

   A: No. The author uses the phrase "proper sobriety" to describe the appropriate reaction to a warhead carrying a megaton of explosive power, indicating his belief that this is a serious amount of power.

   B: Yes. The author's use of the phrase "proper skepticism" provides strong support for this answer choice by indicating his opinion that such figures are likely exaggerated.

   C: No. While in paragraph 3 the author cites statistics on the likelihood of drowning and dying in a car crash, he does not explicitly relate these to swimming or being the driver of a car.

   D: No. The passage states in paragraph 6 that slipping between millions and billions or between billions and trillions should be funny but isn't, not that the numbers themselves are funny.

4. **A**   This is a Weaken question.

   A: Yes. In paragraph 3 the author claims that "lacking some feeling for probability" leads to judging the risk of automobile accidents as minor and incorrectly judging the risk of being killed by terrorists as major. In order to weaken this claim, a correct answer choice might describe an exception to the author's claim—either people without some feeling for probability that do not misjudge the risk of being killed by terrorist (that's the easy one), or people with some feeling for probabilities that do misjudge the risk of being killed by terrorists. It is reasonable to assume that most mathematicians would have "some feeling for probabilities." That a group with a feeling for probabilities also acts as if being killed by terrorists is a major threat when going overseas most undermines the author's argument.

   B: No. Even if 34 Americans were killed abroad by terrorists, judging it as a major risk is still in error since the probability is not altered significantly enough. This answer choice is not strong enough to weaken the argument.

   C: No. In paragraph 3 the author cites the risk of dying in a bicycle crash and suggests that the risk is larger than that of being killed by terrorists. However, we don't know from this answer choice or from the passage that dying in a bicycle crash is in fact a significant risk while traveling (thus, we don't know that this is a reasonable risk assessment). Also, this is a small point among many to illustrate the larger point about an overblown fear of the threat of being a victim of terrorism abroad, compared to other risks that are in fact greater. This answer choice does not significantly weaken the point made by that comparison. Finally, the language of the choice is too weak; compare the "many people" in this choice to the "most mathematicians" in choice A.

D: No. The "tendency to personalize" is part of the author's next point in paragraph 4 and is not directly related to the author's discussion of probabilities in paragraph 3.

5. **D** This is an Inference/Roman numeral question.
   I: False. This statement is too extreme. The last sentence of paragraph 1 states that students "have often improved their feelings for numbers dramatically."
   II: **True. This is discussed in paragraph 4.**
   III: **True. This paraphrases the findings of the recent study referenced in the last paragraph.**

6. **C** This is a Structure question.
   A: No. The passage never discusses innumeracy specifically in the elderly.
   B: No. The author makes no personal judgment on whether or not people should divorce.
   C: **Yes. This answer choice paraphrases the first sentence of paragraph 6, which explicitly refers to the joke.**
   D: No. Paragraph 3 discusses errors in judging risks. The joke in paragraph 5 relates to understanding appropriate quantities and times, as the author indicates in the paragraph immediately following the joke itself.

7. **B** This is a Retrieval/Except question.
   A: No. The author describes a conversation he had with a doctor, which qualifies as a personal anecdote.
   B: **Yes. The correct answer will contain a statement that is NOT given as an example of innumeracy among doctors. Death due to heart and circulatory disease is mentioned in paragraph 4 as an example of the tendency to "equate the risk from obscure and exotic malady" with the chances of acquiring a common disease. There is no connection made here to risk assessments made by doctors.**
   C: No. The "recent study" referenced in paragraph 7 is given as an example of doctors' inaccurate risk assessments.
   D: No. The author's phrase "at least eleven people in their waiting room" is an exaggeration intended to be understood in a humorous way. The last sentence links this example to doctors' innumeracy.

Chapter 3
Active Reading

GOALS

1. To develop new—and more effective—active reading habits
2. To get to the Bottom Line of each Verbal Reasoning passage
3. To use annotation in order to be able to retrieve information quickly and accurately

3.1   BASIC APPROACH: THE SIX STEPS

First, here is a review of the six basic steps to approaching the Verbal Reasoning section that we discussed in Chapter 1. In the rest of this chapter, we will focus on steps two, three, and four.

▬ STEP 1: RANK AND ORDER THE PASSAGES

Decide whether to do the passage NOW, LATER, or NEVER (KILLER), based on the difficulty level of the passage text and of the questions.

▬ STEP 2: PREVIEW THE QUESTIONS

Read through the question stems (not the answer choices) before you read the passage. Look for words and phrases that indicate important passage content. Do not worry at this stage about identifying the question type.

▬ STEP 3: WORK THE PASSAGE

As you read through the passage, use the highlighting function (sparingly) to annotate the most important references in the passage, especially words that indicate the logical structure of the author's argument and references that appeared in your preview of the questions. Notice topic sentences that help you to identify conclusions made by the author. Articulate the Main Point of each chunk of information (usually, each paragraph). Use your scratch paper, especially on difficult passages, to jot down these main points. As you read, think about how these chunks relate to each other, and identify the structure of the passage.

▬ STEP 4: BOTTOM LINE

After you have read the passage, sum up the Bottom Line: the main point and tone of the entire passage.

▬ STEP 5: ATTACK THE QUESTIONS

Do the questions in groups: Specific questions first, then General questions, and finally the Complex questions. Read the question word for word, identifying the question type and translating the question task into your own words. Go back to the passage before reading the answer choices and find the relevant information (reading at least five lines above and below the reference). Think about what the correct answer will need to do, and generate an answer to the question in your own words. Use Process of Elimination (POE) actively. Select the "least wrong" answer.

Before you move on to the next passage, scroll through the questions from top to bottom, making sure that you have not left any blank.

▬ STEP 6: INSPECT THE SECTION

At or before the 5-minute mark, double-check to make sure that you haven't left anything blank. You can use the Review function at this stage. Do NOT rethink questions you have already completed.

3.2 STRATEGIES FOR ACTIVE READING: GETTING TO THE BOTTOM LINE

What Is the Bottom Line?

As you've no doubt noticed, MCAT Verbal Reasoning passages are often dense, convoluted, and full of details that you ultimately don't need to know in order to answer the questions. Such passages are impossible to read as closely as you would read a text for school, especially given the time constraint. On the MCAT, your goal is not to develop a deep understanding of every aspect of the passage; your goal is to find the information you need to answer the questions, and to pay as little attention as possible to everything else.

Therefore, do not attempt to understand or memorize every detail. This is time-consuming and counterproductive. Rather than attempt to remember all the details, visualize the passage as comprised of several large chunks of information. Each chunk, which may span part or all of a paragraph, has a Main Point and serves a particular function within the passage as a whole.

As you read, separate the central point of each paragraph from the evidence used to support that point. Translate the Main Point of each paragraph into your own words. What is the author trying to prove? Pay close attention to words that indicate the author's opinion or attitude. Jot down a short sentence summarizing the Main Point of the chunk and/or paragraph on your scratch paper. Link this theme with the Main Points of the previous paragraphs. Imagine that you are reading a mystery novel and predict what the author is going to say next.

After you have read and identified the Main Point of the last paragraph, define the main point and tone of the passage as a whole: this is the Bottom Line of the entire passage.

How to Get the Bottom Line: Active Reading

In order to read the passages effectively (that is, quickly and with a reasonable degree of comprehension), you must become an *active reader*. Imagine yourself attacking each passage. Think of the passage as an argument that you are breaking down into its most basic parts.

Here are the basic principles for active reading:

1. Preview the questions for content (not for question type). Predict what issues will be especially important in the passage you are about to read.
2. Translate the Main Point of each paragraph or chunk of information into your own words. Link it to what you've already read and predict what is to come next.
3. Note the author's tone and purpose. What side is the author on? Why is he or she writing this passage?
4. Notice pivotal words and other transitions: Use them to identify the "chunks" of an argument and how those chunks relate to each other.
5. Highlight the words that indicate the logical structure of the passage— that is, how the parts of the passage relate to each other. Also highlight topics that appeared in the questions.
6. Articulate the Bottom Line of the whole passage to yourself before answering the questions.

3.3 PASSAGE ANNOTATION AND MAPPING

Why Annotate?

Annotation is a crucial part of active reading. Like any successful traveler, you need a *map* to help you navigate the passage. Intelligent annotation can help you to create this map. A smart annotation system is neither too sparse nor too elaborate.

In the course of your undergraduate studies, you may have become accustomed to highlighting large chunks of text. However, this approach is not going to help you on the MCAT. If you highlight everything that "looks important," in the end, all you will have is some big blocks of yellow text. This won't help you to understand the logic of the argument as you read, and you will have to reread huge chunks of text to find the relevant information as you answer the questions.

You must have a specific strategy for annotating or *mapping* the text of the passage. Mapping is an active process that keeps you engaged with the text. It forces you to decide which points are most crucial to the author's argument, and how those points relate to each other to create the Bottom Line. It also marks the breaks between logically important chunks of the passage, which helps you locate information necessary for answering the questions.

Mapping

There are two tools you have to map the passage: *making notes on your scratch paper* and *highlighting the passage*.

Making Notes

Use your scratch paper to jot down the Main Point of each paragraph and the Bottom Line of the passage. Do this for every passage now; eventually, you may only need to write it down for the harder passages. Do NOT, however, use your scratch paper to list every fact mentioned in each paragraph; your goal is to identify the core idea of that chunk, not to write down a detailed outline of it. Also, if there is a time line in the passage, write it down so that you can use it as you answer the questions. You can also use your scratch paper to write down translations of difficult questions and answer choices.

What to Highlight

QUESTION TOPICS   When you see words or phrases that you recognize from your preview, highlight them. However, don't jump out of the passage to answer the question at this point (you don't know yet what else the author might have to say about that subject!). By highlighting them, you make it easy to come back and find them when you do answer the question.

TRANSITIONS: PIVOTAL WORDS

Pivotal words are especially important, so let's discuss them in more detail.

MCAT Verbal Reasoning passages rarely contain a single point reiterated over and over again. Rather, a chain of reasoning is more likely to change direction one or more times. These turns in the overall direction of a passage are often marked by **pivotal words**. Here are some common pivotal words and phrases:

but	although	however
yet	despite	nevertheless
nonetheless	except	admittedly
in spite of the fact that	in contrast	even though

These words indicate *change* or *contrast*. Pivotal words signal that the author is about to shift the course of the argument by:

- placing a condition on the argument;
- introducing an antithetical point;
- shifting from a simple to a more complex level of argument;
- making a concession to an opposing viewpoint.

Think of pivotal words as signposts that appear at crucial turns or refinements in the argument. Highlight them as you work through the passage. Marking pivotal words serves at least two functions:

- First, it increases the visibility of the parts of the passage that are likely to contain key ideas.
- Second, stopping to highlight a pivotal word lets you know that you need to determine *why* a transition is occurring at that point. In other words, the most valuable aspect of marking pivotal words—indeed, of annotating in general—is that it alerts you to the parts of the passage to which you need to pay the most attention, and it helps you track the logic of the author's argument.

TRANSITIONS: CONTINUATIONS

These words indicate that the author is further developing or explaining the point he or she has just made. Here are words commonly used to indicate continuations:

furthermore
additionally
also

3.3

CONCLUSIONS   Authors use these words to sum up their Main Points. Finding and highlighting these words will help you to do the same. Here are some common conclusion indicators:

therefore
thus
so
consequently
clearly

OPINION INDICATORS   One of the most important aspects of the Bottom Line is the author's tone. To accurately identify the author's point of view, look for and highlight phrases that express opinion, and words like:

finally
fortunately
thankfully
unfortunately
sadly

EMPHASIS WORDS   Authors use words like these to catch your attention, because what follows is especially important. Here are some examples of emphasis words:

most important
primarily
chiefly
key
crucial

COMPARISONS AND CONTRASTS   Not only are these words important to the logical structure of the passage; they also alert you to potential traps in the questions. When the passage describes two things as different, a wrong answer will describe them as similar, and vice versa. When the author discusses a change over time, wrong answers will reverse the chronology. By locating and highlighting comparison/contrast indicators, you are already helping yourself get the questions right. Here are some examples:

similarly
like
analogy
unlike
in contrast
the difference between
later
before/after

EXAMPLES   These words tell you that what follows is an example or illustration of a larger, more important point. Highlight them so that you can find these details if they become important to the questions. These markers are especially useful for answering questions that ask you if, or how well, the author's claims are supported. What you should be *thinking* about now as you read, however, is the conclusion being supported by the example. This is what will give you the Main Point of the chunk and eventually the Bottom Line of the passage. Here are some common example indicators:

> for example
> because
> since
> in this case
> in illustration

LIST MARKERS   When the author provides a string of claims or examples, it can be difficult to pull out the relevant item from that list when you are answering the questions. Highlight just the markers, not the entire list. But, just as with example indicators, define what this list is illustrating as you read: what is it a list of? List markers might be:

> first
> second
> thirdly

NAMES   Highlight names now so that you don't have to reread large chunks of text to find them when they show up in the question stems and answer choices.

3.4   HABITS OF EFFECTIVE READERS

Here are some suggestions for learning to read not only faster but more efficiently, the first time through the passage:

- **Focus on big ideas and skim the details.** Don't get bogged down in long descriptions. Practice using the clues provided in the author's wording to distinguish the major claims from the (potentially irrelevant) details.
- **Hit the right pace.** If you read too fast, you won't get anything out of the passage, and will end up rereading the entire passage as you answer the questions. If you go too slowly, however, you will lose focus and/or over think what you are reading.
- **Don't try to memorize.** Remember: this is essentially an open book test. You will be going back to the passage for the facts you need for the questions.
- **Practice reading in chunks of words.** Rather than "sounding out" each word in your mind as if you were reading out loud, think about seeing the words in groups of two or three to get a sense of what is being said. When you are answering the questions, however, always read word-for-word.
- **Push your eyes forward towards the end of the sentence;** don't linger on each word.
- **Visualize as you read.** When you hit an important point in the passage, create an image in your mind that captures the author's meaning.
- **Sit back and relax!** If you have your nose up against the screen, it is harder to think about the "big picture." You will get tired and stiff, and it will be harder to keep focused.

Outside Reading

Many MCAT students feel uncomfortable with the kind of material they encounter in the Verbal Reasoning section. You may not have much experience reading texts from the social sciences and humanities. To further develop your active reading skills, use some of the books listed below. Use these books not to learn more about the subject, but to practice active reading and annotation. Xerox a chapter or two from a few different books. Treat each page as a passage. Highlight the key words and phrases that fall into the categories we have discussed in this chapter. Articulate the Main Point of each paragraph and write it down. Think about how the paragraphs fit together logically to come up with the Bottom Line (including the author's tone) for each page or two.

Suggested Supplemental Reading List

1. Bate, Walter Jackson (1991), *The Burden of the Past and the English Poet*
2. Campbell, Joseph (1949), *The Hero with a Thousand Faces*
3. Durant, Will (1935), *The Story of Civilization*
4. Giroux, Henry A. (1988), *Schooling and the Struggle for Public Life: Critical Pedagogy in the Modern Age*
5. Gould, Stephen Jay
   (1981) *The Mismeasure of Man*
   (1997) *Questioning the Millenenium: A Rationalist's Guide to a Precisely Arbitrary Countdown*
6. Haraway, Donna (1989), *Primate Visions: Gender, Race, and Nature in the World of Modern Science*
7. Lakoff, George and Johnson, Mark (1980), *Metaphors We Live By*
8. Panofsky, Erwin (1955), *Meaning in the Visual Arts*
9. Welleck, Rene and Warren, Austin (1955), *Theory of Literature*

3.5   DOS AND DON'TS FOR ACTIVE READING

Do

- Translate the main idea of each paragraph into your own words.
- Link and predict major themes.
- Take notes on your scratch paper.
- Keep it simple.
- Highlight key words and phrases.
- Summarize the main point and tone of the whole passage before attacking the questions.

Don't

- Read parts of the passage text over and over (instead, move on!).
- Memorize.
- Copy words or phrases on to your scratch paper without knowing what they mean.

3.6 VERBAL READING EXERCISES: ACTIVE READING

Exercise 1: Finding the Bottom Line

Below is a sample MCAT Verbal Passage. Before looking at the outline that follows it, read the passage, focusing on identifying the Main Point of each paragraph without getting caught up in trying to understand every confusing sentence or the details of the examples. Write down the Main Point and purpose of each paragraph on a piece of scratch paper. As you read, think about how the different parts of the passage logically relate to each other to develop the author's argument. Then sum up those Main Points into the Bottom Line of the passage and write it down on your scratch paper.

[T]he… principle… can be paraphrased as "We see the universe the way it is because we exist."

There are two versions of the anthropic principle, the weak and the strong. The weak anthropic principle states that in a universe that is large or infinite in space and/or time, the conditions necessary for the development of intelligent life will be met only in certain regions that are limited in space and time. The intelligent beings in these regions should therefore not be surprised if they observe that their locality in the universe satisfies the conditions that are necessary for their existence. It is a bit like a rich person living in a wealthy neighborhood not seeing any poverty.

One example of the use of the weak anthropic principle is to "explain" why the big bang occurred about ten thousand million years ago — it takes about that long for intelligent beings to evolve. As explained above, an early generation of stars first had to form. These stars converted some of the original hydrogen and helium into elements like carbon and oxygen, out of which we are made. The stars then exploded as supernovas, and their debris went to form other stars and planets, among them those of our solar system, which is about five thousand million years old. The first one or two thousand million years of the earth's existence were too hot for the development of anything complicated. The remaining three thousand million years or so have been taken up by the slow process of biological evolution, which has led from the simplest organisms to beings who are capable of measuring time back to the big bang.

Few people would quarrel with the validity or utility of the weak anthropic principle. Some, however, go much further and propose a strong version of the principle. According to this theory, there are either many different universes or many different regions of a single universe, each with its own set of laws of science. In most of these universes the conditions would not be right for the development of complicated organisms; only in the few universes that are like ours would

intelligent beings develop and ask the question: "Why is the universe the way we see it?" The answer is then simple: if it had been different, we would not be here!

The laws of science, as we know them at present, contain many fundamental numbers, like the size of the electric charge of the electron and the ratio of the masses of the proton and the electron. We cannot, at the moment at least, predict the values of these numbers from theory — we have to find them by observation. It may be that one day we shall discover a complete unified theory that predicts them all, but it is also possible that some or all of them vary from universe to universe or within a single universe. The remarkable fact is that the values of these numbers seem to have been very finely adjusted to make possible the development of life. For example, if the electric charge of the electron had been only slightly different, stars either would have been unable to burn hydrogen and helium, or else they would not have exploded. Of course, there might be other forms of intelligent life, not dreamed of even by writers of science fiction, that did not require the light of a star like the sun or the heavier chemical elements that are made in stars and are flung back into space when the stars explode. Nevertheless, it seems clear that there are relatively few ranges of values for the numbers that would allow the development of any form of intelligent life. Most sets of values would give rise to universes that, although they might be very beautiful, would contain no one able to wonder at that beauty. One can take this either as evidence of a divine purpose in Creation and the choice of the laws of science or as support for the strong anthropic principle.

Material used in this particular passage has been adapted from the following source:
S. F. Hawking, *A Brief History of Time.* © 1988 by Bantam Books.

Bottom Line Exercise (continued)

Now, compare what you have on the page with the following:

1. **Definition** of the [anthropic] principle
2. **Development of theme**
   Explanation of the weak anthropic principle
   One universe with life-supporting regions limited in space and time
3. **Example**
   Weak anthropic principle "explains" big bang happening long ago
4. **Change in direction**
   Explanation of strong anthropic principle: goes further than weak (multiple sets of regions/scientific laws)
5. **Special significance**
   The laws of science, existence of intelligent life, and the strong anthropic principle

Bottom Line: Most people agree that conditions for intelligent life are rare; some propose a stronger version of this anthropic principle, which involves different universes or parts of the universe that have their own laws of science.

It is this information—and, really, not much more—that you need to retain after reading the passage.

Exercise 2: Working the Passage

Previewing the Questions

Read through the five questions below. Identify the words and phrases that indicate the issues in the passage that will be relevant to answering these questions. Don't try to identify the question type at this stage; focus only on clues to passage content. After we preview these questions, we will move on and read the passage attached to them.

1. According to the author, which of the following constitutes a fundamental human characteristic?

2. Which of the following, based on information in the passage, would most strengthen the author's claim in paragraph 6 that the work of economists is necessary to the advancement of civilization?

3. The author claims that human beings find it difficult to survive. What explanation is offered in support of this conclusion?

4. According to the passage, why do economists have such significant influence over society?

5. It can be inferred from the passage that economists are relatively unknown because:

Summing it up: What will this passage be about? _____

_____

_____

_____

_____

_____

The questions you have just previewed are about the passage (in paragraphs) on the following pages. As you work through those paragraphs, keep in mind what you learned from these questions.

Defining the Main Points and the Bottom Line

What we have here is an entire passage. These paragraphs have already been highlighted for you, as an illustration of what you should be (and shouldn't be) highlighting. As you read, think about *why* those words have been highlighted, and what those highlighted words tell you about the important parts of the author's argument.

For each paragraph, define the Main Point of that chunk. Write down the Main Point in the space provided before you move on to the next paragraph. Don't make a list of all the information included. Focus on the claims being made, not the evidence supporting those claims. At the end, we will articulate the Bottom Line of this passage.

3.6

The very fact that man has had to depend on his fellow man has made the problem of survival extraordinarily difficult. Man is not an ant, conveniently equipped with an inborn pattern of social instincts. On the contrary, he is preeminently the creature of his will-o'-the-wisp whims, his unpredictable impulses, and his selfishness. Man is torn between a basic need for gregariousness — to coexist peaceably with his neighbors — and a pronounced tendency toward greediness. Often, his tendency to guard his own interest is at odds with his need to survive in a community. And it is to this clash and conflict that the first great economists addressed themselves.

Main Point: <u>Human morals are governed by economists.</u>

Struggle btwn selfishness/selfless, ind/collective
                                          comm
is addressed by economists.

One would think that in a world torn by economic problems, a world in which we constantly worry about economic affairs and talk of economic issues, the great economists would have an important place in history and be as familiar to us as the great philosophers or statesmen. Yet they seem to be only shadowy figures of the past. In the 1760s an educated traveler in England would probably have heard of Adam Smith, a professor at the University of Glasgow, but today a great many educated people do not know that this gentleman was the father of economics.

Main Point: *Even though economy so imp to us, we do not treat economists as celebrities/famous.*

3.6

No economist has ever been either a national hero or a national villain. Yet what economists have done has been more decisive for history than many acts of statesmen who basked in brighter glory. Often their deeds have been more profoundly disturbing than the shuttling of armies back and forth across frontiers, more powerful for good and bad than the edicts of kings and legislatures. Since economists have shaped and swayed men's minds they have necessarily shaped and swayed the world.

Main Point: *Do not need credit, shaped societal morals, shaped world policy.*

Few economists ever lifted a finger in action. They worked, in the main, as scholars: quietly, inconspicuously, and without much regard for what the world had to say about them.

3.6

Main Point: Economists work behind scenes.

Economists are not well known because most people do not understand the significance of economics and believe it to be a rather uninteresting academic pursuit. But a man who thinks that economics is only a matter for professors forgets that this is the science that has sent men to their battle stations. A man who has looked into an economics textbook and concluded that economics is boring is like a man who has read a primer on logistics and decided that the study of warfare must be dull.

Main Point: Economics seems boring but is the reason why there are wars / lives lost / lives affected.

To be sure, not all the economists were titans. Adam Smith was a stunningly interesting character. But thousands of his followers wrote texts, some of them monuments of dullness, and explored minutiae with all the zeal of medieval scholars. Nonetheless, economists are the worldly philosophers, and their work is essential to the growth and continuation of advanced civilizations. Economists have sought to embrace in a scheme of philosophy the most worldly of man's activities: his drive for wealth. It is not, perhaps, the most elegant kind of philosophy, but there is no more intriguing or important one.

3.6

Main Point: Adam Smith - famous economist = worldly philosopher = work is the drive to grow our world/civilization.
→ ppl are innately greedy → economists answer why / monitor ppl's greed.

Bottom Line of the passage as a whole:

Economists affect every day life and address human selfishness, advance civilization, = Important. profession.

Material used in this particular passage has been adapted from the following source:

R. L. Heilbroner, *The Worldly Philosophers*. © 1999 by Simon & Schuster Inc.

EXPLANATIONS FOR EXERCISE 2: WORKING THE PASSAGE

Previewing the Questions

Summing it up: What will this passage be about?

This passage will be about human nature and survival, economists and their relationship to society, and why economists are not well known.

Defining the Main Points and the Bottom Line:

NOTE: Your own notes may be briefer; these are written out in more complete terms than you may need for your own understanding.

1. Man's independence conflicts with his need to be part of a group for survival.
2. Economists surprisingly fade into the background of history.
3. Economists have great influence over history.
4. Economists are scholarly, removed from the world.
5. People don't "get" economics, and so don't know economists.
6. Economists are vital to civilization

Bottom Line of the passage as a whole: Although they fade into history, economists are crucial to the advancement of society.

Exercise 3: Annotation and Active Reading—Putting It All Together

Read and annotate the following passage. As you read, stop and write down the Main Point of each paragraph on a piece of scratch paper. When you have read the whole passage, write down the Bottom Line. Then, turn the page and read through the sample annotations and explanation of the passage.

Passage for Annotation Exercise 3

There are two major systems of criminal procedure in the modern world —the adversarial and the inquisitorial. The former is associated with common law tradition and the latter with civil law tradition. Both systems were historically preceded by the system of private vengeance in which the victim of a crime fashioned his own remedy and administered it privately, either personally or through an agent. The vengeance system was a system of self-help, the essence of which was captured in the slogan "an eye for an eye, a tooth for a tooth." The modern adversarial system is only one historical step removed from the private vengeance system and still retains some of its characteristic features. Thus, for example, even though the right to institute criminal action has now been extended to all members of society, and even though the police department has taken over the pretrial investigative functions on behalf of the prosecution, the adversarial system still leaves the defendant to conduct his own pretrial investigation. The trial is still viewed as a duel between two adversaries, refereed by a judge who, at the beginning of the trial, has no knowledge of the investigative background of the case. In the final analysis the adversarial system of criminal procedure symbolizes and regularizes punitive combat.

By contrast, the inquisitorial system begins historically where the adversarial system stopped its development. It is two historical steps removed from the system of private vengeance. Therefore, from the standpoint of legal anthropology, it is historically superior to the adversarial system. Under the inquisitorial system the public investigator has the duty to investigate not just on behalf of the prosecutor but also on behalf of the defendant. Additionally, the public prosecutor has the duty to present to the court not only evidence that may lead to the conviction of the defendant but also evidence that may lead to his exoneration. This system mandates that both parties permit full pretrial discovery of the evidence in their possession. Finally, in an effort to make the trial less like a duel between two adversaries, the inquisitorial system mandates that the judge take an active part in the conduct of the trial, with a role that is both directive and protective.

Fact-finding is at the heart of the inquisitorial system. This system operates on the philosophical premise that in a criminal case the crucial factor is not the legal rule but the facts of the case and that the goal of the entire procedure is to experimentally recreate for the court the commission of the alleged crime.

Sample Annotation (Annotation Exercise 3)

There are two major systems of criminal procedure in the modern world — the adversarial and the inquisitorial. The former is associated with common law tradition and the latter with civil law tradition. Both systems were historically preceded by the system of private vengeance in which the victim of a crime fashioned his own remedy and administered it privately, either personally or through an agent. The vengeance system was a system of self-help, the essence of which was captured in the slogan "an eye for an eye, a tooth for a tooth." The modern adversarial system is only one historical step removed from the private vengeance system and still retains some of its characteristic features. Thus, for example, even though the right to institute criminal action has now been extended to all members of society, and even though the police department has taken over the pretrial investigative functions on behalf of the prosecution, the adversarial system still leaves the defendant to conduct his own pretrial investigation. The trial is still viewed as a duel between two adversaries, refereed by a judge who, at the beginning of the trial, has no knowledge of the investigative background of the case. In the final analysis the adversarial system of criminal procedure symbolizes and regularizes punitive combat.

By contrast, the inquisitorial system begins historically where the adversarial system stopped its development. It is two historical steps removed from the system of private vengeance. Therefore, from the standpoint of legal anthropology, it is historically superior to the adversarial system. Under the inquisitorial system the public investigator has the duty to investigate not just on behalf of the prosecutor but also on behalf of the defendant. Additionally, the public prosecutor has the duty to present to the court not only evidence that may lead to the conviction of the defendant but also evidence that may lead to his exoneration. This system mandates that both parties permit full pretrial discovery of the evidence in their possession. Finally, in an effort to make the trial less like a duel between two adversaries, the inquisitorial system mandates that the judge take an active part in the conduct of the trial, with a role that is both directive and protective.

Fact-finding is at the heart of the inquisitorial system. This system operates on the philosophical premise that in a criminal case the crucial factor is not the legal rule but the facts of the case and that the goal of the entire procedure is to experimentally recreate for the court the commission of the alleged crime.

Material used in this particular passage has been adapted from the following source:

M. A. Glendon, *Comparative Legal Traditions in a Nutshell.* © 1982 by West Publishing Company.

Explanation of the Passage

This passage presents a clear argument, using detailed descriptions to support it. The trick to understanding this argument is to keep track of the three kinds of legal systems: the adversarial, the inquisitorial, and the system of private vengeance, and the differences among them.

Notice that there are three major chunks of information here. They roughly correspond to the three legal systems, but they do not correspond to the three paragraphs; paragraph 1 contains two chunks: a description of the system of private vengeance and of the adversarial system. Paragraphs 2 and 3 work together as one chunk to describe the features of the modern inquisitorial system. Your annotation and summation of the Main Points in the passage should focus on the contrast drawn by the author between the three different systems. Good annotation and "chunking" will help you to get to the Bottom Line of a passage and to find the details necessary to answer the questions.

Your articulation of the Bottom Line of the passage should be something like: "The adversarial system of criminal law is similar to the traditional system of private vengeance and is therefore less developed than the modern inquisitorial system."

3.6

Chapter 3 Summary

- Read actively! Take control of the passage. Don't let the passage control you.

- Read efficiently! If a detail is important for a question, you'll find it when you go back to the passage text when answering that question. If it isn't important, don't waste your time.

- Limit your highlighting to words and phrases that relate to the logical structure of the author's argument and to your preview of the questions.

- Find the annotation style that works best for you, and stick to it. It may seem to slow you down at first, but it will save you time and increase your accuracy in the long run.

CHAPTER 3 PRACTICE PASSAGES

Individual Passage Drills

Do the following two passages untimed. Separate the claims (Main Points of each chunk) from the evidence used to support them (details). Use a yellow highlighter to annotate the words and phrases that appeared in your preview of the questions or that related to the logical structure of the author's argument.

As you answer the questions, uses your annotation (notes and highlighting) actively.

Once you have completed the passages, use the Individual Passage Log to evaluate your performance. Think in particular about how and how well you worked the passage, and how that affected your performance on the questions. Did you miss any questions because you didn't get the Bottom Line? Could more effective annotation have helped you find the information you needed? Did you highlight too much or too little, and then didn't know where to go back to in the passage?

CHAPTER 3 PRACTICE PASSAGE 1

Nothing short of this curious sympathy could have brought into close relations two young men so hostile as Roony Lee and Henry Adams, but the chief difference between them as collegians consisted only in their difference of scholarship: Lee was a total failure; Adams a partial one. Both failed, but Lee felt his failure more sensibly, so that he gladly seized the chance of escape by accepting a commission offered him by General Winfield Scott in the force then being organized against the Mormons. He asked Adams to write his letter of acceptance, which flattered Adams's vanity more than any Northern compliment could do, because, in days of violent political bitterness, it showed a certain amount of good temper. The diplomat felt his profession.

If the student got little from his mates, he got little more from his masters. The four years passed at college were, for his purposes, wasted. Harvard College was a good school, but at bottom what the boy disliked most was any school at all. He did not want to be one in a hundred — one per cent of an education. He regarded himself as the only person for whom his education had value, and he wanted the whole of it. He got barely half of an average. Long afterwards, when the devious path of life led him back to teach in his turn what no student naturally cared or needed to know, he diverted some dreary hours of faculty-meetings by looking up his record in the class-lists, and found himself graded precisely in the middle. In the one branch he most needed — mathematics — barring the few first scholars, failure was so nearly universal that no attempt at grading could have had value, and whether he stood fortieth or ninetieth must have been an accident or the personal favor of the professor. Here his education failed lamentably. At best he could never have been a mathematician; at worst he would never have cared to be one; but he needed to read mathematics, like any other universal language, and he never reached the alphabet.

Beyond two or three Greek plays, the student got nothing from the ancient languages. Beyond some incoherent theories of free-trade and protection, he got little from Political Economy. He could not afterwards remember to have heard the name of Karl Marx mentioned, or the title of "Capital." He was equally ignorant of Auguste Comte. These were the two writers of his time who most influenced its thought. The bit of practical teaching he afterwards reviewed with most curiosity was the course in Chemistry, which taught him a number of theories that befogged his mind for a lifetime. The only teaching that appealed to his imagination was a course of lectures by Louis Agassiz on the Glacial Period and Paleontology, which had more influence on his curiosity than the rest of the college

instruction altogether. The entire work of the four years could have been easily put into the work of any four months in after life.

Harvard College was a negative force, and negative forces have value. Slowly it weakened the violent political bias of childhood, not by putting interests in its place, but by mental habits which had no bias at all. It would also have weakened the literary bias, if Adams had been capable of finding other amusement, but the climate kept him steady to desultory and useless reading, till he had run through libraries of volumes which he forgot even to their title-pages. Rather by instinct than by guidance, he turned to writing, and his professors or tutors occasionally gave his English composition a hesitating approval; but in that branch, as in all the rest, even when he made a long struggle for recognition, he never convinced his teachers that his abilities, at their best, warranted placing him on the rank-list, among the first third of his class. Instructors generally reach a fairly accurate gauge of their scholars' powers. Henry Adams himself held the opinion that his instructors were very nearly right, and when he became a professor in his turn, and made mortifying mistakes in ranking his scholars, he still obstinately insisted that on the whole, he was not far wrong. Student or professor, he accepted the negative standard because it was the standard of the school.

Material used in this particular passage has been adapted from the following source:

H. Adams, *The Education of Henry Adams.* © 1918 by Houghton Mifflin Co.

1. Which of the following best characterizes the author's opinion of Adams' college experience?

A) Positive, because Harvard College was a good school.
B) Negative, because the four years at college were a complete waste.
C) Mixed, because while Adams learned little, there was some value to the experience.
D) It cannot be determined from the passage because the opinions expressed are Adams', not the author's.

2. The author's claim that in mathematics "failure was so nearly universal that no attempt at grading could have had value" is most *inconsistent* with which of the following statements also made in the passage?

A) "Instructors generally reach a fairly accurate gauge of their scholars' powers."
B) "The four years passed at college were, for his purposes, wasted."
C) "The entire work of the four years could have been easily put into the work of any four months in after life."
D) "He regarded himself as the only person for whom his education had value, and he wanted the whole of it."

3. Which of the following statements is/are supported by information in the passage?

    I. Adams was a man beholden to vanity regarding his appearance.
    II. Adams returned to teach and was motivated by instilling a new generation with useful information that was well received by his students.
    III. Adams had a predilection for politics and literature.

A) I only
B) III only
C) I and III only
D) I, II and III

4. All of the following are suggested as occupations or interests held by Adams EXCEPT:

    recollection

A) college professor.
B) paleontology.
C) chemistry.
D) military officer.

    Main point/argument

5. The author's primary purpose in the passage is to:

A) detail the academic life of a sub-par college student's experience and lobby for changing the system of education.
B) argue for the necessity of a liberal arts education in order to create a well-educated citizenry.
C) critically recount Adams' college experiences.
D) recount the positive and negative experiences of students at Harvard.

CHAPTER 3 PRACTICE PASSAGE 2

The Lampsilis is a freshwater clam with a decoy "fish" mounted on its rear end. This remarkable lure has a streamlined "body," side flaps simulating fins and tail, and an eyespot added for effect; the flaps even undulate with a rhythmic motion that imitates swimming. This "fish," constructed from a brood pouch (the body) and the clam's outer skin (the fin and tails), attracts the real item and permits a mother clam to shoot her larvae from the brood pouch toward an unsuspecting fish. Since the larvae of Lampsilis can only grow as parasites on a fish's gill, this decoy is a useful device indeed.

I was astounded to learn recently that Lampsilis is not alone. Ichthyologists Ted Pietsch and David Grobecker recovered a single specimen of an amazing Philippine anglerfish, not as a reward for intrepid adventures in the wilds, but from that source of so much scientific novelty — the local aquarium retailer. (Recognition, rather than machismo, is often the basis of exotic discovery.) Anglerfish lure their dinner, rather than a free ride for their larvae. They carry a highly modified dorsal fin spine affixed to the tips of their snouts. At the end of this spine, they mount an appropriate lure… They rest inert on the bottom and wave or wiggle their conspicuous lures near their mouths. "Baits" differ among species, but most resemble — often imperfectly — a variety of invertebrates, including worms and crustaceans. Pietsch and Grobecker's anglerfish, however, has evolved a fish lure every bit as impressive as the decoy mounted on Lampsilis's rear — a first for anglerfish.

The only thing more difficult to explain than perfection is repeated perfection by very different animals. A fish on a clam's rear end and another in front of an anglerfish's nose — the first evolved from a brood pouch and outer skin, the second from a fin spine — more than doubles the trouble. Anti-Darwinian evolutionists have always favored the repeated development of very similar adaptations in different lineages as an argument against the central Darwinian notion that evolution is unplanned and undirected. If different organisms converge upon the same solutions again and again, does this not indicate that certain directions of change are preset, not established by natural selection working on random variation? Should we not look upon the repeated form itself as a cause of the numerous evolutionary events leading toward it?

The Darwinian response involves both a denial and an explanation. First, the denial: It is emphatically not true that highly convergent forms are effectively identical. Two lineages may develop remarkable, superficial similarities as adaptations to a common mode of life. But organisms contain so many complex and independent parts that the chance of all evolving twice toward exactly the same result is effectively nil. Evolution is irreversible; signs of ancestry are always preserved; convergence, however impressive, is always superficial. Consider my candidate for the most astounding convergence of all: the ichthyosaur. This seagoing reptile with terrestrial ancestors converged so strongly on fishes that is actually evolved a dorsal fin and tail in just the right place and with just the right hydrological design. These structures are all the more remarkable because they evolved from nothing — the ancestral terrestrial reptile had no hump on its back or blade on its tail to serve as a precursor. Nonetheless, the ichthyosaur is no fish, either in general design or in intricate detail. The ichthyosaur remains a reptile, from its lungs and surface breathing to its flippers made of modified leg bones, not fin rays.

Second, the explanation: Darwinism is not the theory of capricious change that [some Anti-Darwinians] imagine. Random variation may be the raw material of change, but natural selection builds good design by rejecting most variants while accepting and accumulating the few that improve adaptation to local environments. The basic reason for strong convergence, prosaic though it may seem, is simply that some ways of making a living impose exacting criteria of form and function upon any organism playing the role. Terrestrial vertebrates propel themselves with their limbs and may use their tails for balance. Swimming fish balance with their fins and propel from the rear with their tails. Ichthyosaurs, living like a fish, evolved a broad propulsive tail.

Material used in this particular passage has been adapted from the following source:

S. J. Gould, *The Panda's Thumb: More Reflections on Natural History.* © 1980 by S. J. Gould.

1. In the context of the passage, the claim that "evolution is irreversible" most probably means:

   A) species' adaptations move inexorably toward the optimal form for their environment.
   B) species always resemble their more recent ancestors more closely than any earlier ancestor.
   C) the ichthyosaur could not have re-adapted to a terrestrial environment once it became a water-dwelling species.
   D) once an adaptation appears in a species, some sign of it will persist even as the species continues to evolve.

2. The author provides the example of the ichthyosaur in order to:

A) illustrate how convergent adaptations might not result in species that are truly effectively identical.
B) defend the claim that convergent evolution is actually quite common.
C) demonstrate that not all reptiles must live in terrestrial environments.
D) suggest that the ichthyosaur, though technically a reptile, is almost indistinguishable from some fish species.

3. The passage suggests that the author would be most likely to agree with which of the following statements?

A) The lure used by Lampsilis attracts prey as effectively as that used by Pietsch and Grobecker's anglerfish.
B) Lampsilis and anglerfish most likely share a common ancestor.
C) Lampsilis evolved its lure earlier in its genetic history than did Pietsch and Grobecker's anglerfish.
D) Lampsilis's lure is more convincing than that used by many species of anglerfish.

4. The author suggests that convergent evolution could be the result of:

I. environmental conditions that place similar demands on the function of an organism.
II. random probabilistic coincidence.
III. an optimal form that acts as a target for a large number of small evolutionary steps.

A) I only
B) II only
C) I and II only
D) I and III only

5. The evolutionists described in paragraph 3 would be most likely to interpret the similar adaptations of Lampsilis and the Philippine anglerfish in which of the following ways?

A) The similarity is evidence of an intelligent creator, who designed both species to serve similar purposes.
B) The similarity is merely a chance coincidence, unlikely to be repeated elsewhere in nature.
C) The similarity provides evidence that evolution is not necessarily based in part upon random variation.
D) The similarity is only superficial, and therefore not of special significance.

6. Which of the following best exemplifies convergent evolution, as it is described in the passage?

A) One species of Arctic mammal adapts to the extreme cold of the winter by hibernating, while a closely related species migrates to a warmer environment each winter, returning again when temperatures are no longer dangerously cold.
B) A species of Antarctic fish adapts to its frigid surroundings by evolving a protein that prevents its body fluids from freezing, while a species of Arctic fish evolves a similar mechanism to prevent freezing, despite the fact that the two species' genetic lines diverged long before either evolved their anti-freezing adaptations.
C) A cactus species in the American southwest adapts to the extreme aridity by evolving an extremely shallow and diffuse root system that quickly gathers water on the rare occasion that it rains, while a grass species in the American prairie, where rainfall is plentiful, develops a similar root system that allows the plant to propagate itself over a large area quickly.
D) Two primate species that share a common ancestor inherit the ancestor's long arms, but one species lives primarily in the forest canopy and uses its long arms primarily for climbing and swinging while the other species lives primarily on the forest floor and uses its arms primarily for gathering food.

7. Penguins propel themselves through the water with the short, stiff wings on their sides, rather than with their feet or tails. Given the information in the passage, this fact most strongly suggests that:

A) as penguins continue to evolve, they will eventually begin to use their wings more for balance in the water, and less for propulsion.
B) similar environmental pressures do not always result in instances of convergent evolution.
C) each species of animal adapts to its environment in a completely unique way.
D) the penguin does not move through the water as efficiently as the ichthyosaur did.

SOLUTIONS TO CHAPTER 3 PRACTICE PASSAGE 1

1. **C**   This is a Tone/Attitude question.

   A: No. While the author does state in paragraph 2 that Harvard was a good school, the passage has a largely negative tone about Adam's experience. For example, the author states that Adams "got little more from his masters" than from his peers (paragraph 2), that in mathematics "his education failed lamentably" (paragraph 2), and that Adams got little out of his study of ancient languages, political economy, and chemistry (paragraph 3). The author also criticizes Adams' professors in paragraph 2.

   B: No. While the tone is largely negative, the author states in paragraph 4 that "Harvard College was a negative force, and negative forces have value. Slowly it weakened the violent political bias of childhood, not by putting interests in its place, but by mental habits which had no bias at all." Therefore, "complete waste" is too strong.

   C: **Yes. While the author describes the failings of Adams' education in paragraphs 2 and 3, the author also states that there was some value to the experience: "Harvard College was a negative force, and negative forces have value. Slowly it weakened the violent political bias of childhood, not by putting interests in its place, but by mental habits which had no bias at all" (paragraph 4).**

   D: No. While the passage does suggest Adams' opinion, it also clearly indicates the author's opinion of Adams as a student ("a partial [failure]" (paragraph 1)), of the professors at Harvard ("In the one branch he most needed — mathematics — barring the few first scholars, failure was so nearly universal that no attempt at grading could have had value, and whether he stood fortieth or ninetieth must have been an accident or the personal favor of the professor" (paragraph 2)), and of Adams' education as a whole, including the value Adams did get out of the experience ("Harvard College was a negative force, and negative forces have value." (paragraph 4)).

2. **A**   This is a Structure question.

   Note: **The** correct answer will be the statement made elsewhere in the passage that most contradicts the statement cited in the question stem. If a statement in an answer choice is on a different issue, it will not be inconsistent (that is, the two statements would be consistent in that they could both be true).

   A: **Yes. Following the statement that grading could have had little value, the author states: "whether he stood fortieth or ninetieth must have been an accident or the personal favor of the professor" (paragraph 2). This suggests that grades or rankings did not in fact reflect the skill or accomplishment of the student. This would be inconsistent with the claim cited in choice A (from paragraph 4) that instructors accurately evaluate their students.**

   B: No. The claim that the four years were wasted is consistent with the author's critique of how professors graded.

   C: No. The quote in this choice is on a different issue: that Adams was interested in only a small portion of his course material (paragraph 3). Therefore the two claims are not inconsistent with each other.

   D: No. This refers to a somewhat different issue (Adams' self-centeredness (paragraph 2)), rather than the value or accuracy of the grading. Furthermore, to the extent that this statement relates to the existence of other students (who were also graded by the same standards), it is consistent, not inconsistent with the claim in the question stem.

3. **B**   This is an Inference/Roman numeral question.

    I: False. This statement is not supported by the passage. While Adams' vanity is mentioned in the first paragraph, there was no mention of Adams being vain specifically about his appearance.

    II: False. While it is correct that Adams did teach, the passage states that Adams went "back to teach in his turn what no student naturally cared or needed to know" (paragraph 2). Therefore the claim that Adams was "motivated by instilling a new generation with useful information that was well received by his students" is inconsistent with the text.

    III: **True. By stating that the Harvard experience "weakened the violent political bias of childhood" (paragraph 4), the author suggests that Adams did have an interest in, or predilection towards, politics in the first place. The author also mentions in paragraph 1 that because of Lee's request, "The diplomat felt his profession." As for literature, in paragraph 4 the author states: "Rather by instinct than by guidance, he turned to writing," suggesting that Adams had some interest himself in literature.**

4. **D**   This is an Inference/Except question.

    A: No. Paragraph 2 states: "Long afterwards, when the devious path of life led him back to teach in his turn what no student naturally cared or needed to know, he diverted some dreary hours of faculty-meetings by looking up his record in the class-lists, and found himself graded precisely in the middle." This suggests that Adams returned to Harvard as a professor.

    B: No. Paragraph 3 states: "The only teaching that appealed to his imagination was a course of lectures by Louis Agassiz on the Glacial Period and Paleontology, which had more influence on his curiosity than the rest of the college instruction altogether." This suggests Adams had an interest in paleontology.

    C: No. Paragraph 3 states: "The bit of practical teaching he afterwards reviewed with most curiosity was the course in Chemistry, which taught him a number of theories that befogged his mind for a lifetime." Even if Adams was confused by chemistry, the passage suggests that he did have some interest in or "curiosity" about it.

    D: **Yes. There is no mention of Adams having any interest in military affairs. The passage does talk of Lee accepting a military commission (paragraph 1), but not of Adams doing the same or having any interest in military affairs.**

5. **C**   This is a Main Point/Primary Purpose question.

    A: No. While the passage does provide some details about Adams' education, it does not explicitly lobby for, or make suggestions concerning, education.

    B: No. There is no mention of preparing well-educated citizens.

    C: **Yes. The author casts a critical eye on Adams' college experiences by speaking throughout the passage in largely negative terms; the value gained in lessening Adams' political biases (paragraph 4) still came out of the negative nature of the experiences themselves.**

    D: No. While one could infer that some of the experiences described applied to other students as well (e.g., how they were evaluated), the main focus of the passage is on Adams himself. Furthermore, the emphasis is on the negative experiences; even the positive outcome mentioned in the beginning of the last paragraph came out of *negative experiences*.

SOLUTIONS TO CHAPTER 3 PRACTICE PASSAGE 2

1. **D** This is an Inference question.
   - A: No. This would be the claim made by the anti-Darwinian evolutionists described in paragraph 3, with whom the author disagrees.
   - B: No. The passage only indicates that there is evidence of the evolutionary path taken, not that a species always moves further and further away from earlier ancestors.
   - C: No. This choice is too extreme. The passage does not say that evolution must be a linear, unidirectional path, or that species cannot readapt to formerly inhabited environments.
   - **D: Yes. This is the best interpretation of the cited claim. Note that the phrase "evolution is irreversible" is followed by the explanatory phrase "signs of ancestry are always preserved." By this the author most likely means that evidence of previous forms remains within a species. Note that in that same paragraph, the author discusses the example of the ichthyosaur. This discussion entails the assumption that we can see what features its precursor had; thus, there must be evidence of that evolution in the ichthyosaur itself.**

2. **A** This is a Structure question.
   - **A: Yes. This example serves to support the author's point against the anti-Darwinian evolutionists who are described in paragraph 3. Their claim is that "certain directions of change are preset" toward certain repeated forms. In the example of the ichthyosaur, the author shows how convergence is superficial, or, in appearances only; in this case, that the ichthyosaur did not actually evolve into a fish.**
   - B: No. This choice refers to a claim that is not made in the passage: the author does not discuss how common convergent evolution might be.
   - C: No. The question asks for the purpose of the example, not just what you know to be true based on the passage. This answer refers to something you could infer—indeed, the ichthyosaur would count as an aquatic reptile—but this is not the point the author wants to prove here.
   - D: No. This is inconsistent with the author's argument at the end of paragraph 4.

3. **D** This is an Inference question.
   - A: No. This choice might look attractive, but Lampsilis does not use its lure to attract prey. Rather, it lures fish who will serve as hosts for its larvae (paragraph 1).
   - B: No. The author does not indicate that species with similar physical features are likely to share a common ancestor. In fact, the discussion of convergent evolution later in the passage indicates that "common mode[s] of life" rather than ancestry can be the explanation.
   - C: No. The passage gives no evidence comparing the genetic history of the two species.
   - **D: Yes. This choice is supported by the last sentence of paragraph 2, which tells us that the author only knows of one type of anglerfish (Pietsch and Grobecker's) with a decoy as good as Lampsilis's.**

4. **A** This is an Inference/Roman numeral question.
   - **I: True. This is the main point of paragraph 5.**
   - II: False. The author states in paragraph 5 that "Random variation may be the raw material of change, but natural selection builds good design..."
   - III: False. This is the position of the anti-Darwinian evolutionists in paragraph 3, a position which the author rejects.

5. **C**   This is an Inference question.
    A: No. The passage makes no mention of creationism. Be careful not to attribute other (perhaps familiar) anti-Darwin ideas to these evolutionists.
    B: No. This statement opposes their position, since they argue against the idea that evolution is "unplanned and undirected." Instead, they believe that "certain directions of change are preset."
    C: **Yes. The evolutionists in paragraph 3 argue "against the central Darwinian notion that evolution is unplanned and undirected."**
    D: No. The first part of this choice sounds more like paragraph 4, which is the author's point of view rather than that of the anti-Darwinian evolutionists in paragraph 3. Furthermore, no one in the passage says the similarity is insignificant.

6. **B**   This is an Analogy question.
    A: No. The mammals in this choice solve the problem in different ways, not in the same way.
    B: **Yes. The author defines convergence in paragraph 4 as the development of similarities between two lineages in response to a common way of life. Only this answer choice fits this definition, since the fish have different lineages and adapted in a similar way to similar conditions.**
    C: No. The cactus and the grass in this choice have similar adaptations, but in response to different problems.
    D: No. The two primates in this choice did not develop separately and are not solving the same kind of problem.

7. **B**   This is a New Information question.
    A: No. We can't say anything for sure about penguins' future based on the passage. The author does not suggest that evolution always follows a predictable path.
    B: **Yes. The author doesn't tell us about penguins, but he does tell us that fish (and the ichthyosaur) propel themselves through water differently than the penguin does (see paragraph 5). Therefore, this is evidence that convergent evolution does not always occur, even when animals exist in similar conditions.**
    C: No. This choice may look good, but we can't justify any claims about each and every species. Furthermore, the passage tells us that many species' ways of adapting to a common situation are similar, rather than completely unique.
    D: No. We have no evidence to show how efficient the penguin is compared to the ichthyosaur.

Individual Passage Log

Passage # _____

Q #	Q type	Attractors	What did you do wrong?

Revised Strategy _____

Passage # _____

Q #	Q type	Attractors	What did you do wrong?

Revised Strategy _____

Chapter 4
Question Types
and Strategies

GOALS

1. To learn the types of questions that are likely to be asked and strategies for attacking them
2. To refine the use of Process of Elimination (POE)

4.1 REVIEW: THE SIX STEPS

Here, one last time, is a brief outline of the six basic steps to approaching the MCAT Verbal Reasoning section:

■ STEP 1: RANK AND ORDER THE PASSAGES

Decide whether to do the passage NOW, LATER, or NEVER (KILLER) based on the difficulty level of the passage text and of the questions.

■ STEP 2: PREVIEW THE QUESTIONS

Read through the question stems (not the answer choices) before you read the passage. Look for words and phrases that indicate important passage content. Do not worry at this stage about identifying the question type.

■ STEP 3: WORK THE PASSAGE

As you read through the passage, use the highlighting function (sparingly) to annotate the most important references in the passage, especially words that indicate the logical structure of the author's argument and references that appeared in your preview of the questions. Notice topic sentences that help you to identify conclusions made by the author. Articulate the Main Point of each chunk of information (usually, each paragraph). Use your scratch paper, especially on difficult passages, to jot down these main points. As you read, think about how these chunks relate to each other, and identify the structure of the passage.

■ STEP 4: BOTTOM LINE

After you have read the passage, sum up the Bottom Line: the Main Point and tone of the entire passage.

■ STEP 5: ATTACK THE QUESTIONS

Do the questions in groups: Specific questions first, then General questions, and finally the Complex questions. Read the question word for word, identifying the question type and translating the question task into your own words. Go back to the passage before reading the answer choices and find the relevant information (reading at least five lines above and below the reference). Think about what the correct answer will need to do, and generate an answer to the question in your own words. Use POE actively. Select the "least wrong" answer.

Before you move on to the next passage, scroll through the questions from top to bottom, making sure that you have not left any questions blank.

■ STEP 6: INSPECT THE SECTION

At or before the 5-minute mark, double-check to make sure that you haven't left anything blank. You can use the Review function at this stage. Do NOT rethink questions you have already completed.

In the rest of this chapter, we'll focus on **Step Five: Attack the Questions.**

4.2 ATTACKING THE QUESTIONS

In order to continue to improve your Verbal Reasoning skills, you will need to refine your approach to the questions. In this chapter we will discuss the five basic steps you should take in answering any question, and the specific tactics appropriate to each question type.

Five Steps For Answering Questions

1. Read the question word for word and identify the question type.
2. Translate the question into your own words; identify what the question task is asking you to do with the information in the passage.
3. Identify key words and phrases that refer to specific parts of the passage and *go back to the passage* to locate that information.
4. Answer in your own words; articulate what the correct answer will need to do based on the question type and the information in the passage.
5. Use Process of Elimination (POE), and choose the *least wrong* answer choice.

Let's look at each step in more detail.

1. **Read the question word for word; identify the question type.**
   WHY?
   - If you misread or misinterpret the question now, you may never catch your mistake. Now is not the time to skim, or to get only a vague impression of what the question is asking.
   - No matter how good your annotation and mapping of the passage, if you're headed to the wrong destination, those signposts do you no good. You could have an excellent map of the United States, but if you're supposed to get to Boston, and you think your destination is Biloxi, you are in big trouble. Know your destination!
   - The MCAT writers are highly skilled at predicting likely misinterpretations and at giving you wrong answers with which you could be perfectly happy. If you've ever completed a passage, pleased with how quickly and smoothly it went, only to realize upon checking your answers that you got many questions wrong, you may be reading the questions too carelessly.
   - Different kinds of questions ask for different kinds of information. Most importantly, General questions require general answers and can usually be answered with your own statement of the Bottom Line. Specific answer choices can be very narrow and always require going back to the passage. Complex questions may also require you to go back to the passage, but they ask you to either describe the login or structure of the author's argument, or to apply new information to it. Identifying the question type is important because that will guide the rest of the process.

   HOW?
   - Read the question as if you have never seen it before. Focus on each word rather than taking it in as a chunk.
   - Think of the question as assigning you a task; what mission do you need to accomplish in answering the question? Do you need to find information that matches the passage? Describe the author's argument in the passage (in part or the whole)? Strengthen or weaken the author's argument? Apply new information to it?

2. **Translate the question into your own words; identify what the question task is asking you to do.**
   WHY?
   - You may have noticed by now that questions are not always phrased in an easily comprehensible way. The test writers do this on purpose to see if you can understand difficult, complex writing and ideas.

   HOW?
   - When you come across a long, complex, and convoluted question, take it out of MCAT-speak and put it into your own words. You may find it useful to jot down a few words on your scratch paper.
   - The benefits of translation are two-fold. First, it helps you to clarify exactly what the question is asking. Second, it will enable you to remember exactly what you're looking for when you go back to the passage.

   For example, a question for a passage on Abstract Expressionism may ask,

   > 1. Which of the following would be most inconsistent with Brown's claim that Jackson Pollock did not lack influence within the movement called Abstract Expressionism, as that movement and its subsequent offshoots and internal divisions are described in the passage?

   When you cut away the extraneous stuff and clarify the convoluted wording, all this question is asking is,

   > 1. Which of the following answer choices indicates that Pollock had little or no influence on Abstract Expressionism?

3. **Identify key words/phrases that refer to specific parts of the passage;** *go back to the passage to locate that information.*
   WHY?
   - Going back to the passage to answer questions with specific lead words is mandatory. You simply don't have time to memorize the details. Relying on your ability to recall facts under time pressure will only get you into trouble.
   - If you don't check your answers against the text, you are likely to pick a choice that contains words from the passage taken out of context, or one that is true in the real world, but not supported by the passage.
   - Going back to the passage before you read the answer choices will not only increase your accuracy, but will also increase your overall speed. If you already have a solid grounding in the passage, you will more quickly recognize the correct choice, and you are much less likely to get stuck between two answers.

HOW?

- A key word or phrase is something in the question that appears only a few times in the passage, and it guides you toward the relevant sections in the passage that you'll need to reread.
- Looking again at the sample question above, the phrase "Abstract Expressionism" would not make a good key phrase if the whole passage is about Abstract Expressionism; it's likely to appear many times throughout the passage. The name Jackson Pollock, however, is likely to lead you right to the relevant sections for that particular question.
- Once you've identified the key words, *scan* the passage (using your annotations) until you locate those words, and then read a few sentences above and below until you find what you need. "Five lines above and five lines below" is a good guide. However, you should start reading where the relevant information begins, and keep reading until the passage moves on to another issue.
- Pay attention to the logical structure of the author's argument. For example, if the sixth line below begins with a word like *yet* or *additionally*, you need to keep reading. Pivotal and transitional words indicate that the author may be qualifying what he or she has just said, or adding an additional point that you need to take into account.
- Some Specific (such as, "With which of the following statements would the author be most likely to agree?") and Complex questions do not give you lead words as clues. For these questions, eliminate the choices that are inconsistent with the Bottom Line (or, for a Weaken question, that are consistent with the passage), and then go back to the passage to check each of the remaining possibilities.
- For General questions, you can usually use your own articulation of the Bottom Line. You may, however, still need to go back to the passage when you are down to two choices.

4. **Answer in your own words; articulate what the correct answer will need to do, based on the question type and the information in the passage.**
   WHY?
   - Think of the answer choices as a minefield, full of potentially fatal missteps and pitfalls. Before you enter that minefield, you want to have a detailed map of what a strong answer choice will accomplish.
   - The wording of the credited response may be quite different from what you expect, but with your own answer as a guide, you will recognize it while avoiding the traps.

   HOW?
   - Once you've located the relevant information—and not before—articulate your own answer to the question. For particularly difficult questions, you may wish to jot this down on your scratch paper.
   - This does not mean, however, that you should try to predict the exact wording of the credited response. Instead, come up with a guide to what the correct answer needs to *do* (such as, in the sample question above, to show that Jackson Pollock had little or no influence).

5. **Use Process of Elimination (POE) to choose the *least wrong* answer choice.**
   WHY?
   - POE is the best friend of every strategic test-taker. Very often on the MCAT, there is no perfectly correct answer among the given choices, only better and worse choices. On particularly difficult passages, the credited response can even be a pretty bad answer. However, it will be the *best* answer among the four you have to choose from.
   - There are a number of standard ways in which the MCAT writers make loser choices look like winners. The answer that at first glance "looks good" may in fact be a trap. See the rest of this chapter and Chapter 5 for more information on types of wrong answers.

   HOW?
   - Use your own understanding of the question task and of what the correct choice needs to do in order to eliminate the most clearly wrong answers. This will usually take you down to two choices.
   - Reread the question and compare the choices you have left to each other. Identify what is wrong, if anything, with each choice. The winner is the choice that has the *least wrong* with it. You may not like that winner very much, but you score a point, which is all that matters in this game.
   - When you are down to two choices, actively look for the types of Attractors that commonly appear for that question type.

4.3   QUESTION TYPES AND FORMATS

There are 10 basic question types that you will encounter in MCAT Verbal Reasoning:

1. Retrieval
2. Inference
3. Vocabulary in Context
4. Main Idea/Primary Purpose
5. Tone/Attitude
6. Structure
7. Evaluate
8. Strengthen/Weaken
9. New Information
10. Analogy

These 10 types can appear in one of three formats:

1. **Standard:** The question task is direct.
2. **Except/Least/Not:** The question asks you to find the exception.
   That is, the choice that does NOT address, or that LEAST addresses, the question task (i.e., the statement that is *not* supported by the passage). The three wrong answers will in fact address the task (i.e., *will be* supported by the passage).
3. **Roman Numeral:** The question offers you three items. The correct answer will include all of the items that do appropriately address the question task and none that do not.

Each of the ten question types falls into one of three larger categories: Specific (types 1 through 3), General (types 4 and 5), or Complex (types 6 through 10). Occasionally there might be a variation within a category. For example, a Tone/Attitude question could refer to a particular part of the passage and so qualify as *Specific*. A Structure question could ask for the overall organization of the passage, which would make it a *General* question.

Most people benefit from doing the questions in groups. Do the Specific questions first. By going back to the passage to answer these questions, you will understand the author's argument even better. Then do the General questions, and leave the hard Complex questions until last.

A firm knowledge of all of these types and of the common trap answers that appear in each is necessary for dealing with the questions quickly and accurately. Before you take the MCAT, you will be able to easily identify each question and know immediately what strategy you will need to employ.

In the next part of this chapter, we will go through each question type in the Standard format, as well as the Except/Least/Not and Roman Numeral formats. After a discussion of the basic approach to the type, you will find a sample question and a description of how to apply the Five Steps to that question. The sample questions are attached to the passage on criminal procedure that you annotated for Exercise 3 in Chapter 3. The passage is reproduced here; first rework the passage so that it is fresh in your mind.

4.4 QUESTION TYPES: SAMPLE PASSAGE AND QUESTIONS

There are two major systems of criminal procedure in the modern world—the adversarial and the inquisitorial. The former is associated with common law tradition and the latter with civil law tradition. Both systems were historically preceded by the system of private vengeance in which the victim of a crime fashioned his own remedy and administered it privately, either personally or through an agent. The vengeance system was a system of self-help, the essence of which was captured in the slogan "an eye for an eye, a tooth for a tooth." The modern adversarial system is only one historical step removed from the private vengeance system and still retains some of its characteristic features. Thus, for example, even though the right to institute criminal action has now been extended to all members of society, and even though the police department has taken over the pretrial investigative functions on behalf of the prosecution, the adversarial system still leaves the defendant to conduct his own pretrial investigation. The trial is still viewed as a duel between two adversaries, refereed by a judge who, at the beginning of the trial, has no knowledge of the investigative background of the case. In the final analysis the adversarial system of criminal procedure symbolizes and regularizes punitive combat.

By contrast, the inquisitorial system begins historically where the adversarial system stopped its development. It is two historical steps removed from the system of private vengeance. Therefore, from the standpoint of legal anthropology, it is historically superior to the adversarial system. Under the inquisitorial system the public investigator has the duty to investigate not just on behalf of the prosecutor but also on behalf of the defendant. Additionally, the public prosecutor has the duty to present to the court not only evidence that may lead to the conviction of the defendant but also evidence that may lead to his exoneration. This system mandates that both parties permit full pretrial discovery of the evidence in their possession. Finally, in an effort to make the trial less like a duel between two adversaries, the inquisitorial system mandates that the judge take an active part in the conduct of the trial, with a role that is both directive and protective.

Fact-finding is at the heart of the inquisitorial system. This system operates on the philosophical premise that in a criminal case the crucial factor is not the legal rule but the facts of the case and that the goal of the entire procedure is to experimentally recreate for the court the commission of the alleged crime.

Material used in this particular passage has been adapted from the following source:

M. A. Glendon, *Comparative Legal Traditions in a Nutshell.* © 1982 by West Publishing Company.

[handwritten margin note: Similarities btwn adv & priv. vers. exist.]

Type 1: Retrieval Questions

Retrieval questions test your ability to locate information in the passage. They may also involve simple paraphrasing and summarizing, but they do not require any substantial analysis or interpretation. They will include some reference to a detail in the passage (a person's name, a theory, a time period, etc.).

Retrieval questions may be phrased in these ways:

- "According to the passage, the three components of Brown's theory are…"
- "The passage states that Brown's theory is rejected by…"
- "Which of the following statements is *not* mentioned as a characteristic of Brown's theory?" (Except/Least/Not format)

Sample Question 1:

Retrieval

1. According to the author, the inquisitorial system is two steps removed from:

A)   the adversarial system.
B)   the system of punitive vengeance.
C)   pretrial discovery.
D)   regularized punitive combat.

1. **Read the question word for word and identify the question type.**
    The words "according to the passage" tell us that this is a Retrieval question.

2. **Translate the question into your own words; identify what the question task is asking you to do with the information in the passage.**
    Retrieval questions tend to be fairly straightforward. Here, the question is asking us to locate information in the passage about the inquisitorial system, and to find an answer choice that is best supported by that information.

3. **Identify key words and phrases that refer to specific parts of the passage and *go back to the passage* to locate that information.**
    The word "inquisitorial" appears in all three paragraphs. However, "two historical steps" is found only in the beginning of paragraph 2. That is where we will find the answer to this question.

4. **Answer in your own words; articulate what the correct answer will need to do, based on the question type and the information in the passage.**
    The correct answer will state what the "inquisitorial system" is two steps removed from. If we start at the beginning of paragraph 2 and read five lines down, we see that it is "two historical steps removed from the system of private vengeance." The correct answer needs to state or paraphrase this. Also note that paragraph 1 describes the two systems that preceded the inquisitorial system; any choice that mixes up the three systems will be incorrect.

5. **Use Process of Elimination (POE) to choose the *least wrong* answer choice.**
    As we indicated earlier, each question usually has at least one trap or Attractor answer, that is, a choice that "sounds good" but in fact has some significant flaw. (See Chapter 5 for further discussion of Attractors.)
    Because Retrieval questions tend to be relatively easy, the MCAT writers often try to distract you from the credited response by pairing it with an answer choice that sounds very similar to

the passage but *is not* directly supported by it. These Attractors often copy words and phrases directly from the passage text, but don't capture the meaning of those words in the passage. The test writers may also give you an answer choice that *is* directly supported by the text, but that is not an appropriate answer to that particular question. They may also change or reverse a relationship (for example, the passage says A leads to B, and the wrong answer says that B leads to A).

The only way to spot and avoid these traps is to go back to the passage and reread the relevant sections.

Let's take a look at each answer choice for our sample question:

A: No. The first sentence of paragraph 2 states that "the inquisitorial system begins historically where the adversarial system stopped its development." We also know from paragraph 1 that the adversarial system followed "the system of private vengeance." Therefore, the inquisitorial system is one step, not two steps, removed from the adversarial system. This is a classic trap answer on a Retrieval question; it gives us something that is discussed in the same part of the passage, but that doesn't match the specific reference in the question task.

B: **Yes. Notice that that the author uses "punitive combat" at the end of paragraph 1 to describe what came before the adversarial system (the adversarial system regularized that punitive combat). Thus "punitive vengeance" is another way of saying "private vengeance." Therefore, this choice is directly supported by the relevant part of the passage.**

C: No. This choice takes words from the passage out of context, and doesn't directly address the question task. Pretrial discovery is part of the inquisitorial system; it isn't something that the inquisitorial system is removed from.

D: No. This choice is tricky because it sounds a lot like choice B. But when we compare the two, we see that choice D mentions *regularized* punitive combat. The end of paragraph 1 states that "the adversarial system…symbolizes and regularizes punitive combat." "Punitive combat" itself describes the system of private vengeance. So, this is just another way of saying "the adversarial system," and just like choice A it is incorrect.

Type 2: Inference Questions

Inference questions are the most common question type. They require you to choose the answer that is best supported by the passage. There is no such thing as being "too close" to the passage to qualify as an inference. An answer that directly paraphrases the passage may in fact be (and often is) the correct answer.

To approach an Inference question, find the relevant section or sections of the passage. Check each answer choice against that information, choosing the one that has the most support. The credited response may seem like a stretch (for example, something that you think is not particularly "reasonable" to conclude), but it will be the best supported of the four. Be flexible; the correct answer may be something that you would never have come up with on your own, but there will be some evidence for it in the passage.

Inference questions are often phrased in the following ways:

- "It can inferred from the passage that…"
- "Based on the passage, it is reasonable to assume that…"
- "The author implies that Brown's theory is most closely linked to…"
- "Implicit in the passage is the contention that Brown's theory is…"
- "The author suggests that…"
- "Based on information in the passage, it can be most reasonably concluded that…"
- "With which of the following statements would the author be most likely to agree?"
- "Which of the following statements is best supported by the passage?"

Sample Question 2:

2. The passage suggests that the inquisitorial system differs from the adversarial system in that:

    A) it provides the judge with information about the findings of the pretrial investigation.

    B) it makes the defendant solely responsible for gathering evidence.

    C) it guarantees that all defendants get a fair trial.

    D) a defendant who is innocent would prefer to be tried under the inquisitorial system.

1. **Read the question word for word and identify the question type.**
   The words "The passages suggests that" identify this as an Inference question.

2. **Translate the question into your own words; identify what the question task is asking you to do with the information in the passage.**
   This question is asking us how the author contrasts the inquisitorial with the adversarial system.

3. **Identify key words and phrases that refer to specific parts of the passage and *go back to the passage* to locate that information.**
   This is where many students falter, thinking that they don't need to go back to the passage because the question is asking us to infer something (or, in this case, what is suggested). The correct answer still must be closely based on the passage text, not on your own ideas or deductions.
   The words "inquisitorial" and "adversarial" appear in multiple places. However, the words "in contrast" at the beginning of paragraph 2 indicate that this is the beginning of the author's discussion of the differences between the two systems. Your annotation should alert you to the fact that there are a variety of differences listed in this paragraph. Don't reread the whole paragraph at this point, but you will need to check the answer choices against it.

4. **Answer in your own words; articulate what the correct answer will need to do, based on the question type and the information in the passage.**
   The credited response will need to not only match the description of the two systems, but will also need to correctly describe a difference between them.

5. **Use Process of Elimination (POE) to choose the *least wrong* answer choice.**
A wide variety of Attractors appear in Inference answer choices. One of the most common is a statement that puts information from the passage into overly absolutist or extreme language. For example, the passage may say that something *often* occurs, while the trap answer will say that same thing *always* occurs.

Do not, however, eliminate a choice for an Inference question only because it is narrower or more moderate than the scope or wording of the passage.

Be careful to eliminate answer choices that are out of scope; that is, answer choices which refer to issues that could be tangentially related but that are never discussed in the passage. Just like for Retrieval questions, look out for Attractors that take words out of context, or that are supported by the passage but not relevant to the question.

Let's take a look at each answer choice for our sample question:

A: **Yes. At the end of paragraph 2, the author states (in the context of differences between the two systems) that "the judge takes an active part in the conduct of the trial that is both directive and protective." Earlier in that same paragraph, the author also states that the inquisitorial system requires "full pretrial discovery." From this we can infer that in the inquisitorial system the judge would have access to information uncovered in the pretrial investigation or discovery.**

B: No. The passage suggests that this is true of the adversarial, not the inquisitorial system.

C: No. This choice is too extreme. The passage suggests that the inquisitorial system may lead to increased fairness, but not that fairness is guaranteed.

D: No. Although many of these words appear in the passage, there is nothing to suggest which system an innocent person would prefer. While this choice makes common sense, it is too much of a stretch, especially when compared with choice A which is directly supported by the passage text.

Type 3: Vocabulary in Context Questions

Vocabulary in Context questions ask you to define what the author means by a certain word or phrase. They are very similar to inference questions, in the sense that they are asking what the author is suggesting or implying by the use of those terms.

The correct answer must fit in the context of the relevant sentence and the paragraph containing that sentence, and must be consistent with the Bottom Line of the passage as a whole. As for all specific questions, you must go back to the passage and read in context.

Vocabulary in Context questions are often worded as follows:

- "As it is used in the passage, the phrase *theoretical rigor* refers to…"
- "With respect to Brown's model, *theoretical rigor* (paragraph 1) most likely indicates…"
- "The term *theoretical rigor* refers implicitly to Brown's…"
- "The phrase *theoretically rigorous conduct* means that a researcher should…"
- "The word *rigorous* (paragraph 1) is used in the sense of…"

Sample Question 3:

3. It can be inferred from the passage that the phrase *pretrial discovery* (paragraph 2) most nearly means:

A) the obligatory sharing of evidence between the prosecution and defense. ·
B) the directive and protective role of the judge.
C) the duty of the prosecutor to present evidence for conviction.
D) the evidence that is gathered before the trial.

1. **Read the question word for word and identify the question type.**
   While this question may at first appear to be an Inference question, it is asking us what the author means by "pretrial discovery." This makes it a Vocabulary in Context question.

2. **Translate the question into your own words; identify what the question task is asking you to do with the information in the passage.**
   The question is asking us to find a definition or description of "pretrial discovery" that fits into the context of the relevant part of the passage.

3. **Identify key words and phrases that refer to specific parts of the passage and *go back to the passage* to locate that information.**
   We can find those words in the last third of paragraph 2. The passage says that under the inquisitorial system "the public prosecutor has the duty to present to the court not only evidence that may lead to the conviction of the defendant but also evidence that may lead to his exoneration. This system mandates that both parties permit full pretrial discovery of the evidence in their possession."

4. **Answer in your own words; articulate what the correct answer will need to do, based on the question type and the information in the passage.**
   The correct answer needs to fit with the idea that both the prosecutor and the defendant must disclose all "evidence in their possession."

5. **Use Process of Elimination (POE) to choose the *least wrong* answer choice.**
   Eliminate the choices that are clearly inconsistent with the text, or that don't correspond to the appropriate issue.

   Then, take any remaining choices back to the text and substitute them for the word or words to be defined. The credited response will be the answer that, when inserted into that sentence, makes sense without changing the meaning of the sentence. It must also be consistent with the main idea of that paragraph and of the passage as a whole.

   Be on the lookout for Attractors that give legitimate dictionary or colloquial/common sense definitions of a word that are not consistent with the passage.

   Also beware of choices that over-generalize or that are too narrow in scope to accurately represent the author's meaning.

Let's take a look at each answer choice for our sample question:

A: **Yes. In the sentence before the one in question, the author discusses the duty of the prosecutor to present all of the evidence that has been discovered, whether it helps or hinders the prosecutor's case. This duty applies to the defense as well. Therefore, "pretrial discovery" refers to the requirement that all evidence is shared.**

B: No. While this is mentioned in the same paragraph, it is not relevant to the question. Note the word "finally" in the passage. This is a clue that we have moved on to another difference between the inquisitorial and adversarial systems; we are no longer talking about the issue of sharing information.

C: No. This choice is too narrow. The prosecutor has to also present evidence that would not support conviction. Furthermore, the defense has the same duty; it is not limited to the prosecutor.

D: No. This is a classic trap for Vocabulary in Context questions! While this would fit a common-sense definition, it doesn't fit with the meaning of the passage. "Pretrial discovery" refers to the sharing of the evidence by both sides, not to the evidence itself.

Type 4: Main Idea/Primary Purpose Questions

These questions require you to summarize claims and implications made throughout the passage in order to formulate a general statement of the central point or primary activity of the passage. Think of the passage as an argument. The Main Idea is the overall claim, supported by specific evidence in the various paragraphs, which the author wants to convince you to accept as true. The Primary Purpose is then very closely related; it will express what the author *does* in order to convey the Main Idea.

Good active reading is the key to these questions; don't wait until you encounter a Main Idea question to think about the Main Point or Bottom Line of the passage. Synthesize the major themes as you read the passage. Distill these themes into a summary of the content and tone of the author's argument or presentation. This is your foundation for answering any question, not just Main Idea and Primary Purpose questions.

Main Idea questions are often phrased in these ways:

- "The main idea of the passage is that…"
- "The central thesis of this passage is…"

Primary Purpose questions are often phrased as follows:

- "The author's primary purpose is to explain that…"

Sample Question 4:

4. The primary purpose of the passage is to:

A) explain why the inquisitorial system is the best system of criminal justice.

why?

B) explain how the adversarial and the inquisitorial systems of criminal justice both evolved from the system of private vengeance.

→ Main Idea - what?

C) show how the adversarial and inquisitorial systems of criminal justice can both complement and hinder each other's development.

D) analyze two systems of criminal justice and deduce which one is more advanced.

1. **Read the question word for word and identify the question type.**
   General questions are generally very easy to identify. Here, the words "primary purpose" tip us off.

2. **Translate the question into your own words; identify what the question task is asking you to do with the information in the passage.**
   The question is asking us to summarize the author's overall goal in writing this passage. A good translation of this question would be: "Why did the author describe the two modern criminal procedure systems, as well as the pre-modern system of private vengeance?"

3. **Identify key words and phrases that refer to specific parts of the passage and *go back to the passage* to locate that information.**
   On Main Idea and Primary Purpose questions you will not usually need to go back to the passage before reading the choices. Use your original articulation of the Bottom Line to take a first pass or cut through the choices. You may, however, need to go back to the passage when you are down to two or three choices.

4. **Answer in your own words; articulate what the correct answer will need to do, based on the question type and the information in the passage.**
   For this type, the correct answer needs to include (explicitly or implicitly) all of the major themes of the passage, without going beyond the scope of the author's argument. Our own answer to this question would be something like: "The author describes the pre-modern system of private vengeance in order to set up contrast between the adversarial and inquisitorial systems; the adversarial system is closer to the system of private vengeance, and the inquisitorial system is more highly evolved."

5. **Use Process of Elimination (POE) to choose the *least wrong* answer choice.**
   Common Attractors for Main Idea and Primary Purpose questions will understate or overstate the author's point. Choices that summarize the main idea of a paragraph or two but which leave out other major themes are too narrow. Vague or overly inclusive choices that go beyond the scope of the passage are too broad. Take the "Goldilocks approach": eliminate what is too big or too small, and find the one that is just right.
   For Primary Purpose questions, focus in part on the verb in each answer choice, and eliminate the ones that are inappropriate; that is, too opinionated, too neutral, or that go in the opposite direction from the passage.
   Eliminate choices that are too extreme. Is the author really *proving* or *disproving* a claim, or just *supporting* or *challenging* that claim? Eliminate any verb that expresses an opinion

(*criticizing*, *propounding*, etc.) on a neutral passage (*explaining*, *describing*, etc.) and vice versa. Be very careful to read and evaluate all parts of each answer choice. An answer choice may begin beautifully, but change halfway through to bring in something inconsistent with or irrelevant to the author's argument. If any part of the choice is wrong, the whole thing is wrong.

Let's take a look at the choices for this question:

A: No. This choice is too extreme ("the best"), and also too broad in scope. The passage only compares the inquisitorial system to the adversarial and private vengeance systems, not to all other systems of criminal justice.

B: No. This choice is too narrow in scope. The author not only explains this evolutionary connection, but explicitly contrasts the inquisitorial with the adversarial system in order to judge the former to be "historically superior."

C: No. This choice is out of scope. The passage never suggests that these two systems coexist, or that one would either contribute to, or get in the way of, the other.

D: Yes. While this choice does not explicitly mention the system of private vengeance, it doesn't need to; the author discusses the pre-modern system of private vengeance in order to argue that the inquisitorial system is historically superior to the adversarial system (because the adversarial system is closer to the system of private vengeance).

Type 5: Tone/Attitude Questions

Tone and Attitude questions ask you to evaluate whether or not the author expresses an opinion regarding the material in the passage, and if so, to judge how strongly positive or negative that opinion is. Pure Tone or Attitude questions are fairly rare (however, Main Idea and Primary Purpose questions always involve assessing the tone of the passage).

Just as for Main Idea and Primary Purpose questions, you must identify the tone of the author through active reading before you begin any of the questions.

When pure Tone/Attitude questions do appear, they are usually general questions, as in the following:

- "In this passage, the author's tone is one of…"
- "The author's attitude can best be described as…"

These questions may also ask about the author's attitude towards a particular part of the passage, as in:

- "The author's attitude toward Brown's claim can best be described as…"
- "What is the tone of the author's response to Brown's critics?"
- "The author's attitude towards the controversy surrounding Brown's theory can best be characterized as exhibiting…"

Sample Question 5:

5. The author's attitude regarding the evolution of criminal procedure systems can best be characterized as:

A) condemnatory.
B) instructive. *(contra word)* *directive, protective;*
C) admiring.
D) ambivalent.

1. **Read the question word for word and identify the question type.**
   The word "attitude" is a pretty clear indication of a tone question. Because the passage as a whole is about the evolution of criminal procedure systems, this is a General Attitude question.

2. **Translate the question into your own words; identify what the question task is asking you to do with the information in the passage.**
   This question is asking us what the author thinks about how criminal procedures have changed over time.

3. **Identify key words and phrases that refer to specific parts of the passage and *go back to the passage* to locate that information.**
   As with most General questions, you already have an answer, based on the passage, in mind. Therefore you may not need to go back to the passage before you begin evaluating the answer choices. However, you may well need to refer back to the passage during POE.

4. **Answer in your own words; articulate what the correct answer will need to do, based on the question type and the information in the passage.**
   The correct answer must be fairly neutral in tone. The author is describing how criminal procedure has evolved, not condemning or advocating any particular system. The author does state that the inquisitorial system is superior, but in the context of being "historically superior;" that is, more highly evolved.

5. **Use Process of Elimination (POE) to choose the *least wrong* answer choice.**
   Common Attractors on Attitude and Tone questions are choices that take the author's opinion to extremes. If the passage expresses qualified or moderate admiration, for example, an Attractor may incorrectly describe the author as "enthusiastic."
   If the author expresses both positive and negative thoughts about a subject, incorrect answer choices may leave out the positive or ignore the negative. Also, positive and negative comments don't cancel each other out to create a neutral tone.
   If the passage is neutral, any choice that expresses an opinion one way or the other is incorrect. Beware of choices that express strange attitudes rarely seen in MCAT passages. For example, if you see a choice like "obtuse ambiguity," you should be highly suspicious of it.

Let's apply POE to our sample question:

A: No. This choice is too strong, and too negative. The author does not condemn earlier criminal procedure systems; the passage only labels them as less highly evolved. The author definitely does not condemn "the evolution of criminal procedure systems" as a whole; the author says nothing negative about the inquisitorial system, which is the most highly evolved version.

B: Yes. The author is describing this evolution in a fairly neutral tone. Thus we can say that the tone of the passage is instructive; its goal is to teach us about the evolution of criminal procedure.

C: No. This choice is too strong and too positive. It is tempting, given that reference to "historically superior." However, the passage isn't praising the inquisitorial system, but just describing it as the most recent system. Even if you think that the author might have positive feelings about the inquisitorial system, "instructive" is still the better, safer choice.

D: No. "Ambivalent" means uncertain, or torn between multiple options. Nothing in the passage suggests that the author is torn between different opinions regarding the evolution of criminal procedure systems.

Type 6: Structure Questions

Structure questions ask you to describe how the author makes his or her argument. They differ from other questions in that they address the passage's construction or logical structure along with its content. This is what puts them into the category of Complex Questions, even though they almost always relate to one specific area of the passage. Structure questions ask for the purpose of a particular reference within the passage. That reference could be to an example, a conclusion, a contrasting point of view, etc. For example, the question stem might cite evidence from the passage and ask you to find the answer that describes the claim or larger point which is supposed by that evidence.

To answer these questions, it is crucial to identify the Main Point of the paragraph or chunk of information in which the reference cited in the question appears. Look for words—like *for example* or *for instance*—that indicate that what comes next is the support or evidence, and conclusion words—like *therefore, thus, so,* or *hence*—that indicate that what comes next is the claim being supported.

It is also possible for Structure questions to appear in General form, asking you to describe the organization of the passage as a whole. When answering a General Structure question, separate the choices into pieces and check for pieces that are out of order, that have an inappropriate tone, or that describe things that never happened in the passage.

Specific Structure questions may be worded as follows:

- "The author probably mentions the controversy surrounding Brown's ideas in order to…"
- "The three experiments carried out by Brown are cited in the passage as evidence that…"
- "The author describes Brown's unique methodology in order to make the point that…"

General structure questions can be phrased as:

- "Which of the following best describes the overall organization of the passage?"
- "Which of the following statements best describes the logical progression of the author's argument?"

Sample Question 6:

> 6. The author cites the slogan "an eye for an eye and a tooth for a tooth" (paragraph 1) in order to:
>
> A) show how aspects of the private vengeance system persist in today's legal system.
> B) criticize pre-modern systems of justice as overly violent.
> C) characterize private vengeance as a system that required the victim himself to seek justice.
> D) demonstrate how the legal rule rather than the facts of the case provided the foundation of the system of private vengeance.

1. **Read the question word for word and identify the question type.**
   The words "in order to" tell us that this is a Structure question.
2. **Translate the question into your own words; identify what the question task is asking you to do with the information in the passage.**
   The question is asking us to describe why the author used this phrase at this point in the passage.
3. **Identify key words and phrases that refer to specific parts of the passage and *go back to the passage* to locate that information.**
   The quote "An eye for an eye…" appears in paragraph 1. The author argues that it "captures the essence" of the private vengeance system, in which "the victim of a crime fashioned his own remedy and administered it privately…."
4. **Answer in your own words; articulate what the correct answer will need to do, based on the question type and the information in the passage.**
   The correct answer must connect the quote to the system of private vengeance, and describe it as part of the author's explanation of how victims themselves had to administer punishments to those that had wronged them.
5. **Use Process of Elimination (POE) to choose the *least wrong* answer choice.**
   For Structure questions, beware of Attractors that describe claims that are made in the passage but that are not relevant to or directly supported by the reference given in the question. Also beware of half right, half wrong choices. All parts of the correct answer choice must check out.
   The correct choice must be consistent with the Main Point and tone of the relevant chunk of passage, as well as with the Bottom Line of the passage as a whole.

Let's evaluate the answer choices for our sample questions:

A: No. The author argues that while the adversarial system does share some aspects with private vengeance, we have moved on to a system based on "fact-finding" where the judge directs the proceedings. Our modern inquisitorial system is "two historical steps removed from the system of private vengeance" (paragraph 2). Therefore, today's legal system is shown to be very different from the system of private vengeance.

B: No. The tone of this choice does not match the passage. While we might think of "an eye for an eye" as a violent way to mete out justice, the author does not describe it that way, or criticize it as such.

C: Yes. The quote appears in a sentence describing private vengeance as "a system of self-help." The preceding sentence also discusses how "the victim had to fashion his own remedy and administer it privately...." This choice fits with both the content and tone of the passage and with the specific reference in the question.

D: No. This choice takes words from the end of the passage out of context. There is no direct connection made by the author between basing a system on a legal rule, and the "eye for an eye" approach to justice.

Type 7: Evaluate Questions

Evaluate questions are similar to Structure questions in that you need to identify the logical structure of the author's argument. Evaluate questions, however, go a step farther by asking either *whether or not* a particular claim is supported within that passage, or *how well* that claim is supported.

To answer these questions, you need to pay close attention to words that show the logical structure of the passage (e.g., *for example, in the following instance, in conclusion, thus, however,* etc.). If the question asks which claim is supported, look for words indicating examples, descriptions, citation of authority, etc. Choose the answer choice that is supported in the appropriate way. If the question asks which claim is NOT supported, eliminate the answer choices that *are* supported by specific examples, illustrations, etc. (depending on the wording of the question).

If the question asks whether the claim is supported strongly or weakly, look to see if examples or explanations are given. If not, or if they are not directly relevant to the issue being discussed, the claim is supported weakly or not at all. Sample Question 7 below is of this type.

These questions may be phrased as follows:

- "Which of the following claims made in the passage is supported by an example or reference to authority?"
- "For which of the following of the author's claims is NOT support provided in the text of the passage?" (Except/Least/Not format)
- "The author asserts that Brown's theoretical model is 'dangerously incomplete.' The support offered for this conclusion is..."
- "Is Brown's analysis of the implications of Herrera's theoretical model well supported?"

Sample Question 7:

7. How well supported is the author's claim that the adversarial system still retains some features of private vengeance?

A) Strongly, because the claim is inherent in the meaning of the word "adversarial"
B) Strongly, because examples of similarities between the two are provided by the author
C) Weakly, because the claim is logically inconsistent with the author's description of the inquisitorial system
D) Weakly, because no evidence is cited to bolster the claim

1. **Read the question word for word and identify the question type.**

   The question asks *how well* supported the author's claim is, which makes it an Evaluate question. Notice that it doesn't just ask *what* the author's claim is (this would be a Retrieval or Inference question) or *how* the claim is supported (which would be a Structure question).

2. **Translate the question into your own words; identify what the question task is asking you to do with the information in the passage.**

   The question is asking if there are any significant flaws or weaknesses in the author's argument about the relationship between private vengeance and the adversarial system. If so, what are those flaws? If not, why is it a strong argument?

   If the question had asked, for example, "Which of the following is supported by reference to a relevant authority," the question would be asking us to go back to the passage for each choice to find the one that does in fact have citation from a relevant authority supporting it.

3. **Identify key words and phrases that refer to specific parts of the passage and *go back to the passage* to locate that information.**

   This question sends us back to paragraph 1. The claim cited in the question comes in the middle of the paragraph. Immediately after the claim, the author discusses particular similarities (as well as some differences) between private vengeance and the adversarial system.

4. **Answer in your own words; articulate what the correct answer will need to do, based on the question type and the information in the passage.**

   Read through the examples supporting the claim: the defendant must conduct "his own pretrial investigation," and "the trial is still viewed as a duel between two adversaries." This leads the author to the conclusion that the adversarial system "symbolizes and regularizes punitive combat;" punitive combat characterizes private vengeance.

   Because the author gives relevant examples, and draws reasonably well-supported conclusions based on those examples, we can say that the claim is strongly supported.

5. **Use Process of Elimination (POE) to choose the *least wrong* answer choice.**

   Answer choices that mischaracterize the strength of the argument are incorrect.

   Once you have narrowed it down to the choices that fall on the correct side (in this case, "strongly" or "weakly") narrow it down further by analyzing precisely what is either good or bad about the author's logic.

   If the question had asked, for example, "Which of the following is supported by reference to a relevant authority?", we would eliminate the choices that either 1) had no reference to authority supporting them or 2) were supported by reference to an irrelevant authority.

4.4

Let's go through the answer choices for our sample question:

A: No. While the claim is in fact supported strongly, it is not because of the definition of "adversarial." Instead, it is because the author provides relevant examples.

B: Yes. The fact that the defendant must carry out his own pretrial investigation; and that the trial is still seen as a duel, show that the adversarial system retains aspects of private vengeance, even if they are in a somewhat more symbolic or institutionalized form.

C: No. There is no inconsistency in the logic of the author's argument (which claims that the adversarial and inquisitorial systems are in fact quite different).

D: No. Direct, relevant evidence is in fact given (note the phrase "for example" in the passage, directly following the claim cited in the question).

Type 8: Strengthen/Weaken Questions

A Strengthen/Weaken question asks you to evaluate the *answer choices* in terms of how *they* may support or undermine the passage (as opposed to Structure and Evaluate questions, which ask how, if, or how well *the author* has supported his or her own argument).

Notice that Strengthen and Weaken questions often use the phrase, "which of the following, if true...." Take those words *if true*—whether implied or explicitly stated—seriously. Do not try to find the answer choices *in* the passage. Take each statement as if it were true and find the one that does what it needs to do *to* the relevant part of the passage. These questions are quite different from the question types we have discussed up to this point in that they give you new information in the answer choices; the correct answer will change, not just describe or reflect, the passage.

Strengthen questions may be phrased as follows:

* "Which of the following would provide the *best support* for the author's conclusion in the last paragraph?"
* "Which of the following, if true, would most *strengthen* the author's claims?"

Weaken questions look very similar, but go in the opposite direction:

* "Which of the following would most *weaken* the author's point?"
* "Which of the following, if true, would most *undermine* the author's claims?"

You might also see a variation on Weaken questions that cites a statement from the passage, and asks you to decide which *answer choice* would be most weakened by that statement. For example,

* "The claims made by Brown, if true, would cast the most *doubt* on which of the following statements?"

Regardless of the wording, you are doing the same thing in answering any Weaken question: finding the answer choice that is most inconsistent with the cited part of the passage.

Sample Question 8:

8. Which of the following, if true, would be most inconsistent with the author's main argument in the passage?

A) The vengeance system did not precede all systems of criminal procedure in the world.
B) The inquisitorial and adversarial systems have many things in common.
C) The adversarial system is a system of self-help.
D) Personal vengeance is at the heart of the inquisitorial system.

1. **Read the question word for word and identify the question type.**
   The words "most inconsistent with" identify this as a Weaken question. The question is asking us to undermine the author's central argument.

2. **Translate the question into your own words; identify what the question task is asking you to do with the information in the passage.**
   We will need to take each choice as true, rather than looking for support for the right answer in the passage. We will still need to go back to the passage, however, to pin down the credited response. We need the response that most undermines the author argument as a whole.

3. **Identify key words and phrases that refer to specific parts of the passage and *go back to the passage* to locate that information.**
   Because the question asks us to weaken the author's main argument, we can use our own articulation of the Bottom Line of the passage. With that already clearly defined, we don't need to go back to the passage before we start evaluating the choices.
   If the question stem had asked us to weaken or strengthen a particular claim within the passage, we would need to first go back and find and paraphrase that part of the author's argument.

4. **Answer in your own words; articulate what the correct answer will need to do, based on the question type and the information in the passage.**
   The correct answer will suggest that the adversarial and inquisitorial systems are more similar than the author claims, and/or that the inquisitorial system is not in fact historically superior.

5. **Use Process of Elimination (POE) to choose the *least wrong* answer choice.**
   For a Weaken question, the best answer will go the furthest toward making it impossible for the claim made in the passage to be true. Look for the answer choice that is most inconsistent with the relevant part of the passage.
   For a Strengthen question, look for the choice that 1) provides additional empirical evidence for the claim, or 2) fills in a logical gap in the argument made in the passage, or 3) anticipates and blocks a potential argument against the claim made in the passage.
   When using POE on Strengthen and Weaken questions, eliminate choices that are irrelevant to the cited part or issue in the passage (that is, that are out of scope). Remember, however, that the correct answer will bring in new information: "irrelevant" is not the same thing as "never mentioned."
   Do *not* eliminate choices on the basis of absolute or extreme wording. It is impossible on these questions (in contrast to Specific and General questions) for an answer to be wrong solely on the basis of being too strong. The more it strengthens or weakens the passage, the better.

In fact, choices on this question type may be wrong because they don't go far enough to have a significant impact on the author's argument.

Finally, look out for Attractors that weaken on a Strengthen question, or that strengthen on a Weaken question.

Let's use POE on our Sample Question:

A: No. The author does not claim that private vengeance was the very first system used to punish criminals. For all we know, there could have been other pre-modern systems that preceded private vengeance. This choice attacks a claim that is never made by the author; it is therefore out of scope.

B: No. The passage itself suggests some similarities: e.g., there is a judge, and there is a private investigator searching for evidence to support the prosecution (the inquisitorial system just broadens those duties to include finding evidence for the defense as well). Because the author's main argument is not founded on the assumption that there are few or no similarities between the two, this choice does not go far enough to weaken the passage.

C: No. This choice is entirely consistent with the author's depiction of the adversarial system in paragraph 1. This choice strengthens, not weakens, the author's contrast between the adversarial and inquisitorial systems.

D: **Yes. The author argues that the inquisitorial system is historically superior because it is "two historical steps removed from the system of private vengeance" (paragraph 2) and because it is based on "the facts of the case" (paragraph 3). The adversarial system, in contrast, "is only one historical step removed from the private vengeance system and still retains some of its characteristic features" (paragraph 1). If private vengeance was in fact at the heart of the inquisitorial system, this would undermine the author's argument about the historical character and evolutionary place of the inquisitorial system. Thus, choice D is the best answer.**

Type 9: New Information Questions

All New Information questions have one thing in common: They provide new facts or scenarios in the question stem that are never mentioned in the passage. That said, the question may require you to do a variety of things with that new information. New Information questions break down into two general types.

Type 1: New Information/Inference questions

These questions give you new facts that are in the same general issue area of the passage and then ask what, according to the passage, is likely to be true. In essence, you're inserting the new facts into the existing passage, and then drawing an inference from both the new and the old information. Before you read the answer choices, answer the question in your own words, based on the information already in the passage and on the new facts in the question stem.

For example, the question might ask:

- "If China experienced an unusually rainy winter, what would also be true, based on the passage?"
- "According to the passage, what would likely happen if China experienced an unusually rainy winter?"
- "What would the author recommend as the best way to predict whether China is likely to experience an unusually rainy winter next year?"
- "If a meteorologist were to claim that China's climate can be studied in isolation, how would the author respond?"

Type 2: New Information/Strengthen/Weaken questions

These questions provide you with new facts in the question stem (as opposed to pure Strengthen/Weaken questions that give the new information only in the answer choices). They then ask you to evaluate what effect those new facts would have on the author's argument as a whole, or on one specific claim made or described in the passage.

Approach these questions much like you do Strengthen/Weaken, and Evaluate questions. Identify the issue of the question, and go back to the passage to find the relevant sections. Pay close attention to the logical structure of the author's argument. Define what the correct answer needs to do based on the passage, the information in the question stem, and the direction (strengthen or weaken) the correct choice must take.

This type of New Information question may be phrased as follows:

- "Suppose it was shown to be true that when winters in China are unusually rainy, summers in Latin America are unusually dry. What effect would this have on the author's argument as it is described in the passage?"
- "Which of the following claims made in the passage would be most strengthened by data showing that industrialization has affected global weather patterns?"
- "Recent studies have shown that the jet stream has shifted 10 degrees in latitude over the past five years. This fact tends to undermine the author's claim that…"
- "El Niño has been proven to be a recurring and invariant pattern. This fact tends to support the author's claims in paragraph 2 because…"

The following Sample Question falls into the *Type 1* category.

Sample Question 9:

4.4

9. Suppose that in an inquisitorial system of justice a judge perceives that the prosecution is misdirecting the trial by introducing irrelevant evidence. The author would most likely advise the judge to:

A) protect the prosecution by turning a blind eye to the proceedings.
B) admonish the prosecution and get the trial back to the issues at hand.
C) call a mistrial and free the defendant.
D) refuse to participate in the trial.

1. **Read the question word for word and identify the question type.**
   The word "suppose" is our first indication that this is a New Information question. What follows is a scenario that does not already appear in the passage. The question asks us what the author of the passage would advise, making this a *Type 1* question.

2. **Translate the question into your own words; identify what the question task is asking you to do with the information in the passage.**
   The question is asking us to find an answer choice that is consistent both with the passage and with the new situation in the question stem; in this new scenario, the judge discovers that the prosecution is breaking the rules.

3. **Identify key words and phrases that refer to specific parts of the passage and *go back to the passage* to locate that information.**
   The role of the judge in the inquisitorial system is described at the end of paragraph 2. The judge must "take an active part in the conduct of the trial, with a role that is both directive and protective."

4. **Answer in your own words; articulate what the correct answer will need to do, based on the question type and the information in the passage.**
   Based on the passage, the judge in this situation must take action to protect the defense from the unfair tactics used by the prosecution, and must direct the trial in a way consistent with the system's rules.

5. **Use Process of Elimination (POE) to choose the *least wrong* answer choice.**
   A common Attractor for any New Information question is an answer choice that focuses on the wrong part of the passage.
   Also beware of answer choices that are inconsistent with the passage (for all but the Weaken version of this question type), or that deal with irrelevant issues. This means choices that do not connect to the passage, or that are not relevant to the theme of the new information in the question.
   For *Type 1* questions, beware of extreme language. The correct answer can't go too far beyond the scope and tone of the passage.
   For *Type 2* questions, beware of choices that go in the opposite direction (e.g., that strengthen instead of weaken or vice versa).

Let's go through POE on our sample question:

A: No. This is inconsistent with the author's claim that in the inquisitorial system, the interests of the defense as well as of the prosecution should be protected. This is also inconsistent with the author's claim that the judge must take an active role to direct the proceedings.

B: **Yes. This is consistent with the author's claim that the judge has a protective role (protecting the rights of the defense by admonishing the prosecution) and a directive role (getting the trial back on track). This choice is relevant to the theme of the new information and is consistent with the passage (as required by the question task). Thus, it is the "least wrong" of the four choices.**

C: No. This choice is too extreme; the passage does not indicate that prosecutorial misbehavior would invalidate the trial as a whole. This choice is also out of scope; the issue of calling a mistrial arises in neither the passage nor the question stem.

D: No. As in choice A, this is inconsistent with the author's claim that judges in the inquisitorial system must play an active role.

Type 10: Analogy Questions

These questions ask you to take something described in the passage, abstract it, and then apply it to an entirely new situation. They differ from New Information questions in that the new information is in the answer choices, not in the question stem. They differ from Strengthen questions in that the new information in the correct choice will not make the original argument stronger than it already was. It will be similar to it in logic, but is likely to be on a different issue or subject matter.

These questions can be tricky, as all the answers at first glance may seem to have nothing to do with the passage. However, you are matching the logic or purpose of the author's argument, not the informational content of the passage. Therefore, the correct answer can match the logic of the passage (or relevant part of the passage) while still bringing in entirely new content.

Take for example a passage in which the author argues the following: "Weather is the result of a global interactive system. Therefore, to understand and predict the weather in a particular region, you must analyze how the climates of all regions interact with each other, and not limit your focus to the weather patterns in that region alone."

The question might ask:

* "Which of the following approaches to educational reform would most likely be advocated by a school board member following the same logic as the author of the passage?"

To answer this question, you must *first* generalize the author's own claims to create an abstracted model that could be applied to other situations. For example, you might say, "Large interactive systems cannot be understood by looking at the parts in isolation from the whole; you must understand how those parts relate to and affect each other," or, more simply, "the whole is more than the sum of its parts."

Now, take this generalized version into the answer choices, and look for a choice that has the same theme. The school board member might place the school system within the context of larger socioeconomic

4.4

forces that also affect educational performance. Or, she might argue that the school itself is a large interactive system, and that you can't improve education by addressing only one piece of the puzzle (standardized testing, for example). As you can see, a wide variety of answer choices are possible. Don't waste time coming up with specific scenarios; generalize the passage's argument as much as possible, and then match each answer choice against that abstracted model.

Remember that the correct answer must depend solely on the content of the passage, not on outside information or your own opinion!

Sample Question 10:

10. The author's discussion of the history of systems of criminal procedure is most similar to which of the following?

A) a study of the transmission of infectious diseases
B) a proposal for civil rights reforms
C) an evolutionary biologist's study of plant species
D) an architect's blueprint

1. **Read the question word for word and identify the question type.**
   The phrase "most similar to" tells us that this is an analogy question.
2. **Translate the question into your own words; identify what the question task is asking you to do with the information in the passage.**
   The question is asking us to describe the overall logic and purpose of the passage, in order to match it to a similar logic and purpose (but, in a different subject area) in the correct answer.
3. **Identify key words and phrases that refer to specific parts of the passage and *go back to the passage* to locate that information.**
   Because this question asks us to make an analogy to the author's overall logic and purpose in the passage as a whole, we don't necessarily need to go back the passage at this point; use your own articulation of the Bottom Line, and your understanding of the logical structure of the passage, as a guide.
4. **Answer in your own words; articulate what the correct answer will need to do, based on the question type and the information in the passage.**
   The passage describes the historical evolution of criminal procedure: how private vengeance evolved into the adversarial system, which then evolved into the inquisitorial system. Therefore, we need an answer that has this theme of evolution or change over time.
5. **Use Process of Elimination (POE) to choose the *least wrong* answer choice.**
   Keep in mind that all of the answer choices may be on different topics (i.e., not on criminal procedure).
   The correct choice will be the one that is most similar in logic to the author's overall argument in the passage.
   Eliminate choices that have the wrong tone (compared to the passage).
   When you are down to two, pick the choice that has the most similarities. If one of the two remaining choices has one similarity, but the other remaining choice is similar in two ways, the latter choice will be the credited response.

Let's use POE on our sample answer choices:

A: No. First of all, this choice has a negative tone that does not match the passage. While the passage does describe how the adversarial system maintained some of the characteristics of private vengeance, the author doesn't use language suggesting it was "infected" (which has an overly negative tone) by the earlier system. Furthermore, this theme of transmission of a disease from one thing to another doesn't fit with the passage's theme of difference and contrast (between the adversarial and inquisitorial systems).

B: No. The tone of this choice does not match the tone and purpose of the passage. The author describes change over time, but does not recommend further change.

C: **Yes. An evolutionary biologist studying plant species would look at change over time through the succession of species. This choice is most similar to the logic and purpose of the passage, and matches the tone reasonably well.**

D: No. Compare this choice to choice C. While there are some aspects of a blueprint (describing the structure a system), there is no theme in this choice of change over time. Also, the author of the passage is describing structures themselves (that already exist) not plans for structures.

Now that we have looked at the 10 question types in the Standard format, let's look at examples of the other two formats: Except/Least/Not and Roman Numeral questions.

Except/Least/Not Questions

This question type can appear in combination with most of the question tasks described above. Because of its potentially confusing structure (looking for the worst instead of the best), students often misread or misapply the question. In fact, the correct answer to this question type can be the wacky or totally irrelevant answer choice that you are used to eliminating first.

To avoid making a mistake, use your scratch paper. Write down the passage number (if you haven't already) and the number of the question. Next to the question number jot down a translation of the question, including what kind of choices you will be eliminating. Do this before looking at the answer choices. For example, for a Weaken Except question, write down,

"eliminate what weakens, pick what strengthens or has no effect."

Also jot down the four letters. As you evaluate each answer choice, write Y (in this case, for *yes*, it does weaken the passage) or N (for *no*, it does not weaken the passage) next to the choice. Cross it off on your scratch paper as you strike it out on the screen. At the end, you should have three Ys and one N. Pick the one that is not like the others!

Sample Question 11:

4.4

11. The author would be most likely to agree with all of the following statements EXCEPT:

A) the judge actively participates in the inquisitorial system.
B) the prosecutor in the adversarial system need not disclose evidence to the defense.
C) the inquisitorial system regularizes punitive combat.
D) the vengeance system was a system of self-help.

1. **Read the question word for word and identify the question type.**
   Except/Least/Not questions are quite easy to recognize. Here, the key word is *except*. This is an Inference question ("The author would be most likely to agree") in Except/Least/Not format.
2. **Translate the question into your own words; identify what the question task is asking you to do with the information in the passage.**
   This question is asking us to eliminate the choices that are supported by the passage (that is, statements that the author of the passage would accept as true), and to pick the one that is most inconsistent with the author's argument.
3. **Identify key words and phrases that refer to specific parts of the passage and go back to the passage to locate that information.**
   In this question, there is no specific reference to the passage. You will need, however, to go back to the passage as you work through the answer choices.
   If the question had given us a specific reference (e.g., to "the police department"), you would go back to the passage and read above and below that reference before moving on to the next step.
4. **Answer in your own words; articulate what the correct answer will need to do, based on the question type and the information in the passage.**
   The correct choice will contradict the passage in some way. The incorrect answers will be consistent with the passage information as well as consistent with the author's tone and purpose.
5. **Use Process of Elimination (POE) to choose the *least wrong* answer choice.**
   As you might predict, the most common Attractor is the opposite: a choice that would be the correct answer to a Standard Format question. Approach Except/Least/Not questions carefully and methodically to avoid falling into this (very annoying) trap.
   Keep in mind that your reasons for eliminating choices on a Standard question (e.g., language that is too extreme, or a statement that mixes up two different things in the passage) now become your reasons for keeping and perhaps selecting an answer.

Let's take a look at our answer choices:

A: No. This choice is directly supported by the end of paragraph 1.
B: No. This choice is supported by the discussion of pretrial discovery in paragraph 2. If the inquisitorial system is different in that it does require the prosecutor to disclose its evidence to the court (and so to the defense), the author would agree that the prosecutor need not disclose it under the adversarial system.
C: **Yes. This is true of the adversarial, not the inquisitorial system (see the end of paragraph 1). This choice contradicts the passage; therefore, it is the credited response.**
D: No. This choice is supported by the middle of paragraph 1.

Roman Numeral Questions

Like Except/Least/Not questions, Roman Numeral questions can appear in combination with a variety of question tasks.

To approach these questions, evaluate numeral I (unless it appears in all four choices, in which case it must be true). If it is not an appropriate answer to the question, strike out all of the choices that include it. If it *is* appropriate, eliminate the choices that do *not* include it. Compare the choices you have left to each other. If numeral II or III appears in all of them, read it but don't over-think it. Unless there is something terribly wrong with it, it must also be true based on the combinations you have.

Use your scratch paper: jot down the three numerals so that you can cross them off or circle them as you evaluate each one (on a CBT you can only strike out the lettered answer choices, not the Roman numerals.)

Sample Question 12:

12. According to the passage, which of the following is a duty of the prosecutor in the inquisitorial system?

   I. To present evidence that may lead to the defendant's exoneration
  II. To disclose all evidence in his/her possession
 III. To assume a role that is both protective and directive

A) II only
B) III only
C) I and II only
D) I and III only

1. **Read the question word for word and identify the question type.**
   This is a Retrieval question ("According to the passage") in Roman Numeral format.
2. **Translate the question into your own words; identify what the question task is asking you to do with the information in the passage.**
   The question is asking which of the three statements accurately represent things that are required of a prosecutor within the inquisitorial system.
3. **Identify key words and phrases that refer to specific parts of the passage and *go back to the passage* to locate that information.**
   The inquisitorial system is described in paragraphs 2 and 3. Prosecutor's duties are specifically mentioned in the context of pretrial discovery, in the second half of paragraph 2 (after the word "additionally," and before the word "finally").
4. **Answer in your own words; articulate what the correct answer will need to do, based on the question type and the information in the passage.**
   Prosecutors in the inquisitorial system must permit full disclosure of all evidence they have uncovered, even if that evidence would help the defense. They must also comply with all of the other rules of the inquisitorial system.

5. **Use Process of Elimination (POE) to choose the *least wrong* answer choice.**
    In some ways, you are approaching the choices just as you would for a Standard question (in our Sample, a Retrieval task). For each numeral, ask yourself if this statement accomplishes the question task (here, if it describes a prosecutor's duty in the inquisitorial system). However, you can also often use the combinations in the answer choices to your advantage. If, for example, you are sure that numeral I is supported, and unsure about numeral III, but no choice includes both I and III, you know that numeral III is in fact not supported (as it doesn't appear in any of the possible correct answer choices).
    If you tend to miss Roman Numeral questions, diagnose the most common reasons for your mistakes. If you tend to pick incomplete answers that are missing one or two numerals, you may be reading the numerals too quickly, picking only the ones that are the most obvious, and missing the more subtly supported statements. If you tend to pick choices that include too many, you may not be going back to the passage enough to check your answers carefully against the text.

Let's go through POE on our Sample Question item by item:

I: True. This statement is supported by the author's discussion of pretrial discovery in paragraph 2. Therefore, we can eliminate choices A and B, because neither includes Roman numeral I. We are now down to choices C and D. The difference between them is that choice C includes II but not III, and choice D includes III but not II. It is now a battle between choices II and III— only one of them can be correct!

II: True. This is also supported by the author's description of pretrial discovery. Note that we essentially have the correct answer at this stage, as there is no answer that includes all three numerals.

III: False. This is the role of the judge, not of the prosecutor (see the end of paragraph 2, after the word "finally").

So, our credited response is **Choice C: I and II only.**

4.5 VERBAL REASONING EXERCISE: IDENTIFYING QUESTION TYPES

Here are 10 sample questions. Read each question carefully, and identify the question type and format. Also think about what this question type is asking you to do.

1. Nevitt lists the duties of City Council representatives in order to: *structure*

2. If it is shown to be true that only two species of egg-laying mammals exist, the author would most likely conclude that the platypus:

   Main Idea

3. The passage suggests which of the following to be true of the Treaty of Versailles?

4. According to passage information, the Sahara Desert:

   retrieval.

5. Which of the following claims, if true, would most *undermine* the author's contention that most environmental regulation is counterproductive?

6. Which of the following is most similar to Professor Bybee's experimental methodology?

7. By "quarantine" the author most likely means:

   Vocab context

8. Which one of the following *least* strengthens the author's claim that caps on jury awards should be lifted?

9. The author's criticism of deconstructionist literary theory is supported:

10. Which of the following assertions is *least* believable based on claims made in the passage?

Answers for Verbal Reasoning Exercise: Identifying Question Types

1. **Structure:** What role does this list play in Nevitt's argument?
2. **New** Information *Type 1*: What would the author say is true about the platypus, based both on the new information and on the existing information in the passage?
3. **Inference:** Which statement about the Treaty of Versailles is best supported by information in the passage?
4. **Retrieval:** Which statement about the Sahara Desert is best supported by information in the passage?
5. **Weaken:** Which answer choice goes farthest to suggest that environmental regulation *is* productive?
6. **Analogy:** Which choice most describes the same kind of methodology or process as that used, according to the passage, by Bybee?
7. **Vocabulary in Context:** Which definition of quarantine best fits with the author's use of that word in the passage?
8. **Least Strengthen:** Which choice either weakens that claim (by indicating caps should not be lifted) or has no effect on that claim? Eliminate the choices that do suggest that caps should be lifted.
9. **Evaluate:** Is the author's criticism of deconstructionist literary theory strongly or weakly supported? If strongly, then how? If weakly, then what are the flaws in the argument?
10. **Inference/Except:** Look for the answer that is least supported by (most inconsistent with) the passage. Eliminate the choices that are supported by the passage.

Chapter 4 Summary

Know the five steps you should take in answering any question:

1. Read the question carefully and identify the question type.

2. Translate the question into your own words.

3. Identify key words and phrases [for Specific questions] and go back to the passage to find the relevant information.

4. Answer the question in your own words.

5. Use Process of Elimination.

Know the ten basic question types that you will encounter in MCAT Verbal Reasoning:

1. Retrieval

2. Inference

3. Vocabulary in Context

4. Main Idea/Primary Purpose

5. Tone/Attitude

6. Structure

7. Evaluate

8. Strengthen/Weaken

9. New Information

10. Analogy

Monitor your progress and improve your accuracy by keeping a Self-Evaluation Log.

CHAPTER 4 PRACTICE PASSAGES

Individual Passage Drills

Do the following two passages untimed. Use these passages to focus on answering the questions in your own words.

Get a stack of Post-it® Notes. Paste a Note over each set of answer choices, leaving the questions themselves visible. Work the passage as usual, but when it comes time to answer the question in your own words, write your answer on the Note. When finished, lift up the Post-it® Note and look for the choice that's closest to what you wrote down, while actively using POE to eliminate choices that sound similar but are flawed.

Once you have completed the passages and checked your answers, fill out an Individual Passage Log for each passage.

In your self-evaluation focus in particular on question types. Did you correctly identify the question type? Did you understand what the question was asking you to do? Did you apply the 5 Steps in a way that was appropriate for the question task? Which question types were easier and harder for you to complete and why? And, what kinds of Attractors did you fall for? Finally, how can you change your approach to answering questions to improve your accuracy and efficiency?

CHAPTER 4 PRACTICE PASSAGE 1

It is a remarkable fact that no sooner does a wild animal or plant become intimately associated with man, than it at once departs more or less widely from its ancient type. Our conquests from the vegetable world have to a great extent so far lost their original character that we can no longer determine the species from which they sprang. Botanists cannot find the wild forms which have given us the cabbage, wheat, and most other small grains, and a host of other important varieties. So, too, the origin of our dogs is as yet unsolved and bids forever to remain a mystery. In addition to this changed character which we observe in the forms of domesticated animals and plants alike, we note that the mental characteristics of the former undergo vast alterations. The mental change which has come about in dogs, partly by selection, partly from association with man, has gone so far that the species may be fairly said to have replaced its pristine motives with those which it has derived from ourselves. In many cases it has become, so far as its ways are concerned, even more man than dog.

Now that we are beginning to know something of the laws of inheritance, it is high time for us deliberately to consider what our relations to the organic world are hereafter to be, and how we can guide ourselves in these relations by the light of modern learning. It is in the first place clear that the subjugation of the earth which necessarily accompanies the development of civilization, inevitably tends to sweep away a large part of the organic life which is not adopted and protected by man. New as civilization is on this continent, it has already brought the moose and the buffalo to a point where they are on the verge of extinction, and in the Old World the wild ancestors of the horse and the bull have quite disappeared from the wildernesses. Within a few centuries the greater birds, the Dinornis and Epiornis, as well as the interesting Dodo, have vanished from the southern isles which they inhabited. In the century to come we can foresee that this process of effacement of the ancient life will go on with accelerated velocity.

It seems inevitable that man should play the part of a destroyer. It is his place to break down the ancient order determined by what we call natural forces and in its stead to set a new accord in which the economy of the earth will be in a great measure controlled by his intelligence. Even those who most keenly sympathize with the wilderness life are not likely to object to the changes which are necessary to open the way for this new dispensation. They may fairly ask, however, that hereafter the displacement of the ancient life shall be brought about with foresight and with the exercise of the utmost care in minimizing the sacrifices which we are called on to make. Naturalists may fairly ask men to remember that each of these species which we are forced to destroy represents the toil and pains of unimaginable ages, and that when these creatures are swept away they can never be recovered.

To take only the case of the great birds which have recently been swept from the earth, we see clearly that we have with them lost precious opportunities for enlarging our understanding of nature and have at the same time been deprived of the chance to domesticate creatures which would most likely have proved of much economic value. With each of these species which disappears we lose what may be a precious chance of adding to the small store of animals or plants which may contribute to the well being of our kind. These considerations make it plain that it is our duty by our civilization, to do all in our power to save these species and at the same time to essay their domestication, for only when under the protection of man can they be regarded as insured from destruction.

Material used in this particular passage has been adapted from the following source:

N. S. Shaler, *Domesticated Animals: Their Relation to Man and to his Advancement in Civilization.* © 1895 by Charles Scribners' Sons.

1. The passage suggests domestication:

    I.   alters the evolutionary course of species.
    II. protects species from extinction.
    III. can affect form as well as character.

A) I and II only
B) I and III only
C) II and III only
D) I, II, and III

2. In paragraph 2, the word "effacement" is used to mean:

A) eradication.
B) replacement.
C) evolution.
D) understanding.

3. The author agrees with the naturalists he references in the passage largely on the basis of:

A) morality.
B) scientific analysis.
C) environmentalism.
D) pragmatism.

4. At the time this passage was written, the moose and the buffalo were at the edge of extinction but the horse and the bull continued to flourish. Based on information in the passage, which of the following explanations for this phenomenon would the author most likely support?

A) Random mutations gave the horse and the bull a survival advantage over other species.
B) Horses and bulls are too numerous in the Old World to be wiped out entirely.
C) Domestication has removed the incentive for man to hunt horses and bulls to extinction.
D) As the New World was settled, moose and buffalo were essential sources of food, and so, subject to over-hunting.

5. Which of the following most nearly parallels man's relationship to animals as the author portrays it in the passage?

A) An employer concerned about burning out young employees
B) A store owner concerned about running out of inventory
C) An industrial tycoon concerned about depleting the world's supply of a raw material
D) A behavioral scientist trying to learn how best to condition animals to respond to commands

6. The support given for the argument in paragraph 4 that extinction represents a loss of economic value is:

A) strong: the concept follows logically from the author's description of the naturalists' point of view.
B) strong: the author cites the Dinornis, Epiornis, and Dodo as examples of birds whose economic value has been lost.
C) weak: no evidence is given to link bird species with intellectual or economic value.
D) weak: the author makes a contradictory argument earlier in the essay.

7. Paragraph 1 suggests the origins of species have been:

A) masked by deliberate cross-breeding and modification.
B) altered by natural selection.
C) obscured by association with man.
D) tainted by overzealous hunting, fishing, and harvesting.

CHAPTER 4 PRACTICE PASSAGE 2

The challenge of any [Supreme] Court-led politics of representation is to raise conceptions of political identity to the surface, bringing critical attention to bear on how the judiciary fashions the political community as it shapes its own political power.

The first step toward meeting this analytical challenge requires an examination of the public debate over the adjudication of minority representation under the Voting Rights Act of 1965. Three basic positions have prevailed on the debate, distinguished largely by their different views on whether the Voting Rights Act should be rolled back, pushed forward, or simply maintained. Given these differences in orientation, these ideological responses to the act can be called conservative, progressive, and centrist. The conflicting claims of conservatives and progressives set the outer limits of debate, making discussion of minority representation a sharply contested and exceedingly polarized affair. In such a context of mutually exclusive assertions, the centrist attempt to strike a reasonable balance appears immediately appealing.

On the whole, while conservatives and progressives are united in their rejection of the status quo, they diverge sharply in their reasons for seeking change. Where conservatives see a politics that has been held hostage to the demands of civil rights elites, progressives describe a politics increasingly dominated by white racism and retrenchment. It is in this polarized context of claims and counterclaims that the centrists attempt to fashion a reasonable middle position. Dismissing both conservative and progressive claims as exaggerated rhetoric, centrists argue that the debate over the Voting Rights Act is actually quite narrow. While name calling and finger pointing have drawn the lion's share of attention, centrists claim that most of the disputants are actually concerned with achieving a color-blind society. Beneath the barbed polemics, controversies over minority representation amount to a disagreement over means rather than ends. Bernard Grofman and Chandler Davis suggest that the "highly abstract" mode of the current debate only breeds misunderstanding and conflict; a better approach is to be found in a "consideration of the empirical evidence of the actual consequences of the [Voting Rights Act].

In the centrist view, then, the Voting Rights Act is neither a racially balkanizing nor a broadly empowering document. In essence, the act takes limited steps to ameliorate specific and concrete inequities. The incrementalist, case-by-case nature of voting-rights policy means that remedial measures can be crafted without raising larger issues of democratic theory. Big questions such as "What is fair minority representation?" never need to be asked because judges and other federal officials are simply correcting what is obviously wrong given the specific facts at hand.

What can be made of the centrist attempt to steer a middle course between conservative and progressive claims? Centrists make the claim for a responsive political process largely by insisting that the incrementalism of voting rights policy avoids theoretical questions. The very realism and reasonableness of the Voting Rights Act inheres in its atheoretical design. Thus, the centrist argument amounts to more than a simple corrective of exaggerated views. If the centrists are right, the entire polarized debate between conservatives and progressives should be set aside as a distraction. We will do just fine if the country and the courts continue to muddle through the issue of minority representation a case at a time.

On what grounds is the centrist evasion of theoretical issues warranted? The Voting Rights Act itself hinges on contestable issues such as "equal political opportunity," which Congress has defined only in the broadest manner. Such imprecision would seem to encourage a wide range of judicial interpretations, suggesting an opportunity for judicial theorizing somewhat antithetical to the ideal centrist reform.

One could argue that so long as the Court is effectively constrained by its own canons of statutory construction, voting-rights reform need not plunge into any conceptual morass. The difficulty with such an argument is that the judiciary has historically employed a number of canons, many of which point interpretation in different directions. It is true that some legal commentators have spoken of the judge "worth his salt" or with the right "sense of the situation" who can negotiate among the various canons, consistently producing an accurate rendering of the statute's meaning or purpose. Despite such claims, widespread consensus on what should count as the proper "sense of the situation" has not emerged. Easy agreement has proved elusive because the choice between interpretive strategies itself depends on what Cass Sunstein calls "background principles" — principles that express particular visions of how government ought to operate and, thus, provide the baseline against which statutes should be understood.

In general, one can say that the process of statutory interpretation is critically concerned with normative disputes over how the government ought to operate. By stressing measurable facts and hard evidence, the centrist argument as a whole sidesteps the debate's key issue. The progressive and conservative views are not simply "mistakes" that can be corrected by a more accurate set of facts. Each of these camps anchors its claims in different conceptions of fair representation, which serve as guides for how the Voting Rights Act's promise of equal political opportunity ought to be realized. Thus, conservatives and progressives do not simply disagree on what the "facts" of the debate are. More importantly, they disagree on what the same "facts" mean in light of what fair minority representation is taken to be.

Material used in this particular passage has been adapted from the following source:

K. Bybee, *Mistaken Identity: The Supreme Court and the Politics of Minority Representation.* © 1998 by Princeton University Press.

1. Which of the following statements best expresses the main thesis of the passage?

A) Three positions have emerged in the debate over the Voting Rights Act, which may be labeled progressive, centrist, and conservative.

B) While imperfect, the centrist approach is the most reasonable, given that it avoids the ideological extremes embodied in the conservative and progressive positions and that it advocates a case-by-case evaluation of the impact of the Voting Rights Act.

C) The centrist position on the Voting Rights Act represents a flawed understanding of the nature of the act, and of how the act relates to the construction of political identity.

D) Examining the debate over the Voting Rights Act is an important step in evaluating the impact of the judiciary on politics.

2. The author most likely refers to commentators who speak of judges with the correct "sense of the situation" in order to:

A) illustrate a way in which a common understanding of basic principles of fair representation might be reached)

B) raise difficulties with an argument that could be used to support the centrist approach.

C) criticize judges for arriving at overly personal solutions to complex theoretical problems.

D) support the claim that the Voting Rights Act turns on the contestable issue of "equal political opportunity."

3. Suppose it were shown that progressives believe fair representation of a minority group can only by achieved through electing representatives who are members of that group, while conservatives believe that minority interests are well protected by any representative who works for the good of society as a whole. If this is true, which position described in the passage would be most *undermined*?

A) The author's argument that background principles determine how facts are interpreted

B) The conservative position that the Voting Rights Act should be rolled back

C) The centrist position that application of the Voting Rights Act need not consider big abstract questions

D) The progressive position that politics is dominated by white racism

4. The author's argument in paragraph 8 that the progressive and conservative camps locate their claims in different conceptions of fair representation is supported:

A) weakly, because no descriptions or examples of these different concepts are provided

B) weakly, because this claim conflicts with the centrist argument that the Voting Rights Act is atheoretical.

C) strongly, because it is based on Sunstein's conception of "background principles."

D) strongly, because it implies that the same facts may be interpreted in different ways by different people.

5. In the context of the passage, "incrementalism" (paragraph 5) most likely refers to a policy that:

A) causes fundamental societal change.

B) considers problems on a case-by-case basis.

C) is concerned with achieving a color-blind society.

D) takes a step by step approach to reaching agreement on basic theoretical principles.

6. Which of the following would be most analogous to the centrist approach, as it is described in the passage?

A) A mediator who seeks to find middle ground by encouraging each side to make concessions to the other in order to come to a mutual understanding of what would constitute a fair resolution

B) A sociologist who uses economic theory to analyze social interactions

C) A political scientist who categorizes political systems based on levels of fair representation and equality

D) A psychologist who treats patients by looking at each person's experience and perceptions in order to help him or her to achieve "a good life" as defined by commonly accepted standards

7. Which of the following, if true, would most support the author's evaluation of the centrist position?

A) Different ideas of what constitutes fair representation are inextricably bound up with differing ideas about the proper role of the state within society.

B) Controversy about how to delineate electoral districts in order to ensure fair representation is often based on disagreements about population statistics.

C) The original writers of the Voting Rights Act did not believe that the implementation of the act would require debate on abstract questions of principle.

D) The conflicting claims set out by progressives and conservatives differ more in terms of vocabulary than on the basic ideas intended to be expressed through the rhetoric employed by each side.

SOLUTIONS TO CHAPTER 4 PRACTICE PASSAGE 1

1. **D** This is an Inference/Roman Numeral question.

   I: True. The general idea of paragraph 1 is that "association with man" has fundamentally changed plant and animal species such that "no sooner does a wild animal or plant become intimately associated with man, than it at once departs more or less widely from its ancient type."

   II: True. In the last line of the passage, the author says: "only when under the protection of man can they be regarded as insured from destruction." Remember that Inference questions can and frequently do draw their answers from more than one part of the passage.

   III: True. See paragraph 1: "In addition to this changed character which we observe in the forms of domesticated animals and plants alike, we note that the mental characteristics of the former undergo vast alterations."

2. **A** This is a Vocabulary in Context question.

   A: Yes. Even if you're not familiar with the term "effacement," you can figure out that this is the most likely answer from the context. When the passage refers to "this process of effacement," notice that the pronoun "this" is referring back to something. A quick look back at the previous sentence shows "this" is a process of making species "vanish." "Eradication" is the best match.

   B: No. The passage does not suggest the "vanishing" species are being replaced.

   C: No. This answer disregards the context. Paragraph 2 is discussing extinction, not evolution.

   D: No. The author is not discussing how we might come to understand this process, but rather the process itself.

3. **D** This is an Inference question.

   Note: In paragraph 3, the author explains that naturalists believe we should avoid causing extinctions because each species is unique. The author then develops that argument in paragraph 4 in his own voice. The answer must follow from what the author presents as his own beliefs rather than only from what the naturalists believe.

   A: No. This is one interpretation of the naturalists' argument—that it is immoral to destroy a unique species. This is also a common sense answer, but not one supported by paragraph 4.

   B: No. The author does not engage in scientific analysis.

   C: No. Although this passage seems to exemplify a form of environmentalism, the author's rationale for avoiding extinctions does not stem from wanting to preserve the natural environment.

   D: Yes. See paragraph 4. The author's reasons for preserving species concern how those species can benefit people. Thus the argument is that animals are useful, not that they should be preserved for their own sake.

4. **C** This is a New Information question.

   A: No. Although the author does make passing reference to evolution due to human influence, this choice is not supported by the passage as we do not know whether the moose and bull were nearing extinction because of evolutionary forces.

   B: No. The author does not mention population as a factor in species' survival.

C: Yes. While not directly stated, this answer is the best supported of the choices presented. The last line of the passage states: "it is our duty by our civilization, to do all in our power to save these species and at the same time to essay their domestication, for only when under the protection of man can they be regarded as insured from destruction." This is an idea from the passage that can be applied to this situation: horses and bulls have been protected from hunting because of their usefulness whereas the moose and buffalo have not been domesticated.

D: No. Be careful not to use outside knowledge. The credited answer will be supported by the text, and there is no discussion of over-hunting in the passage.

5. **C** This is an Analogy question.

A: No. There is no suggestion people are working animals too hard.

B: No. This answer is close, but a store owner who runs out of inventory can generally reorder more stock, whereas a species that becomes extinct can not be renewed or replaced.

C: **Yes. The author portrays man as interested in using animals for his own (partly economic) reasons, but also as being in danger of exploiting animals to the point of extinction (see in particular paragraph 4).**

D: No. While paragraph 1 does discuss the minds of dogs, animal training is not the author's key concern in the relationship between people and animals.

6. **C** This is an Evaluate question.

A: No. The idea that extinction represents a loss of economic value is different from, and not necessarily the logical result of, the naturalists' argument that every species is unique and irreplaceable. Even if it did follow logically, it would be hard to characterize this kind of reasoning as support for the idea.

B: No. The author mentions specific bird species but does not explain or make reference to their economic value, which would be necessary to support the argument at issue.

C: **Yes. While specific bird species are mentioned, they are not linked to economic value.**

D: No. No earlier argument specifically contradicts or argues against the idea that species have economic value.

7. **C** This is an Inference question.

A: No. This answer is very similar to choice C but goes a step farther than what's supported by the passage; cross-breeding, or the combination of different species, is not explicitly mentioned.

B: No. Natural selection affects which species and qualities survive as they change over time, but it does not itself change the original species.

C: **Yes. This is the main idea of paragraph 1, which states: "Our conquests from the vegetable world have to a great extent so far lost their original character that we can no longer determine the species from which they sprang. Botanists cannot find the wild forms which have given us the cabbage, wheat, and most other small grains, and a host of other important varieties. So, too, the origin of our dogs is as yet unsolved and bids fair ever to remain a mystery."**

D: No. It is not clear how the origin of a species can be "tainted"; this is not an issue addressed in the passage.

SOLUTIONS TO CHAPTER 4 PRACTICE PASSAGE 2

1. **C**   This is a Main Idea/Primary Purpose question.

   A: No. This choice is too narrow to be the correct answer to a Main Idea question. While the statement is supported by the passage, it leaves out the heart of the author's argument, which is his evaluation of the validity (or lack thereof) of the centrist position.

   B: No. This choice misrepresents the author's opinion. While the author does state that "the centrists attempt to fashion a reasonable middle position" (paragraph 3), and that their position "appears immediately appealing" (paragraph 2),the author argues in paragraphs 6-8 that this position is fundamentally flawed in its assumption that discussion and implementation of the Voting Rights Act can avoid theoretical discussion. Always make sure to take the entire passage into account for a general question, and to clearly define the author's opinion.

   C: **Yes. In the beginning of the passage, the author connects discussion of the Voting Rights Act to issues of political identity (paragraph 1). The author discusses the centrist response to progressive and conservative positions in paragraphs 2-5. Finally, in paragraphs 6-8, the author argues that the centrists are fundamentally wrong in their assertion that the act can be understood or implemented without confronting abstract issues: for example, what constitutes fair representation. Note that the author's claim about the need to consider theoretical issues ties back to paragraph 1 and the beginning of the second.**

   D: No. As in choice A, this answer is supported by the passage (paragraphs 1 and 2), but is too narrow to be the main thesis of the passage. For example, it leaves out the author's negative evaluation of the centrist position.

2. **B**   This is a Structure question.

   A: No. The author suggests the opposite. He states: "Despite such claims, widespread consensus on what should count as the proper sense of the situation" has not emerged (paragraph 7). Furthermore, the commentators themselves are not referring to judges who achieve a common understanding of basic principles, but rather to those who supposedly can come to an accurate understanding of the meaning or purpose of a statute (and how to apply it to a particular case).

   B: **Yes. A centrist might use the argument that abstract principles need not be considered by voting-rights reform because judges are able "negotiate among the various canons" to interpret and apply statutes without relying on theoretical interpretation. The author goes on to say that this is not in fact the case, because deciding how to interpret a statute requires choosing between basic principles regarding "how the government ought to operate" (paragraphs 7 and 8). Thus, theory cannot be avoided, and the purely empirical approach advocated by the centrists is not possible.**

   C: No. There is no criticism of the judges themselves expressed by the author. The implied criticism is of the commentators who make this argument about judges. Also, the problem identified by the author isn't that their approach is too "personal," but rather that it cannot in fact avoid theoretical issues.

   D: No. This is the wrong issue. While the author does make this argument in the beginning of paragraph 6, the discussion of judges in paragraph 7 does not itself give evidence that the act depends or hinges on the particular contestable issue of "equal political opportunity."

3.   **C**   This is a New Information question.

Note: The new information suggests a disagreement about what constitutes fair representation. This, if valid, would undermine the centrist claim that "Big questions such as 'What is fair minority representation?' never need to be asked because judges and other federal officials are simply correcting what is obviously wrong given the specific facts at hand" (paragraph 4). And, by undermining the centrists, it strengthens the author's critique of the centrist position.

A: No. This would strengthen rather than weaken the author's position.

B: No. This new information has no impact on the conservative position. The fact that there are different conceptions of fair representation does not by itself suggest that the act is something that should be maintained or extended rather than rolled back.

C: **Yes. The centrist claim that abstract questions do not need to be considered rests in part on their belief that most people agree on basic principles, and that there can be wide agreement on what is "obviously wrong given the specific facts at hand" (paragraph 4). If there is in fact disagreement on what constitutes fair representation, this would weaken or undermine the centrist position. Note that the author states in paragraph 8 that "Each of these camps anchors its claims in different conceptions of fair representation, which serve as guides for how the Voting Rights Act's promise of equal political opportunity ought to be realized." This suggests that the very different ways of conceiving of "fair representation" described in the question stem would qualify as different ends or principles, not just different means.**

D: No. The new information gives no evidence one way or the other about the existence or role of white racism in the political process.

4.   **A**   This is an Evaluate question.

A: **Yes. This statement is weakly supported. The author makes the claim but gives no supportive evidence to prove the claim. We don't know what those different conceptions are, or how significantly they might differ.**

B: No. The first word of the choice is correct, but the rest of it is incorrect. The entire point of the passage is largely to disprove the centrist argument. Simply conflicting with an opposing position is not itself a weakness.

C: No. While the claim cited in the question follows from the discussion of Sunstein's idea (paragraph 7), the concept of the existence of background principles does not itself support the claim that conservatives and progressives have different concepts of fair representation.

D: No. The second part of the choice is accurate (see paragraph 8), but the evaluation ("strongly") is incorrect. This choice essentially reverses the relationship between parts of the argument. The implication of a claim (that is, the conclusion based on it) does not itself provide support for the claim.

5.   **B**   This is a Vocabulary in Context question.

A: No. This is the opposite of what the term expresses in the context of the centrist view. The centrists, who advocate the incrementalist view, believe that application of the act on a case by case basis entails simply correcting mistakes on a relatively small scale.

B: **Yes. "Incrementalism" is essentially defined in the previous paragraph: "The incrementalist, case-by-case nature of voting-rights policy means that remedial measures can be crafted without raising larger issues of democratic theory."**

C: No. This describes what the centrists believe to be true of most people (paragraph 3), but does not define incrementalism itself.

D: No. This choice is half right but half wrong. Yes, it is a step by step approach, but not to reaching agreement on theoretical principles. The centrists (who are identified with incrementalism in the passage) believe that this agreement has already been reached (see paragraph 3).

6.   **D**   This is an Analogy question.
Note: The correct answer will be the one that is most logically similar to the centrist view or approach. In the passage, the author states that according to the centrists, "the act takes limited steps to ameliorate specific and concrete inequities" (paragraph 4), that "Big questions such as "What is fair minority representation?" never need to be asked because judges and other federal officials are simply correcting what is obviously wrong given the specific facts at hand" (paragraph 4), and that "We will do just fine if the country and the courts continue to muddle through the issue of minority representation a case at a time" (paragraph 5).

A: No. This choice is immediately attractive because it mentions a middle ground. However, the centrists aren't trying to get the progressives and conservatives to come to some new agreement through compromise. Rather, the centrists argue that there is already basic agreement or mutual understanding on what is fair, and it's just a practical issue of how to achieve that in particular cases.
B: No. The centrists reject the use of theory, while the sociologist relies on it.
C: No. While this choice mentions fairness and equality, there is no correspondence between the centrist position in the passage and categorization of different systems in the choice.
D: **Yes. This choice has three basic aspects in common with the centrist approach: using a case-by-case approach, an assumption that there is common agreement on basic principles (here, what constitutes a "good life"), and the goal of "fixing" what's wrong in an individual case in order to bring it in line with how we supposedly would all agree things should be.**

7.   A   This is a Strengthen question.
A: **Yes. In paragraphs 7–8, the author critiques the centrist position in part by arguing that agreement on how to apply statute requires agreement on "background principles" about "how government ought to operate"(that is, the proper role of the state in society). He goes on to say that this means that because each camp has a different idea of what "fair representation" means, they disagree on abstract issues of principle regarding how to interpret "facts." The author, however, never directly states that, or explains how, the operation of government relates to fair representation. If the two are in fact fundamentally interrelated, it would support the author's critique of the centrists' claim that there is no fundamental disagreement on principles within the Voting Rights Act debate.**
B: No. This would support the centrists themselves, by suggesting that at least some of the debate is about facts or empirical questions (here, statistics), rather than about matters of principle.
C: No. To the extent that the intent or belief of the writers of the act is relevant, this would go against the author's interpretation.
D: No. This would weaken the author's argument by supporting the centrist claim. This choice suggests that the disagreement between progressives and conservatives is not as stark as it may seem, and there is a fair amount of basic agreement on basic ideas.

Individual Passage Log

Passage # _____

Q#	Q type	Attractors	What did you do wrong?

Revised Strategy _____

Passage # _____

Q#	Q type	Attractors	What did you do wrong?

Revised Strategy _____

Chapter 5
The Process of
Elimination (POE)
and Attractors

GOALS

1. To learn the principles and steps of working through questions using the Process of Elimination (POE)
2. To recognize patterns in Attractors

5.1 THE PROCESS OF ELIMINATION

As we discussed in the last chapter, there are five basic steps you must take in answering any question:

1. Read the question word for word and identify the question type.
2. Translate the question into your own words; identify what the question task is asking you to do with the information in the passage.
3. Identify key words and phrases that refer to specific parts of the passage and *go back to the passage* to locate that information.
4. Answer in your own words; articulate what the correct answer will need to do based on the question type and the information in the passage.
5. Use Process of Elimination (POE), and choose the *least wrong* answer choice.

   In this chapter, we'll focus in more detail on Step 5, Process of Elimination or **POE**.

   It is more effective to attack the question by eliminating the three wrong answer choices than by searching for the perfect choice. The MCAT writers are highly skilled at hiding the credited response in obscure and convoluted language, and at creating wrong answer choices that at first glance look good, but have a subtle yet fatal flaw. Your mission is to avoid the traps on your way to the correct choice.

   Here are the basic steps of POE. In most cases, you will need to take two "cuts" through the choices as you narrow them down.

First Cut

Read Every Word of Every Choice Carefully.

This is not the time to skim! Once you have misinterpreted or skipped over something, it is very difficult to recognize your mistake.

Eliminate Choices Using the Bottom Line of the Passage.

Remind yourself of the Main Point and tone of the passage and read through each answer choice, eliminating any that violate, or directly contradict, the author's argument (unless it's a Weaken or Except question). Understanding the passage's Bottom Line will also allow you to quickly eliminate choices that, although they may not contradict the author's points, are not relevant to the passage, and so are out of scope.

Eliminate Choices Inconsistent with Your Own Answer (When Possible, Given the Question Type).

Use your own answer to the question (which should be based closely on the passage and on the question task) as a guideline for eliminating answer choices. Do not, however, eliminate a choice just because it's not a perfect match. Be flexible.

Second Cut

Reread the Question Stem.

Remind yourself of the question type and issue.

Compare the Remaining Choices to Each Other.

Notice extreme or absolute wording, and any other relevant differences between them.

Go Back to the Passage Again to Pin It Down (When Necessary).

Keep the differences between the choices in mind to help you find where you need to go.

Choose the Least Wrong Answer Choice.

When making your final choice, it's important to keep two things in mind:

1. **Be highly suspicious of absolute or extreme statements.**
   Except on Strengthen or Weaken questions, correct MCAT answer choices will rarely make an extreme claim. Do not use this test carelessly, however. Simple declarative statements (such as, *The inquisitorial system is historically superior to the adversarial system.*) are not necessarily extreme. Look for words that may indicate absolute statements such as *any, all, none, never, always, totally, must, only, exactly, impossible,* etc. Also look out for statements that make extreme claims even without using any of these words.

Notice the wishy-washy or equivocal wording in the previous statement; these words *may,* not *must,* indicate statements that are too extreme for the passage. Whether or not a particular word or statement is extreme depends on how it is used within the context of the answer choice. The following phrases illustrate the difference between extreme and not so extreme statements, in the context of language that should and should not make you suspicious of answer choices.

Extreme	Not Extreme	Comments
will be	will for a time be	The phrase *will be* predicts the future, which may well be beyond the scope of the passage. The phrase *will for a time be* suggests a temporary condition, which is more moderate and therefore more likely to be supported by the text.
the only reason is	the only way to leave the room is	The phrase *the only reason is* rules out all other reasons, and is likely to be too extreme. The phrase *the only way to leave the room is* simply states that there is one door, which is a description, not an absolute claim. Whether or not the word *only* qualifies as extreme depends on context.
the greatest result	a great result	The use of the definite article *the* in combination with the suffix *-est* makes this a very strong statement. The phrase *a great result* is much less absolute, because it could be one of many great results.
kill all the roaches	kill roaches	The statement *kill roaches* sounds extreme because of the word kill, but this is a different kind of extreme—in action not in degree or in logic. *Kill all the roaches* is in fact extreme because the statement is all-inclusive.

2. **If part of an answer choice is wrong, then it's all wrong.**
    Pay attention to every word: One incorrect word or phrase will make the entire answer choice wrong. This is one reason why searching for the correct choice—instead of the three wrong choices—may lead you to an incorrect choice. A wrong answer may have something attractive about it, but the credited response won't have anything incorrect in it (or will at least be the best supported of the four).

Any word can make an answer choice wrong. If the answer choice implies that something is true *all* of the time, and the passage suggests that it is true *some* (but *not all*) of the time, then the answer choice cannot be supported by the passage. Pay special attention to words of negation (such as *no, not, none, never,* etc.).

5.2 ATTRACTORS

Usually, if you understand the Bottom Line of the passage, it is easy to eliminate two of the four answer choices. But, students commonly express this lament: "I always get it down to two choices and then I pick the wrong one!" That's because the test is designed to make you do this.

For each question, there is usually at least one **Attractor**: an answer choice designed to tempt you into choosing it. It will have something attractive about it, such as words from the passage or concepts similar to those discussed by the author. If you're in too much of a hurry, looking only for the "right" answer, you'll fall for an Attractor most of the time. Remember: The test writers know how students think and what kind of logical mistakes they tend to make. Take the control away from them by predicting and avoiding the traps.

Typical Attractors

If you look for it, you'll see some patterns appear in the answer choices. The MCAT utilizes a core group of Attractors to tempt those who rush or who do not understand basic ideas presented in the passage. Here are the most common Attractors, grouped into categories. Learn them, look for them, and, thus, defend yourself against them.

Decoys

These choices are written to sound just like the passage. However, they include something that doesn't match up, either with the passage text or the question task.

- **Words out of context**
  This Attractor uses vocabulary right from the passage. It "sounds good," but the meaning of the words is changed. That is, the answer choice uses the right words but carries the wrong meaning. This is a trap in particular for people who are not going back to the passage, or who are not rereading the relevant parts of the passage carefully enough.

- **Half right/half wrong**
  These are "bait and switch" answers. Part or most of the choice is exactly what you are looking for, but another part is not supported by the passage (e.g., too extreme or out of scope). This is a trap set for people who make up their minds before they read the entire choice, or who try to "rehabilitate" an answer because part of it sounds so good. Remember that one word is enough to make a choice wrong.

- **Opposite/Negations**
  These choices take a sentence or idea directly from the passage, but add or remove a crucial "not" or "un-." The statement therefore sounds just like the passage, but in fact directly contradicts it.

- **Reversals**
  This answer choice extracts a relationship from the passage but then reverses it to go in the opposite direction. It may flip a sequence of cause and effect, or confuse the order of events in a chronology.

- **Garbled language**
  This choice gives you some familiar words, but is difficult or impossible to understand. The test-writers are hoping that you will pick it thinking that because it is confusing it must be correct. However, another version of this trap is to put the correct choice into confusing language, with the hope that you will immediately eliminate it because it doesn't "sound good." So, when you see garbled language, don't automatically pick it, but don't automatically eliminate it either. And, don't spend five minutes trying to decipher it. Use POE aggressively: there may be a better choice, or it may be the only one left after you have eliminated the other three.

- **Right answer/wrong question**
  The statements in these Attractors, unlike in the other members of this category, are in fact directly supported by the passage. However, they aren't relevant to the question being asked. When you are down to two choices, always reread the question stem in order to avoid this trap.

- **Wrong point of view**
  This is a variation on the Right answer/wrong question Attractor. If there is more than one point of view described in the passage, a wrong answer might describe a point of view different from the one referred to in the question stem.

Extremes

These choices go too far in one direction or the other.

- **Absolutes**

  This type of wrong answer uses language that is much stronger than the language in the passage. It may include extreme words such as *none, always, never, only,* etc. Keep in mind, however, that a strongly worded passage may support a strongly worded choice. Also remember that a choice doesn't have to include one of the standard extreme words to be making a claim that is too extreme or absolute in its meaning.

- **Superlatives**

  These wrong answers include words like *first, last, best, most, worst, least* (or anything else ending in *–est*), or *primary*. For instance, it may describe a theory as the *first* or the *best* theory, but the author simply says that it's an important theory.

- **Judgments and recommendations**

  The choice passes judgment on whether something is good or bad, but that thing is described by the author in a neutral tone. Or, the answer choice states that a proposal should be implemented or rejected, when that policy or action is merely described in the passage, or the choice may describe a moderate point of view in overly extreme terms. Finally, a wrong answer may tempt you to intuit the author's state of mind or personal beliefs in a way that is not supported by the passage text.

- **Not strong enough**

  This Attractor is specific to Strengthen and Weaken questions. Rather than being too extreme, it is too wishy-washy to significantly affect the author's argument in the passage. Always compare choices to each other; for this question type, you want the choice that goes farthest in the right direction.

Out of Scope

These answer choices introduce facts, issues, or claims that are never addressed in the passage, or, they do not match the scope of the question task.

- **Not the issue**

  This answer choice brings in ideas or facts that are not discussed in the passage. You will usually eliminate these in your first cut.

- **Outside knowledge**

  The wrong answer makes a statement that is true based on your own knowledge, but isn't directly supported by the text of the passage. Remember that the Verbal Reasoning section tests your ability to read actively and analyze the passage; it does not test your general knowledge.

- **Crystal ball**

  The wrong answer predicts the future (but the passage doesn't) or goes beyond the timeframe of the passage.

- **No such comparison**

  This incorrect choice will take something that is mentioned in the passage and compare it to something that is not. Or, it may take two things that are mentioned by the author and compare them in a way that is not supported by the passage (often by stating that one option is better than the other).

- **Too narrow/too broad**

  The "too narrow" Attractor is typical on General questions: it mentions or contains only part of the author's argument. Keep in mind however that correct answers to Specific questions (including Inference questions) can be quite narrow. Wrong answers that are too broad have the opposite problem: They overgeneralize or go beyond the author's argument. They may describe a general category into which the topic of the passage would fit. On General questions, use the "Goldilocks Approach": Eliminate any answer choices that are too narrow or too broad, and choose the one that's just right.

5.3 POE DOS AND DON'TS

Do

- Read and identify the question carefully—predict the traps.
- Read each answer choice in its entirety.
- Read all four answer choices before deciding.
- Be suspicious—look for traps.
- Notice extreme or absolute wording.
- Eliminate using the Bottom Line.
- Eliminate using your own answer.
- Compare the choices to each other.
- Go back to the passage to check your answers.

Don't

- Skim the answer choices.
- Pick the first choice that "sounds good."
- Ignore information in a choice, or add something to it, in order to make it fit. That is, don't force a square peg into a round hole.
- Eliminate choices on Strengthen/Weaken questions because of strong wording.
- Eliminate choices on Inference questions because of moderate wording.
- Pick D without reading it carefully just because you've eliminated answer choices A, B, and C.
- Answer based on memory.

5.4   STRESS MANAGEMENT

Most students feel some level of stress before an important exam. A certain level of anxiety, while un-comfortable, is beneficial; it sharpens your attention, keeps you alert, and intensifies your focus. However, if you find that your stress and anxiety gets out of control to the point where your performance suffers, there are ways to manage and reduce it to a reasonable level. Here are some tactics and techniques; try them, find the ones that work for you, and use them consistently whenever you feel the need.

Develop and Implement a Clear Strategy

Anxiety comes in part from feeling out of control. Identify the aspects of the test, the testing conditions, and the importance of the test that instill fear in you, and do things that will help you confront and mini-mize those fears. For example:

- Take as many full practice tests as possible. Experience builds confidence.
- Build up your stamina. It is difficult to maintain concentration over many hours, especially under stressful conditions. Prepare for test day by working passages over longer and longer pe-riods with shorter and shorter breaks, until you can comfortably concentrate for a few hours at a time.
- Practice dealing with distraction. Do passages or practice tests under less than ideal condi-tions. Go to a coffee house, or an area of the library where people are moving around. Prac-tice tuning out your surroundings.

Take a Breath

The tenser we get, the shallower our breathing becomes. Lack of oxygen then can contribute to your anxi-ety in a feedback loop. *Stop* this process the minute you realize that your muscles are tightening or your focus is fading. Sit back in your chair and take three deep breaths. Take your eyes off the screen for 10–15 seconds, and move your arms and shoulders around to release the muscles. Don't force yourself onward to the next question if you realize that you're not working at your peak. Rather than wasting a big chunk of time getting questions wrong because you can't think straight, take a few seconds to relax and regroup, and make the most of the rest of your time.

Use Positive Reinforcement

When we place high demands on ourselves, it's easy to fall into negative thinking at moments of frustra-tion. You may find yourself thinking self-critical thoughts while studying or during a practice test such as, "How could I miss that question! I'm so stupid! I'm never going to get this!" Recognize this for what it is: a stress reaction, not a representation of reality. Find words and phrases to replace the negative thoughts, such as "I know I'm smart, I'm working hard, and it will all pay off in the end." It may sound goofy, but it works.

Reward Yourself

Don't let yourself burn out over the next month or two. Yes, study and practice are crucial, but so is maintaining peace of mind. If you are so overworked and tired that you cannot concentrate on what you're doing, give yourself a break. Set a goal (e.g., a certain number of hours of study time, or a particular number of practice passages). Once you achieve that goal, go to a movie, hang out with friends, go to the gym, do whatever you enjoy most for a few hours.

Practice Creative Visualization

Creative visualization, if practiced over time, can offer significant long-term anxiety reduction. Lie on the floor (at home, not during the test!) on your back, with your arms and legs stretched out. Adjust your position until you feel comfortable and relaxed. Then close your eyes and picture the most wonderful, relaxing place you have ever visited or would like to visit, or a situation that makes you feel safe and at peace. It may be a tropical island, a quiet forest, a deserted beach, or a gathering at home with friends and family. See your surroundings clearly, smell the air, hear the birds, or picture the faces of the people who make you happy. When you are ready to stop, picture the most relaxing part of the scene one last time. Count to three slowly, then open your eyes. If you practice this regularly for a few weeks, especially at times when you feel tense, you should begin to feel less anxious. Then, if you do find yourself becoming anxious during the test, close your eyes, breath deeply, and imagine yourself back in that peaceful place. You will find yourself relaxing quickly, because you've trained yourself to respond that way.

Chapter 5 Summary

- Use POE aggressively.

- Know and eliminate the common Attractors.

- Read carefully—do not skim the questions or the answer choices.

CHAPTER 5 PRACTICE PASSAGES

Individual Passage Drills

Do this exercise *untimed* at first. Work and Annotate the passages as usual (remember to preview the questions). As you work the questions, for each answer choice you eliminate, write down the reason next to the choice, and/or highlight the word or words within the choice that make it wrong. Keep a list of Attractors near by, and feel free to refer to it as you work. Take time to remind yourself which Attractors commonly appear on particular question types. If you cannot tell the difference between two choices and must guess between the two, note that next to the question.

When you check your answers, for each question you missed, note down in the Individual Passage Log what was wrong with the incorrect answer you chose, and what you thought was wrong with the correct answer. Look for patterns in your mistakes. Do you consistently choose the same kind of Attractor? Do you tend to eliminate the correct answer too quickly, and then talk yourself into a wrong answer choice further down the list? Do you pick the choice that sounds right, instead of eliminating the wrong answer choices and picking the least wrong choice? Devise a strategy to avoid making those same mistakes in the future.

Continue to do this exercise over the next few weeks, doing at least two passages back to back at a time. Eventually you can do the passages timed, but give yourself an extra minute or two to annotate the answer choices. Continue to monitor your progress and to diagnose any changing patterns in your performance.

CHAPTER 5 PRACTICE PASSAGE 1

The Depression yielded not only misery but also tremendous energy and radicalism. Union-organizing and reform movements of all kinds flourished as the crisis challenged Americans to abandon the constraints of the past and move forward, boldly, into the future. Recovery in the family, as in the economy, would be achieved not simply by returning to ways of the past, but by adapting to new circumstances. The economic crisis opened the way for a new type of family based on shared breadwinning and equality of the sexes.

But by the time the Depression was over and World War II had come and gone, it was clear that millions of middle-class American families would take the path toward polarized gender roles. What caused the overwhelming triumph of "traditional" roles in the "modern" home?

Although most Americans experienced some form of hardship during the Depression, it was the nation's male breadwinners—fathers who were responsible for providing economic support for their families—who were threatened or faced with the severest erosion of their identities. Those who lost income or jobs frequently lost status at home, and self-respect as well. Economic hardship placed severe strains on marriage. Going on relief may well have helped the family budget, but it would do little for the breadwinner's feelings of failure.

With the breadwinner's role undermined, other family roles shifted dramatically. Frequently wives and mothers who had never been employed took jobs to provide supplemental or even primary support for their families. Given the need for women's earnings, the widespread employment of women might have been one of the most important legacies of the Depression era. But discriminatory policies and public hostility weakened that potential. Although many families depended on the earnings of both spouses, federal policies supported unemployed male breadwinners but discouraged married women from seeking jobs. Section 213 of the Economy Act of 1932 mandated that whenever personnel reductions took place in the executive branch, married persons were to be the first discharged if married to a government employee. As a result, 1,600 married women were dismissed from their federal jobs. Many state and local governments followed suit; three out of four cities excluded married women from teaching, and eight states passed laws excluding them from state jobs. These efforts to curtail women's employment opportunities were directly related to the powerful imperative to bolster the employment of men.

If the paid labor force had been more hospitable, and if public policies had fostered equal opportunities for women, young people in the 1930s might have been less inclined to aspire to prevailing gender roles. Viable long-term job prospects

for women might have prompted new ways of structuring family roles. In the face of persistent obstacles, however, that potential withered. The realities of family life combined with institutional barriers to inhibit the potential for sustained radical change among white middle-class American families.

The prevailing family ideology was gravely threatened when women and men adapted to hard times by shifting their household responsibilities. In the long run, however, these alternatives were viewed as temporary measures caused by unfortunate circumstances, rather than as positive outcomes of the crisis. Young people learned, on the one hand, to accept women's employment as necessary for the family budget; on the other hand, they saw that deviations from traditional roles often wreaked havoc in marriages. Children who grew up in economically deprived families during these years watched their parents struggle to succeed as breadwinners and homemakers, and they suffered along with their parents if those expectations proved impossible to meet. The sociologist Glen Elder, in his pioneering study of families during the Depression, found that the more a family's traditional gender roles were disrupted, the more likely the children were to disapprove of the altered balance of power in their homes.

Material used in this particular passage has been adapted from the following source:

E. T. May, "Myths and Realities of the American Family," *A History of Private Life*, Volume V. © 1991 by The Belknap Press of Harvard University Press.

1. In paragraph 1, families are compared to the economy. This comparison is based on:

A) a contrast between the workplace and the home.
B) the possibility of new forms of social organization.
C) the actions of radicals hoping to undermine the status quo.
D) the unfortunate results of an economic crisis.

2. The author's argument about the impact of the Depression on male breadwinners would be best supported by a study that found:

A) married men were more likely to lose jobs than unmarried men.
B) government welfare programs helped ease financial hardship for the unemployed.
C) unemployment was a reliable predictor of psychological depression.
D) unfair wages meant many wives were unable to replace the breadwinner's income by entering the workforce.

3. The support for the author's view about government's
   role in the changing form of marriage is:

A) strong: the author provides several examples suggesting
   government inhibited change.
B) strong: the author supports his view thoroughly with
   relevant analogies.
C) weak: the author's examples do not effectively support
   the author's view.
D) weak: the author does not significantly address the
   government's role.

4. To the author, the events of the passage best represent
   which of the following?

A) A missed opportunity
B) A tragic development
C) A traditional pattern
D) A radical change

5. The author most likely feels that marriage based on
   equality of the sexes:

A) can be successful, given the right circumstances.
B) is untenable because government cannot accept women's
   equal right to work.
C) is typical in the modern home.
D) inevitably causes conflict within the family.

6. Glen Elder's study describes children who were likely to
   "disapprove of the altered power balance in their homes."
   Which of the following statements best represents the
   most likely source of that disapproval?

A) Mothers who entered the workforce had less time to
   spend at home parenting.
B) Fathers who became unemployed would experience great
   feelings of failure which would permeate family life and
   lead to an increased incidence of domestic violence.
C) Children raised in traditional households were unfamiliar
   with non-traditional forms of marriage, and so tended to
   distrust them.
D) Families in which the traditional order had been disrupted
   were also likely to be families undergoing the trials of
   economic hardship.

7. Suppose a study were to find evidence of widespread
   discrimination in employers' hiring practices during
   the Depression. Specifically, when less qualified male
   candidates and more qualified female candidates were
   in direct competition for jobs, the males were very
   frequently hired. Furthermore, the government took little
   to no action to rectify these supposed injustices. How
   would the author most likely respond?

A) This is consistent with public and government attitudes
   during the Depression: men's employment was seen as
   more important than women's.
B) Since prejudices are first shaped by family life, a radical
   change toward more equitable gender roles in marriage
   was necessary before society could reject gender
   discrimination in the workplace.
C) Public and institutional viewpoints such as these, which
   prevented women from providing supplemental or even
   primary support for their families, were unfair and
   regrettable.
D) Government's lack of response is surprising; the
   Economy Act of 1932 suggested government was
   interested in employment demographics at the time.

CHAPTER 5 PRACTICE PASSAGE 2

German anthropologists understood nature as a static system of categories that allowed them, in their study of "natural peoples," to grasp an unchanging essence of humanity, rather than the ephemeral changes historians recorded. However, the concept of nature was anything but stable in nineteenth-century Germany. Since the early part of the century there had been a deep tension between Kantian models of natural science and idealist *Naturphilosophie*, conflicts in which many anthropologists themselves were active participants. Furthermore, in nature anthropologists sought a realm free from historical change just as Darwinians began asserting that nature, like humans, did in fact change over time. The boundary between history and nature, which formed an important basis for both humanism and anthropology, came to appear more unstable than ever....

The idea of nature and natural science that informed German anthropology was based on elements from two conflicting approaches, conventionally associated with Immanuel Kant and Friedrich Schelling. The founders of German anthropology belonged to a generation of natural scientists who, in the second half of the nineteenth century, rejected Schelling's romantic *Naturphilosophie* in favor of a return to Kant's more secular and rationalist notion of nature and natural science. As is the case with so many philosophical rejections, however, anthropologists preserved as much *Naturphilosophie* as they cast off, and their understanding of nature was really a synthesis of the two philosophers' approach.

From Kant anthropologists took an idea of nature as a static and objective system that could be conclusively known by scientists. In his *Metaphysical Basis of Natural Science*, Kant had maintained that an "authentic natural science" consisted exclusively of a priori deductions of necessary laws. He thus applauded a version of Newtonian mechanics based solely on mathematics as a perfect natural science and dismissed chemistry as a "systematic art" rather than a science because its laws were derived from sensory experience of "given facts." Unlike Newton, Kant excluded theological considerations from natural science, founding a tradition in Germany of strictly separating natural science and religion, a tradition sharply distinct from British natural theology. While this law-based, objective, totally secular, and perfectly knowable nature would have appealed to anthropologists, they would not have subscribed to the Kantian notion of science as the a priori deduction of mathematical laws. Indeed, anthropology was above all a science of the given facts, which Kant had rejected as a source of natural scientific knowledge.

It was precisely over this issue of the empirical that Schelling had originally broken with Kant, and it was in their empiricist approach to nature that anthropologists retained their allegiance to Schelling. Schelling had justified experience and empirical knowledge of nature against Kant's insistence that true knowledge of nature had to be deductive, a priori, and law-like. Thus, a science of qualities, such as chemistry with its qualitatively different elements, could count as a science for Schelling but not for Kant. For Schelling, the rehabilitation of the empirical in natural knowledge was part of an idealist project to overcome the difference between theological and natural knowledge, mind and nature, and speculation and experience. When anthropologists denounced *Naturphilosophie*, it was not for its empiricism. Worse than the idealism of *Naturphilosophie* was, for anthropologists, its view of nature as becoming rather than being, a view antithetical to the concept of nature that anthropologists wanted to use against historicist humanism. Thus, Virchow asserted that, "while the facts teach that the races of humans and the species of animals are immutable," *Naturphilosophie* (wrongly, in Virchow's view) teaches that they can change. Furthermore, anthropologists separated religious and scientific questions, following Kant's rather than Schelling's understanding of the relation of natural and theological knowledge. Allowing theology and development to enter into discussions of nature would undermine the basic project of anthropology as an antihumanist science of natural peoples outside history. When they spoke of *Naturphilosophie*, anthropologists thought as much about Darwinism as about the philosophical writings of Schelling and his followers.

Anthropologists saw in the science of botany a model for their own antievolutionist synthesis of Kant's systematizing with Schelling's empiricism. There were a number of botanists active in the Berlin Anthropological Society, including the latter-day *Naturphilosoph*, Alexander Braun. Braun argued that the study of plants allowed one to observe the essence of nature relatively directly because plants do not disguise themselves with culture, as humans do. Adolf Bastian extended Braun's understanding of plants to natural peoples, whom he compared to cryptograms, flowerless plants such as algae, mosses, and ferns. As botanists had gained general knowledge about plants by studying the flowerless cryptograms, which had previously been "despised and crushed underfoot," so too would anthropologists solve the "highest questions of culture" by considering natural peoples, who lack the "flowers of culture."

Material used in this particular passage has been adapted from the following source:

A. Zimmerman, *Anthropology and Antihumanism in Imperial Germany.* © 2001 by University of Chicago Press.

THE PROCESS OF ELIMINATION (POE) AND ATTRACTORS

1. The primary purpose of the passage is most likely to:

   A) describe the analogy drawn by German anthropologists between botany and anthropology.
   B) criticize 19th century German anthropologists for drawing inspiration from two mutually inconsistent schools of thought regarding natural science.
   C) explain the views of 19th century German anthropologists regarding the proper approach to studying human beings in the context of natural science.
   D) describe how 19th century German anthropology synthesized Kant's views on theology with Schelling's belief that science consists of a priori deductions of natural laws.

2. Which of the following claims, if true, would most *undermine* the German anthropologists' view that botany is a valid model for anthropology?

   A) Human beings inherently exist within a social context, and therefore there is no such thing as a people not influenced by culture.
   B) Some botanists believe that the study of flowerless cryptograms can tell us little about the structure and function of flowering plants.
   C) Alexander Braun abandoned *Naturphilosophie* early in his academic career, and therefore his ideas about botany have little in common with the views of that school of thought.
   D) It is impossible to study theology without taking into account cultural influences.

3. Which of the following statements, based on the passage, most accurately represents a relationship between the German anthropologists' views on natural science and those of Kant and Schelling?

   A) The German anthropologists accepted Kant's view that science consists of deductions from necessary laws and rejected Schelling's belief that empiricism requires combining theological and natural knowledge.
   B) The German anthropologists accepted Schelling's empiricist approach and rejected Kant's belief that science consists of deductions from mathematical laws.
   C) The German anthropologists rejected Kant's inclusion of theological considerations within natural science and accepted Schelling's belief that human beings are mutable.
   D) The German anthropologists rejected Kant's systematizing and accepted Schelling's empiricism.

4. Which of the following, based on the passage, would be most analogous to a historicist view of anthropology?

   A) A belief that physics consists of a set of unchangeable laws that govern all actions and interactions between objects.
   B) A belief that chemistry is a science rather than a systematic art, given that its laws can be discovered through empirical evidence.
   C) A belief that political science is the study of how different political systems create and shape, and are themselves shaped by, human beliefs and values over time.
   D) A belief that economics is inherently the study of how inherent and consistent human motivations play themselves out in different contexts.

5. Elsewhere, the author of the passage writes that in 19th century Germany the study of geology, within natural science, was divided into *Geognosie*, the study of the present-day, essential, and inherent characteristics of the earth, and *Geologie*, the study of how geological features evolve and come into being. Based on information in the passage, how would the German anthropologists most likely view these two fields of study?

   A) They would accept both as related and equally essential approaches to a scientific understanding of the earth.
   B) They would reject both as irrelevant to a scientific understanding of human beings.
   C) They would accept *Geologie* as a scientific approach to understanding the nature of the earth, while seeing *Geognosie* as a questionable attempt to impose rigid categories on inherently changeable features.
   D) They would see *Geognosie* as a more scientific approach to geology than *Geologie*.

6. With which of the following statements would the German anthropologists discussed in the passage be LEAST likely to agree?

A) Culture can obscure qualities common to all humans.
B) Nature can be described through a set of objective and unchanging categories.
C) Chemistry cannot be legitimately labeled as a science.
D) Newton erred in including theological considerations within natural science.

7. Which of the following statements made in the passage most directly supports the author's assertion that "in nature anthropologists sought a realm free from historical change" (paragraph 1)?

A) The concept of nature was unstable in 19th century Germany.
B) British natural theology combined religion with natural science.
C) According to Virchow, while *Naturphilosophie* teaches that the races of humans and species of animals can change, they are in fact immutable.
D) There was a tension between Kantian models of natural science and idealist *Naturphilosophie*.

SOLUTIONS TO CHAPTER 5 PRACTICE PASSAGE 1

1. **B** This is a Structure question.
    A: No. The author does not contrast (i.e., illustrate differences between) the workplace and the home. Rather, the author states that they are similar in that adaptation to new circumstances was needed (paragraph 1).
    B: **Yes. In paragraph 1, the author states that "Recovery in the family, as in the economy, would be achieved not simply by returning to ways of the past, but by adapting to new circumstances."**
    C: No. The author does mention "radicalism," but does not describe radicals hoping to make changes to the family.
    D: No. This choice is too negative. This comparison follows shortly after the sentence, "The Depression yielded not only misery but also tremendous energy and radicalism" (paragraph 1). The author also states in that paragraph that "the crisis challenged Americans to abandon the constraints of the past and move forward, boldly, into the future." Therefore, the author recognizes positive as well as negative results of the economic crisis.

2. **C** This is a Strengthen question.
    Note: The author's argument about the impact of the Depression on male breadwinners suggests breadwinners who lost their jobs were personally hurt, and that this had a negative impact on families (paragraphs 3 and 6).

    A: No. This evidence would not strengthen the argument. The author's argument is about the effect of unemployment on married men on an individual and family level. Knowing that married men overall were more likely to lose their jobs would not strengthen the author's point about the impact of unemployment on individual men and their families.
    B: No. Although paragraph 2 does mention "relief," keep your eye on the argument. The passage specifically says financial relief had little impact on unemployed men's feelings (paragraph 3).
    C: **Yes. A study like the one described by this answer choice would act as evidence supporting the idea that married men were personally hurt ("faced with the severest erosion of their identities") by losing their jobs.**
    D: No. The passage suggests men's sadness is caused by an "erosion of their identities," i.e., that losing a job entails losing one's purpose. Whether or not their income is replaced by someone else is, therefore, not key to the argument as it's set out in the passage.

3. **A** This is an Evaluate question.
    A: **Yes, paragraph 4 provides numerous examples in which the government tries to manipulate the job market in favor of men.**
    B: No. The author does not use analogy to support her argument. The only analogy drawn is between the economy and the family (paragraph 1), but there is no direct connection between that comparison and the author's specific discussion of the role of the government.
    C: No. The examples in paragraph 4 do directly support the idea that "federal policies supported unemployed male breadwinners but discouraged married women from seeking jobs," and later, "Many state and local governments followed suit."
    D: No. The author does address government's role in paragraph 4, on a federal, state, and local level.

4.   **A**   This is a Tone/Attitude question.

   Note: This question is essentially asking about the author's overall attitude toward the events of the passage. Thus, use your sense of the author's overall purpose in writing the passage.

   A: **Yes. See paragraph 4: "Given the need for women's earnings, the widespread employment of women might have been one of the most important legacies of the Depression era. But discriminatory policies and public hostility weakened that potential." The word choice in paragraph 5 also suggests the author might have supported changes to traditional roles in marriage: "Viable long-term job prospects for women might have prompted new ways of structuring family roles. In the face of persistent obstacles, however, that potential withered."**

   B: No. While there reason to believe the author might like to have seen more lasting change take place (see the explanation for choice A), the word "tragic" is too strong to describe the tone of the passage.

   C: No. According to paragraph 1, the events of the passage were new, not traditional. While traditional roles triumphed in the end (paragraph 2), the events of the passage as a whole represent at least a temporary break with traditional patterns.

   D: No. This choice represents a misreading of the main idea of the passage. The potential for radical change to gender roles in marriage did not turn into lasting change during the Depression.

5.   **A**   This is an Inference question.

   A: **Yes. The author believes external obstacles (i.e., government and social resistance) prevented family roles from changing. In paragraph 5, the author says if those obstacles were removed, we might have seen real change.**

   B: No. The use of the word "cannot" implies government still holds this view; the attitudes of government today are beyond the scope of this passage. Also, government did not discourage women from working because it "could not accept" women working, but because men's employment was seen as more important.

   C: No. This choice contradicts paragraph 2, which refers to the "overwhelming triumph of 'traditional' marriage in the 'modern' home".

   D: No. This choice is too extreme. The word "inevitably" is absolute, whereas paragraph 6 says "deviations from traditional roles *often* wreaked havoc in marriages."

6.   **D**   This is an Inference question.

   A: No. Be careful not to use outside knowledge. While this may be true in reality, the issue is not addressed in the passage.

   B: No. While it is reasonable to conclude that male breadwinners' unhappiness contributed to children's attitudes as children "watched their parents struggle to succeed as breadwinners and homemakers" (paragraph 6), the author does not discuss domestic violence.

   C: No. While non-traditional forms of marriage may well have been unfamiliar, the author does not connect lack of familiarity to children's disapproval.

   D: **Yes. The clearest interpretation here is that Glen Elder's study is used as support for the claim that "[young people] saw that deviations from traditional roles often wreaked havoc in marriages." The following sentence suggests this was not because children were uncomfortable with the change in roles, but because changing roles usually accompanied economic struggle (paragraph 6).**

7. **A**   This is a New Information question.
    Note: Questions that give new information are often most relevant to a specific part of the passage. This one corresponds most closely to paragraph 4; the credited answer will reflect that.

    A: **Yes. See paragraph 4: "But discriminatory policies and public hostility [emphasis added] weakened that potential. Although many families depended on the earnings of both spouses, federal policies supported unemployed male breadwinners but discouraged married women from seeking jobs."**

    B: No. This answer choice puts forward a general theory—changes to the family are required for changes to the workplace—while the author suggests the opposite. That is, that government action in the workplace limited the possibility of change within the family (see paragraph 5).

    C: No. This choice suggests the author's general approach is to criticize or lament obstacles to women's progress. It would be more accurate to say the author is explaining why more equitable gender roles did not take hold at the time. Secondly, the passage suggests that women were able to provide financial support for their families at the time, at least to some extent (paragraph 4); "prevented" is too strong to be supported by the passage.

    D: No. This choice uses familiar language but is inconsistent with the passage. Government would not be expected to stop such discrimination; its inaction would not be a surprise. In fact, government institutionalized discrimination in the Economy Act of 1932 (paragraph 4).

SOLUTIONS TO CHAPTER 5 PRACTICE PASSAGE 2

1. **C**   This is a Main Idea/Primary Purpose question.

    A: No. This choice is too narrow. While the analogy described in the last paragraph is part of the author's discussion of the views of German anthropologists, it is one piece of evidence supporting the larger argument, not the main point or primary purpose of the passage as a whole.

    B: No. This choice has the wrong tone. The author is not criticizing the anthropologists, but rather is giving a neutral description of their views and of some of the sources of those views.

    C: **Yes. This choice is broad enough to cover the content of the passage without going beyond its scope, and it has an appropriately neutral tone. Paragraph 1 introduces the idea that the anthropologists studied "humanity" and "natural peoples," as well as the idea that this study occurred within the larger context of natural science. The rest of the passage relates to the views of these German anthropologists, and/or sources of inspiration for those views.**

    D: No. While German anthropology was based on a synthesis of views of these two men (paragraph 2), this choice partially misrepresents the pieces from each that were synthesized. The anthropologists did follow Kant's "exclusion of theological considerations from natural science" (paragraphs 3 and 4). However, it was Kant, not Schelling, who believed that science consists of a priori deductions of natural laws, and the passage states that the anthropologists "would not have subscribed to the Kantian notion of science as the a priori deduction of mathematical laws" (paragraph 3).

2. **A** This is a Weaken question.

Note: According to the last paragraph, anthropologists saw botany as a model because as botany "allowed one to observe the essence of nature relatively directly because plants do not disguise themselves with culture, as humans do," the study of so-called "natural peoples" (analogized to flowerless cryptograms) allowed anthropologists to understand culture and humanity through studying people who supposedly had no culture.

A: **Yes. The anthropologists saw botany as a model, according to the passage, largely because they believed that one could learn about an "unchanging essence of humanity" (paragraph 1) by studying people with no culture, just as botanists can learn about an "essence of nature" by studying plants with no flowers. If there is no such thing as a people without culture, however, this would significantly undermine the validity of botany as a model for anthropology.**

B: No. This choice does not go far enough to undermine the anthropologists' view. "Some botanists" could be two or three, and we don't know from the answer choice that their claim is valid. Beware of choices that are too weak to have a significant impact when answering Strengthen and Weaken questions.

C: No. While Braun is identified as a "latter-day *Naturphilosoph*," the relevance of his views to those of the anthropologists does not depend on Braun representing that school of thought (keep in mind that the anthropologists rejected much of *Naturphilosophie* (paragraph 2).

D: No. This choice is not relevant to the question. The anthropologists believed that theology was not a legitimate part of natural science (paragraph 4). Therefore, even if the study of theology requires the study of culture, this has no impact on the anthropologists' views on the study of humanity within natural science.

3. **B** This is an Inference question.

A: No. The first part of this choice is incorrect. The anthropologists rejected Kant's view that science consists of deductions from necessary laws (see end of paragraph 3).

B: **Yes. Both parts of this choice are supported by the passage. The passage states in paragraph 4 that "it was in their empiricist approach to nature that anthropologists retained their allegiance to Schelling." In paragraph 3, the author writes that the anthropologists "would not have subscribed to the Kantian notion of science as the a priori deduction of mathematical laws. Indeed, anthropology was above all a science of the given facts, which Kant had rejected as a source of natural scientific knowledge."**

C: No. This choice is accurate up until the very last word. However, it was the idea that "the facts teach that the races of humans and the species of animals are immutable" or unchangeable that the anthropologists accepted, rather than an idea that humans are mutable or changeable (an idea that Schelling did not, according to the passage, propose).

D: No. The first part of this choice is incorrect: "Anthropologists saw in the science of botany a model for their own antievolutionist synthesis of Kant's systematizing with Schelling's empiricism" (paragraph 5). Thus, they accepted rather than rejected Kant's systematizing.

4. **C** This is an Analogy question.

Note: The non-historicist view of the German anthropologists was that nature is "a static system of categories that allowed them, in their study of 'natural peoples,' to grasp an unchanging essence of humanity, rather than the ephemeral changes historians recorded." The author also states that "in nature anthropologists sought a realm free from historical change."(paragraph 1). Later in the passage the author states: "Worse than the idealism of *Naturphilosophie* was, for anthropologists, its view of nature as becoming rather than being, a view antithetical to the concept of nature that anthropologists wanted to use against historicist humanism" (paragraph 4). Therefore, a historicist view of anthropology would be based on studying changes over time rather than some unchanging "essence of humanity." To answer the question, you need to eliminate choices that would be similar to the German anthropologists' approach, and to find the answer that represents studying changes or development over time.

A: No. This, in its study of unchanging laws, would be a non-historicist approach.

B: No. There is no suggestion that this approach to chemistry involves studying changes over time. The reference to the discovery of empirical laws, in fact, suggests the opposite.

C: **Yes. This approach to political science would involve studying how political systems and human beliefs and values interact and change over time, or, through history.**

D: No. A belief in the existence of inherent and consistent human motivations (similar to an "unchanging essence of humanity") suggests consistency rather than change over time.

5. **D** This is a New Information question.

Note: The German anthropologists saw nature as a "static and objective system that could be conclusively known by scientists" (paragraph 3), and believed that "Worse than the idealism of *Naturphilosophie* was…its view of nature as becoming rather than being, a view antithetical to the concept of nature that anthropologists wanted to use against historicist humanism." While the anthropologists studied human beings, they saw this study as existing within the realm of natural science. Therefore, we can infer that they would accept "*Geognosie*, the study of the present-day, essential, and inherent characteristics of the earth" as a more legitimate scientific approach than "*Geologie*, the study of how geological features evolve and come into being."

A: No. The passage suggests that they would prefer *Geognosie* over *Geologie*, as more scientific.

B: No. There is no evidence in the question stem or in the passage that the anthropologists would see either, especially *Geognosie*, as totally irrelevant.

C: No. The passage suggests that the anthropologists themselves were looking for strict categories to apply to humanity (paragraph 1). Therefore, there is no reason to infer that they would see categorization as a problem. Furthermore, the anthropologists believed natural science should look for unchanging, rather than changeable, elements.

D: **Yes. *Geognosie* fits better with the anthropologists' view of legitimate natural science.**

6. **C** This is an Inference/LEAST question (that is, it asks which statement is least supported by the passage).

A: No. This statement is supported by paragraph 5, where the author writes: "Braun argued that the study of plants allowed one to observe the essence of nature relatively directly because plants do not disguise themselves with culture, as humans do." Braun's ideas were part of the reason why the anthropologists saw botany as a model for their own approach.

B: No. In paragraph 1, the author states that "German anthropologists understood nature as a static [or unchanging] system of categories." In paragraph 3, the author claims: "From Kant anthropologists took an idea of nature as a static and objective system that could be conclusively known by scientists." Therefore, the anthropologists would agree with this statement.

C: **Yes. While Kant believed chemistry was not a science, the anthropologists disagreed on this point. For Schelling and for the anthropologists (who followed Schelling's empirical approach), "a science of qualities, such as chemistry with its qualitatively different elements, could count as a science" (paragraph 4). Therefore the anthropologists would least agree with this statement.**

D: No. In paragraph 3, the author states that "Unlike Newton, Kant excluded theological considerations from natural science" and that "this law-based, objective, totally secular, and perfectly knowable nature would have appealed to anthropologists." In paragraph 4, the passage states that "anthropologists separated religious and scientific questions, following Kant's rather than Schelling's understanding of the relation of natural and theological knowledge. Allowing theology and development to enter into discussions of nature would undermine the basic project of anthropology as an antihumanist science of natural peoples outside history." Therefore, the anthropologists would agree, not disagree, with this choice.

7. **C** This is a Structure question.

Note: All of the claims cited in the choices are in the passage. The question is, which claim is used by the author to most directly support the assertion cited in the question stem.

A: No. The existence of a debate over the concept of nature doesn't itself directly support or explain the author's claim about the anthropologists' own views. The fact that this statement appears in the same paragraph is not enough to show that it acts to logically support the assertion cited in the question.

B: No. The fact that British natural theology, unlike the anthropologists' approach to natural science, combined religion with science doesn't by itself support the author's claim about the actual content or nature of the anthropologists' views on historical change.

C: **Yes. Virchow is quoted in paragraph 4, in the context of the author's explanation of the anthropologists' view that "Worse than the idealism of *Naturphilosophie* was, for anthropologists, its view of nature as becoming rather than being, a view antithetical to the concept of nature that anthropologists wanted to use against historicist humanism." (Note the word "thus" at the beginning of the next sentence, which indicates that the Virchow quote is part of the discussion of the anthropologists' view.) This is a continuation of the discussion that begins in paragraph 1 of the anthropologists' anti-historical approach. Therefore, even though Virchow's statement appears in a different paragraph, it still acts to support and explain the assertion made in paragraph 1.**

D: No. While discussion of this tension is part of the author's overall argument, it doesn't itself directly support the author's claim about the specific assertion cited in the question stem. The fact that it appears in the same paragraph as the assertion doesn't guarantee that it acts to support that assertion.

Individual Passage Log

Passage # _____

Q#	Q type	Attractors	What did you do wrong?

Revised Strategy _____

Passage # _____

Q#	Q type	Attractors	What did you do wrong?

Revised Strategy _____

Chapter 6
Ranking and Ordering
the Passages

GOALS

1. To understand the organization of the MCAT Verbal Reasoning section
2. To learn to assess the difficulty levels of passages
3. To learn a strategy for attacking the section as a whole

6.1   WHY RANK THE PASSAGES?

As we have discussed, to maximize your efficiency and accuracy within each passage you must take control of the material and not let the material control you. In the same way, you'll maximize your score by taking control of the section *as a whole*, working through the passages in a way that helps you get the easy questions and not waste time on the most difficult questions.

This chapter outlines what you need to know about how the MCAT Verbal Reasoning section is organized in terms of level of difficulty, and how you can assess any seven passages to design your best plan of attack.

How Are the MCAT Verbal Passages Organized?

The MCAT does not follow a strict pattern in how they organize the seven passages; they are presented more or less randomly. Needless to say, the AAMC will not disclose specific information concerning how the passages are chosen, how many are at an easy, medium, or difficult level, etc. Moreover, each administration is different, and every time the test is administered there are multiple forms of the test. So, where does that leave us?

Let's begin with what we know. During the many years that we have been developing these materials, we have discovered some patterns. A lot of experience has led us to the following conclusions about the structure of the Verbal Reasoning section.

Passage Organization

Although one might think that the seven passages would be arranged in order of level of difficulty (that is, easy passages first, medium next, and difficult last), this is generally *not* the case. What would be the point of putting all the difficult passages at the end in a section that students often don't finish? In fact, the passages are in a seemingly random order; often, the last passage in the section is an easy or medium passage that you want to be sure to complete, and the hardest passage is in the middle of the section.

Most Verbal Reasoning sections will have at least one passage that merits the rank of KILLER, meaning it's so difficult that spending even 30 or 40 minutes wouldn't allow you to answer all—or even most of—the questions correctly. Killer passages are not worth your valuable time—guess on the questions or, at least, do them last.

Therefore, it's up to you to strategically reorganize your seven passages in order to address them most effectively.

Passage Division

Division of the seven passages generally looks like this:

- 2–3 easy passages
- 3–4 medium passages
- 1–2 difficult passages

Unless your goal is to score an 11 or above, you probably should be randomly guessing on one or two passages; that is, the one or two most difficult passages in the section. And if your goal *is* to score an 11 or above, you may still do best by guessing on a few of the questions on the most difficult passage (the one you are leaving until last).

6.2 ASSESSING DIFFICULTY LEVEL: NOW, LATER, AND KILLER

Your first objective when beginning the section is to assess the relative difficulty of the passages. A passage should be ranked NOW if it seems relatively straightforward. The passages that appear to be more challenging should be ranked as LATER. The most difficult passage or passages (the ones on which you will be randomly guessing) get a rank of KILLER.

Although it's tempting to associate topic or subject matter with difficulty level, remember that—unlike the science sections—the Verbal Reasoning section of the MCAT does not test outside knowledge. Everything you need to correctly answer the questions is in the passage. In fact, bringing in outside knowledge can actually hurt your score.

Students will often want to skip easier passages simply because they're about, say, poetry or opera (or any other topic that tends to be unfamiliar). However, what really makes a passage difficult is the way it's written *and* the types of questions that are asked about it.

The Passage Text

What Should You Look For?

The following criteria should be used to evaluate the difficulty of the passage text itself.

1. **Level of concreteness or abstraction:** Passages that are highly theoretical and that discuss abstract concepts will be much harder to follow than passages that are concrete and descriptive. Would you rather read a passage about the "philosophic contemplation of the Not-Self" or one on the "doubling of the cost of living in the last ten years"? And again, subject matter is not the key to difficulty. For example, an art passage that is essentially a painter's biography may be very concrete and factual, and therefore quite easy to comprehend. A science passage about the philosophical implications of recent theories regarding the origins of the universe may be very difficult, because it is highly abstract.

2. **Language level:** While the Verbal Reasoning section cannot expect you to know technical language specific to a particular discipline (without defining the terms in context), difficult passages will often include esoteric language that no one really uses in everyday conversation. If the author uses such words as *lugubrious*, *phlegmatic*, *synesthesia*, or *flagitious* in the first few sentences, she's probably not going to start using "plain English" in the next few. Lots of unfamiliar vocabulary will make the passage more difficult to understand, regardless of the topic.

3. **Sentence structure:** Extremely long, convoluted sentences are harder to read, especially under a time constraint. Short, direct sentences will be easier to follow.

How to Evaluate the Passage Text

Skim the first few sentences of the first or second paragraph. Try to paraphrase what you have just read. If all you can do is repeat the exact wording of the passage because the meaning of those words is so unclear, this indicates a more difficult passage. If, on the other hand, you can easily put the meaning of those lines into your own words, the passage is likely to be fairly straightforward.

Think of it this way: If in 15 seconds, you could explain to your six-year-old sister what those two sentences are saying, then the passage will probably make sense to you too.

Do NOT rank a passage solely on the basis of its length. The few moments it may take you to read five or six extra lines will not significantly affect your performance, but choosing a short yet difficult passage over a longer but easier passage certainly will.

The Questions

What Should You Look For?

To benefit most from your personalized strategy, you'll need to focus on determining which question types are more challenging for you. For example, some people find Except/Least/Not and Roman Numeral questions to be more difficult, while others do not. However, certain question types do tend to be harder for everyone.

Complex questions, especially New Information, Strengthen, Weaken, Analogy, and some Evaluate questions, require you to apply new information to the passage and/or judge the strength of the author's argument. These questions can be challenging, even when the passage itself is relatively straightforward.

Specific questions like Retrieval and Vocabulary in Context, however, tend to be easier, requiring only a paraphrase of the text. Inference questions can also be very straightforward, especially when the passage text is concrete and descriptive. In the same way, a General question on a comprehensible passage is quite doable.

How to Evaluate the Questions

Quickly scroll through the set of questions. Do not read them carefully. Rather, scan them and notice if there are lots of long question stems and choices, and if there are many Complex question types (or types of questions that you tend to struggle with).

Adding It Up

It is the reading level of the passage plus the difficulty level of the accompanying questions that determine the passage's overall difficulty level.

6.3 ORDERING THE SECTION

Now that you have the criteria with which to rank your passages, let's discuss the overall ordering of the section.

The Two-Pass System

1. Read the first two sentences of the first passage and scroll through the questions. If it's a NOW passage, do it now. If it's a LATER or KILLER passage, "mark" and fill in a random guess for each question. Note the passage number at the top of your scratch paper, and go on to the next passage. Complete all the NOW passages in the section: this is your first pass.
2. Once you've completed all the NOW passages, take a second pass through the section and do all the LATER passages. You can use the Review function, if necessary, to find the passages you have marked.

At the 5-minute mark, inspect the section to make sure that you haven't left any questions blank.

If you have a few extra minutes left over for a KILLER passage, quickly read the first and last line of each paragraph. Identify the easiest Specific questions (Retrieval and Vocabulary in Context), and do as many as you can by going to the relevant sections of the passage text. Again, be careful to leave time to fill in random guesses for the questions you cannot complete.

6.4   VERBAL REASONING EXERCISES: RANKING

Exercise 1: Evaluating the Passage Text
Each of the following paragraphs represents the first two sentences of a Verbal Reasoning passage. Using the criteria described earlier, decide if these are likely to be Easy, Medium, or Difficult passages to understand. You can find answers at the end of the exercise.

Passage I

It is often argued that the attempt to regulate the behavior of corporations through legislation is at best futile and at worst deleterious; in making their argument, advocates of nonregulation assume a distinction between the morality of duty and the morality of aspiration. They argue that duties, which specify the minimum standards of human conduct, lend themselves to legal enforcement better than do aspirations, which exhort one to realize one's full potential.

Passage II

A fundamental element of the American criminal justice system is trial by impartial jury. This constitutionally protected guarantee allows the defendant to challenge prospective jurors who are clearly prejudiced in the case.

Passage III

Imagining a primal state of existence, one in which there is no notion of space or time as we know it, pushes most people's powers of comprehension to the limit.… We run up against a clash of paradigms when we try to envision a universe that is, but somehow does not invoke the concepts of space or time.

Passage IV

The KT boundary, as it is called, marks one of the most violent events ever to befall life on Earth. Sixty-five million years ago, according to the current theory, the Cretaceous period was brought to a sudden conclusion by the impact of an asteroid or comet ten kilometers in diameter.

Passage V

A satisfactory explanation of the deepest significance of the fluoridation controversy remains elusive. Despite decades of research on the topic, the persistence and the passion of the fluoridation debates are yet incompletely understood by social scientists and social philosophers.

Passage VI

Trust and its violation have intrigued sociologists for decades. Trust is no more than an attribute of individuals; trust also describes a form of social organization, and interorganizational dynamics of trust violations offer a challenge to regulatory models that are largely intercorporate and involve individual or organizational self dealing.

Passage VII

The secret of all art, also of poetry, is, thus, distance. Thanks to distance the past preserved in our memory is purified and embellished; when what we remember was occurring, reality was considerably less enticing, for we were tossed, as usual, by anxieties, desires, and apprehensions that colored everything.

Passage VIII

Mention the word "surrealism" today, and certain visual images spring immediately to mind, and these images inevitably lead to certain assumptions about Surrealism: that it was primarily concerned with the visual arts, that it was about jokes, and that it was designed with a beady eye to the market. Nothing could be further from the truth, however.

Passage IX

Punishment appears to have unintended consequences. According to social theory, for example, punishment may increase the incidence of aggression because the target may imitate the behavior of the punishing agent, and offenders who are labeled are likely to behave consistently with expectations associated with that label.

Passage X

Nietzsche sees morality in much the same way that he sees epistemology. There is a gradual emptying out of that which is living in morality.

Explanations for Exercise 1: Evaluating the Passage Text

1. **Difficult:** This paragraph includes abstract concepts such as "the morality of duty and the morality of aspiration" that are difficult to paraphrase. Also, the vocabulary level is high— "deleterious," "nonregulation," "aspiration"—and will likely remain so throughout the passage.

2. **Easy:** This passage seems straightforward and factual.

3. **Difficult:** This passage is very abstract. "Primal state of existence" and "paradigms" are red flag phrases.

4. **Easy:** This passage seems straightforward, and it seems to have a clear viewpoint.

5. Medium: A passage about the "deepest significance" of a controversy is likely to be fairly abstract. This is also indicated by the fact that social scientists and philosophers are trying to understand it, meaning the passage may be a challenge for test-takers to understand as well.

6. **Difficult:** The second sentence in particular is very abstract with a complex structure that makes it difficult to follow—the passage is likely to continue in the same vein.

7. **Medium:** This text, although not as abstract (in an academic way) as passage I, is vague in a way that will require a certain amount of effort to follow and translate.

8. **Easy:** Although it is about art, which is usually considered an abstract topic, the paragraph is fairly descriptive and concrete rather than being highly theoretical.

9. **Medium:** There are some fairly abstract references here (e.g., "aggression," "the target," and "the punishing agent") which may muddy up the clarity of the passage.

10. **Difficult:** Try doing the six-year-old sister test on this paragraph. The vocabulary level, the sentence structure, and the abstractness of the subject matter indicate that this will be an extremely difficult passage.

6.4

Exercise 2: Evaluating the Questions

Classify each of the following Verbal Reasoning questions as Easy or Hard. You can find answers at the end of the exercise.

6.4

1. It can be inferred from the passage that the availability of temperature-depth records for any specific area of the United States depends primarily on the:

2. In order to support his view with respect to Wilson's *Declining Significance of Race*, Hill would be most likely to discuss which one of the following?

3. Which of the following statements would most *weaken* the author's claim that voir dire fails to ensure a jury's impartiality?

4. Suppose that it was demonstrated that the capacity of the human brain to distinguish regular from irregular cycles developed through the operation of natural selection. What impact would this have on the author's claims in the second paragraph?

5. According to the passage, which of the following was most important in creating the modern trend toward redistribution?

6. The phrase "potent political opposition" (paragraph 1) refers to:

7. The author's attitude towards insider trading can best be described as:

8. In their evaluation of the fossil record, the author states that Cutler and Behrenmeyer did all of the following EXCEPT:

6.4

9. Of the following, which would be most logically similar to the way in which a majority of fatalities from malaria occur, as the process is described in the passage?

10. The author claims that the art market rises and falls in concert with the stock market. How well is this claim supported by the author?

EXPLANATIONS FOR EXERCISE 2: EVALUATING THE QUESTIONS

1. **Easy:** Inference questions with specific references to the passage often have straightforward answers. In this case, you would probably just need to find where these records are discussed in the passage.

2. **Hard:** This is a Strengthen question that involves two speakers – you need to keep both of their perspectives in mind and conclude what approach Hill would take to support his or her own position in comparison (or contrast) to Wilson's.

3. **Hard:** A Weaken question requires taking new information provided in the answer choices and using reasoning to apply it to the passage.

4. **Hard:** The word "suppose" indicates that this question is going to require evaluating new information in the question stem and then taking multiple steps to answer the question. Also, the question stem is quite lengthy.

5. **Easy:** This is a Retrieval question, so the answer can be found in the passage text.

6. **Easy:** This question tells you where to go to find the information you need. As long as you remember to read above and below, it should not be difficult to answer.

7. **Easy:** The author's attitude can usually be determined with little difficulty.

8. **Easy:** The wording "The author states" tells you that this is a Retrieval question. The fact that it is an "EXCEPT" question shouldn't make it significantly more difficult, as long as you keep track of the question format, and of why you are eliminating each choice.

9. **Hard:** The phrase "logically similar" indicates that this is an Analogy question, which involves a higher level of reasoning and abstraction than do most question types.

10. **Hard:** This is a difficult version of an Evaluate question: you will have to decide if the support given is strong or weak and why.

6.4

Exercise 3: Evaluate Your Ranking

Ranking is a skill, like any other, that needs to be learned, practiced, and refined over time. If you ever rank an easy passage as LATER (or KILLER), or a difficult passage as NOW, review the passage and the questions to see what made it easy or difficult, and how you could have evaluated it better the first time through.

Compare the language of each passage, the length and difficulty level of the questions, and your own performance on each passage. Determine the order of attack that would have worked best for you.

- Were there any KILLER passages that you should have skipped and guessed on? How could you have known it was a KILLER before you wasted any time on it?
- Did you fail to get to any easy passages lurking at the end of the section?
- How will you change your approach on your next MCAT Practice Test you take?

Chapter 6 Summary

- The seven passages in the MCAT Verbal Reasoning section are "organized" in a seemingly random way. The level of difficulty of each passage depends on both the reading level of the passage text and on the difficulty level of the question types.

- To maximize your score, you must attack the passages strategically. Don't waste your time on KILLER passages!

CHAPTER 6 PRACTICE PASSAGES

Individual Practice Drills

Rank the two passages that follow. Do the passage that you rank as easier first. Keep track of the time you spend on each passage, but don't give yourself a set time limit.

Once you have completed the passages and checked your answers, fill out an Individual Passage Log for each passage. In particular, decide if you ranked and ordered them correctly. If not, define what you could have recognized about the passage text and/or the questions in order to rand and order the passages more accurately and effectively.

By now, you should be taking full timed Verbal Reasoning sections and full practice tests from online or other resources. Always evaluate your ranking after completing a Verbal Reasoning test section.

Don't agonize over your decisions or panic if every choice you make isn't perfect. Ranking is simply another way to gain more control over the test (and to take that control away from the test writers).

CHAPTER 6 PRACTICE PASSAGE 1

While I would certainly not want to disparage the efforts of vegetarians to limit violence toward animals in their personal lives and in public institutions and practices involving the slaughter and consumption of animals, I think it is important also to underscore that vegetarianism is itself fundamentally deconstructible. Vegetarianism is not just a passion for other animals but a series of practices involving animals and a series of discourses about animals. And if we follow the logic of Derrida's thought on the question of the animal, then it is necessary both to support vegetarianism's progressive potential but also interrogate its limitations. I have already shown how animal ethics in general (and animal rights theory, in particular) tends to reinforce the very metaphysics of subjectivity it seeks to undercut inasmuch as animal ethicists rely on a shared subjectivity among human beings and animals to ground their theories. But there are other limitations in vegetarian and pro-animal practices that should be noted. First, no matter how rigorous one's vegetarianism might be, there is simply no way to nourish oneself in advanced, industrial countries that does not involve harm to animal life (and human life, as well) in direct and indirect forms.... Simply tracking the processes by which one's food gets to the table is enough to disabuse any consumer of the notion that a vegetarian diet is "cruelty free." As such, a vegetarian diet within the context of advanced, industrial societies is, at best, a significant challenge to dominant attitudes and practices toward animals, but it remains far from the kind of ethical idea it is sometimes purported to be. Second, there are other ethical stakes involved in eating that go beyond the effects consumption of meat and animal byproducts has on animals. All diets, even organic and vegetarian diets, have considerable negative effects on the natural environment and the human beings who produce and harvest food. Consequently, if we consider ethical vegetarianism to constitute an ethical stopping point, these other concerns will be overlooked. And it is precisely these other concerns, concerns about the other, often-overlooked forms of violence, that should *also* impassion a deconstructive approach to the question of the animal.

Although these critical points are certainly in line with the logic of a deconstructive approach to animal ethics, they do not form the focus of Derrida's analysis. Derrida draws attention, instead, to a different limitation to pro-animal ethics and politics, one that he associates with "interventionist violence" against animals. The violence at issue here takes a *symbolic* rather than literal form, and this symbolic violence against animals, Derrida seems to think, is one of the most pressing philosophical and metaphysical issues facing thought today. In view of this notion of symbolic violence, he makes the following statement: "Vegetarians, too, partake of animals, even of men. They practice a different mode of denigration." What

does he mean by this? Clearly, ethical vegetarianism aims at avoiding consumption of animal flesh — and presumably human flesh, as well. So, in what manner do vegetarians partake of animals and other beings toward which they aim to be nonviolent? Derrida's remark here is part of a complicated argument about the ethical questions concerning eating, incorporation, and violence toward the Other. While Derrida, like Levinas, posits a nonviolent opening to the Other... he does not believe that a wholly nonviolent relation with the Other is possible. On his line of thought, violence is irreducible in our relations with the Other, if by nonviolence we mean a thought and practice relating to the Other that respects fully the alterity of the Other. In order to speak and think about or related to the Other, the Other must — to some extent — be appropriated and violated, even if only symbolically. How does one respect the singularity of the Other without betraying that alterity? *Any* act of identification, naming, or relation is a betrayal of and a violence toward the Other. Of course, this should not be taken to mean that such violence is immoral or that all forms of violence are equivalent.... [Within vegetarianism] the ethical question should not be "How do I achieve an ethically pure, cruelty-free diet?" but rather, "What is the best, most respectful, most grateful, and also most giving way of relating" to animals and other Others?

Material used in this particular passage has been adapted from the following source:

M. Calarco, *Zoographies: The Question of the Animal from Heidegger to Derrida.* © 2008 by Columbia University Press.

1. Which of the following assertions is/are made in the passage?

   I. Derrida believes that symbolic violence against animals is currently one of the most important issues in metaphysical thought.
   II. Symbolic violence against the Other is as bad as literal violence.
   III. Eating in an advanced industrialized society inherently entails harming others.

   A) II only
   B) I and II only
   C) I and III only
   D) I, II, and III

2. The author most likely believes that:

A) vegetarianism is pointless since it cannot be freed from a relation of cruelty with the Other.
B) Levinas is short-sighted in believing a non-violent relationship with the Other is possible.
C) vegetarianism is noble in its efforts to limit violence against human and nonhuman animals, but it is not above questioning and criticism.
D) Derrida is overly extreme in asserting that "vegetarians partake of animals, even men."

3. Suppose that a young girl rescues a formerly abused greyhound dog from an animal shelter. She names him Odysseus after the Greek explorer to honor the dog's past and celebrate his arrival in a safe and loving home. Based on information provided in the passage, how would Derrida respond to this situation?

A) Derrida would allow that, even though the act of naming entails treating the animal as Other, the respect signified by the name balances against the violence done to the dog in the past.
B) He would point out that even naming the Other is an act of violence, albeit a symbolic one, no matter what the intention behind the name.
C) He would praise the girl for choosing such a historically significant and noble name, saying that this reflects her love of animals.
D) Derrida would criticize the girl for committing an act of violence as severe as those committed by the dog's former owners.

4. What definition of the word "disabuse" (paragraph 1) best fits in the context of the passage?

A) Treating something kindly and/or healing it after a period of abuse
B) Chastising someone for misguided views
C) Affirming someone's views
D) Convincing a person that his or her views are fallacious

5. What is the primary purpose of the passage?

A) To question the Derridian view of animals as Others to whom we owe an ethical responsibility, whether we are vegetarians or not
B) To critique, with the help of Derrida's philosophy, the central motivations of vegetarianism and to suggest a new basis for a discussion concerning how best to treat animals
C) To suggest that vegetarianism is fundamentally misguided since nobody can practice a completely "cruelty free" diet
D) To interrogate the notion of "ethical purity" and argue that such a state of being is impossible

6. All of the following are claims made by the author EXCEPT:

A) ethical vegetarianism aims to avoid the consumption of animal and human flesh.
B) vegetarianism remains far from the ethical ideal it is purported to be.
C) animal ethicists rely on a shared subjectivity between humans and animals to ground their theories.
D) vegetarianism is fundamentally deconstructive.

7. The author provides the most support for which of the following claims?

A) Derrida draws attention to a limitation of pro-animal ethics which is associated with "interventionist violence."
B) There is simply no way to feed oneself in advanced, industrialized countries without causing some harm to animal life.
C) All diets have considerably negative effects on the environment and on the humans who produce and harvest food.
D) Vegetarians are not as ethically pure as vegans, who avoid all animal byproducts in their diets, thereby reducing their environmental harm.

CHAPTER 6 PRACTICE PASSAGE 2

Hispanics are the fastest growing minority in the United States. "Hispanics," "Latinos," "Chicanos," "Mexican Americans," "Puerto Ricans," "Cuban Americans," and so on, are all designations used to describe this large, heterogeneous population with different cultural, ethnic, geographic, and social backgrounds. There is still no clear definition of the term "Hispanic." The data available regarding the incidence, morbidity, and mortality from cancer in "Hispanics" are scarce, scattered, outdated, and often incomplete.

From the studies looking at the accessibility and availability of medical care to this population, few have examined in detail the variability within the entire Hispanic population. The aggregation of culturally distinct subgroups, which have resided in the United States for different periods of time, into a more inclusive "Hispanic" category assumes that all persons of Mexican, Central and South American, Cuban, and Puerto Rican extraction have similar perceptions, true or not, of cancer risks and share needs and experience similar barriers in using health services. There is, however, no clear evidence for this assumption.

On the contrary, there is evidence that each group has specific characteristics that make them different and independent from one another, despite the fact that they also share some commonalities. Recruitment of minorities, specifically Hispanics, to clinical trials has been a significant problem that can potentially be overcome by adequate protocol development and investigator education regarding specific knowledge, attitudes, and needs of minority populations. It is timely and refreshing to see a recent anthropological evaluation of the problem of cancer in (female) Hispanics. It reviews the knowledge, attitudes, and barriers (KAB) for breast and cervical cancer in four different groups of women of Hispanic/ Latino origin and compare them among themselves and against a group of physicians' KAB.

Unfortunately, there are no complete data regarding cancer in all Hispanic groups. We currently do not know the true number of cancer cases in Hispanics, nor do we have accurate morbidity, mortality, and survival data from these groups. As a result, we are not really able to fully understand or appreciate the physical, emotional, and financial impact of cancer in Hispanic patients and their families. Mortality from cancer in Hispanics is difficult to assess because of the limited data that are available. Utilizing existing community groups and organizations and helping to create strong community bonds could improve the potential for success of minority cancer control efforts and patient recruitment to clinical trials. These programs can become networks of information with inherent trust from their respective communities. In developing these interventions, we should increase our awareness of the needs of all different Hispanic groups and assure that programs are developed together with these communities, in order to assure that they are culture- and community-sensitive, respecting and complementing the Hispanic heritage.

[The recent anthropological study reminds] us that perhaps there are no true knowledge deficits, but rather misconceptions regarding the true cancer risks. Thus, it emphasizes two facts: (1) we must get to know and understand the population(s) with whom we plan to work; and (2) there is a strong need for education, not only of the communities with whom we work but, perhaps more important, of the scientific teams (physicians, nurses, anthropologists, social workers, etc.) that will work in and with those communities. Preliminary data from our group have shown that community-based lay health educators ("Promotoras de Salud"), working together with local health departments can be successful in reaching, educating, and increasing recruitment of Hispanic (Mexican-American) women to cervical cancer screening programs and to cancer clinical trials. This program is now being piloted through the Southwest Oncology Group in San Antonio's (Texas) Hispanic community. The time has come to revise and update our sources of information and data gathering. Careful study of each Hispanic subgroup is essential in order to have a realistic picture of the overall cancer problem in the United States today. These studies must include a clearer definition of the differences among the many Hispanic subgroups with their respective problems and barriers to cancer care.

Material used in this particular passage has been adapted from the following source:

M. R. Modiano, "Breast and Cervical Cancer in Hispanic Women," *Medical Anthropology Quarterly*, ©1995.

1. The primary purpose of the passage is to:

A) prompt others to create a better, more accurate definition of "Hispanics."

B) promote a better understanding of Hispanic populations in order to recognize and serve their cancer health needs.

C) advocate for the term "Hispanic" to be discarded for its ineffectively inclusive description of diverse peoples.

D) educate Latino cancer patients about available resources.

2. The author characterizes Hispanics as which of the following?

A) A large, diverse minority of Spanish speaking people in the United States with unusually strong community bonds

B) A population whose various members face similar obstacles in the health care system

C) A group whose known epidemiological cancer data may be lacking

D) A heterogeneous people who are represented well in clinical trials

3. Which of the following are limitations that exist currently, as stated by the passage?

    I. The view of Hispanics as a culturally monolithic people

    II. Language barriers between healthcare professionals and patients

    III. Interference by medically untrained community groups

A) I only

B) I and II only

C) I and III only

D) II and III only

4. It can be inferred that the author would be in favor of a program with all of the following aspects EXCEPT:

A) a careful study of each Hispanic subgroup focusing on commonalities between them.

B) a community based initiative that is congruent with Hispanic cultures.

C) an emphasis on cancer screening in women.

D) education of medical professionals about the populations they serve.

5. The author deems all of the following as positive aspects of the recent study discussed EXCEPT:

A) pointing out potentially helpful ways in which clinical trial recruitment can be improved.

B) separating "Hispanic" women in the study into specific groups.

C) utilizing an anthropological approach in analyzing cancer data in Hispanics.

D) gathering data on all of the different Hispanic subgroups.

6. The tone of the passage can best be described as:

A) derisive and accusatory.

B) distressed but indifferent.

C) optimistic and analytical.

D) clinical and regretful.

7. The intended audience of this passage is most likely:

A) cancer hospitals or research center administrators.

B) the American public at large.

C) Hispanic women with breast or cervical cancer.

D) the Southwest Oncology Group.

SOLUTIONS TO CHAPTER 6 PRACTICE PASSAGE 1

1. **C** This is a Retrieval/Roman Numeral question

   I: **True. In paragraph 2, the author states: "The violence at issue here takes a *symbolic* rather than literal form, and this symbolic violence against animals, Derrida seems to think, is one of the most pressing philosophical and metaphysical issues facing thought today."**

   II: False. Near the end paragraph 2, the author states: "Of course, this should not be taken to mean that such violence is immoral or that all forms of violence are equivalent." There is no statement made that equates symbolic violence with literal violence.

   III: **True. While this answer choice may sound extreme, its language is backed up in paragraph 1, when the author says: "there is simply no way to nourish oneself in advanced, industrial countries that does not involve harm to animal life."**

2. **C** This is an Inference question.

   A: No. This answer choice is too extreme. While the author critiques vegetarianism, he never goes so far as to dismiss it as "pointless." Note that in paragraph 1, the author states: "It is necessary both to support vegetarianism's progressive potential but also interrogate its limitations."

   B: No. The author does not evoke such critical language with regards to Levinas. Also, we don't know from the text that Levinas does in fact believe that a nonviolent relationship with the Other is possible, only that Levinas, like Derrida, "posits a nonviolent opening to the Other."

   C: **Yes. The author expresses admiration for vegetarians' efforts to limit their role in violence against animals, but spends the passage highlighting some flaws in the reasoning behind vegetarianism. See paragraph 1: "It is necessary both to support vegetarianism's progressive potential but also interrogate its limitations."**

   D: No. The author does not criticize Derrida in any way. Note that when the author asks in the middle of paragraph 2, "What does he mean by this," and goes on to say that clearly vegetarians eat neither animals nor people, he is not suggesting that this (literal consumption) is in fact what Derrida is referring to. Rather, the author goes on to explain that Derrida uses "partake" in the sense of symbolic violence towards "the Other."

3. **B** This is a New Information question.

   A: No. Derrida believes that the act of naming "the Other" is itself an act of violence (see middle of paragraph 2). Although Derrida would most likely allow or admit that this act of violence is less severe than physical abuse, it is still (symbolic) violence. Therefore the naming adds to, rather than balances against, the violence done to the dog.

   B: **Yes. In paragraph 2, the author discusses Derridian thought and states: "*Any* act of identification, naming, or relation is a betrayal of and a violence toward the Other." This answer choice is therefore the most appropriate one based on information from the passage.**

   C: No. There is no evidence in the passage to support this interpretation of Derrida's reaction. There is no suggestion that Derrida would care what the name is or what the intentions of the namer are.

   D: No. The author, in the context of explaining Derrida's argument, makes an effort to acknowledge that not all forms of violence are equivalent: "Of course, this should not be taken to mean that such violence is immoral or that all forms of violence are equivalent" (paragraph 2).

4. **D**   This is a Vocabulary in Context question.

    A: No. This answer is inappropriate given the context in which the word appears. The word is used in relation to changing one's mind about an opinion: In this case, the author is talking about exposing the reality that vegetarian diets are not in fact "cruelty free."

    B: No. This answer is too strong in tone: there is no personal chastising or reprimanding of the people who held views that vegetarian diets are "cruelty free."

    C: No. This answer choice is antithetical to the context of the word "disabuse" in the passage: disabusing is not about affirming someone's views but rather changing or eliminating them.

    D: **Yes. This answer is the best fit according to the passage. The author suggests that thinking about how food gets to us is enough to convince anyone that a vegetarian diet is not in fact "cruelty free."**

5. **B**   This is a Main Idea/Primary Purpose question

    A: No. The author does not question Derrida's views about animals but rather employs them to make his analysis.

    B: **Yes. This answer choice best captures the ideas presented in the passage and the purpose of the author's use of Derrida's philosophy. In paragraph 1, the author begins the discussion of vegetarianism's limitations by saying: "And if we follow the logic of Derrida's thought on the question of the animal, then it is necessary both to support vegetarianism's progressive potential but also interrogate its limitations." Paragraph 2 follows in kind, focusing on Derrida's views on the Other and how they relate to vegetarianism. The last sentence suggests a new way of approaching the issue: "[Within vegetarianism] the ethical question should not be 'How do I achieve an ethically pure, cruelty-free diet?' but rather, 'What is the best, most respectful, most grateful, and also most giving way of relating' to animals and other Others?"**

    C: No. The words "fundamentally misguided" are too extreme given the tone of the passage. For example, the author states: "it is necessary...to support vegetarianism's progressive potential" as well as to look into its limitations (paragraph 1).

    D: No. This answer is too broad, since it does not address the idea of vegetarianism which is central to the passage. Furthermore, the author does not argue that ethical purity is never possible, but only that vegetarianism cannot itself be an ethically pure position (which relates back to the issue of the choice being too broad).

6. **D**   This is a Retrieval/Except question

    A: No. This claim is made in paragraph 2: "Clearly, ethical vegetarianism aims at avoiding consumption of animal flesh—and presumably human flesh, as well."

    B: No. This statement is made in paragraph 1: "A vegetarian diet within the context of advanced, industrial societies is, at best, a significant challenge to dominant attitudes and practices toward animals, but it remains far from the kind of ethical idea it is sometimes purported to be."

    C: No. This statement is made word for word in paragraph 1 of the passage.

    D: **Yes. In paragraph 1 the author states that "Vegetarianism is fundamentally deconstructible." This is different from saying it is "deconstructive," since the former term indicates that vegetarianism can be deconstructed, while the latter suggests it can deconstruct other things.**

7. **A**   This is an Evaluate question

   A: **Yes. After the author mentions Derrida's concept of "interventionist violence" in paragraph 2, he elaborates upon this term and defines it by means of discussion and example (i.e., naming the Other). Therefore, this, out of the four claims, is the one for which the author provides the most support within the passage.**

   B: No. This claim is made in the passage (paragraph 1) but the author does not elaborate upon it by providing an explanation of how a vegetarian diet entails harm to animals. First, the following reference to the process by which food arrives at the table still does not explain what the direct or indirect harm might be. Second, the later reference to harm done to the environment hints at an explanation, but only a vague one (there is still no discussion of what that harm might be). Therefore, when comparing this choice to choice A, the statement in choice A is much more strongly supported within the passage.

   C: No. This claim is made in the passage (paragraph 1) but the author does not offer specific examples or further explanation of the negative effects mentioned.

   D: No. This statement is not made in the passage. The author mentions animal byproducts (second half of paragraph 1), but does not connect this to veganism (which itself is never mentioned—making this connection would require using too much outside knowledge) or suggest that people who avoid animal byproducts are more ethically pure than vegetarians.

SOLUTIONS TO CHAPTER 6 PRACTICE PASSAGE 2

1. **B**   This is a Main Idea/Primary Purpose question.

   A: No. The focus on simply the definition of "Hispanics" is too narrow. This answer choice ignores many of the central ideas of the text, including using community organizing and education to gain understanding about cancer information in Hispanic populations and to provide proper care.

   B: **Yes. The correct answer will be the one of the four choices that best captures and covers all the major themes of the passage. The last four lines of the passage describe what the author believes is important (understanding the Hispanic populations) and the changes he believes should be made to help the affected people by creating "a realistic picture" of the situation. The rest of the passage explains why this better understanding is needed, and suggests ways in which it might be achieved.**

   C: No. This choice is both too extreme and too narrow. While the author agrees that the use of the overly inclusive term "Hispanic" results in barriers to discovering important information about cancer in those populations, he never advocates discarding the term. He simply believes that each subgroup of the population should be examined separately. Furthermore, while the term "Hispanic" may be problematic in some ways, this is not the focus of the entire passage.

   D: No. The passage states that education is an important facet that needs to be addressed, but the text itself does not offer much educational information regarding using cancer resources. The mentions of the "Promotoras de Salud" and "Southwest Oncology Group" are only to provide examples for the author's argument about the need for such organizations and programs.

2. **C** This is an Inference question.
    A: No. "Hispanics" are described as a large, diverse group of people (paragraph 1). However, the author never states or suggests that Hispanics speak Spanish. Be careful not to use outside knowledge or assumptions when picking an answer choice. Furthermore, while the author does discuss measures that would help to "create strong community bonds" (paragraph 4), the passage does not suggest that Hispanics have unusually strong community bonds compared to other groups.
    B: No. The passage states the opposite of this statement: the use of the " 'Hispanic' category" assumes all the people "experience similar barriers" in health services (paragraph 2). However, "each group has specific characteristics that make them different and independent from one another" (paragraph 3).
    C: Yes. The last line of paragraph 1 states that "The data available regarding the incidence, morbidity, and mortality from cancer in Hispanics are scarce, scattered, outdated, and often incomplete."
    D: No. The author states that the Hispanic population is indeed heterogeneous, but notes in paragraph 3 that they are actually underrepresented in clinical trials. This is another example of an "opposite" Attractor.

3. **A** This is a Retrieval/Roman Numeral question.
    I: True. The passage states that clumping together the culturally diverse groups that make up the Hispanic population results in a limited and inaccurate picture of "the physical, emotional, and financial impact of cancer in Hispanic patients and their families" (paragraph 4).
    II: False. While barriers, in general, are mentioned within the passage, specific language barriers are not addressed and are outside of the scope of the passage.
    III: False. The author states that "community-based lay health educators" working with "health departments…can be successful" (paragraph 5).

4. **A** This is an Inference/Except question.
    A: Yes. The correct answer choice will have the *least* support from the passage text. While the first part of this choice is supported, the second part is not. The author calls for study and understanding of "variability" or differences between the subgroups. The author argues throughout the passage that a focus on, or assumption of, commonalities is misguided.
    B: No. Paragraph 4 emphasizes the importance of both a community based approach and a program "complementing the Hispanic heritage."
    C: No. Paragraph 5 mentions, positively, the successful "cervical cancer screening programs" carried out by community based coalitions.
    D: No. Paragraph 5 highlights the importance of the education of "physicians, nurses, anthropologists, social workers, etc."

5. **D** This is an Inference/Except question.
    A: No. Paragraph 3 states, "Recruitment of minorities, specifically Hispanics, to clinical trials has been a significant problem that can potentially be overcome by adequate protocol development and investigator education regarding specific knowledge, attitudes, and needs of minority populations."
    B: No. In paragraph 3, the author mentions that the subjects were divided into "four different groups of women of Hispanic/Latino origin."

C: No. The author states in paragraph 3 that it is "timely and refreshing to see an anthropological evaluation of the problem of cancer in (female) Hispanics."

D: **Yes. The correct answer choice will have the *least* support from the passage. The study in question divided the women into four categories. However, the author does not suggest that there are only four subgroups, or that the study covered all existing subgroups.**

6. **C** This is a Tone/Attitude question.

A: No. While the author points out the inefficiencies of the healthcare system stemming in part from the inclusive term "Hispanics," he does not point fingers or accuse anybody specifically. He simply notes that the term is one with flaws: "There is still no clear definition of the term 'Hispanic.'" In addition, there are no words that indicate contempt or ridicule as the word "derisiveness" would.

B: No. The author feels that there is a problem, but the word "distressed" is too extreme to describe his attitude. In addition, the author is not indifferent. He promotes ideas that he hopes will cause change. This can be noted through statements like: "The time has come to revise and update our sources of information and data gathering" (paragraph 5).

C: **Yes. The author describes, in paragraph 5, progress that is occurring already, and what more improvements can be made. This indicates optimism. His explanation of the problem and situation is analytical—he discusses different aspects of the problem and provides supportive evidence.**

D: No. "Clinical" does describe the relatively objective tone of the author. The text lacks passionate claims, but is, instead, professional, as the term "clinical" may indicate. However, the word "regretful" is too extreme to describe the author's attitude. While he would like the healthcare system to be reformed, the author does not use words that would indicate regret or disappointment. If one part of the choice is incorrect, the whole choice is wrong.

7. **A** This is an Inference question.

A: **Yes. The author's intent is to encourage enactment of changes that will positively benefit Hispanics. Note wording such as "In developing these interventions, we should increase our awareness of the needs of all different Hispanic groups" (paragraph 4) or "we must get to know and understand the population(s) with whom we plan to work" (paragraph 5), which suggests that the passage is intended for people working within the field of health care. Administrators at cancer institutes or researchers have the ability to utilize his suggestions and advice, such as by carrying out useful research, or coordinating community based initiatives to reach more Hispanics.**

B: No. The tone and content of the passage indicate that it is not intended for the general reader, but rather for people with a specific interest, and role to play, in this particular issue.

C: No. The primary purpose of this passage (as noted in the solution for question 1) is not to educate Hispanic women, but to create changes in our understanding how cancer affects Hispanics, and in how Hispanic people are educated, tested and treated. While one could imagine that Hispanic women with breast or cervical cancer might be interested in this information, this group is too narrowly defined to be the "intended audience." The passage is geared towards people who would be able to carry out research, education, and treatment, rather than towards potential subjects of research, education, or treatment.

D: No. The Southwest Oncology Group already participates in the practices advocated by the author (paragraph 5). There would be little or no benefit seen by presenting the group with the information of the passage.

Individual Passage Log

Passage # _____   Time spent on passage _____

Q#	Q type	Attractors	What did you do wrong?

Revised Strategy _____

Passage # _____   Time spent on passage _____

Q#	Q type	Attractors	What did you do wrong?

Revised Strategy _____

Chapter 7
MAPS:
Focus on Structure

GOALS

1. To better understand, summarize, and locate passage information
2. To manage stress effectively

7.1 THE STRUCTURE OF A PASSAGE

As you know by now, mastery of the Verbal Reasoning section requires working the passage efficiently during your first read-through, understanding the major themes, and locating turning points and transitions in the logic without getting bogged down in the details. Over the past few chapters, you've learned specific strategies for attacking the questions and the answer choices. Now it is time to return to the passage itself and further refine your reading and analytical skills.

At this point in the process, you know what the major components of a passage are. Now, how do you use that knowledge to improve your reading comprehension and your efficiency and accuracy in answering the questions? In this chapter, we will look at the familiar aspects of the passage from a new angle. That is, how the author structures the passage to communicate his or her core ideas. By recognizing and following that structure, you can both better understand the important parts and the Bottom Line of the passage (Logic), and quickly find the relevant information as you are answering the questions (Location).

Three Levels of Structure

The structure of a passage can be identified on three levels.

- **Level 1:** The structure of individual sentences. Look for how the parts of the sentence work together, and how the words used by the author indicate the meaning of that sentence. Don't get caught up in parsing out the structure of every line of every paragraph. But, when sentences contain **indicator words** like *however, although, therefore, on one hand, for example*, etc., it is important to use those words to figure out the meaning of that sentence.

  For example, pivotal words signal a shift in meaning or subject. When you identify a pivotal word in the sentence, ask, "What is it shifting from, and what is it shifting to? How do the two parts of a sentence (or the pair of sentences, if the indicator words come at the beginning of a sentence) relate to each other, and what does this tell me about the author's argument?" Or, if you see the word *therefore*, your immediate question should be, "What is the conclusion or claim being made and where is the evidence supporting that claim?" (especially important for answering Structure and Evaluate questions). The words *for example* should raise the question, "what larger claim is being supported by this example, and how does it relate to the author's argument in the passage as a whole?"
  By paying attention to indicator words (see Chapter 3), you can identify the sentences that will play a particularly important role in constructing the author's argument, and skim over the sentences that are less important at this stage.

- **Level 2:** The structure of a paragraph or chunk of information. If you ask these questions about individual sentences, it naturally leads you to the structure and intent of the entire paragraph. Did it introduce an opposing point of view? Did it provide specific evidence and support for a conclusion drawn earlier? Does it introduce another stage of development, or continue to develop a description of a particular phase?

  Separate the paragraph into **claims** and **evidence**. The claims being made are important in understanding the main point of the paragraph, whereas the details of the evidence supporting those claims are usually important only when answering the questions.
  Look for **topic sentences.** Often (but not always) the author uses the first or last sentence of the paragraph to sum up the theme or main point of the paragraph as a whole.

- **Level 3:** The structure of the passage as a whole. The relationship between the individual paragraphs creates or constructs the logical structure of the author's argument. This leads you naturally into an understanding of the Bottom Line (logic of the passage). Having this map of the passage in mind also helps you to quickly locate the information you need as you are answering the questions.

Some common passage structures are:

- Compare and contrast
- Steps and stages
- Cause and effect
- Thesis with evidence
- Rebuttal
- Narration or description
- Analysis of different aspects of an issue or idea
- Old and new theory
- Chronology

7.2 THE MAPS OF A PASSAGE
There are four basic components to any passage that, when clearly identified and articulated, give you a firm grounding in the text and build a foundation for the process of answering the questions.

These components are the **MAPS** or:

Main Point

Attitude

Purpose

Support

1. The **MAIN POINT** of each paragraph encapsulates the core of *what* the author is trying to communicate. It includes the main idea of each paragraph or chunk of information, and defines and delimits the scope of the passage. The **MAIN POINT** of the passage is the Bottom Line.
2. The **ATTITUDE** expresses *who* the author is through the tone of the passage. Is the author presenting himself or herself as a critic? An advocate? A neutral observer?
3. The **PURPOSE** is the intent of each chunk of the passage and of the passage as a whole. *Why* did the author write it? Was it to compare and contrast two theories? To propose a new theory? To trace the evolution of an idea? To describe a process?
4. The SUPPORT is the evidence the author uses to support his or her claims. *How* does the author construct the passage?

You are, or at least should be, quite familiar with these four aspects by this point. However, if you want to further improve your score, the task is to better understand how to quickly identify these aspects not in isolation, but as part of an interactive system. That is, to see how they relate to and build upon each other.

Think about a real map. It is constructed in a particular way with a particular purpose: to guide you to your destination. When you use a map, you don't need to pay attention to every street or highway or reference; you only need to find the streets and the connections between those streets which are relevant to your particular goal at that particular time. Memorizing the entire map is not only unnecessary, it's impossible. If you look at the entire picture without separating out the important from the unimportant sections, you will be lost—it's just too much information!

By breaking a passage down into MAPS, you define both Logic and Location. The Logic gives you the Bottom Line, which is crucial for all questions. Location "labels" the different parts of the passage, enabling you to use your map to find the specific information you need as you are answering each question.

So, let's look at our four MAPS components in more detail in connection to passage structure. To follow the process you actually go through as you work a passage, we will reverse the components to SPAM, starting at the lowest level and working up to the Main Point.

Support

How does the passage use evidence to support the author's larger claims?

As you've discovered on the Writing Sample section of the MCAT, support is crucial to expository writing. Claiming that "Cooperation works better than violence," or "Advertising encourages social conformity," is relatively easy. It takes more effort to convince anyone of when and why such an idea would be true, and it requires a sophisticated understanding of how an idea or claim is supported by evidence to evaluate that claim and the overall argument within which it appears.

You need to identify the support used by the author in order to 1) decide to skim through it in your first read-through, as it is less important to the logic of the passage, and 2) re-locate it, if and when it becomes relevant to the questions. Many Verbal Reasoning questions require you to enumerate or to characterize evidence presented in a passage.

So, how do you recognize the support?

There are many ways to support a Main Point. The following are the most common:

1. **Examples:** The author illustrates the Main Point with an example from the real world or with a hypothetical example meant to reflect the real world. Examples are often introduced with standard words or phrases that help you to identify them: *in this case, in illustration, for example.*
2. **Generalizations:** To make a point about Christmas, for example, an author might generalize about something larger—like holidays in general. Or the author might make a point about Christmas by discussing Christmas trees. In other words, a generalization supports a main idea by giving an example of something larger—or something smaller—than the subject.
3. **Steps/stages:** Many passages describe the development of an idea, a historical time line, or an evolutionary process. Generally, each paragraph will describe one of those stages. Or, a passage may describe how one thing preceded another in order to support a larger claim about cause and effect.
4. **Comparisons/contrasts:** An effective way to explain something is to compare it to, or contrast it with, something else. Through differences and similarities, the specific characteristics of an idea can be highlighted. A specific type of comparison is an *analogy*, where one situation is described in order to communicate something about another, supposedly similar situation.
5. **Statistics:** Statistics can be any type of numerical information: percentages, ratios, probabilities, populations, prices, etc. It is especially important to avoid getting bogged down in these details. You will be able to find them again later, if you need to.
6. **Studies:** The author cites studies, research, or polling data to support a conclusion.
7. **Definitions:** The author defines key terms in order to communicate something about the context or issues within which those terms are used.
8. **Quotes or citation of others:** The passage includes either direct quotes or citation of other works. It is important to ask yourself if the author is agreeing or disagreeing with these other writers or speakers.
9. **General opinion:** The author describes a past or present common belief. Authors often do this in order to introduce a different or alternative idea. Always define if the common belief is consistent or inconsistent with the author's point of view.
10. **Anecdotes:** The author tells a story, often from his or her personal experience.

Purpose

Why was the passage written?

Purpose is closely related to structure, and it can be broken down to three levels in a similar way:

1. What is the purpose of the support provided by the author? What larger claim is being supported? Answering this question will lead you to the next level.
2. What is the purpose of the paragraph? What role does it play within the logical structure of the passage? How do the different paragraphs relate to each other? Answering this question leads you to the final level.
3. What is the purpose of the passage as a whole? Why did the author write it? What overall claim or point is being made?

The purpose of the passage as a whole is very closely tied to the author's attitude. The intent of neutral passages is to describe or explain something. In a purely descriptive passage, it is likely that each paragraph will deal with a different characteristic of the thing being described.

An explanatory passage often includes both generalizations as well as specific examples as illustrations of those generalizations. Identify transition words to ascertain when the author is moving from one point to another (*additionally, also, furthermore*, etc.) or from a generalization to a specific case or illustration (*for example*).

On the other hand, evaluative, critical, or persuasive passages often present one idea or position, a contrasting idea or position, and the author's opinion, which may involve choosing one of those sides over the other or presenting a separate alternative altogether. A common purpose is to contrast old with new theories, or to present and evaluate a debate or controversy.

Keep in mind the strength of the tone and the language. For example, the author may be rejecting the validity of a claim or simply raising questions about or problems with that claim. Keep track of pivotal words (*however, but, yet, conversely, although*, etc.) that indicate when the author is shifting in the discussion from one side to the other, or introducing a qualification. (Pivotal words, however, are not limited to opinionated passages, just as transitional words do not appear exclusively in neutral passages.) Difficult passages may have several such shifts.

Attitude

Who wrote the passage? What is the author's tone?

An author may position herself as a neutral observer, simply describing or explaining without expressing an opinion. The author may even describe a debate or conflicting points of view without directly entering into that debate.

In other passages, the author is more present—speculating, evaluating, criticizing, praising, or advocating. To define the attitude of the author, look for words that indicate the tone of the passage (e.g., *unfortunately, shamefully, at last, thankfully*, etc.), or statements that embody the voice or opinion of the author. If the author does have an opinion, evaluate how strongly negative or positive it is. Look out for qualifying language (e.g., *might, could, in some cases, while it is sometimes true that*, etc.) that authors often use to moderate their tone.

Rarely, a question will directly ask for the attitude or tone of the author. However, attitude can play a role in any question type. It is particularly central to Main Point or Primary Purpose questions, to any question that asks how the author would respond to new information, and to Strengthen and Weaken questions.

Main Point

What is the passage trying to prove?

Articulating the main point or main idea is one of the most important steps you can take to maximize both your accuracy and your speed in working through the questions. A question may directly ask for the main point or central thesis. However, even if there is no such question, the main point can be used on a variety of question types to quickly eliminate answer choices that are out of scope or not the issue of the passage. The main point may be summarized in the first or last paragraph of the passage, but this is not always the case. In many passages, parts of the main point are scattered throughout, and it can be defined only by synthesizing or piecing together the main idea of each chunk of information.

Students often fall into one of two traps when attempting to identify the main point. On the one hand, they might state it too broadly, as a vague category or idea that includes—but goes beyond—the passage. On the other hand, they may define it too narrowly, focusing on only one among several of the points made by the author.

7.3 VERBAL REASONING EXERCISES: MAPS

Exercise 1: Separating Claims from Evidence

Read and highlight each of the following paragraphs. As you read, identify the evidence used and the claims made based on that evidence. Note the wording and/or paragraph structure used by the author to distinguish the evidence from the main point. Note any topic sentences (sentences that express the main point of the paragraph). Finally, answer the three questions following each paragraph. Answers follow at the end of the Exercise.

Paragraph 1

Drug activity was the life force of Coco's new building. There was no pretense of security: doors were propped open, and the interior hallway made for a nerve-wracking trip from the sidewalk to the hall. Pigeon droppings formed a putrid sand castle in the building's crumbling fountain. The mailboxes were bashed in, their little doors dented and askew. People snatch the light bulbs from the hallways.

     1. What is the Main Point? Is it expressed in a topic sentence?

     2. What is the evidence supporting that Main Point, and what is the nature of that evidence?

     3. What language or paragraph structure did the author use to distinguish the evidence from the claims?

Paragraph 2

To assert, as one is tempted to, whether friendly or hostile to Nietzsche, that his results were flashes of poetic insight, or brilliant intuition, misses, I think, the real thrust and importance of his position. The fundamental intention of Nietzsche's work must be to recover and make manifest these underlying presuppositions which were the foundations of the coherence of Greek culture. It is apparent, for instance, that he does not intend a historical portrait of Greece shortly after the Cliesthenian reforms. In another context, speaking of Myerbeer's opera, he will argue that "it is *now* a matter of *indifference*" that the founders of opera were revolting against the Church, and that "it is *enough* to have perceived" that they were in fact engaged in *sub rosa* glorification of natural man.

     1. What is the Main Point? Is it expressed in a topic sentence?

     2. What is the evidence supporting that Main Point, and what is the nature of that evidence?

     3. What language or paragraph structure did the author use to distinguish the evidence from the claims?

Paragraph 3

English serfs were not slaves—human chattels—as in the Roman Empire and American South. They had legal rights to strips of arable land of their own to work (after putting in around two-thirds of their time working the lord's personal lands, called his demesnes). The serf villagers had a right to pasturage of a modest number of domesticated animals. They could hunt for boar and rabbits (not deer, which were reserved for the ruling class) in the neighboring forests or haul fish out of a nearby stream to eat on Catholic Fridays and during Lent. They could plant vegetable gardens next to their houses. The lord had to provide in each village a mill to grind the peasant's grain for their heavily cereal diet.

1. What is the Main Point? Is it expressed in a topic sentence?

2. What is the evidence supporting that Main Point, and what is the nature of that evidence?

3. What language or paragraph structure did the author use to distinguish the evidence from the claims?

Paragraph 4

The *Nude Descending a Staircase* is now one of the most celebrated milestones of modern art, but when the show's organizers saw it, far from being dazzled, they were horrified. Their view of what Cubism was, or ought to be, centered increasingly narrowly upon the mathematics of the Golden Section. Marcel's *Nude* owed nothing to this. In fact, it was clearly influenced as much by the Futurists as the Cubists. The Futurists were concerned with speed, noise, movement: their works had been exhibited the previous month at Bernheim Jeune's gallery, an exhibition which Duchamp visited several times. He was at this time concerned not with pure form, but with the problem of describing movement on a static canvas: he said later that the idea had come from Marey's serial photographs of people and animals in movement, and described its geometry a 'sport of distortion other than Cubism.'

1. What is the Main Point? Is it expressed in a topic sentence?

2. What is the evidence supporting that Main Point, and what is the nature of that evidence?

3. What language or paragraph structure did the author use to distinguish the evidence from the claims?

Paragraph 5

The discrepancy between people who had rats and people who did not was underscored in 1959. It was a time when Americans and New Yorkers were thinking pretty highly of themselves, when people on Park Avenue felt safe from rats. It was during the Cold War, and Soviet officials were in Manhattan visiting a technology show that highlighted Soviet inventions. A headline in the *Daily News* boasted U.S. EXPERTS WANDER AT RED SHOW AND WONDER AT NOTHING. The same week, however, a three-year old baby died in Coney Island. His mother had heard him crying in the night and thought he wanted a bottle but soon discovered he was being bitten by rats…. Between January of 1959 and June 1960, 1,025 rat bites were reported in New York…. Sixty thousand buildings were identified as rat harborages by the city's health department—buildings constructed before 1902 that had been designed to house a few families and were now housing dozens. In 1964, nine hundred thousand people were reported living in forty-three thousand old tenements.

1. What is the Main Point? Is it expressed in a topic sentence?

2. What is the evidence supporting that main point, and what is the nature of that evidence?

3. What language or paragraph structure did the author use to distinguish the evidence from the claims?

Answers to Exercise 1: Separating Claims from Evidence

Paragraph 1:

1. Topic sentence: "Drug activity was the life force of Coco's new building."

2. The paragraph uses anecdotal evidence to illustrate the Main Point.

3. The paragraph flows from the assertion into the description.

Paragraph 2:

1. Topic sentence: "The fundamental intention of Nietzsche's work must be to recover and make manifest these underlying presuppositions which were the foundations of the coherence of Greek culture."

2. The author quotes from Nietzsche's work to support his position.

3. The author starts by contradicting the "tempting" position, then asserting his own, and supporting that assertion with evidence from Nietzsche's writings.

Paragraph 3:

1. Topic sentence: "English serfs were not slaves…"

2. The author lists the legal rights that the English serfs did have, as evidence that they were not outright slaves.

3. The claim is presented in the topic sentence, and the rest of the paragraph works to support that claim.

Paragraph 4:

1. The Main Point of this passage is that Marcel Duchamp's painting, *Nude Descending a Staircase*, was influenced by Futurism as much as, or more than, by Cubism. There is no single topic sentence in this paragraph.

2. The author uses general evidence about the artistic philosophy of the Cubists and the Futurists to prove his point about this painting. The contrast between how the painting was seen at the time and how it is now viewed reinforces this point.

3. The author's claim needs to be pieced together from the historical and general evidence she provides. The initial contrast between the painting's reception in its time and now introduces the point, however.

Paragraph 5:

1. The Main Point of the passage is that rats were an identifiable city-wide problem for many people in New York in 1959. There is no single topic sentence in this paragraph.

2. The author uses both anecdotal evidence (the baby on Coney Island) and statistical evidence to demonstrate the rat problem. He also contrasts people on Park Avenue with people living in tenements to show that some people did not have to worry about the rat problem, while others were severely affected by it.

3. An initial contrast is suggested ("The discrepancy..."), and then developed by discussion of the complacency of many people as opposed to the rat-related suffering of others. The latter is introduced by a pivotal phrase: "The same week, however..."

Exercise 2: MAPS Exercise

Read the following passage in 3–4 minutes, and then write down the Main point, Attitude, Purpose, and Support. Don't just think about the answers; *write them down* to ensure that you have clearly articulated each component. Explanations follow the exercise.

Race relations and racial attitudes in the United States have changed dramatically over the past quarter of a century. Although many of these changes are well documented, controversies persist about whether, in fact, race has declined in its significance as a determinant of social, economic, and political statuses and outlooks.

An intriguing argument which attempts to reconcile and make sense of the discrepant findings about the status of blacks vis-à-vis whites is the "polarization thesis." William Julius Wilson, for example, argues that the black community is becoming socially, politically, and economically polarized. He points out that a number of blacks are completing college educations and moving into the kinds of prestigious jobs that provide economic security, higher standards of living, and homes in the suburbs. These blacks, he argues, have been able to take advantage of the opportunities which emerged as a result of the civil rights movement. On the other hand, many other blacks are trapped in inner-city ghettos where schools are poor and where opportunities for employment and advancement are limited. As the black community becomes more socioeconomically differentiated, race becomes a less important determinant of the life chances and outlooks of individual blacks than does socioeconomic status. Implicit in this argument is the idea that as race decreases in importance as a stratifying agent, blacks will become more similar to non-blacks with the same socioeconomic position than they will be to other blacks with vastly different socioeconomic statuses.

When it was first published in 1978, Wilson's *Declining Significance of Race* touched off much controversy and debate. Critics of the book marshaled a great deal of evidence and numerous counter-arguments to undermine Wilson's declining significance of race thesis. Charles V. Willie, for example, basing his arguments on data concerning income, education, and housing, put forth the idea that not only was race not declining in its import, but it was actually increasing as a determinant of the quality of life for blacks.

Similarly, Robert Hill argued that conditions for blacks as a group were not improving, and on some fronts things were actually getting worse. For example, he pointed out that recessions continued to affect blacks disproportionately. Unemployment rates for blacks remain twice those of whites. The number of blacks living in poverty continued to rise at the same time that the number of whites living in poverty decreased.

Recent empirical investigations have provided both support for Wilson's declining significance hypothesis and evidence against this position. For example, through the 1960s and 1970s blacks improved their relative standings in education, occupational status, and personal income, but failed to make substantial gains when compared with whites in such areas as family income, unemployment rates, housing patterns, and rates of poverty. To date, however, no study has indicated whether changes in stratification patterns have simultaneously led to a convergence between blacks and non-blacks in their social, political, and economic outlooks and a polarization among blacks.

Material used in this particular passage has been adapted from the following source:
C. Herring, "Convergence, Polarization, or What? Racially Based Changes in Attitudes and Outlooks," *Sociological Quarterly*. © 2005.

Main Point: _____

_____

_____

_____

_____

_____

_____

_____

_____

_____

Attitude: _____

Support: _____

_____

_____

_____

_____

_____

_____

_____

_____

_____

_____

_____

_____

_____

_____

Purpose: _____

_____

_____

_____

_____

_____

_____

_____

_____

_____

Analysis of the Passage

Here is one possible MAPS outline for the preceding passage:

Main Point:	Although blacks have made gains in some areas and suffered losses in others, it is difficult to know whether polarization has occurred, and if it has, what its effect might be.
Attitude:	Interested in Wilson's thesis, but not convinced without empirical evidence
Purpose:	To describe a promising theory, present critics of the theory, and suggest there is no clear resolution to date
Support:	Illustrates a controversy by citing authors on both sides, and describes how they back up their claims. Cites own evidence showing that empirical support exists for both sides.

Exercise 3: Putting It All Together

To break down and explore each of these components in more detail in the context of tracking the structure of the passage, let's visit a sample MCAT Verbal Passage, which is reproduced on the following pages.

Preview the questions and work the passage. For each example provided, ask yourself why the author uses that example. Identify wording that indicates the author's tone. For each paragraph, identify how that paragraph relates to the rest of the passage. Articulate the Bottom Line of the passage.

Then answer the questions, specifically looking for how your understanding of MAPS and passage structure applies. Finally, read through the explanation that follows.

From Romania to Germany, from Tallinn to Belgrade, a major historical process — the death of communism — is taking place. The German Democratic Republic does not exist anymore as a separate state. And the former GDR will serve as the first measure of the price a post-Communist society has to pay for entering the normal European orbit. In Yugoslavia we will see whether the federation can survive without communism, and whether the nations of Yugoslavia will want to exist as a federation. (On a larger scale, we will witness the same process in the Soviet Union.)

One thing seems common to all these countries: dictatorship has been defeated and freedom has won, yet the victory of freedom has not yet meant the triumph of democracy. Democracy is something more than freedom. Democracy is freedom institutionalized, freedom submitted to the limits of the law, freedom functioning as an object of compromise between the major political forces on the scene.

We have freedom, but we still have not achieved the democratic order. That is why this freedom is so fragile. In the years of democratic opposition to communism, we supposed that the easiest thing would be to introduce changes in the economy. In fact, we thought that the march from a planned economy to a market economy would take place within the framework of the *nomenklatura* system, and that the market within the Communist state would explode the totalitarian structures. Only then would the time come to build the institutions of a civil society; and only at the end, with the completion of the market economy and the civil society, would the time of great political transformations finally arrive.

The opposite happened. First came the big political change, the great shock, which either broke the monopoly and the principle itself of Communist Party rule or simply pushed the Communists out of power. Then came the creation of civil society, whose institutions were created in great pain, and which had trouble negotiating the empty space of freedom. And only then, as the third moment of change, the final task was undertaken: that of transforming the totalitarian economy into a normal economy where different forms of ownership and different economic actors will live one next to the other.

Today we are in a typical moment of transition. No one can say where we are headed. The people of the democratic opposition have the feeling that we won. We taste the sweetness of our victory the same way the Communists, only yesterday our prison guards, taste the bitterness of their defeat. And yet, even as we are conscious of our victory, we feel that we are, in a strange way, losing. In Bulgaria the Communists have won the parliamentary elections and will govern the country, without losing their social legitimacy. In Romania the National Salvation Front, largely dominated by people from the old Communist *nomenklatura,* has won. In other countries democratic institutions seem shaky, and the political horizon is cloudy. The masquerade goes on. dozens of groups and parties are created, each announces similar slogans, each accuses its adversaries of all possible sins, and each declares itself representative of the national interest. Personal disputes are more important than disputes over values. Arguments over labels are fiercer than arguments over ideas.

1. Which of the following best expresses the main idea of the passage?

A) Communism will never completely vanish from the Earth.
B) Democracy is the highest good that any Eastern European country can ever hope to achieve.
C) Market economies do not always behave as we might predict.
D) Although many formerly Communist countries are now "free," this does not always mean that they have a democracy.

2. The author originally thought that the order of events in the transformation of society would be represented by which of the following?

A) The totalitarian structure would collapse, leaving in its wake a social structure whose task would be to change the state-controlled economy into a free market.
B) The transformation of the economy would destroy totalitarianism, after which a different social and political structure would be born.
C) The people would freely elect political representatives who would then transform the economy, which would then undermine the totalitarian structure.
D) The change to a democratic state would necessarily undermine totalitarianism, after which a new economy would be created.

3. Which of the following best represents the relationship between freedom and democracy, as it is described by the author?

A) A country can have freedom without having democracy.
B) If a country has freedom, it necessarily has democracy.
C) A country can have democracy without having freedom.
D) A country can never have democracy if it has limited freedom.

4. Which of the following best describes the author's attitude toward what has taken place in communist society?

A) He is relieved that at last the democratic order has surfaced.
B) He sees the value of returning to the old order.
C) He is disappointed with the nature of the democracy that has emerged but nevertheless pleased with the victory of freedom.
D) He is confident that a free economy will ultimately provide the basis for a true democracy.

5. When the author mentions "the same process" (paragraph 1), it can be inferred from the passage that he is most likely referring to:

A) the gradual shift away from authoritarian politics.
B) the potential disintegration of the Soviet Union.
C) the possible breakdown in the general distribution systems in the Soviet Republic.
D) the expected sale of state-owned farms to private enterprise.

6. Which of the following does the author imply has contributed to the difficulties involved in creating a new democratic order in Yugoslavia?

I.   The people who existed under a totalitarian structure did not have the experience of "negotiating the empty space of freedom."
II. Mistaking the order in which political, economic, and social restructuring would occur
III. Changes in the economy were more difficult than anticipated.

A) II only
B) I and III only
C) II and III only
D) I, II, and III

7. It can be inferred from the passage that the democratic opposition feels that it is "in a strange way, losing" (paragraph 5) because:

A) some of the old governments are still unwilling to give in to freedoms at the individual level.
B) the new governments are not strong enough to exist as a single federation.
C) newly elected officials have ties to old political parties.
D) no new parties have been created to fill the vacuum created by the victory of freedom.

Answers to Exercise 3: Putting It All Together

7.3

Answers to questions:

1. D

2. B

3. A

4. C

5. B

6. B

7. C

Support

This passage supports its main thesis by contrasting what *actually* happens with the expectation that formerly communist nations would evolve into democracies, and then cites specific cases in the first and last paragraphs to illustrate the point. Your paragraph-by-paragraph outline might look like this:

1. examples of the death of communism
2. generalization and contrast nature of freedom and democracy
3. expected progression
4. real progression
5. examples of incomplete transition

Knowing where and how the author supports his claims is particularly important in answering questions 2, 5, 6, and 7.

Purpose

In this passage, the purpose is to analyze how and why sociopolitical transformation in the formerly communist nations did not follow the expected path, and to express regret that this has left their evolution into democracies incomplete.

Take a look at questions 2 and 5, and consider the role played by the Purpose of the author in each of the credited responses.

Attitude

The author is clearly present in this passage. Note the repeated use of the word "we"; the author presents as a participant (paragraph 3) as well as an informed expert (paragraph 1), not as a disinterested outsider. Note also the tone and language of the passage. Democracy is something to be "achieved," from which we can infer that it is a desirable thing. The author speaks of the "sweetness of our victory," telling us that freedom in this sense, while limited, is greatly appreciated. Yet at the same time the author feels that "we are, in a strange way, losing." This indicates the author's discontent with the incomplete nature of the transformation.

Now take a look at question 4, which directly asks for the author's attitude. Choices A and D are too positive (and A is wrong for other reasons as well; it is inconsistent with the author's analysis). Choice B is too negative. The author appreciates the changes that have occurred, and wants the transformation to continue. Only choice C reflects the mixture of appreciation and regret that defines the author's attitude in this passage.

Main Point

In this passage, the author argues that many formerly communist nations have overthrown totalitarian regimes and achieved political freedom. However, because the transformation of the economy and civil society of these countries is as yet incomplete, true democracy does not exist. A student without a firm grasp on the driving theme and scope of the argument might incorrectly identify the main point as, "One can have freedom without democracy," which is too broad. A student who gets too caught up in one part of the passage might say the Main Point is that, "In Bulgaria and Romania, members of the old communist order still hold positions of power." A student who gets it just right, however, might say that the Main Point is something like this: "Many countries have overthrown communism and are now free, but they have not yet achieved democracy."

Now take a look in particular at questions 1, 3, and 4. Notice how useful it is to have a clear statement of the Main Point as a tool to eliminate traps and choose the correct answer.

Exercise 4: Practice MAPS

7.3

Use copies of this log to outline the MAPS for at least 8 passages from online or from other resources. While you do not need to actually write down the MAPS of a passage during an MCAT, by practicing this technique, you will improve your ability to characterize and evaluate the passage's central thesis, its logical structure, and the nature and strength of its claims.

MAPS Log

Passage #

MAIN POINT:

ATTITUDE:

PURPOSE:

SUPPORT:

7.4 DEALING WITH STRESS

We've discussed some possible ways of dealing with the stress and anxiety that most people experience when preparing for and taking the MCAT. By now, you should have settled on a method that you can use effectively whenever anxiety or loss of concentration becomes a problem. Remember, stress won't go away, but it can be managed so that all that extra adrenaline coursing through your system can work for you, not against you.

Describe any symptoms of anxiety you may have experienced when taking a practice test or doing homework, and the method or methods you use to help manage it.

Symptoms:

_____

_____

_____

_____

_____

Management Methods:

_____

_____

_____

_____

_____

Along with stress, losing control of your pacing strategy can be a problem, especially toward the end of the test. On your next practice test or timed Verbal Reasoning section, monitor your pacing throughout. If you begin to panic about the time, or rush through questions without feeling reasonably secure in most of your answers, STOP and take three deep breaths. Remind yourself of the strategy and techniques you have spent so much time and effort learning. Don't let yourself lose your form at the finish line. Regain control of yourself and of the test before moving on.

Chapter 7 Summary

- Identify and articulate the MAPS of a passage, and think about how the author uses the wording and structure of the passage to communicate the Bottom Line of the passage as a whole.

- Main Point: *What* is the passage trying to prove?

- Attitude: *Who* wrote the passage? What is their tone?

- Purpose: *Why* was the passage written?

- Support: *How* does the passage make its points?

- Note that the tone can indicate the purpose for writing the passage.

- Don't decide on the main point or Bottom Line too quickly. Remember that important clues to the Main Point are likely to be scattered throughout the passage.

- Find a way to manage stress and maintain concentration, and use it consistently.

CHAPTER 7 PRACTICE PASSAGES

Individual Passage Drills

Complete these two passages, keeping track of the time you spend on each, but without giving yourself a set time limit. As you work each passage, pay special attention to MAPS.

Once you have completed the passages and checked your answers, fill out the Individual Passage Logs. Focus in particular on the relationship between your analysis of the structure of each passage and how well you did on the questions.

CHAPTER 7 PRACTICE PASSAGE 1

The language of efficiency, or cost-effectiveness, is all around us. We hear it everywhere, in our private lives as well as in public conversation. I recently read an advertisement in a local newspaper for a fully wired kitchen that would allow me to program my microwave and stove from the office simply by flicking a button on my hand-held computer. By the time I reach home, dinner will be ready to eat. The alarm system will disengage as I reach the front door. "How efficient!" the ad proclaims in bold lettering.

But the ad misses, not by accident, I suspect, one crucial piece of information. It does not tell me *at what* this newly wired, very expensive kitchen will be efficient. At improving the quality of my food? At saving time? What, I worried, will I be expected to accomplish with the time saved? Is it legitimate to use the twenty minutes I might gain to read a novel I have been longing to read? Or am I expected to engage in "productive" work in the time I save? How will this time-saving kitchen improve my satisfaction? My welfare?

The seduction of efficiency is not restricted to the latest advances in labor-saving devices for the beleaguered working mother. The language of efficiency shapes our public as well as our private lives. Those who provide our public services are expected to do so efficiently. Physicians and nurses in the hospital where my mother was treated are expected to work efficiently. So are teachers, governments, and civil servants. They are constantly enjoined to become efficient, to remain efficient, and to improve their efficiency in the safeguarding of the public trust. Efficiency, or cost-effectiveness, has become an end in itself, a value often more important than others. But elevating efficiency, turning it into an end, misuses language, and this has profound consequences for the way we as citizens conceive of public life. When we define efficiency as an end, divorced from its larger purpose, it becomes nothing less than a cult.

Our public conversation about efficiency is misleading. Efficiency is only one part of a much larger public discussion between citizens and their governments. Efficiency is not an end, but a means to achieve valued ends. It is not a goal, but an instrument to achieve other goals. It is not a value, but a way to achieve other values. It is part of the story but never the whole.

Even when efficiency is used correctly as a means, when it is understood as the most cost-effective way to achieve our goals, much of our public discussion is fuzzy about its purpose. What does effectiveness mean? What, for example, is an effective education? To answer that question, we would first have to discuss the purposes of education, a discussion that is informed by values, and only then could we come to some understanding of the criteria of effectiveness. At times, however, even the

mention of effectiveness is absent, and the conversation slides over to focus only on costs. And when the public discussion of efficiency focuses only on costs, the cult becomes even stronger.

Yet the word "efficiency" is not only misused in public conversation as an end rather than a means. Our public conversation is not merely bedeviled by a simple technical error. The cult of efficiency, like other cults, advances political purposes and agendas. In our post-industrial age, efficiency is often a code word for an attack on the sclerotic, unresponsive, and anachronistic state, the detritus of the industrial age that fits poorly with our times. The state is branded as wasteful, and market mechanisms are heralded as the efficient alternative. This argument, we shall see, is based on a fundamental misunderstanding of the importance of the "smart" state in the global, knowledge-based economy.

Material used in this particular passage has been adapted from the following source:

J. G. Stein, *The Cult of Efficiency*. © 2002 by Anansi.

1. The author draws an important distinction between:

A) goals and the ways those goals are accomplished.
B) efficient and inefficient technology.
C) representative and misleading advertising.
D) public and private dialogues about efficiency.

2. The author suggests which of the following to be true of cults?

A) They can influence society at large.
B) They promote illogical and unreasonable beliefs.
C) They are simply groups of like-minded individuals.
D) They are usually organized around a focus on costs.

3. The author most likely supports a view of government as an institution that:

A) finds the most cost-effective ways to provide for society's needs.
B) is wasteful and fits poorly with our times.
C) has an important role to play in the modern economy.
D) is not as efficient as market mechanisms.

4. Suppose a public school board were to demand teachers use fewer hours to prepare instruction so that the school board can save money. In response, the author would most likely:

A) praise the board for striving to find more efficient ways to deliver services.
B) support the board's commitment to quality education.
C) withhold judgment and suggest the decision be considered within a larger context.
D) criticize the school board for undermining public education.

5. Which of the following assertions about language is LEAST supported by the passage?

A) Language has the power to shape how citizens think about their relationships with each other and government.
B) Language can be misused to advance political agendas.
C) Vague language sometimes leaves out important information.
D) Government uses language to mislead us in the public conversation about efficiency.

6. Elsewhere, the author writes in more detail about public hospitals in Canada. Based on the information in the passage, these hospitals are most likely:

A) offering a lower standard of care than private hospitals do.
B) unable to afford efficient, time-saving technology.
C) under pressure to provide better care without increased resources.
D) overly focused on costs rather than patient care.

7. Throughout the passage, the author suggests which of the following to be true of efficiency?

A) It is a deceptively attractive idea.
B) It is the foundation of a well-run state.
C) It is just as important to public life as to private life.
D) It is never a worthy goal.

CHAPTER 7 PRACTICE PASSAGE 2

A college class on the American novel is reading Alice Walker's *The Color Purple* (1982). A student raises her hand and recalls that the Steven Spielberg film version (1985) drew angry responses from many African American viewers. The discussion takes off: Did Alice Walker "betray" African Americans with her harsh depiction of black men? Did Spielberg enhance this feature of the book or play it down? Another hand goes up: "But she *was* promoting lesbianism." "Spielberg *really* played that down!" the professor replies. A contentious voice in the back of the room: "Well I just want to know what a serious film was doing with Oprah Winfrey in it." This is answered by another student, "Dude, she does have a *book* club on her show!" Class members respond to these points, examining interrelationships among race, gender, popular culture, the media, and literature. This class is practicing cultural studies.

Cultural studies approaches generally share four goals. First, cultural studies transcends the confines of a particular discipline such as literary criticism or history. Cultural studies involves scrutinizing the cultural phenomenon of a text — for example, Italian opera, a Latino telenovela, the architectural styles of prisons, body piercing — and drawing conclusions about the changes in textual phenomena over time. Cultural studies is not necessarily about literature in the traditional sense or even about art. Henry Giroux and others write in their *Dalhousie Review* manifesto that cultural studies practitioners are "resisting intellectuals" who see what they do as "an emancipatory project" because it erodes the traditional disciplinary divisions in most institutions of higher education. For students, this sometimes means that a professor might make his or her own political views part of the instruction, which, of course, can lead to problems. But this kind of criticism, like feminism, is an engaged rather than a detached activity.

Second, cultural studies is politically engaged. Cultural critics see themselves as "oppositional," not only within their own disciplines but to many of the power structures of society at large. They question inequalities within power structures and seek to discover models for restructuring relationships among dominant and "minority" or "subaltern" discourses. Because meaning and individual subjectivity are culturally constructed they can thus be reconstructed. Such a notion, taken to a philosophical extreme, denies the autonomy of the individual, whether an actual person or a character in literature, a rebuttal of the traditional humanistic "Great Man" or "Great Book" theory, and a relocation of aesthetics and culture from the ideal realms of taste and sensibility, into the arena of a whole society's everyday life as it is constructed.

Third, cultural studies denies the separation of "high" and "low" or elite and popular culture. You might hear someone remark at the symphony or at an art museum: "I came here to get a little culture." Being a "cultured" person used to mean being acquainted with "highbrow" art and intellectual pursuits. But isn't *culture* also to be found with a pair of tickets to a rock concert? Cultural critics today work to transfer the term *culture* to include *mass culture*, whether popular, folk, or urban. Transgressing of boundaries among disciplines high and low can make cultural studies just plain fun. Think, for example, of a possible cultural studies research paper with the following title: "The Birth of Captain Jack Sparrow: An Analysis." For sources of Johnny Depp's funky performance in Disney's *Pirates of the Caribbean* movies, you could research cultural topics ranging from the trade economies of the sea two hundred years ago, to real pirates of the Caribbean such as Blackbeard and Henry Morgan, then on to memorable screen pirates, John Cleese's rendition of Long John Silver on *Monty Python's Flying Circus*, and, of course, Keith Richards's eye makeup.

Finally, cultural studies analyzes not only the cultural work, but the means of production. Marxist critics have long recognized the importance of such paraliterary questions as, Who supports a given artist? Who publishes his or her books, and how are these books distributed? Who buys books? For that matter, who is literate and who is not? These studies help us recognize that literature does not occur in a space separate from other concerns of our lives. Cultural studies thus joins *subjectivity* — that is, culture in relation to individual lives — with *engagement*, a direct approach to attacking social ills. Though cultural studies practitioners deny "humanism" of "the humanities" as universal categories, they strive for what they might call "social reason," which often (closely) resembles the goals and values of humanistic and democratic ideals.

Material used in this particular passage has been adapted from the following source:

W. Guerin et al, *A Handbook of Critical Approaches to Literature.* © 2005 by Oxford University Press.

1. Which of the following would be LEAST consistent with the author's description of cultural studies?

A) An analysis of Missourian Mark Twain's "A Connecticut Yankee in King Arthur's Court" that examined questions regarding the oppressive inequality embodied in monarchical social etiquette and regional class structures.

B) A discussion of female image and intelligence as presented by reality TV dating shows such as VH1's "Rock of Love" with rock star Bret Michaels.

C) An exploration of whether Steven Spielberg's absent father characters in "E.T.", "Catch Me If You Can", and the "Indiana Jones and the Last Crusade" are a response to his own father being absent in his childhood.

D) An examination of the influence of gospel hymns on the speechwriting of civil rights leaders such as Rev. Dr. Martin Luther King, Jr. and Medgar Evers.

2. If a hard-line cultural studies practitioner were to conclude, after researching the text, that white supremacist Asa Earl Carter's novel *The Education of Little Tree* about the traditional upbringing of a Native American boy was written free of his opinions about non-Caucasian peoples, it would most *undermine* the author's assertion that:

A) cultural studies is not exclusively about literature or even art.

B) the oppositional nature of cultural studies, carried to an extreme, denies the sovereignty of individual will.

C) analyzing the means of production is one of the important goals of cultural studies.

D) cultural studies is politically engaged.

3. When the author quotes Henry Giroux's description of cultural studies practitioners as "resisting intellectuals" (paragraph 2), he most nearly means that:

A) professors approaching literature this way reject an overly academic approach.

B) the cultural studies movement began as an underground movement.

C) professors reveal their own opinions in class in order to provoke disagreement and discussion from students.

D) such academics take a multifarious approach to analyzing phenomena in a text.

4. The author's reference to a rock concert serves to indicate that:

A) rock music combines both highbrow and lowbrow culture.

B) music can serve political purposes.

C) culture includes musical expression.

D) popular artistic forms have not always been considered to be highly sophisticated.

5. Elsewhere the author writes, "Images of India circulated during the colonial rule of the British raj by writers like Rudyard Kipling seem innocent, but reveal an entrenched argument for white superiority and worldwide domination of other races." This, if taken as an example of cultural studies, illustrates the author's belief that such studies:

A) deny the separation between lowbrow culture like Kipling's innocent stories and highbrow culture like discussions of political power.

B) examine questions of power and influence, such as the structure of colonial society in India, and raise questions about who was circulating Kipling's writing.

C) include mass culture such as Kipling's stories "The Jungle Book" and "Rikki-Tikki-Tavi."

D) transcend historical analysis.

6. In the context of the passage as a whole, "emancipatory" (paragraph 2) most nearly means:

A) excusing from an obligation.

B) freeing from service.

C) endorsing a wider perspective.

D) promoting equality

7. Suppose a critic were to propose a comparative analysis between Shakespeare's 16th-century play *Romeo and Juliet* and Tennessee Williams's 20th-century play *A Streetcar Named Desire*, focusing entirely on how the number of acts in each play affects the development of the main female character. Which of the following statements best represents how the author of the passage would most likely view this study and/or its author?

A) This critic is not a cultural studies practitioner because she limits her investigations to questions internal to the plays.

B) The critic is resisting historical disciplines by cutting across several centuries in her analysis.

C) The critic should include an analysis of Shakespeare's and Williams's lives and the impact of personal events on their writing.

D) Questions of who supported Shakespeare and Williams financially are irrelevant.

SOLUTIONS TO CHAPTER 7 PRACTICE PASSAGE 1

1. **A** This is an Inference question.

   A: **Yes. See paragraph 4: "Efficiency is not an end, but a means to achieve valued ends." This answer choice uses different words to refer to "ends" and "means," and this distinction is central to the author's main idea about efficiency.**

   B: No. While the example of the automated kitchen in paragraph 1 does introduce the idea of efficient technology, the author does not explicitly describe a distinction between different types of technology.

   C: No. The author does suggest in paragraph 2 that the advertisement referred to in paragraph 1 is intentionally vague—"But the ad misses, not by accident, I suspect, one crucial piece of information..."—but no distinction is drawn between different types of advertising.

   D: No. See paragraph 3: "The language of efficiency shapes our public as well as our private lives." This suggests our public and private views of efficiency are similar, rather than distinct.

2. **A** This is an Inference question.

   A: **Yes. In paragraph 6, the author says, "The cult of efficiency, like other cults, advances political purposes and agendas." Advancing a political purpose entails making an impact on the political conversation. Cults, as the author defines them, therefore can influence society.**

   B: No. Be sure to choose answers that are supported by the passage text. This choice is a common-sense view of cults that is not expressed in the passage. The author does not go so far as to call the cult of efficiency "illogical."

   C: No. The author uses the word "cult" in the context of describing how the "cult of efficiency" "misuses language" in a way that "has profound consequences for the way that we as citizens conceive of public life" (paragraph 3). She also writes that the "cult of efficiency, like other cults, advances political purposes and agendas" (paragraph 6). To label cults as *simply* groups of people who agree with each other would be inconsistent with the author's tone.

   D: No. This choice uses language that is too absolute. The "cult of efficiency" may be based on a discussion of costs, but the passage does not apply this idea to other cults.

3. **C** This is an Inference question.

   A: No. The author discusses the value of government in paragraph 6, but does not say that its value lies in cost-effectiveness.

   B: No. This is the view of "the cult of efficiency" as described in paragraph 6, which the author says "is based on a fundamental misunderstanding of the importance of the "smart" state in the global, knowledge-based economy."

   C: **Yes. See paragraph 6: "The state is branded as wasteful, and market mechanisms are heralded as the efficient alternative. This argument, we shall see, is based on a fundamental misunderstanding of the importance of the "smart" state in the global, knowledge-based economy." The author believes the state is still relevant.**

   D: No. The author defends the value of the state in paragraph 6. While the passage doesn't indicate that the government is as efficient as the market (the author rejects efficiency as a valid stand-alone standard of judgment), neither does the author indicate that it is less efficient.

4. **C**   This is a New Information question.

   A: No. See paragraph 4: "Efficiency...is not a goal, but an instrument to achieve other goals." The author would not necessarily see cutting costs as an important goal in its own right for the school board.

   B: No. In the passage, the author argues that efficiency in and of itself does not equate with quality: "Efficiency is not an end, but a means to achieve valued ends" (paragraph 4). In paragraph 5, the author writes: "What, for example, is an effective education? To answer that question, we would first have to discuss the purposes of education, a discussion that is informed by values, and only then could we come to some understanding of the criteria of effectiveness." Therefore, the author would not automatically equate saving money with quality education (more likely, the opposite).

   C: **Yes. Consider paragraph 5: "Even when efficiency is used correctly as a means, when it is understood as the most cost-effective way to achieve our goals, much of our public discussion is fuzzy about its purpose. What does effectiveness mean? What, for example, is an effective education?" So, any discussion of the merits of cutting costs depends on a larger discussion of the *goals* of cutting costs. Thus, this is the author's most likely response.**

   D: No. The author's main idea is that efficiency should be used as a means rather than an end, but this answer takes that idea too far by implying the author is opposed to the idea of efficiency (in education) altogether.

5. **D**   This is an Inference/Except question.

   A: No. This assertion is supported in paragraph 3: "The language of efficiency shapes our public as well as our private lives." In paragraph 6, the author specifically discusses how the language of efficiency relates to and affects our view of the state.

   B: No. This assertion is supported in paragraph 6: "Yet the word "efficiency" is not only misused in public conversation as an end rather than a means...The cult of efficiency, like other cults, advances political purposes and agendas." Since the former statement is the author's opinion and the latter the explanation of that opinion, it is reasonable to infer that the cult of efficiency misuses the term.

   C: No. In paragraphs 1 and 2, the author states that the phrase "How efficient!" intentionally obscures "one crucial piece of information. It does not tell me *at what* this newly wired, very expensive kitchen will be efficient."

   D: **Yes. The passage does not suggest the government itself uses language to mislead. Thus, this is the correct choice.**

6. **C**   This is a New Information question.

   A: No. The author does not compare public and private hospitals.

   B: No. Technology is the subject of paragraphs 1 and 2, not paragraph 3 in which the author discusses the state of hospitals and other publicly funded institutions. There is no evidence in the passage that public hospitals are unable to afford any particular type of technology, only that they are under pressure to be cost-effective.

   C: **Yes. See paragraph 3: "Those who provide our public services are expected to do so efficiently. Physicians and nurses in the hospital where my mother was treated are expected to work efficiently...They are constantly enjoined to become efficient, to remain efficient, and to improve their efficiency in the safeguarding of the public trust." This answer choice paraphrases the idea that hospitals and their employees are under pressure to be more efficient. We are not told what country the author is writing about in the passage; however, this choice represents a reasonable (compared to the other choices) analogy to draw, even if the author is not discussing Canada in the passage text.**

D: No. The author describes the demands placed on public services from the outside. The hospital's own focus is outside the scope of the argument. This choice is also too extreme; the existence of pressure to reduce costs does not necessarily guarantee that costs have taken precedence over patient care within the hospital itself.

7. **A** This is an Inference question.

A: **Yes. In paragraph 1, the example of the ad illustrates that efficiency is attractive. In paragraph 2, the author then explains this promise lacks substance. In paragraph 3, she refers to this advertisement process as a "seduction," a process based on attraction.**

B: No. On one hand, the author does say efficiency is important. In paragraph 4, she says it can be "used correctly as a means...to achieve our goals". However, the author also states in the same paragraph that "Efficiency is only one part of a much larger public discussion between citizens and their governments." That is, it would be one means (perhaps among many) to a goal of a well-run state, whatever "well-run" might mean in context.

C: No. The passage makes no comparison between the importance of efficiency itself in public and private life (only that the *language* of efficiency is used in both).

D: No. This is too extreme; it is inconsistent with the author's argument that efficiency can be an important means to an end (paragraph 4).

SOLUTIONS TO CHAPTER 7 PRACTICE PASSAGE 2

1. **C** This is an Inference/Least question.

A: No. This is consistent with the author's description of cultural studies in paragraph 2, where the author states that cultural studies transcends traditional boundaries between academic disciplines. It is also consistent with the author's discussion in paragraph 3: "Cultural critics see themselves as 'oppositional,'... to many of the power structures on society at large. They question inequalities within power structures..."

B: No. This examination of gender depictions is consistent with the discussion of gender depictions in paragraph 1's example of cultural studies.

C: **Yes. This analysis is not consistent with any description of cultural studies laid out in the passage because it limits its scope to the artist's own life rather than the culture within which he created his movie.**

D: No. This is consistent with paragraph 2's assertion that "Cultural studies involves scrutinizing the cultural phenomenon of a text—for example, Italian opera," as well as with paragraph 4's examples of the types of cultural phenomena, including "mass culture," examined by cultural studies practitioners.

2. **B** This is a New Information question.

A: No. The analysis of Carter's book would be consistent with the idea that history and traditional customs are also a part of cultural studies.

B: **Yes. Someone who is extremely committed to a cultural studies approach, according to the author, would be unlikely to assert that an artist could create a text in which he effectively and consciously omitted all trace or influence of his cultural context. According to the passage, an individual author would not be seen by this type of cultural critic as having this kind of autonomy (paragraph 3).**

C: No. There is no indication, either way, whether the critic examined questions of the means of production. Thus, the new information neither strengthens nor weakens this claim of the author.

D: No. There is no reason, based on the passage, to believe that political engagement in this case would require a hard-line cultural critic to identify racist themes within the novel itself.

3. **D** This is an Inference question.

A: No. While these practitioners are resisting traditional divisions in academia between disciplines (e.g., between literary criticism and history), being "academic" is not identified in the passage with respecting these divisions. Therefore, there is no evidence to support the idea that what they are rejecting is an "overly academic" approach.

B: No. There is no evidence that cultural studies began as a secretive movement. This is taking the word "resisting" out of the context of the passage.

C: No. This choice is wrong first because there is no evidence that professors introduce their own viewpoints *in order to* provoke disagreement, only that introduction of the professor's own political views may be part of instruction. Second, introduction of the professor's own views is given as perhaps one aspect of the "emancipatory project," but not as part of a definition of what the term "resisting intellectuals" itself means.

D: **Yes. The author states that these intellectuals "see what they do as 'an emancipatory project' because it erodes the traditional disciplinary divisions" by "scrutinizing the cultural phenomenon of a text" (paragraph 2). This means that rather than studying only the text itself (or other aspects traditionally seen as "literary" issues related to it) cultural critics bring in other issues relating to the culture within which the text appears. This aligns with what the author said earlier in the paragraph, that "cultural studies transcends the confines of a particular discipline." Therefore, these academics take a multifarious or diverse approach to a text.**

4. **D** This is an Inference question.

A: No. There is no indication rock music is *both* highbrow and lowbrow—on the contrary, the passage indicates that rock music has traditionally been considered lowbrow instead of highbrow.

B: No. Politics is not an issue in this paragraph. In addition, to the extent that the author discusses political motivations elsewhere in the passage, the issue is the political engagement of cultural critics, not of culture itself.

C: No. The point of the reference is not to show that culture includes music; an earlier reference to the symphony suggests that at least some forms of music are already seen as cultural expression. Furthermore, the point being made is that cultural critics deny the distinction between high (the symphony) and low (the rock concert) culture.

D: **Yes. In paragraph 4, the author writes that "cultural studies denies the separation of 'high' and 'low' or elite and popular culture...Being a 'cultured' person used to mean being acquainted with 'highbrow' art and intellectual pursuits. But isn't *culture* also to be found at a rock concert?" The change cultural studies has created from what culture "used to mean" has been to include forms (such as the rock concert) that were once considered not to be elite, intellectual, highbrow, or highly sophisticated.**

5. **B**   This is a New Information question.

   A: No. Nothing indicates that Kipling's stories are or would have been considered lowbrow.

   B: Yes. This is consistent with the author's description of the second major goal of cultural studies ("They question inequalities within power structures"), as detailed in paragraph 3; it is also consistent with the author's description of the fourth major goal of cultural studies ("Marxist critics have long recognized the importance of such paraliterary questions as, Who supports a given artist? Who publishes his or her books, and how are these books distributed?") as described in paragraph 5. (Note: Marxist critics are referred to as part of the description of cultural critics.)

   C: No. Nothing indicates that Kipling's stories constitute mass culture. Note that A and C are saying basically the same thing, and thus have the same problem—so you can cross them both out.

   D: No. This perspective is rooted in history, so it doesn't illustrate how cultural studies transcends, or goes beyond, history.

6. **C**   This is a Vocabulary in Context question.

   A: No. There is no indication of obligation in the passage. This choice takes the meaning of the word out of context.

   B: No. There is no indication of service in the passage. As in choice A, this answer represents a common definition of emancipation, but one that does not fit in the context of the passage.

   C: Yes. Paragraph 2 says cultural studies practitioners see their field "as 'an emancipatory project' because it erodes the traditional disciplinary divisions." Eroding divisions would produce a "wider perspective;" that is, one not limited by the practices or assumptions of a particular academic field.

   D: No. While the author indicates in paragraph 3 that cultural critics "question inequalities," this is not the context in which the word "emancipatory" appears in paragraph 2. This choice then has two problems: it uses a common definition of the word that does not fit in the context of the relevant part of the passage, and it refers to an issue that arises elsewhere in the passage but not in this paragraph.

7. **A**   This is a New Information question.

   A: Yes. Because the question the critic asks is limited to the form of the plays and the development of characters within that structure, and because it does not address culture or any of the goals of cultural studies as they are outlined in the passage, the author is most likely to argue that the critic is not practicing cultural studies.

   B: No. If anything, comparing texts from two different periods in history would be embracing a historical approach, not resisting it.

   C: No. Examining the text in terms of the events of the author's life is not one of the goals of cultural studies.

   D: No. We have no evidence the author disagrees with the fourth goal of cultural studies, as he described it in paragraph 5, which asserts the relevance of questions of finance and production.

Individual Passage Log

Passage # _____   Time spent on passage _____

Q#	Q type	Attractors	What did you do wrong?

Revised Strategy _____

Passage # _____   Time spent on passage _____

Q#	Q type	Attractors	What did you do wrong?

Revised Strategy _____

Chapter 8
Strategy and Tactics

GOALS

1. To make the most of your time
2. To find ways to improve through self-evaluation
3. To refine your pacing strategy

8.1   MAXIMIZING YOUR PERFORMANCE

Now is the time to ask yourself a serious question: are you diligently and consistently implementing and refining a strategic approach to the test? Or, are you just doing passage after passage and taking test after test in the belief that simple repetition will continue to improve your score? If it's the latter, you must ask yourself WHY you are making the mistakes that you are and HOW you can change to improve your performance.

The Big Picture

Imagine two students. The first (say, the one who isn't using these materials) approaches the Verbal Reasoning section as she would any test in college. The second, a student using this book, uses the strategies she has learned. How will these students use their time on the test?

First Student, with No Specialized Test Strategy

- **On Easier Passages:** Overconfident and complacent, this student rushes through the easier passages, relying on her memory and failing to check her answer choices back to the passage text. She chooses the first answer that sounds good, and is perfectly happy with her choices, not realizing that she has fallen into all of the test writers' traps.

- **On Harder Passages:** This student, doing the passages in the order given by the test writers, hits a difficult passage in the middle of the section. Frustrated and confused, she slows down, reading everything three times, trying to understand exactly what the author is saying. She spends five minutes on a question, believing that she can't move on until she is sure of the correct answer. She becomes more and more anxious about the time, which makes it even harder to focus on the passage. This student tries to use sheer effort where strategy would be more effective.

Second Student, with MCAT-Appropriate Strategies

- **On Easier Passages:** Knowing that the majority of her correct answers will come from the easier passages, this student works through them with steadiness and focus. She clearly articulates the Bottom Line of the passage before answering the questions. She answers the questions in her own words before attacking the answer choices, and checks each choice back to the passage.

- **On Harder Passages:** This student knows that not all passages will be completely comprehensible, and has an appropriate strategy for the harder passages. She uses POE to the fullest, remembering that she is looking for the "least wrong" choice, not an ideal answer. She asks questions of the answer choices (such as, *Is the language too extreme to be an inference? Is this choice too narrow for a Main Idea question?*) based on her knowledge of question types and common Attractors. This student gains points based on her intelligent, test-appropriate strategy.

Narrowing It Down

Let's revisit our first student. When asked why she misses questions, she responds, "I don't know. I always get it down to two choices, and then I pick the wrong one."

The second student, having done an extensive evaluation of her own performance to date, might respond, "On Inference questions, I tend to forget to look for absolute language, and I pick choices that are too extreme. Sometimes I get too impatient to define the Bottom Line, and then I pick Main Point answer choices that are too narrow. I also sometimes have too much confidence in my own memory, don't go back to the passage, and then miss easy Retrieval questions by choosing answer choices from the wrong part of the passage." The second, self-aware student knows exactly what she needs to work on over the next few weeks, and has a clear path to continued improvement. The first student will most likely continue to make the same mistakes over and over again. Remember, those who don't know and understand their own history are doomed to repeat it.

If you are identifying a bit too much with our first student, now is the time to ask yourself the following questions:

1. **Are you having trouble articulating the Bottom Line?**
   Is it difficult to locate the relevant parts of the passage when you are working the questions?
   The Diagnosis
   Both of these issues go back to articulating the main point of each paragraph or chunk, and synthesizing those themes as you read. If you don't identify the author's main points as you read, separating out the claims from the evidence, it is almost impossible to distill it down at the end to a core argument. And, if you aren't identifying the location of these different themes, the passage runs together in your mind as an undifferentiated block of information, and you will have trouble remembering and locating where different topics appeared.

   The Cure
   Review Chapter 3 on Active Reading.
   Break the argument into chunks and define the Main Points as you read; don't wait to think about it until after you have finished reading the passage. If you haven't been using your

scratch paper much (or at all), make yourself write down the Main Points as you go. Articulate how each new chunk logically relates to what you have already read. Preview the questions for content, so that you have some context within which to translate what you are reading, and you are alerted to some of the important issues in the passage.

2. **Do you tend to miss certain question types?**

   The Diagnosis

   Use your passage and practice test logs to identify which types give you the most trouble. Is it an overall category (e.g., Specific questions)? Is it a few particular question types or formats?

   The Cure

   Review Chapter 4 on Question Types.

   Identifying these patterns is the first step towards figuring out the exact causes of your mistakes. Here are some common problem areas and solutions.

   - Main Point/Primary Purpose: Pay attention to tone, and break down the passage by defining its logical structure. Avoid choices that are too narrow.
   - Specific questions: Keep track of the specific reference in the question stem, and go back to the passage *before* you take the first cut through the answer choices.
   - Structure/Evaluate: Pay attention to words in the passage that distinguish claims (*therefore, thus, in conclusion*) from evidence (*for example, in illustration, in these three cases*).
   - New Information: Treat the new information in the question stem like a paragraph of the passage: what is the main point of this chunk, and how does it relate to the logic of the author's argument? Use your scratch paper to translate complicated questions.
   - Strengthen/Weaken: Clearly define what the correct answer needs to do: what is the relevant issue, and must the correct answer be consistent or inconsistent with the passage? With what part of the passage? Keep close track of direction.
   - Except/Least/Not: Define not only what the right answer needs to do but what kind of choices you will be eliminating. Use your scratch paper to keep track of POE.

3. **Do you tend to fall for certain types of Attractors?**

   The Diagnosis

   Use your logs and look for patterns!

   The Cure

   Review Chapter 5 on POE.

   Each time you do a new passage or test section, pick out ahead of time two types of Attractors you will be on the lookout for. Define a specific tactic for recognizing and avoiding these traps. For example:

   - Extreme wording: Look out for words like *only, most, all, must, never*, etc. Also, evaluate the strength of the statements in each choice; an answer choice can be too extreme even if it doesn't use these particular words.
   - Partially correct: Force yourself to read the entire choice word for word. Actively look for that one word that can make it incorrect. Suspend all judgment on the validity of the choice until you have read every word.
   - Right answer/wrong question: Always go back to the passage, with the specific reference in the question clearly in mind. Reread the question before you take your second cut through the choices.

4. **Are you going too slow or too fast?** Problems with pacing can underlie all of the above issues. So, lets move on to discuss it in more detail.

8.2   FOCUS ON PACING

By this point, you should begin timing yourself on your practice passages. If your reasonable goal is to complete six passages with high accuracy and randomly guess on one passage, as a rule of thumb it should take you 3 minutes plus a minute per question ("Q + 3 minutes") per passage. This is an approximation of the total time for the passage, not a suggestion that you spend one and only one minute to answer each question. What does that mean in practice? A five-question passage should take you approximately 8 minutes to complete. For a seven-question passage, you should take approximately 10 minutes.

Diagnosing the Problem

Let's look in more detail at three basic pacing issues.

1. **Going too fast**
   There are three signs that your score will improve if you slow down and do fewer questions:
   - If you are finishing six or seven passages but consistently missing two or more questions on every passage, or if you often miss more than half of the questions for a passage (that is, you do well on some passages but crash and burn on others).
   - If you realize that you often miss easy questions. This means that when you go over a test, many or most of the questions that you got wrong look obvious in retrospect. You can't imagine why you didn't pick the credited response, and you can't really remember why you liked that wrong answer so much.
   - If you are completing all seven passages and not scoring at least a 12.

2. **Going too slow**
   If one or more of the following describes you, increasing your speed and efficiency will improve your score:
   - You consistently get all or most of the questions that you do correct, but you are doing five or fewer passages.
   - You spend a disproportionately high amount of time on a few passages or a few questions.
   - You spend 6 or more minutes reading the passage text the first time through.

3. **Getting bogged down in a KILLER passage**
   Let's return to our two students and compare their different approaches to the KILLER passage:
   - **What the first student, untrained in strategy, does with the KILLER passage:**
     She slows down, gets lost and distracted while reading, and spends too much time going back and rereading long sections of the passage. She gets caught up in deciphering fancy vocabulary words.
     When she moves into the questions, she goes even slower; she has spent so much time reading the passage that she feels that she has to get all of the questions right to justify it. At some point, the student realizes anxiously that too much time has passed and she guesses on the last two or three questions of the passage before moving on, stressed out and perspiring. She then speeds through the other easier passages, trying to make up for lost time, making foolish errors and throwing away easy points.

- **What the second, trained student does with the KILLER passage:**
  Skips it.
  By randomly filling in all of the answer choices on the KILLER Passage, the second student frees up at least 10–15 minutes that would have been wasted on getting questions wrong.

8.3 REFINING YOUR PACING

Once you have decided if you need to slow down or speed up, the next question is HOW?

Slowing Down

This is not as obvious as it seems. Don't spend the time that you save by doing fewer questions or passages on excessive rereading. Also, don't sit and ponder difficult parts of the passage at great length, or come up with elaborate justifications for why a variety of answer choices might be correct. It is still important to be tightly focused and efficient, even when slowing down your pace.

Instead, invest the extra time in the following:

- translating the question and clearly identifying the question type and task,
- reading the answer choices more carefully; that is, word for word,
- comparing choices to each other and specifically looking out for common traps,
- and—most importantly—in going back to the passage to find the relevant information and defining what the correct answer needs to do.

Speeding Up

There are four common ways in which students get bogged down and lose time.

1. **Reading the passage too carefully the first time through**
   If you are reading every word, and highlighting the passage heavily, then you're reading the passage like a college course book rather than a Verbal Reasoning passage. You may feel safer going into the questions having spent 6 or more minutes with the passage, but the test doesn't allow you the time to do so. Cut to the chase the first time through, and save the more careful rereading for answering the questions. (Review Chapters 3 and 7.)
2. **Not reading and translating the question carefully**
   If you go into the passage without a clear idea of what you're looking for, you are likely to get lost and waste precious time backtracking to reread the question, or getting stuck in the answer choices because nothing fits what you first thought the question was asking. Spend a few more seconds translating the question, and the correct answers will come a lot more quickly. (Review Chapter 4.)

3. **Not aggressively using POE**

   You can waste a huge amount of time looking for a perfect answer instead of the "least wrong" answer. Trying to make a watertight case for the credited response when it is one of those "not great, but the best of what I've got" answers will not only suck up a lot of time and energy, it will also often cause you to talk yourself out of the correct choice. Maintain a critical focus through the entire POE process. (Review Chapter 5.)

4. **Overcommitting to one question or one passage**

   - Learn to recognize quickly whether you understand a test question or not. Are you rereading it over and over? Are you bouncing repeatedly (three or more times) from passage to question and back again? If so, these are clear signs that this question is not working for you (that is, it's very difficult). Use POE, take your best shot, and move on.

   - However, don't go to the opposite extreme. If you are getting it down to two and then guessing on a majority of questions, your accuracy will significantly suffer and your score will go down, not up.

   - Don't spend a high percentage of your resources on a single passage. More difficult passages should take a bit more time, but you need to keep moving. Remember that in many cases hard passages have been edited such that some things are never fully explained or clarified; you could read it ten times over and still not really "get it." Luckily, in most cases you don't need to understand every aspect of the passage to get most of the questions right.

Try Pacing Exercise 1 at the end of this chapter if your accuracy is good but you need to increase your speed.

Avoiding KILLER Passages

Use your previous experience to refine your ranking technique. Each time you rank a passage as NOW and it turns out to be a LATER or KILLER, go back and re-evaluate the passage and the questions to see what made it harder than you expected, and how you could have recognized it earlier.

Conversely, every time you misidentify an easy passage as a difficult passage, do the same. Look in particular for passages with unfamiliar subject matter that you ranked as LATER or KILLER that were relatively easy once you got into them.

It is dangerous to rank passages on the basis of familiarity; it is really the difficulty of the language and of the question types that makes for a hard passage.

Review Chapter 6 if you are having trouble ranking passages accurately.

8.4

8.4   VERBAL REASONING EXERCISES: PACING AND SELF-EVALUATION

Exercise 1: Speeding Up

Do this exercise if you have excellent accuracy on the passages that you actually complete, but can only complete a limited number of passages under timed conditions. You may wish to spread this exercise out over a few days or weeks.

Do a seven-passage section (or look at your most recent practice test), and note the average time spent per passage here:_____

Now do four more passages back to back (or, an entire seven-passage test section), but give yourself one less minute per passage. Use the suggestions in this chapter to diagnose areas where you may be wasting time, and to work through those areas more efficiently. If you complete those passages with good accuracy, reduce your time per passage by another 30–60 seconds and do another set of passages.

Continue this process until your accuracy begins to suffer. Note the average time spent per passage here:

Carefully diagnose the reasons for your mistakes, and continue to work at that pace until your accuracy improves to your previous level.

Continue this exercise until you hit the appropriate pace for you.

Exercise 2: 5-Minute Drill

If you have about 5 minutes left when you've finished a passage, do not begin to carefully read the next LATER passage in your ranking. If you do, you will run out of time with few or no questions answered. Instead, quickly read the first and last line of each paragraph. If it's a two-sentence paragraph, just read the first line. Next, pick out the easier Specific questions (such as Retrieval, Vocabulary-in-Context, and Inference questions with lead words and/or paragraph references) and do those first, going back to the passage to hunt down and read the relevant sections. You have a good chance of getting those easier questions right, even with little time remaining.

If you have time left after doing these Specific questions, take a shot at any Main Idea or Primary Purpose questions, using what you have now learned about the major themes of the passage. Be sure to rely heavily on POE, thinking actively about identifying and avoiding common Attractors. Even if you only have a minute left, you can probably at least eliminate one or two answer choices on one General question, or even a Complex question.

So, imagine that the 5-minute warning has come up on the screen, just as you have completed a passage. Your goal now is to get what you can out of the seven questions for the passage on the next pages in the few minutes you have left.

Formal and informal reactions to crime are distinguished by whether they are administered by representatives of the state. Government officials administer formal reactions, such as penal sanctions. Informal reactions are sanctions imposed by non-state functionaries, usually ordinary citizens. These sanctions include all the detrimental consequences that convicted offenders experience that are not formally specified by law or pronounced by a judge in the disposition. To lose one's job or be ridiculed by others are examples of informal sanctions. Since equality before the law is such a symbolically important part of the criminal justice system, many investigators have examined the legal and extralegal determinants of formal sanctions. For example, the effects of offense and offender characteristics on variations in criminal sentences have been investigated extensively. By contrast, informal reactions to crime have received minimal analytic attention. This failure to explore the determinants of informal sanctions distorts understanding of the links between social structure and social control.

Position in the stratification hierarchy is one of the factors that determine susceptibility to law. Those in low positions are more susceptible to law in that, among other things, their crimes are more harshly sanctioned. The same is true for non-governmental forms of social control. Just as inequality in wealth and power influences decision making in courtrooms, it also affects how offenders are treated in workplaces and in the community. Criminal conviction has been shown to reduce the employment opportunities of working-class defendants. Case studies of powerful corporate executives who have committed egregious offenses find that they often continue to hold respected positions in both the economic and social worlds. These studies suggest that the "stigmatizing effects" of criminal conviction are not damaging for some white-collar offenders.

Less powerful white-collar offenders may be more stigmatized by criminal conviction than business executives. For example, professionals and public-sector workers convicted of white-collar crimes lose occupational status more often than business executives convicted of similar offenses. The consequences of legal stigma may be influenced more by the offender's class position than by his or her criminal conduct.

The extent of social condemnation presumably varies directly with the seriousness of offense and severity of the criminal sentences received. In theory, those who commit minor offenses provoke little censure from the community-at-large and receive lenient treatment in the legal system. Those who commit more serious offenses do not fare as well: they may receive both stronger social condemnation and harsher punishment. Since judges supposedly deem informal sanctions, such as loss of status, sufficient punishment for white-collar offenders, they may impose less severe sentences on those who experience those sanctions. Consequently, formal and informal reactions to white-collar crime may not be consistent.

Material used in this particular passage has been adapted from the following source:

M. L. Benson, "The Influence of Class Position on the Formal and Informal Sanctioning of White-Collar Offenders," *Sociological Quarterly*. © 1989.

1. It can be inferred from the passage that the courts would treat social isolation of an accused business executive as:

A) an expected consequence of public accusations but not relevant to the judicial process.
B) a more potent form of punishment than even a prison sentence.
C) a situation that, since not truly measurable, cannot be considered punitive.
D) a legitimate form of punishment that is often considered before a sentence is determined.

2. According to the passage, which of the following is a ramification of the failure to examine the determining factors of informal sanctions?

A) A misunderstanding of the relationship between the structure of society and sanctions that are used to control criminal behavior
B) A reduction of employment opportunities for working-class defendants
C) An inability to establish effective punitive measures using formal sanctions on criminal behavior
D) The ability of numerous business executives convicted of criminal offenses to maintain respectable positions

3. Which one of the following best describes the author's reaction to the two forms of sanctions discussed in the passage?

A) Frustration that class position is a factor in the severity of both formal and informal sanctions
B) Concern about the injustices frequently occurring because governmental and nongovernmental sanctions against offenders are both solely determined by the hierarchy of class position
C) Advocating further study of nongovernmental sanctions to address inconsistent treatment of criminal offenders
D) Favoring formal sanctions as the fairest method of punishing criminal offenders

4. The phrase " 'stigmatizing effects' of criminal conviction" (paragraph 2) refers to which one of the following?

A) The severity of formal sanctions imposed upon working-class defendants after criminal convictions
B) The less severe formal sanctions received by white-collar criminals after criminal convictions
C) The informal sanctions a defendant receives as a result of being convicted of a crime
D) The inequality of treatment before the law of working-class and white collar offenders

5. Which of the following questions about the two forms of sanctions could not be answered by using the information provided in the passage?

A) What is the difference between formal and informal sanctions?
B) Why have formal sanctions received extensive analytic treatment?
C) Why have informal sanctions not received thorough investigation?
D) Why are formal and informal sanctions of white-collar crimes sometimes inconsistent?

6. Which of the following sentences would best serve as a completion to the passage?

A) As the justice system progresses, the determinants of informal sanctions should receive more investigation.
B) Accordingly, judges should not consider informal sanctions when imposing sentences on criminal offenders, regardless of their position on the social hierarchy.
C) If this trend continues, it will remain impossible for criminal defendants to receive fair sentences until more attention is paid to the study of informal sanctions.
D) It is clear that the seriousness of the offense alone should determine the formal sanctions imposed upon criminal conviction.

7. Which of the following best expresses the main idea of the passage?

A) The extent to which a person is stigmatized by criminal conviction depends in large part on their social status or class.
B) To understand how individual behavior is influenced by society, we must learn more about the effect of social stigma on criminal offenders.
C) Informal sanctions have an even greater effect than formal sanctions on those accused or convicted of crimes and so must be studied in more depth.
D) The workings of law and society cannot be studied in isolation from each other; the two are inherently intertwined in our institutions and cultural beliefs.

8.4

ANSWERS TO 5-MINUTE DRILL:

1. D

2. A

3. C

4. C

5. C

6. A

7. B

Exercise 3: Test Assessment Log

This Log should look familiar; there is a copy of it in Chapter 2. If you haven't been using it to evaluate your practice tests, now is the time to start.

In particular, use it to evaluate your pacing. Are you spending the time you need on the easier passages in order to get most of those questions right? Keep track of how much time you spent (roughly) on the NOW passages and on the LATER passages. If you find that you are spending the bulk of your 60 minutes on the harder passages with a low level of accuracy, you need to reapportion your time. Also evaluate your ranking; are you choosing the right passages?

Time	Psg # NOW	Questions Attempted	Number Correct	Number Incorrect	Question Types	Reasons for Mistakes
Start NOWs _____						
End NOWs _____						

Total NOW Passages _____   Total Q Attempted _____

Total Q Correct _____   Total Q Incorrect _____   % Correct _____

Time	Psg # LATER	Questions Attempted	Number Correct	Number Incorrect	Question Types	Reasons for Mistakes
Start LATERs _____						
End LATERs _____						

Total NOW Passages _____   Total Q Attempted _____

Total Q Correct _____   Total Q Incorrect _____   % Correct _____

KILLER Passages(s) Skipped # _____

Revised Strategy _____

Chapter 8 Summary

- Manage your 60 minutes well by maintaining a steady pace throughout the entire section. Take your time to get most of the easier questions right. Don't spend too much time on difficult passages; use POE and your knowledge of Attractors to help you through.

- Evaluate your own performance so that you can refine your pacing strategy appropriately.

- If you have an awkward amount of time left over after completing a passage (e.g., 5 minutes), shift your strategy to make sure that you can get to at least one or two easier questions on another passage. Make sure that you select random guesses for any passages that you don't have time to complete.

CHAPTER 8 PRACTICE PASSAGES

Individual Passage Drills

Complete the two passages back-to-back, timed, using the "six of seven passage rate" from section 8.2.

Once you have completed the passages and checked your answers, fill out the Individual Passage Logs. Focus in particular on:

1. Evaluating your pacing. Were you going too fast or too slow?
2. Identifying types of mistakes that you have also made in the past and strategizing on how to avoid making those same mistakes in the future.

CHAPTER 8 PRACTICE PASSAGE 1

No empirical studies show what proportion of the United States population would have to participate in disruptive and violent demonstrations to seriously threaten the political system. Surely the level of antiregime violence of recent years has not been sufficient to undermine the viability of the American system. Although the actual participants in peaceful demonstrations or violent protests are far fewer in number than the individuals who approve of these activities, most Americans do not approve of either peaceful or violent protests. In both 1968 and 1972, less than one in five Americans approved of peaceful demonstrations and less than one in ten approved of violent, disruptive protests. Although the level of support for these activities did not increase between 1968 and 1972, the level of opposition declined. Increasing numbers of people seem to be willing to tolerate demonstrations and protests under some circumstances.

If the present relationships persist into the future, increasingly greater tolerance but not necessarily more widespread participation can be anticipated. Among college graduates under age thirty, more than 50 percent approve of peaceful demonstrations, and only 10 percent disapprove. These relationships suggest that as education levels increase, approval of demonstrations will increase. These attitudes suggest a growing unwillingness to be repressive against political interests expressed through peaceful demonstrations, perhaps because the claims of participants are granted some legitimacy.

In these terms, there is some uneasiness about the public support for American democracy — and perhaps for any democratic regime. It is possible to view the United States as a democratic system that has survived without a strong democratic political culture because governmental policies have gained a continual, wide-spread acceptance. If that satisfaction erodes, however, as it has begun to do, the public has no deep commitment to democratic values and processes that will inhibit support of antidemocratic leaders or disruptive activities.

It is argued that in the absence of insistence on particular values and procedures, democratic regimes will fail. Clearly, a mass public demanding democratic values and procedures is stronger support for a democratic system than a mass public merely willing to tolerate a democratic regime. This does not mean, however, that the stronger form of support is necessary for a democratic system, although superficially it appears desirable. Quite possibly, strong support is nearly impossible to attain, and weaker support is adequate, given other conditions.

In our view, the analysis of support for democratic regimes has been misguided by an emphasis on factors contributing to the establishment of democracy, not its maintenance. Stronger public support probably is required for the successful launching of a democracy than it is for maintaining an already established democracy. Possibly, preserving a regime simply requires that no substantial proportion of the society be actively hostile to the regime and engage in disruptive activities. In other words, absence of disruptive acts, not the presence of supportive attitudes, is crucial.

On the other hand, the positive support by leaders for a political system is essential to its existence. If some leaders are willing to oppose the system, it is crucial that there be no substantial number of followers to which the leaders can appeal. The followers' attitudes, as opposed to their willingness to act themselves, may provide a base of support for antisystem behavior by leaders. In this sense unanimous public support for democratic principles would be a more firm basis for a democratic system. The increasing levels of dissatisfaction, accompanied by a lack of strong commitment to democratic values in the American public, appear to create some potential for public support of undemocratic leaders. In this light, the public's loyalty to political parties and commitment to traditional processes that inhibit aspiring undemocratic leaders become all the more important.

Material used in this particular passage has been adapted from the following source:

W.H. Flanigan and N.H. Zingale, *Political Behavior of the American Electorate.* ©1979 by Allyn Bacon.

1. Elsewhere, the author describes factors that led to the founding of American democracy. If his account is consistent with the information in the passage, such a discussion would most likely include which of the following?

A) Heroic descriptions of violent uprisings against the British such as the Boston Tea Party
B) Anecdotes concerning George Washington's idealistic motivations
C) Data suggesting vigorous support for democracy was widespread in America at the time
D) A suggestion that more peaceful forms of protest would have given way to a more effective democracy

2. Which of the following, if true, would most strengthen the author's assertion that public support for peaceful protest is likely to increase over time?

A) A hunger strike by a charismatic dissident leader gains some public support
B) Clashes between protestors and police lead to increased participation in violent protests
C) Five years prior to the survey of college graduates cited by the author, 70 percent of college graduates were shown to approve of nonviolent demonstrations
D) Increased government funding will allow colleges to admit larger classes in the future

3. The author suggests all of the following are generally necessary for a democracy to thrive EXCEPT:

A) public distaste for violent antigovernment activity.
B) leaders committed to the pursuit of democratic ideals.
C) an electorate that insists upon democratic values in government.
D) an insufficient dissident population to support an undemocratic leader.

4. The primary purpose of the passage is to:

A) contrast the relative merits of violent and nonviolent protest.
B) describe conditions in which a government would fail.
C) argue that free speech has deleterious effects.
D) consider factors that determine the stability of a certain type of political system.

5. Suppose a set of American national politicians were to renounce their loyalty to existing political parties and create a new party founded on communist ideals. Given the information in the passage, their success at creating political change would most likely depend on:

A) acceptance of their ideas among a critical mass of the populace.
B) support among more educated Americans.
C) a loyal following willing to actively campaign on their behalf.
D) a clearly delineated party platform.

6. The author implies that between 1968 and 1972:

A) acceptance of protest increased and opposition to protest did not decline.
B) social unrest led to greater acceptance of protest as a necessary part of political life.
C) Americans' objection to certain types of protest decreased.
D) there was no change in Americans' attitudes toward protest.

7. The American populace is portrayed as generally:

A) distrustful of government and prone to take political action against its violations of democratic ideals.
B) accepting of America's long history of violence and unrest.
C) willing to passively accept a government that meets its basic requirements.
D) patriotic and unwilling to tolerate dissent.

CHAPTER 8 PRACTICE PASSAGE 2

The most famous sentence in Igor Stravinsky's autobiography reads: "Music is by its very nature powerless to express anything at all." When it appeared, this sentence surprised his audience. After all, Stravinsky had composed some of the most expressive music of the twentieth century, from the lyrical *Petrouchka* to the dramatic *Le sacre du printemps* (The Rite of Spring) to the elegiac *Symphony of Psalms*. But ever the polemicist, Stravinsky was in actuality blasting those whom he regarded as his aesthetic opponents, such as the followers of Richard Wagner; such "impurists" were always marshaling music in the service of extramusical ends, from national solidarity to religious freedom. Seeking to repair a perceived imbalance, Stravinsky portrayed the musician as a craftsman whose materials of pitch and rhythm in themselves harbor no more expression than the carpenter's beams or the jeweler's stone.

Stravinsky may have been right that in the absence of an externally imposed "program," music is simply music. He spoke of the "poetics" of music, which in its literal sense refers to the making (*poiesis*) of music. Unintentionally, however, Stravinsky vividly illustrated a different point through his own life: the extent to which the making of music is *not* possible without the externally triggered factor of politics. All creative individuals - and especially all musicians - must deal with a set of associates who not only help the creators realize their vision but also, eventually, with a wider public, determine the fate of the creators' works. Stravinsky's embroilment in personal and professional politics was extreme for an artist of any sort, yet by throwing the political aspects of creation into sharp relief, Stravinsky reveals the extent to which an artist must work with the field that regulates his chosen domain. Whether they do so well or poorly, eagerly or reluctantly, nearly all creative individuals must devote significant energies to the management of their careers.

Stravinsky's early training came in the form of an apprenticeship with Nikolay Rimsky-Korsakov, the dean of Russian composers. Rimsky-Korsakov guided Stravinsky in orchestration, teaching him how to compose for each instrument; they would each orchestrate the same passages and then compare their versions. Stravinsky was an apt pupil, whose rapid advances pleased his mentor; and, perhaps for the first time in his life, Stravinsky found himself in a milieu that fully engaged him.

A dramatic turning point in Stravinsky's career occurred shortly after his mentor's death when Stravinsky was approached by Serge Diaghilev to compose a nocturne for his theatrical project, *The Firebird*. Suddenly, instead of working alone, Stravinsky had almost daily intercourse with the ensemble — a new and heady experience for someone who had craved the companionship of individuals with whom he felt comfortable. Stravinsky turned out to be a willing pupil, one who learned quickly and reacted vividly to everything. He was sufficiently flexible, curious, and versatile to be able to work with the set designers, dancers, choreographers, and even those responsible for the business end of the enterprise. From Diaghilev young Igor learned two equally crucial lessons for ensemble work: how to meet a deadline and how to compromise on, or mediate amongst, deeply held but differing artistic visions. Yet, he may have learned Diaghilev's lessons too well. As Stravinsky gained in knowledge and confidence, he found himself engaged in strenuous disputes about characterization, choreography, and instrumentation.

The most notable creators almost always are perfectionists who have worked out every detail of their conception painstakingly and are unwilling to make further changes unless they can be convinced that such alterations are justified. Few intrepid creators are likely to cede any rights to others; and even if they are consciously tempted to do so, their unconscious sense of fidelity to an original conceptualization may prevent them from following through. Stravinsky was no exception in this, and his goals were well-defined and impassioned. Suppressing whatever revolutionary impulses may have existed in his own person and animated his earlier music, ignoring the rich emotional associations of his early masterpieces, Stravinsky stressed the importance of conventions and traditions, and the utility of self-imposed constraints. He loathed disorder, randomness, arbitrariness, the Circean lure of chaos. Music was akin to mathematical thinking and relationships, and one could discern powerful, inexorable laws at work. In the paradox-packed closing lines of *The Poetics of Music*, Stravinsky declared: "My freedom will be so much greater and more meaningful, the more narrowly I limit my field of action and the more I surround myself with obstacles. Whatever diminishes constraints, diminishes strength. The more constraints one imposes, the more one frees one's self of the chains that shackle the spirit."

Material used in this particular passage has been adapted from the following source:

H. Gardner, *Creating Minds: An Anatomy of Creativity Seen Through the Lives of Freud, Einstein, Picasso, Stravinsky, Eliot, Graham, and Gandhi.* © 1993 by Basic Books.

1. Which of Stravinsky's learning experiences or observations is most *inconsistent* with the author's statement in the last paragraph that "the most notable creators are almost always perfectionists"?

A) Orchestration techniques learned while working with Rimsky-Korsakov
B) Lessons learned from Diaghilev and involvement in the ensemble
C) The need to engage in protracted political battles
D) The observation that "the more constraints one imposes, the more one frees one's self of the chains that shackle the spirit"

2. The word "political" is used in paragraph 2 in order to refer to:

A) collaboration and artifice.
B) greed and expediency.
C) interpersonal relations.
D) cleverness and guile.

3. We can reasonably infer that the perceived imbalance that Stravinsky was seeking to repair was one of:

A) an over-dependence on inspiration rather than craftsmanship in making music.
B) some composers' tendency to inject extraneous elements into their music.
C) too great an involvement in the political side of theatrical staging and production.
D) an over-emphasis on choreography as compared to instrumentation in theatrical productions.

4. The author's discussion of Stravinsky's actions and statements suggests that which two aspects of Stravinsky's character or career may have been at odds with each other?

A) His desire to create music and his involvement with choreography and set design
B) The artistic independence expressed in *The Poetics of Music* and his dependence on others in managing his career
C) His desire to create and his inability to escape interpersonal politics
D) His desire for a strict approach to making music and his willingness to work in a highly collaborative setting

5. In the author's view, Stravinsky's collaboration with others in musical composition and theater can best be summarized as:

A) productive yet contentious.
B) accepted with reluctance.
C) onerous and ultimately destructive.
D) fruitful and harmonious.

6. According to the passage, Stravinsky believed which of the following to be a condition necessary for creativity in music?

A) A willingness to collaborate and compromise
B) Situations of total freedom
C) Openness to new and revolutionary ideas
D) Limitations to lend it structure

7. A study shows that painters who hire agents and business managers early in their careers tend to be more prolific. What effect would this information have on the author's argument regarding an artist's involvement in his own career?

A) It would be contrary to the author's claim that artists need to manage their own careers.
B) It would be relevant to evaluating the notion that the essence of Stravinsky's artistic vision was shaped by collaboration.
C) It would support the author's implication that artistic fields of endeavor are also businesses.
D) It would justify Stravinsky's engagement in strenuous disputes regarding theatrical elements.

SOLUTIONS TO CHAPTER 8 PRACTICE PASSAGE 1

1. **C** This is a New Information question.

   A: No. Nowhere does the author suggest the conditions for starting a democracy require violence. Nor does the author's tone suggest violence is "heroic."

   B: No. First, although the author does discuss the importance of leaders committed to a democratic system for the existence or maintenance of a democracy in paragraph 6, this is not described as "idealism," and the motivation of those leaders is not the issue, but rather their behavior. Second, this idea is not explicitly tied to the requirements for *founding* a democracy. Third, this choice, in its reference to George Washington, relies on too much outside knowledge for its relevance to the information in the question stem.

   C: **Yes. In paragraph 5, the author says, "Stronger public support probably is required for the successful launching of a democracy than it is for maintaining an already established democracy…"**

   D: No. The author does not equate peaceful protest with a stronger democracy.

2. **D** This is a Strengthen question.

   A: No. An isolated incident such as this one is not enough evidence to suggest a trend will continue. Also notice the mild wording; the fact that it gained "some public support" is not enough to "most strengthen" the author's claim.

   B: No. There is no connection made by the author between some level (we don't know if it's a significant level) of increased participation in violent protest and increased support for peaceful protest.

   C: No. Because it suggests the number of educated people who support peaceful protest is in some level of *decline*, this answer choice would weaken the argument. Note that even if you were thinking that "more than 50 percent" could be 70 percent, this answer still gives no evidence of an increase over time, or of a likely increase in the future.

   D: **Yes. The author explains that "as education levels increase, approval of demonstrations will increase," but does not explicitly support the premise that education levels will increase. If colleges were to accept more applicants, it is fair to assume education levels would increase, thus strengthening the premise.**

3. **C** This is an Inference/Except question

   A: No. One part of the main idea of the passage is that widespread acceptance of disruptive antigovernment activity can threaten democracy (see paragraph 5). Since the question stem asks you to find an answer choice that is not a requirement for democracy, this can not be the answer.

   B: No. See paragraph 6: "the positive support by leaders for a political system is essential to its existence."

   C: **Yes. Paragraphs 4 and 5 explain that the population does not need to actively campaign for democratic ideals for democracy to work. In fact, such strong support for democratic values may be "impossible" (paragraph 4). At the end of paragraph 5, the author states that "absence of disruptive acts, not the presence of supportive attitudes, is crucial." Although paragraph 6 suggests public support for democracy is necessary when antigovernment leaders come to prominence, this is a specific situation, as opposed to the "general" view that the question stem asks for. Because this idea is not supported by the passage, it is the *correct* answer to this "EXCEPT" question.**

   D: No. See paragraph 6: "If some leaders are willing to oppose the system, it is crucial that there be no substantial number of followers to which the leaders can appeal."

4. **D** This is a Main Idea/Primary Purpose question.
    A: No. The author makes no such evaluation of different forms of protest. Be sure not to be overly influenced by paragraph 1 of the passage when determining the author's primary purpose.
    B: No. This answer uses language that is too extreme; the author's does not go so far as to assure us democracy will fail under certain circumstances.
    C: No. This answer choice is too broad. The correct answer must focus on the key issues of the passage: protest, public support, and the stability of democracies. Furthermore, this answer is too negative. While the passage does suggest that free speech is related to peaceful protest (paragraph 2), the author doesn't go so far as to suggest that it has harmful effects.
    D: **Yes. Although it uses vague language to do so, this answer does address the main focus of the passage. The factors that would influence stability of a democratic political system (a "certain type of political system"), according to the passage, would be the level and type of support and/or dissent.**

5. **A** This is a New Information question.
    A: **Yes. Paragraph 6 states, "If some leaders are willing to oppose the system, it is crucial that there be no substantial number of followers to which the leaders can appeal. The followers' attitudes, as opposed to their willingness to act themselves, may provide a base of support for antisystem behavior by leaders."**
    B: No. It would be too large of an inference to take the author's claim that educated Americans are more likely to be tolerant of protest (paragraph 2) to mean their support would be the key to such an insurgent political group's success.
    C: No. The correct answer must be supported by the passage text, rather than by common sense or real world experience. The passage says in paragraph 6 that "it is crucial that there be no substantial number of followers to which the leaders can appeal" and that the "followers' attitudes, as opposed to their willingness to act themselves, may provide a base of support for antisystem behavior by leaders." While you might think that campaigning by a loyal following would help create widespread public support for the dissidents, there is no evidence for this in the passage. Compare this answer to choice A, which does have direct support in the passage text.
    D: No. The passage gives no evidence, in paragraph 6 or elsewhere, that having a clear party platform would influence the public one way or the other.

6. **C** This is an Inference question.
    A: No. This is a reversal of the information in paragraph 1. Acceptance or support of protest stayed the same, while opposition to protest declined.
    B: No. Although this may be historically accurate, the answer must be supported by the text of the passage. There is no suggestion in the passage that social unrest lead to this kind of change in attitude.
    C: **Yes. In paragraph 1, the author states: "Although the level of support for these activities did not increase between 1968 and 1972, the level of opposition declined."**
    D: No. Paragraph 1 clearly states there was such a change; opposition to protest declined.

7. **C** This is an Inference question.
    A: No. Paragraph 1 establishes that "most Americans do not approve of either peaceful or violent protests."
    B: No. The passage does not address America's history of violence or public attitudes towards it.

C: Yes. In paragraph 1, Americans are portrayed as quietly accepting the status quo. Most oppose antigovernment protest and the majority of those who tolerate dissent don't participate. Also, in paragraph 3, the author describes the American populace as merely "satisfied": "It is possible to view the United States as a democratic system that has survived without a strong democratic political culture because governmental policies have gained a continual, wide-spread acceptance."

D: No. The passage does not describe Americans as patriotic. Furthermore, the author states in paragraph 1 that "Increasing numbers of people seem to be tolerating demonstrations and protests under some circumstances." Even if this is still a minority of the population, it would be too extreme to describe Americans as a whole as "unwilling to tolerate dissent."

SOLUTIONS TO CHAPTER 8 PRACTICE PASSAGE 2

1. **B** This is an Inference question.

Note: The author makes this statement in the context of discussing Stravinsky's faithfulness to his own artistic vision. The passage states that perfectionists "have worked out every detail of their conception painstakingly and are [often] unwilling to make further changes" or "cede any rights to others," and that "Stravinsky was no exception in this."

A: No. This choice may be tempting, but we have no basis for supposing compromise or acceptance of "imperfection" was required, as we're only told that they composed separately for later comparison.

B: **Yes. It was from Diaghilev that Stravinsky is said to have learned "to compromise on, or mediate amongst, deeply held but differing artistic visions (paragraph 4). The quote cited in the question stem, in the context of paragraph 5, relates to an unwillingness to "cede any rights to others" or to diverge from the artist's own "original conceptualization."**

C: No. Paragraph 2 indicates that Stravinsky had to engage in political battles in order to "realize [his] vision" and to manage his career. However, there is no indication that these battles involved compromising or going against his perfectionism about the work itself.

D: No. This answer is consistent with the statement in the question stem. This observation appears in paragraph 5, in the context of the author's description of Stravinsky's dedication to realizing his own goals.

2. **C** This is a Vocabulary In Context question.

A: No. While "collaboration" fits, "artifice" or falsehood does not. Be careful not to import your own associations with politics into the passage.

B: No. While "expediency" is not clearly wrong, there is no suggestion of greed. The fact that political battles were necessary in the management of an artist's career doesn't by itself show that the artists are greedy or money-hungry.

C: **Yes. Paragraph 2 says, in the context of discussing the necessary role of politics, that artists "must deal with a set of associates who...help the creators realize their vision."**

D: No. While "cleverness" is not clearly wrong, there is no suggestion of "guile" or deception.

3. **B** This is an Inference question.

   A: No. There is no suggestion in paragraph 1, or elsewhere in the passage, that Stravinsky discounted the importance of inspiration ("expression" is not equated with "inspiration"), or that he believed that he himself or other composers displayed insufficient craftsmanship.

   B: Yes. This choice is supported by information in the lines above the reference to the "imbalance" in paragraph 1, in which the author refers to Stravinsky's intention of "blasting…his aesthetic opponents" whose goals were extramusical, attempting to further such things as national solidarity or religious freedom.

   C: No. The author does not suggest that Stravinsky tried to reduce his, or others', involvement in the political aspects specifically of presenting music or theater to an audience. Stravinsky's complaint was about injecting non-musical aspects into the music itself.

   D: No. While paragraph 4 mentions Stravinsky's involvement in disputes about choreography and instrumentation, it doesn't suggest that he believed choreography had been given too much importance.

4. **D** This is an Inference question.

   A: No. Paragraph 4 suggests that his desire to create and present music and his interest in choreography and set design went hand in hand.

   B: No. While paragraph 2 does suggest that all artists are dependant on others in realizing their vision and managing their career, this doesn't necessarily apply to artistic independence involved in making or creating the music itself.

   C: No. Paragraph 2 suggests that Stravinsky believed that interpersonal politics were necessary to some aspects of the process of creation (such as career management), rather than an impediment to it.

   D: Yes. Stravinsky expresses a strong attachment to making music in particular ways, untainted by extramusical intentions, and it's hinted in paragraph 5 that he would be unlikely to change his compositions. However, the discussion in paragraph 4 indicates that Stravinsky had learned to compromise artistically and to be open to differing artistic visions.

5. **A** This is an Inference question.

   A: Yes. This choice is supported by paragraph 4, where the author describes how Stravinsky benefited from the new experience of collaboration, and yet found himself "engaged in strenuous disputes."

   B: No. "Reluctance" contradicts paragraph 4, which suggests that Stravinsky eagerly took on this new opportunity to collaborate, and "destructive" is too extreme to be supported by the author's mention of "strenuous disputes."

   C: No. "Onerous" is unsupported; we have no evidence that Stravinsky found these disputes to be burdensome. Furthermore, "ultimately destructive" is too extreme.

   D: No. This choice is half right/half wrong. "Fruitful" or productive is supported, but the process was not always "harmonious", as indicated in the matter of "strenuous disputes" mentioned in paragraph 4.

6. **D** This is a Retrieval question.

    A: No. This choice reflects some points made by the author in paragraphs 2 and 4, but we don't know that Stravinsky shared in this belief. The author states that Stravinsky's experience "reveals the extent to which an artist must work with the field that regulates his chosen domain," but not that Stravinsky himself expressed this idea. Note that in paragraph 2, the author states that Stravinsky's life "unintentionally" illustrates the importance of collaboration.

    B: No. This choice contradicts Stravinsky's statements in paragraph 5, where he talks about the importance of constraints and obstacles.

    C: No. The passage states that he eventually believed in "suppressing whatever revolutionary impulses may have existed in his own person" (paragraph 5).

    D: Yes. This comes directly from Stravinsky's quote in paragraph 5.

7. **C** This is a New Information question.

    A: No. This choice may be tempting, but it takes words out of context from the passage. The author indicates in paragraph 2 that the artist must manage his or her career, but also suggests that this usually requires interaction with, and help from, other people.

    B: No. This choice may also be somewhat tempting, but the study would be relevant to evaluating collaboration in the business of the artist's career, including presentation of artistic work to the public, rather than in the essence or fundamental character of the artistic vision itself.

    C: Yes. The author's argument in paragraph 2 is that an artist needs to be involved with the business of his or her own career, whether personally or through agents, so a study that indicates that a business manager increases artistic productivity would support the author's argument.

    D: No. A study about the effects of business management would not be directly relevant to issues of theatrical production.

Individual Passage Log

Passage # _____   Time spent on both passages _____

Q#	Q type	Attractors	What did you do wrong?

Revised Strategy _____

Passage # _____

Q#	Q type	Attractors	What did you do wrong?

Revised Strategy _____

Chapter 9
Refining Your Skills

GOALS

1. To continue the self-evaluation process
2. To further refine your skills
3. To prepare mentally for test day

9.1   CONTINUING THE SELF-EVALUATION PROCESS

At this point in your preparation, you have acquired a variety of tools with which to attack the passages and the Verbal Reasoning section as a whole. Over the remaining time leading up to MCAT day, take the opportunity to further refine those skills, taking your own individual strengths and weaknesses into account. If you don't have a clear list of those strengths and weaknesses (and if you have not been consistently filling out the Individual Passage Logs and Test Assessment Logs), *now* is the time to generate it.

It is still not too late to recognize and correct some of the persistent mistakes you may be making. There is no point in doing passage after passage if you spend little or no time evaluating your performance on those passages. You should spend just as much time evaluating your performance as you do on doing the passage itself. If not, each passage you do reinforces rather than corrects bad habits and blind spots you may still have.

Some things to consider:

- Are you still trying to finish (or almost finish) the entire section and yet are missing a large number of the questions you complete? If so, think about how much time you're spending getting questions wrong. Instead, try two test sections guessing on at least one additional passage, giving yourself more time to carefully consider the questions. See how slowing down affects your overall percentage of correct answers.
- Are you defining the Main Point of each paragraph and articulating the Bottom Line of the passage before addressing the questions? This is one of your most powerful tools. Use it!
- Are you consistently going back to the passage and answering the questions in your own words before evaluating the answer choices?
- Are you actively using POE? Are you approaching the answers skeptically, looking out for traps?

9.2 REFINING YOUR SKILLS

Below are a series of exercises, focusing on the passage, the questions, and the answer choices. They will help you continue to improve your performance in each of those areas, especially on the harder passages.

Exercise 1: Paraphrasing the Passage

Often the difficult or LATER passages are characterized by complex, abstract wording. To make your way through these passages with a reasonable level of comprehension (that is, enough to articulate the main point of each chunk and of the passage as a whole), you need to put the author's convoluted, obscure wording into your own clear language.

Read each of the paragraphs below, and write down the main point in the space provided. If you have difficulty with a section of a paragraph (or a paragraph as a whole), don't just go back to the beginning and read it again "harder." Often after multiple readings, a paragraph makes less, not more sense. Instead, pay attention to the structure of the sentence or paragraph. Find an "anchor," or one piece that you understand, and use it to make sense of the rest. Break the reading down into pieces, and the whole will begin to make a lot more sense.

Note: Some of these paragraphs represent the difficulty level of language found in KILLER passages. Don't panic, and don't give up; just keep your focus and do the best you can. Practicing on the hardest examples will contribute to your performance on any level of passage. These are not meant to be different paragraphs from the same passage, so don't worry about finding a relationship between them. Explanations follow the exercise.

Paragraph 1

Modern medicine has fixed its own date of birth as being in the last years of the eighteenth century. Reflecting on its situation, it identifies the origin of its positivity with a return — over and above all theory — to the modest but effecting level of the perceived. In fact, this supposed empiricism is not based on a rediscovery of the absolute values of the visible, nor on the predetermined rejection of systems and all their chimeras, but on a reorganization of the manifest and secret space that opened up when a millennial gaze passed over men's sufferings. Nonetheless, the rejuvenation of medical perception, the way colors and things came to life under the illuminating gaze of the first clinicians is no mere myth. At the beginning of the nineteenth century, doctors described what for centuries had remained below the threshold of the visible and the expressible, but this did not mean that, after overindulging in speculation, they had begun to perceive once again, or that they listened to reason rather than to imagination; it meant that the relation between the visible and the invisible — which is necessary to all concrete knowledge — changed its structure, revealing through gaze and language what had previously been below and beyond their domain. A new alliance was forged between words and things, enabling one *to see* and *to say*.

Notes: This is a good example of how a passage about a familiar topic (medicine) may in fact be extremely difficult. When taken as a whole, it is almost impossible to understand. Therefore, take it bit by bit. Find a sentence, or a part of a sentence, that you do understand, and use it to make some sense of the parts around it. Don't get stuck on unfamiliar vocabulary. Do you really need to know what a "chimera" or "millennial gaze" is to get the gist of the paragraph? Do, however, pay attention to the series of contrasts provided (indicated by pivotal words and phrases) to get a sense of what the author is describing.

Main Point: _____

_____

_____

_____

_____

_____

_____

_____

Paragraph 2

We have so far discussed the "absent person" in ads. But since this person is always signified by objects (and above all, the product) in the ad, interchangeable with them in that they represent his absence with their presence, it follows that the other side of the exchange, the product, may likewise be absent from the ad, and signified by the people in it. There is a series of lager ads on TV where the lager itself is never there. In one of these ads, two workers in a factory pick up two empty glasses from the conveyer belt and start drinking "lager" from them.... In another ad the two men come into a pub which turns out not to have this particular brand of lager when they order it. So they take two empty mugs and again "drink" the invisible lager. Although the product is actually absent in these cases, it is sufficiently signified in the ad — by the two men — by their attitude towards it, by their taste, and so on. There is also a definite place for it to fill: the surrounding presence of the mugs makes the actual presence of the lager redundant. Thus with absence in an ad, the thing meant to fill the gap is always defined, not by a simple replacement but by what is contingent: it is what surrounds the gap that determines its shape.

Notes: Notice how this paragraph is organized. This structure—a claim followed by one or more examples, and then a further conclusion—is a very common one, and you can use it to help you puzzle through difficult sections of a passage. If you have difficulty with the claims, work backwards from the examples. If you have trouble understanding the examples, start with the claim.

Main Point: _____

_____

_____

_____

_____

_____

_____

_____

Paragraph 3

At a certain point in their historical lives, social classes become detached from their traditional parties. In other words, the traditional parties in that particular organizational form, with the particular men who constitute, represent, and lead them, are no longer recognized by their class (or fraction of a class) as its expression. When such crises occur, the immediate situation becomes delicate and dangerous, because the field is open for violent solutions, for the activities of unknown forces, represented by charismatic "men of destiny."

Notes: It is always more difficult to wrap your brain around the abstract than the concrete. If the author doesn't give a specific example or illustration, imagine one of your own to help solidify your understanding of the text.

Main Point: _____

_____

_____

_____

_____

_____

_____

_____

Paragraph 4

As a label, "cyberpunk" is perfection. It suggests the apotheosis
of postmodernism. On one hand, pure negation: of manner,
history, philosophy, politics, body, will affect, anything mediated
by cultural memory; on the other, pure attitude: all is power,
and "subculture," and the grace of Hip negotiating the splatter
of consciousness as it slams against the hard-tech future, the
techno-future of artificial impermanence, where all that was once
nature is simulated and elaborated by technical means, a future
world-construct that is as remote from the "lessons of history" as
the present mix-up is from the pitiful science fiction fantasies
of the past that had tried to imagine us. The oxymoronic conceit
in "cyberpunk" is so slick and global it fuses high and low, the
complex and the simple, the governor and the savage, the techno-
sublime and rock and roll slime.

Notes: Even sentences that seem like just a cascade of words do have a structure. Try breaking up the long
sentences in this paragraph into shorter, more manageable ones before trying to synthesize them into the
main idea of the passage.

Main Point: _____

_____

_____

_____

_____

_____

_____

_____

Paragraph 5

But physiologists have also begun to see chaos as health. It has long been understood that nonlinearity in feedback processes serves to regulate and control. Simply put, a linear process, given a slight nudge, tends to remain slightly off track. A nonlinear process, given the same nudge, tends to return to its starting point.

Notes: Phrases like *simply put, in other words,* or *that is to say* should be music to your ears. These phrases indicate that the author is going to say it again, in different words, in case it wasn't clear the first time. Make sure you notice and take advantage of these "second chances."

Main Point: _____

_____

_____

_____

_____

_____

_____

_____

Paragraph 6

Western academic philosophy may have a hard time agreeing
on its own definition, but any definition must be responsible
to certain facts about the application of the concept. In the
Euro-American tradition nothing can count as philosophy, for
example, if it does not discuss problems that have a family
resemblance to those problems that have centrally concerned
those we call "philosophers." And nothing that does address
itself to such problems but does so in a way that bears no family
resemblance to traditional philosophical methods ought to count
either. And the Wittgensteinian notion of family resemblance,
here, is especially appropriate because a tradition, like a family,
is something that changes from one generation to the next. Just as
there may be no way of seeing me as especially like my remote
ancestors, even though there are substantial similarities between
the members of succeeding generations, so we are likely to be
able to see the continuities between Plato and Frege only if we
trace steps in between.

Notes: Another important tool at your disposal is the analogy. Where is an analogy used in this paragraph
and what is its relationship to the author's main point?

Main Point: _____

_____

_____

_____

_____

_____

_____

_____

Paragraph 7

This is not to disparage the efforts of the experimenters. They are important as catalysts. For the writer is not alone is his or her endeavor, but is, rather, participating in a collaborative enterprise. The Kriges would not impress us so if it were not for the cooperation of the publishing house (which lends the nobility of its name and ensures that the cloth covers of the book are expensively textured and soberly colored), the librarian (who places the book in the anthropology shelves rather than on those reserved for science fiction) and the teacher (who secures it a place on the anthropology-class reading list). Above all, the Kriges rely on readers' skills in filling out and making sense of scientific discourse, a peculiar one in which data are presumed autonomous, interpretations are either confirmed or disconfirmed by facts that are independently specified, and the discovery of orderliness and the production of definitive accounts are normal and expected.

Notes: What is it about this author's writing style that can make this paragraph difficult to read quickly? How might you deal with this "listing" tendency? How could you actually use it to your advantage?

Main Point: _____

_____

_____

_____

_____

_____

_____

_____

Paragraph 8

The aestheticians of painting, especially the modern ones, are the great advocates of "significant form," the movement of the line, the relations of color and tone. Of these critics, the most consistent, the clearest (and the most widely accepted), that I know is the late Mr. Bernhard Berenson. Over sixty years ago in his studies of the Italian Renaissance painters he expounded his aesthetics with refreshing clarity. The merely accurate representations of an object, the blind imitation of nature, was not art, not even if that object was what would commonly be agreed upon as beautiful, for example, a beautiful woman. There was another category of painter superior to the first. Such a one would not actually reproduce the object as it was. Being a man of visions and imagination, the object would stimulate in his impulses, thoughts, memories visually creative. These he would fuse into a whole and the result would be not so much the object as the totality of the visual image which the object had invoked in a superior mind. That too, Mr. Berenson excluded from the category of true art (and was by no means isolated in doing so): mere reproductions of objects, whether actually in existence or the product of the sublimest imaginations, was "literature" or "illustration." What then was the truly artistic? The truly artistic was a quality that existed in its own right, irrespective of the object represented.

Notes: What is the importance of the sentence, "That too, Mr. Berenson excluded from the category of true art"? Were you a bit surprised, given what had come before? What role does this statement play in defining the author's main point?

Main Point: _____

_____

_____

_____

_____

_____

_____

_____

Explanations for Exercise 1: Paraphrasing the Passage

Paragraph 1

Main Point: Modern medicine developed at the end of the 18th Century, with the merging of the visible and the invisible in physicians' understanding.

Paragraph 2

Main Point: Advertising sometimes uses the strategy of showing the environment in which a product exists, but not the product itself.

Paragraph 3

Main Point: When the representational party of a social class no longer accurately reflects the perceived reality of that class, violent or drastic actions may be taken.

Paragraph 4

Main Point: The word "cyberpunk" encapsulates all of the contradictory elements present in a postmodern world.

Paragraph 5

Main Point: A nonlinear feedback process can be at least as effective as a linear process, because it has the ability to self-correct.

Paragraph 6

Main Point: Western academic philosophy must trace the steps between generations of philosophical thought in order to accurately include the relevant subject matter.

Paragraph 7

Main Point: The full publication process of this textbook is defined by collaboration.

Paragraph 8

Main Point: Aestheticians of painting (such as Bernhard Berenson) do not judge a painting's beauty on the accuracy of its reproduction of reality, but on a higher level of artistry and creativity.

Exercise 2: Paraphrasing the Questions

One common characteristic of hard passages is complexly worded and structured questions. As we discussed in Chapter 3, if you don't understand the question itself, you are likely to spend a lot of time on it, only to arrive at an incorrect answer at the end. For each of the questions below, identify the question category (Specific, General, or Complex), question type (e.g., Inference, Strengthen, Evaluate, etc.) and then translate the question into your own words, defining what this question is requiring you to do. Explanations follow the exercise.

1. The information in the passage suggests that the author would be most likely to agree with which of the following statements concerning the use of HDRs as an alternative energy in the event of a failure of other, more traditional recovery systems?

Question category: _____

_____

Question type: _____

_____

Translation: _____

_____

_____

_____

_____

2. The reference to labor negotiation as an example of third party intervention is meant to illustrate which of the following theories in the context of the author's discussion of triadic and quadratic models?

Question category: _____

_____

Question type: _____

_____

Translation: _____

_____

_____

_____

3. The author's claim that the behavior of certain unusual stars has helped "account for previously unexplained phenomena" (paragraph 4) would be most justified by an astronomer's ability to measure the luminosity and pulsation of which of the following types of stars?

Question category: _____

_____

Question type: _____

_____

Translation: _____

_____

_____

_____

4. According to the passage, the author considers each of
   the following good advice to an owner who has arranged
   for fast-track construction of a building on his land
   EXCEPT:

Question category: _____

_____

Question type: _____

_____

Translation: _____

_____

_____

_____

5. The author suggests that the most valid criticism of
   the enactment of laws governing large corporations
   that encourage aspiration that has been raised by the
   advocates of non-regulation is which of the following?

Question category: _____

_____

Question type: _____

_____

Translation: _____

_____

_____

_____

6. It has been argued that when "nation" and "state" are not viewed as unrelated concepts, methodology takes a back seat to political concerns in nonacademic arenas. This claim would be LEAST inconsistent with the author's argument that:

Question category: _____

_____

Question type: _____

_____

Translation: _____

_____

_____

_____

7. Suppose that a veterinarian specializing in the care of large animals were to experience "differential empathy," as that term is used in the passage. This would be most similar to a lawyer who professed that:

Question category: _____

_____

Question type: _____

_____

Translation: _____

_____

_____

_____

8. In addressing the issue of land reform, Stunwitznow predicted that the unearned benefits accrued to landowners from prior, unregulated transactions would not, in a purely laissez-faire system, be taxed at a higher rate than earned benefits from that same classification or type of transaction given a similar absence of pre-exiting regulatory jurisdiction or activity. This prediction would most undermine the author's expectation that:

Question category: _____

_____

Question type: _____

_____

Translation: _____

_____

_____

_____

Explanations for Exercise 2: Paraphrasing the Questions

1. Question Category: Specific
    Question Type: Inference
    Translation: What does the author think about the use of HDR as an alternative energy when traditional recovery systems fail?

2. Question Category: Complex
    Question Type: Structure
    Translation: Why does the author use the example of labor negotiation in the discussion of triadic and quadratic models?

3. Question Category: Complex
    Question Type: Strengthen
    Translation: The luminosity and pulsation of which type of star would best prove the author's argument regarding the behavior of certain unusual stars?

4. Question Category: Specific
    Question Type: Retrieval EXCEPT
    Translation: What WOULDN'T the author recommend to the owner of land where building is being fast-tracked?

5. Question Category: Specific
    Question Type: Inference
    Translation: What is the most valid criticism raised by the advocates of non-regulation regarding these corporations?

6. Question Category: Complex
    Question Type: Weaken EXCEPT (which is not exactly the same as Strengthen)
    Translation: When "nation" and "state" are viewed as related concepts, political concerns take precedence over methodology outside of academia – what part of the author's argument is this most consistent with?

7. Question Category: Complex
    Question Type: New Information - Analogy
    Translation: How would "differential empathy" apply to a lawyer (like it does to a large-animal vet)?

8. Question Category: Complex
    Question Type: New Information/Weaken
    Translation: Stunwitnow's prediction that the taxation of unearned benefits would be the same as that of earned benefits would undermine what expectation held by the author?

Exercise 3: Process of Elimination

Choose a passage from your practice materials. You can use the Individual Passage Drills or other printed passages. Put a sheet of paper over the passage, so that only the questions and answer choices are visible. Read each question carefully. Based on your knowledge of question types and common Attractors, eliminate the most suspicious choices and choose what you believe to be the most likely credited response.

For example, consider the following question:

1. The primary purpose of the passage is to:

A) urge consumers to demand quicker development of HDR resources for the production of energy.

B) denounce the federal government for its resistance to necessary changes in its long term energy policy.

C) compare and contrast the energy policies of developed and less-developed nations.

D) discuss the advantages and disadvantages of HDRs as an alternative energy source.

MCAT passage authors rarely call on the reader to take action, nor do they commonly denounce or severely criticize anybody. Thus choices A and B are likely to be inconsistent with the author's attitude and purpose. Choice C is more neutral in tone, but is it really possible to undertake such a wide-ranging study in the course of a few paragraphs? This choice is probably too broad. Choice D is more narrow than choice C, but not too narrow to describe a discussion carried out over 60–70 lines. It is also middle-of-the road in tone, as are most MCAT passages. Thus choice D is the most likely choice. (It is, in fact, the credited response.)

Of course you should never answer the questions without reading the passage on the test! However, after completing this exercise for several passages, you'll be surprised how often you do arrive at the credited response. You'll also increase your sensitivity to, and awareness of, the kinds of suspicious wording that often shows up in Attractors.

Exercise 4: Writing Your Own Questions

Take a passage from your practice materials. Put a piece of paper or a series of Post-It® Notes over the questions and the answer choices, so that only the passage itself is visible. Read the passage, mapping and annotating as usual. Based on what you see in the passage (for example, comparisons and contrasts, use of examples or lists, unexpected changes in direction, the author's tone or attitude, etc.), predict what questions would likely appear attached to this passage, and what kind of trap answers they will employ.

Now, write your own questions and answer choices, based on those predictions. At this point, feel free to go back to the passage and read it more carefully then you normally would the first time through. Imagine that you are an MCAT writer, trying to confuse the test taker with complex questions or trick the test taker into choosing Attractor answer choices. Try to write at least one question from each of the most common question types (Retrieval, Inference, Vocabulary in Context, Structure, Strengthen/Weaken, New Information, Main Point/Primary Purpose), but come up with as many, from any category of question, as you can. Now lift up the paper or the Post-It® Notes and work through the questions they give you. How accurately did you predict the questions? Did predicting the questions and trap answer choices help you more effectively answer their questions?

A variation on this exercise is to keep the existing questions but write your own sets of answer choices.

If you are studying with other people, exchange questions on the same passage with each other. Use your knowledge of Attractors to write questions that are defensible but difficult. See how often you fall for each other's Attractors.

You will find that by doing this exercise, you deepen your understanding of how this test is written, and that you are more able to predict and eliminate tricky wrong answers.

9.3 MANAGING STRESS: PREPARING FOR THE DAY OF THE TEST

There are a variety of things you can do in the time remaining to make the day of the MCAT as comfortable and familiar as possible.

- Make peace with your anxiety. Everyone experiences it, including the highest scorers. Feel free to be nervous on test day and the several days (or weeks) before. Even if you don't sleep well the night before the test, you'll be fine. Nervousness can be a good thing; adrenaline intensifies your ability to concentrate intensely.

- Let go of the need to be perfect. You don't need to complete every question, or get every question that you complete correct, to get a high Verbal score.

- This is not the time to quit smoking (do that *after* the MCAT) or give up caffeine, but take care of your health. Keep eating well and exercising up until the test date. And, don't turn to drugs or alcohol for stress management, and definitely don't start experimenting with black-market ADHD drugs! Maintain a habit of 7–8 hours of sleep (per night, not per week). Get up at roughly the same time each morning as you will on test day.

- Whenever possible, practice Verbal Reasoning at the same time of day as the real test, especially if you are taking an early morning test.

- Make a plan for getting to your testing site, and practice it. What time will you get up? What will you eat? What route will you take to the test site? Make sure that you plan to leave in plenty of time to get there a little early. Drive to the site at the same time as you will on the day of the test to see how long it takes you.

- Visualize success. Elite athletes, before each competition, visualize themselves going through each step of a successful performance. This both calms their nerves and focuses them on the task at hand. Remember a time in which you worked through a passage or set of passages with good results, and mentally run through the steps you took. Recall the sense of control and confidence you have when you stay calm and focused, use the techniques you've learned, and take charge of the material. If you begin to feel stress or anxiety, close your eyes and remember that feeling.

Chapter 9 Summary

- Continue to evaluate your performance and diagnose reasons for mistakes. Focus on correcting bad habits, rather than on doing as many practice passages as possible.

- Continue to hone your skills in the three basic areas: working the passage, translating the questions, and POE.

- Monitor your stress level and find ways to relax. Don't wait to feel overwhelmed; build "vacations" into your weekly study schedule.

CHAPTER 9 PRACTICE PASSAGES

Individual Passage Drills

You may wish to use these passages for Exercises 3 and 4 from this chapter. If not, do them back-to-back, timed, at the pace you have determined works best for you (for most people, this will be the Q + 3 rate).

Once you have completed the passages and checked your answers, fill out the Individual Passage Logs. Focus in particular on identifying continuing patterns in the mistakes you are making, as well as identifying times when you successfully implemented appropriate strategies.

CHAPTER 9 PRACTICE PASSAGE 1

"To live as our fathers and grandfathers lived will not do. The village resident more and more feels that his life is connected by thousands of invisible threads not only with his fellow villagers, with the nearest rural township, but this connection goes much farther. He dimly perceives that he is a subject of a vast state, and that events taking place far from his place of birth can have a much greater influence on his life than some event in his village." — Petr Koropachinskii, Ufa Provincial Zemstvo Chairman, 1906

When Koropachinskii wrote these words, he viewed the "invisible threads" connecting the villager with the state as a new political consciousness gained primarily through the political mobilization of the 1905 revolution. Salient features of this mobilization, such as political parties, their programs, and a freer press, drew the attention of political actors at the time and, subsequently, of historians of late imperial Russia. We might consider these connections from another perspective, however: that of the state and the "invisible threads" it used to connect with its subjects. Furthermore, many of these connections were not so much invisible threads as paper trails — written documents found in the files of bureaucracies staffed by officials who sought to extend the regime's knowledge about its population.

[One such method,] registration through the state church, presented complications in an empire composed of many religious groups. Not all of the tsar's subjects were Orthodox. What to do about the rest? As Gérard Noiriel has pointed out, the Old Regime in France had faced a similar problem. Registration by Catholic priests left many Jews and Protestants without civil status. In 1792, the revolutionary Republic addressed this situation by secularizing registration and requiring municipal authorities to register all French citizens. This option held little attraction for the Russian state, where an autocrat ruled an empire organized by legal estates. Tsar Nicholas had no interest in creating citizens. As protector of the Orthodox Church, Nicholas I did not desire to eliminate religious registration, either.

Nonetheless, Nicholas I and his officials did seek to identify the tsar's subjects and to include them in the civic order. The tsarist regime attempted to achieve the civic inclusion of the non-Orthodox by insisting that they register with their own religious institutions. Between 1826 and 1837, the tsar decreed that Catholic priests, Muslim imams, Lutheran pastors, and Jewish rabbis must keep metrical registers. These laws did not extend civil status to all religious groups. Religious dissenters known as Old Believers, numbering as much as 10 percent of the empire's population, and animist peoples were notable exceptions. The Orthodox Church claimed Old Believers as part of its flock, but the dissenters had rejected seventeenth-century reforms in the liturgy and generally wanted nothing to do with the Orthodox clergy. Furthermore, the expansion of metrical registration came at the expense of uniformity. Muslim imams did not report estate status. Religious leaders who did not know Russian could maintain the books in their native languages — the imams could use Tatar, for instance. Nonetheless the expansion of metrical books in the 1820s and 1830s represented a major step toward the inclusion of the empire's non-Orthodox residents into legally recognized subjecthood.

[Decades later, under a different regime,] the Great Reform era brought a new governing ethos to the empire, one that changed the role of metrical registration. Reform-minded bureaucrats sought to increase the population's participation in the administration of the empire and to reduce the importance of estate distinctions. The state emancipated the peasantry, introduced a new court system, and allowed elected units of self-administration (zemstvos) a limited role in local affairs. The military service reform of 1874 marked a shift toward the equalization of male subjects in law. Before 1874, military service was an obligation for those of lower status. The military reform of 1874 made males of all estates liable for military service. A universal military obligation, with reduced burdens based on educational achievement, replaced an estate-based system. After the Great Reforms, the autocracy took the first, halting steps toward a more inclusive, less particularistic civic order.

Material used in this particular passage has been adapted from the following source:

C. Steinwedel, "Making Social Groups, One Person at a Time: The Identification of Individuals by Estate, Religious Confession, and Ethnicity in Late Imperial Russia," *Documenting Individual Identity: The Development of State Practices in the Modern World.* © 2001 by Princeton University Press.

1. Nicholas I's regime ordered inhabitants of Russia to register with their particular religious institutions because:

A) the Orthodox Church would have required registrants to convert.

B) the tsar did not want to extend civil rights to all people by having the state register them.

C) some political parties, such as the Old Believers, rejected the authority of the Catholic Church.

D) the military service reform of 1874 had not yet been enacted to equalize the status of the male population.

2. Suppose a Russian peasant in the early 20th century returning home from a day's work first told his wife of rumors from St. Petersburg that the tsar had been deposed and only later mentioned to her, as an afterthought, that the local Orthodox Church had new priest. Based on the information in the passage:

A) the peasant's conversation with his wife supports the claim that Old Believers did not value the Orthodox Clergy.

B) the tsar's hope of including subjects in the civic order through registration had been fulfilled.

C) the peasant is likely part of a minority religious group not recognized by the Orthodox Church.

D) the peasant's behavior may strengthen Koropachinskii's assertions in paragraph 1.

3. Which of the following is LEAST supported by the passage?

A) Nicholas I's new court system sought to increase the population's participation in the administration of his empire.

B) Some residents of Russia were not citizens prior to the reign of Nicholas I.

C) Nicholas I had an interest in maintaining the power of the Orthodox Church.

D) Not all Russian residents understood the official language.

4. Which of the following events, if it occurred, would most support the author's description of the changes happening in Russian society and politics in the 1870s?

A) Old Believers and animists united to oppose registration and were granted independent civil status in 1835.

B) A peasant attended university in 1880 and was then elected chairman of the zemstvo.

C) A man in early 20th century Russia had a life different from his father's.

D) The progress of the so-called Great Reform era was reversed upon Nicholas II's ascent to the throne.

5. The author's discussion of Koropachinskii's assertions most supports which of the following statements?

A) The changes Koropachinskii identified were possible only after the advent of political parties and a freer press.

B) Religion was less important in people's lives than were the affairs of government.

C) Koropachinskii did not believe the threads were actually invisible.

D) Part of the chairman's statement may not be entirely accurate.

6. The passage includes discussion of Gérard Noiriel's work in order to do all of the following EXCEPT:

A) help place events in Russia in a broader context.

B) provide a precedent for the author's analysis of Nicholas I's policies.

C) offer one solution Nicholas I declined to pursue.

D) illustrate another situation where the Orthodox Church served a majority but not all of the population.

CHAPTER 9 PRACTICE PASSAGE 2

One difficulty in following Adam Smith's account of self-interest is that he had discussed the matter thoroughly in the *Theory of Moral Sentiments*, and he assumed that the reader of the *Wealth of Nations* would not think that he, Smith, considered self-interest the only or even the main motive, or virtue, of humanity. His teacher, Hutchenson, indeed, had taught that the only virtue was benevolence; but Smith, while agreeing that this was the major virtue and the one which aimed "at the greatest possible good," felt strongly that the system of benevolent ethics was too simple and left no room for the "inferior virtues." Therefore he devoted himself to a more naturalistic theory of morals, in which man's nature was accepted as it was.

In the *Wealth of Nations*, Smith combined the two doctrines: God's providential benevolence and man's earthly self-interest. The result is his famous "invisible hand" theory in which the individual, intending only his own gain, is led "to promote an end which was no part of his intention," the well-being of society. The view that personal self-interest is the best regulator of public affairs had been put forward before: it is expressed in Bernard de Mandeville's, *Private Vices, Public Benefits*. When Smith wrote, this view was already familiar to eighteenth-century thinkers. What Smith did was to give it a reasoned economic exposition which made it acceptable and, so to speak, respectable. From then on, the inevitable benefits of self-interest become a doctrine to which rising manufacturers and owners of newly enclosed land constantly appealed. However, he was constantly inveighing against the farmers, the workers, the manufacturers, and the banks, complaining that they did not understand their own particular interests. He chided the mercantilists that their very cupidity, by imposing a heavy duty on certain goods, called into being a smuggling of the goods which ruined their business. Country gentlemen were told that in their demand for a bounty on corn "they did not act with that complete comprehension of their own interest" which should have directed their efforts.

Smith's method was to form out of experience an abstract principle, to state this as a general rule and to give evidence and examples to support it. Thus, he and his science of economics could show "how" and "in what manner." In order to discover such a science of economics, however, Smith had to posit a faith in the orderly structure of nature, underlying appearances and accessible to man's reason. This, in our judgment, is what Smith really meant by the "invisible hand"; that, so to speak, an "order of nature" or a "structure of things" existed which permitted self-interest, if enlightened, to work for mankind's good.

Man's task, therefore, was to understand the nature or structure of things and to adjust himself harmoniously to the necessary results of this structure. On one level, this might mean the acceptance of a "natural" price of things (reached when the supply, whether of goods or of labor, exactly equaled the demand). On another level, Smith applied his faith in a structure of things when he said: "A nation of hunters can never be formidable to the civilized nations in their neighbourhood. A nation of shepherds may." This is true, he thought, because the nature of hunting is such that large numbers cannot indulge in it; the game would be exterminated. On the other hand, shepherds can grow in number as their flocks grow: and can carry war into the hearts of civilized nations because they carry with them their food supply.

What effect did Smith's work actually have? First, it gave the rising manufacturers and merchants a rationale for their desire to change existing government policy. (Existing policy, as we have pointed out, favored the older trades, methods, and classes against the new "Lunar Society" type of individual and enterprise.) Thus, for example, it helped Pitt to pass a free-trade agreement, the Eden Treaty of 1786 with France, through Parliament.

The second effect of Smith's work was in the shaping of thought. His influence in introducing historical method into political economy was far-reaching. He made the foundation of all subsequent economics the notion that wealth was created by labor. But, more than any of these things, he introduced science into the study of economics. Although he talked much about the "invisible hand" and the "natural course of things," Smith really freed man from the tyranny of chance by forming for him the analytical tools with which he might learn to control his economic activities.

Material used in this particular passage has been adapted from the following source:

J. Bronowski and B. Mazlish, *The Western Intellectual Tradition.* ©1960 by HarperCollins Publishers.

1. The author states that Smith draws which of the following relationships between nature and economics?

A) Humans are selfish, and always take as much from the marketplace as they can.
B) Humans are inherently communal beings, and share all their resources.
C) Humans fundamentally act in their own interest.
D) Humans are generous, and act in defense of others.

2. Which of the following statements, if true, would most *undermine* the author's characterization of Smith?

A) Smith extrapolated his theories from real-life observations.
B) Smith's work was wholly theoretical.
C) Smith based part of his work on an older idea.
D) Smith's theory influenced the work of later economists.

3. Which of the following items of information from the passage most supports the author's claim that Smith believed that the economy can be not only studied but influenced by human actions?

A) Smith felt that the system of benevolent ethics was too simple and left no room for the "inferior virtues."
B) Smith combined two doctrines to create his "invisible hand" theory.
C) Smith introduced a historical method into the study of economy.
D) Smith criticized businessmen who did not act in their own best interest.

4. According to the information provided, the attitude of the author towards Smith's theories can best be described as:

A) exuberant support.
B) informed approval.
C) qualified praise.
D) inexplicable disappointment.

5. A reasonable supposition from passage information about Smith and de Mandeville is that they agreed that:

A) individual motivation can provide a benefit to society.
B) benevolence is the only virtue.
C) a naturalist theory of morals would prove the most accurate.
D) economics is a science.

6. The term "invisible hand" in Smith's economic theory is most defined by the principle that:

A) there is a "natural" price of things.
B) individual action can influence society.
C) economics can be quantified through analytical tools.
D) manufacturers can change existing government policy.

7. According to the author, Smith's most important contribution to economics was:

A) identifying benevolence as man's only virtue.
B) identifying the role of nature in economics.
C) identifying self-interest as the best regulator of public affairs.
D) identifying a method by which to analyze economic activity.

SOLUTIONS TO CHAPTER 9 PRACTICE PASSAGE 1

1. **B**   This is an Inference question.

   A: No. The passage does not suggest that the Orthodox Church would *require* conversion.

   B: **Yes. See the end of paragraph 3 and the beginning of paragraph 4. Nicholas rejects the French solution, municipal registration, because "Nicholas had no interest in creating citizens…Nicholas I and his officials did seek to identify the tsar's subjects and to include them in the civic order. The tsarist regime attempted to achieve the civic inclusion of the non-Orthodox by insisting that they register with their own religious institutions."**

   C: No. The Catholic Church is not the church from which the Old Believers (who also aren't described as a political party) dissented—they rejected the Orthodox Church (paragraph 4).

   D: No. Even though this choice includes an accurate description of the military service reform of 1874, lack of equality is not, according to the passage, the reasoning behind Nicholas's religious registration.

2. **D**   This is a New Information question.

   A: No. The peasant and his wife were not identified as Old Believers. Furthermore, there is no suggestion in the new information that the actions of the peasant indicate anything about ideas of Old Believers regarding the value of the Orthodox Church.

   B: No. This situation doesn't specifically relate to the issue of religious registration.

   C: No. The peasant and his wife were not identified with any fringe or minority religious group.

   D: **Yes. Koropachinskii notes that a Russian villager, "dimly perceives that he is a subject of a vast state and that events taking place far from his place of birth can have a much greater influence on his life than some event in his village." The fact that the peasant reports rumors regarding the distant tsar before he reports more concrete news about his own village could support Koropachinskii's assertion.**

3. **A**   This is an Inference/Except question.

   A: **Yes. The correct answer will be the statement that is NOT supported by the passage. The author does not state that Nicholas I instituted a new court system. This came "decades later, under a different regime" (paragraph 5).**

   B: No. In paragraph 3 and paragraph 4, the author states that "Nicholas had no interest in creating citizens" through registration. Note that although the passage doesn't say that Nicholas made everyone citizens, this choice is still correct in saying that not everyone was a citizen before his reign (even if during and after his reign that may still have been the case).

   C: No. The end of paragraph 3 says, "As protector of the Orthodox Church, Nicholas I did not desire to eliminate religious registration either." If Nicholas sought to protect a function of the Church, this suggests that he had an interest in maintaining the Church's power.

   D: No. The end of paragraph 4 states that some religious groups in Russia whose leaders "did not know Russian could maintain the books in their native languages."

4. **B** This is a Strengthen question.

    A: No. This would likely undermine the author's description of events; the passage indicates in paragraph 4 that Nicholas I was opposed to extending civil recognition to these groups.

    B: Yes. If a peasant had access to higher education and was then able to rise to a position of power in local government, it supports the claim in paragraph 5 that eventually measures were taken to promote a "more inclusive, less particularistic civil order."

    C: No. This is consistent with Koropachinskii's description of Russian life in paragraph 1, but the question asks you to support the author's description, not Koropachinskii's.

    D: No. Ultimately, this choice is irrelevant to the author's description. The passage never argues or suggests that the changes were temporary. Furthermore, the passage never discusses the reign of Nicholas II, only that of Nicholas I.

5. **D** This is an Inference question.

    A: No. The author does say that the changes Koropachinskii noted occurred as a result of shifts in 1905 that included the advent of a freer press and political parties, but the author never says that those were the *only* things that could have led to these changes. This choice is too extreme.

    B: No. The author's discussion does not suggest that religion became less important than government, just that the state's actions served to make people aware that they were part of something larger than simply their individual townships.

    C: No. While the author notes in paragraph 2 that "these connections were not so much invisible threads as paper trails — written documents," this is the author's belief, not Koropachinskii's.

    D: Yes. The author states in paragraph 2 that "these connections were not so much invisible threads as paper trails — written documents."

6. **D** This is a Structure/Except question.

    A: No. When the author says "the Old Regime in France had faced a similar problem," he's announcing a parallel between Old France and the events in Russia, creating a broader context.

    B: No. The events in France occurred prior to the events in Russia. Therefore, the case of France can be seen as a precedent.

    C: No. This choice is in line with the author's analysis of Noiriel's parallel: that the French option "held little attraction" for Nicholas (paragraph 3).

    D: Yes. The correct answer will be the statement that doesn't explain why the author cited Noiriel. The Orthodox Church was never mentioned as being in France—the only cited French religious authority is the Catholic Church (paragraph 3).

SOLUTIONS TO CHAPTER 9 PRACTICE PASSAGE 2

1. **C** This is a Retrieval question.

   A: No. This overstates Smith's contention that self-interest is the primary motivation of humans. While one might call acting in one's self interest "selfish," the author does not indicate that self-interest always involves taking as much as one can. For example, in the second half of paragraph 2 the author suggests that self-interest is more complex.

   B: No. Although the passage mentions benevolence (paragraph 1) and Smith's acceptance of it as "the major virtue," this answer choice misrepresents how Smith saw human nature as fundamentally self-interested (paragraphs 1 and 2).

   C: **Yes. The author most directly discusses the relationship between nature and economics in paragraph 3: "In order to discover such a science of economics, however, Smith had to posit a faith in the orderly structure of nature...This...is what Smith really meant by "the invisible hand"; that...an "order of nature" or a "structure of things" existed which permitted self-interest, if enlightened, to work for mankind's good." Also, in paragraph 1 and the beginning of paragraph 2 the author discusses how Smith believed that humans are motivated by their own self-interest, which grows out of man's very nature.**

   D: No. Despite the mention of benevolence in paragraph 1, the passage does not indicate that humans are fundamentally generous, nor that they act in defense of others as a general rule.

2. **B** This is a Weaken question.

   A: No. The author characterizes Smith as forming an abstract principle out of real-life experience (paragraph 3.) Therefore, this choice is consistent, not inconsistent, with the passage.

   B: **Yes. The author stresses the real-life evidence formulating Smith's theories, and the real-life impact they had (see paragraph 2 for examples). Therefore this statement, if true, would undermine the author's characterization of Smith.**

   C: No. Smith did base his work in part on the work of Hutchenson and de Mandeville (see paragraphs 1 and 2). This choice is consistent with the passage.

   D: No. The author states that Smith's work laid the foundation of all subsequent economic studies (see paragraph 6). This choice is consistent with the passage.

3. **D** This is an Evaluate question.

   Note: This question asks you to decide which of the four statements cited in the choices is most directly used within the passage as support for the author's own claim that Smith believed the economy can be influenced.

   A: No. This statement represents the inspiration for Smith's theory, but does not demonstrate that Smith feels that the economy can be influenced.

   B: No. The fact that the "invisible hand" theory combines two different elements (the doctrines of "God's providential benevolence and man's earthly self-interest" (paragraph 2) does not show that Smith feels that the economy can be influenced. These are two separate issues in the passage.

   C: No. This answer speaks to how the economy is now studied (paragraph 6), but has no direct relevance to whether or not the economy can actually be influenced.

   D: **Yes. The fact that Smith actively tried to get farmers, workers, and manufacturers to act in their own best interest (and not just their perception of it) clearly indicates that by changing their behavior, he feels that he can change the marketplace (see paragraph 2). Therefore, out of the four choices (all of which are from the passage), this information most acts to give support for the claim cited in the question stem.**

4. **B**   This is a Tone/Attitude question.

   A: No. This answer is too extreme. The author does give Smith's work credit, but in a balanced manner.

   B: **Yes. The author provides concrete reasons for his support of Smith's work.**

   C: No. There is no qualification of, or stepping back from, the praise that the author has for Smith's work.

   D: No. The passage is complimentary towards Smith, and gives no indication of disappointment.

5. **A**   This is an Inference question.

   A: **Yes. As we can see in paragraph 2, they both believe that "personal self-interest is the best regulator of public affairs."**

   B: No. This is Hutchenson's idea, not de Mandeville's. Also, we know from paragraph 1 that Smith does not agree with this idea, because his work is based on a modification of it.

   C: No. We are not told how de Mandeville (mentioned only in paragraph 2) would feel about such a statement.

   D: No. According to the passage, it was Smith who "introduced science into the study of economics" (paragraph 6); we have no way of knowing whether de Mandeville would agree or not.

6. **B**   This is an Inference question.

   A: No. While Smith does believe in the possibility of a "natural" price of things (see paragraph 4), this is not the primary principle underlying his "invisible hand" theory. The idea of the "natural" price level creates a backdrop within which Smith's "invisible hand" (human self-interest) may act.

   B: **Yes. Smith believes that people acting in self-interest will have an inadvertent affect on the "well-being of society" (see paragraph 2). This is at the heart of Smith's theory of the "invisible hand."**

   C: No. Although Smith did introduce analytical tools to the study of economics (paragraph 6), the idea of quantification is not presented as an underlying principle of the "invisible hand" theory.

   D: No. While paragraph 5 that explains that Smith's theory provides manufacturers a rationale for desiring change in government policy, the author does not present this very specific possibility as an underlying principle (nor do we know that the manufacturers were successful).

7. **D**   This is a Retrieval question.

   A: No. This was Hutchenson, not Smith (see paragraph 1).

   B: No. Smith used the term "nature" but the passage does not suggest that he was the first to connect human nature (or the nature of things in general) to economics, or that this was the most important aspect of Smith's work.

   C: No. This was an aspect of his contribution, but the author specifically describes the "science" that Smith provides as his most important contribution to the study of economics (paragraph 6).

   D: **Yes. The author stresses that his lasting and most important contribution was introducing a scientific methodology to economics (paragraph 6).**

Individual Passage Log

Passage # _____

Q#	Q type	Attractors	What did you do wrong?

Revised Strategy _____

Passage # _____

Q#	Q type	Attractors	What did you do wrong?

Revised Strategy _____

Chapter 10
Final Preparation

GOAL

- To stay relaxed and focused

10.1 MENTAL PREPARATION

Yes, the MCAT is very important to your future. Medical schools put a lot of emphasis on the MCAT score and therefore you're likely to feel a great deal of pressure and anxiety about the test. We know this. You know this.

More importantly, however, the AAMC knows this. In fact, they are counting on it to "standardize" you. They want you to become nervous about finishing, to wonder how well you are doing compared to the person next to you, and to start watching the clock, rushing, and re-thinking your strategy. (This is one of the reasons that the Verbal Reasoning section is too long to do it well in the time allotted.)

However, having completed your entire Verbal Reasoning preparation with us, you will be much better prepared for the test than most of your peers. Nobody else will have had a more rigorous experience. You've learned about how the test is put together, you've practiced the types of reading strategies needed for the exam, you've evaluated your strengths and weaknesses, and have un-learned the habits the AAMC is counting on to standardize you. In other words, you are as well-prepared as humanly possible to beat the odds and to score well on the MCAT.

Take time to prepare mentally also. Visualize yourself calm and confident on the day of the exam. See yourself alert and rested. Imagine beginning the test with confidence because you have seen and practiced on dozens of tests just like it.

Your main job in the last week before the exam is to keep yourself relaxed and focused. Don't burn yourself out at the end. Taper off the hours you spend per day on homework as you approach the test day. Continue to practice your stress reduction techniques. Make time for some enjoyable activities.

Here are some suggestions for the day before—and of—the MCAT:

- Do not study the day before the test. Try to do some light exercise (don't overdo it), eat well, watch a funny movie, and get to bed at your regular set time.
- While waiting to be seated, if other test-takers are gathered together talking frantically about their fears or, on the other hand, about their superior preparation, step away. Don't let anyone make you nervous or negatively influence your calm, confident state of mind.
- Once the test begins, follow the strategy that you have outlined for yourself. Work calmly and methodically. Do not re-think your strategy or your career choice at this point! If you feel that the test is very hard and that you do not have enough time to finish it, then you are doing it correctly—this is not a reason to panic.
- Put things into perspective—do not overestimate the importance of the results of this particular test. It is not the only thing in your admissions packet. Yes, the test is a big deal, but schools look at a large array of things when evaluating candidates.
- Plan to reward yourself after the test. Make plans with friends or family to do something that you like to do. You deserve a reward!

CHAPTER 10 PRACTICE PASSAGES

Individual Passage Drill

On the following pages are two final individual passages. Do them timed, but with an intense focus on maximizing both your accuracy and your efficiency. After completing the passages and checking your answers, fill out the Individual Passage Logs.

Identify continuing patterns in the mistakes you are making, as well as identifying times when you successfully implemented appropriate strategies.

CHAPTER 10 PRACTICE PASSAGE 1

Basketball, a game of constant movement and a thousand actions, is a difficult game to remember; Leonard Koppett makes this and other excellent points in *All About Basketball*. Football is a series of set plays, as clear in our minds as moves in chess; and the high drama of a baseball game is often distilled in a single pitch, catch, throw, or hit. We remember baseball and football actions as though the players were etched upon our minds like figures on a distant green. In basketball, by contrast, we remember movement, style, flair, but only occasionally a single play. Perhaps we recall the seventh game of the Lakers-Knicks playoff on May 8, 1970, after the Lakers had pounded the Knicks in the sixth game. Willis Reed was injured and out, it seemed, for the season; and we may remember Reed walking stiffly to the floor for that final game just minutes before warm-ups were concluded; remember the sustained ovation; remember his stiff jumps as he put the first two shots of the game through and then had to leave the game in pain; remember that the Knicks, lifted high by his courage, went on to win game seven, bringing to New York basketball a new perspective. But it is hardly ever, even here, individual plays one remembers. A basketball game plays past like a river, like a song.

In basketball as in no other sport, Koppett also notes, the referee is part of the drama. Decisions of the scorer and the timer are critical and affect the outcomes of countless games every year. But the referee is an agent, an actor; he affects the changing tissue of the drama every instant. He cannot call every infraction, but he must control the game. He needs to gain the players' and the crowds' attention, respect, and emotional cohesion. Thus, referees like Pat Kennedy, Sid Borgia, and Mendy Rudolph in the NBA became better known than many of the players. Each blew the whistle in a range of different tones and styles; each had a repertoire of operatic gestures; each had an energy and physical exuberance that added to the total drama. All won respect for coolness under withering emotion.

Basketball players are visible in every action, Koppett notes, and easily singled out by the spectators as football players are not. They handle the ball scores of times and are physically involved in every moment of offense and defense, as baseball players are not. They are subject to many more flukes than baseball or football players, for they pass and run at high speed constantly, forcing dozens of errors, breaks, and opportunities. "Don't shoot!" the coach screams in despair, his voice trailing off to "Nice shot" as he sits down.

Teams move in patterns, in rhythms, at high velocity; one must watch the game abstractly, not focusing on any single individual alone, but upon, as it were, the blurred and intricate designs woven by the paths through which all five together cast a spell upon an opposition. The eye watches five men at once, delighting in their unity, groaning at their lapses of concentration. Yet basketball moves so rapidly and so depends on the versatility of each individual in escaping from the defense intended to contain him that the game cannot be choreographed in advance. Twelve men are constantly in movement (counting two referees), the rebounds of the ball are unpredictable, the occasions for passing or dribbling or shooting must be decided instantaneously; basketball players must be improvisers. They have a score, a melody; each team has its own appropriate tempo, a style of game best suited to its talents; but within and around that general score, each individual is free to elaborate as the spirit moves him. Basketball is jazz: improvisatory, free, individualistic, corporate, sweaty, fast, exulting, screeching, torrid, explosive, exquisitely designed for letting first the trumpet, then the sax, then the drummer, then the trombonist soar away in virtuosic excellence.

The point to stress is the mythic line of basketball: a game of fake and feint and false intention, a game of run, run, run; a game of feet, of swift decision, instantaneous reversal, catlike "moves", cool accuracy, spring and jump. The pace is hot. The rhythm of the game beats with the seconds: a three-second rule, a ten-second rule, a rule to shoot in twenty-four seconds. Only when the ball goes out of bounds, or a point is scored, or a foul is called does the clock stop; the play flows on. Teams do not move by timeless innings as in baseball, nor by set, formal, single plays as in football. Even when a play is called or a pattern is established, the game flows on until a whistle blows, moving relentlessly as lungs heavy and legs weary. It is like jazz.

Material used in this particular passage has been adapted from the following source:
M. Novak, *The Joy of Sports*. © 1976 by HarperCollins.

1. We can justifiably infer from this passage that the appearance of Willis Reed at the seventh game of the Lakers-Knicks playoff in 1970:

A) brought New Yorkers a new perspective on the significance of physical injury.
B) played some part in the Knicks' victory.
C) was at the insistence of his coach.
D) was necessary to the Knick's victory.

2. As it is used in the context of the passage, word "operatic" in paragraph 2 most nearly means:

A) classical.
B) musical.
C) comedic.
D) histrionic.

3. Which of the following would most *undermine* Koppett's position on the difference between basketball and other sports like football and baseball?

A) Days after a basketball game, commentators cite a memorable play made in the third quarter.
B) After a football game, commentators cite a memorable play made in the last few moments of the game.
C) Following a basketball game, commentators discuss the contrasting playing styles of team members.
D) After a basketball game, commentators discuss a particular team member's strengths and weaknesses.

4. The author most likely compares basketball to jazz primarily in order to:

A) claim that because of the fast-paced and unpredictable nature of the sport, basketball players are among the most skilled athletes.
B) suggest that, like jazz, basketball allows for flexibility and individual excellence within a set format.
C) assert that basketball is a newer and more dynamic sport than football or baseball.
D) indicate that basketball requires athletes to be fast.

5. The primary purpose of the passage is most nearly:

A) to describe the unique characteristics and challenges of the sport of basketball.
B) to defend the ideas offered in Leonard Koppett's *All About Basketball* against his critics.
C) to compare and contrast basketball players and musicians.
D) to describe the crucial role of the referee in a basketball game.

6. The role of the individual athlete during a basketball game as described by the author is most analogous to:

A) the role of the solo instrumentalist in an orchestra.
B) the role of the director of a film.
C) the role of a member of a selective think-tank in a brainstorming session.
D) the role of an average student in a class.

7. The author describes the reaction of the coach in paragraph 3 in order to do all of the following EXCEPT:

A) provide an illustration of the various emotions that can be inspired by the game.
B) contrast the limited role of the coach with the central role of the referee.
C) indicate a limitation on the role of the coach during the game.
D) communicate the unpredictable nature of the game.

CHAPTER 10 PRACTICE PASSAGE 2

It is not easy to define Benjamin Franklin's religious and moral beliefs; yet it is important to do so, because they are representative of a large body of men of his time, whose worldly success certainly derived from their beliefs. D. H. Lawrence, who was angered by all success, treats Franklin as a hypocrite who found the rules which lead to success and turned them into a religion. This analysis is certainly false, but even if it were true, it would not take us far enough. For it would not tell us what made Franklin respected by men as different as his American friends, his English enemies, and his French admirers. There was something in Franklin's beliefs which had a symbolic quality for them all.

The charge that Franklin was a hypocrite can be presented simply. He advocated many virtues at a time when he undoubtedly lapsed into some vices. He began his marriage in 1730 by bringing an illegitimate son into the house. Indeed, he may never have been very vigorous in resisting the temptations of the flesh. These lapses from the conventions of family life would not have outraged D. H. Lawrence if they had not been coupled with a certain priggishness in many of the household maxims which Franklin popularized. In 1732, Franklin began publishing *Poor Richard's Almanac*, which was by far the most successful work that he wrote, and in some ways the most influential. Like other almanacs, this is stuffed with those plums of wisdom which most people like to taste and few to digest--"hunger never saw bad bread," and "well done is better than well said." It is these crystallized plums, so eminently homely and homemade, which have made Franklin's beliefs seem commonplace.

But this criticism confuses the manner in which Franklin expressed himself — and expressed himself at all times — with the content of his thought. Franklin had a special gift for putting a thought into a simple and earthy sentence. This is a gift of expression: a rare gift, but Franklin had it to perfection. The gift has a drawback, however. In this form, Franklin's isolated thoughts do indeed wear a simple and sometimes a commonplace air. But it is a crude error to suppose therefore that the totality of Franklin's thoughts, the system into which the isolated thoughts lock and combine, is commonplace. In this respect, the simplicity of Franklin's sentences is as deceptive as the simplicity of Bertrand Russell's, and the outlook which they make up all together is equally complex.

The informality with which Franklin wrote and spoke is, however, just to his thought in one respect: he was opposed to formality and rigidity of belief. It is not merely that he did not care for the fine points of dogma; he thought it wrong in principle to wish to formulate religion in fine points. He did

not acknowledge any sectarian monopoly of truth. For example, when, at the age of 83, he stated his belief in God, he coupled it with another belief, "that the most acceptable service we render Him is doing good to His other children."

At bottom, it is this tolerance in Franklin's make-up which we must understand. He was tolerant of others because he recognized in them the same humanity that he knew in himself. He never hid his motives from himself, but neither did he belittle the motives of others. We should recognize him as honest because he judges others exactly as he judges himself, with a realistic and generous sense of what can be expected of human beings. Sustained by humanity, he could gain the respect of those as religiously diverse as the anticlerical Tom Paine and the evangelist George Whitefield.

Material used in this particular passage has been adapted from the following source:

J. Bronowski and Bruce Mazlish, *The Western Intellectual Tradition.* ©1960 by HarperCollinsPublishers.

1. Which of the following statements best expresses the main point of the passage?

A) Benjamin Franklin's writings were distinctive in his day for arguing against religious dogma and in favor of tolerance, thereby attracting much criticism from other authors.

B) The simplicity of Benjamin Franklin's writing, although somewhat at odds with the sophistication of his thought, was connected to the broad-mindedness that gained him the respect of many of his contemporaries.

C) Despite being accused of hypocrisy, Benjamin Franklin became successful due to his gift for simple speech and to his impressive tolerance.

D) Benjamin Franklin's deep insights into moral and religious questions, although gaining him the respect of many, contrasted sharply with the simplicity of his writing style.

2. It is reasonable to infer from the passage that D. H. Lawrence:

A) was more critical of Franklin's writings than of his behavior.
B) upheld in his own household and writings the accepted conventions of family life.
C) was envious of Benjamin Franklin's wealth and popularity.
D) believed that successful religions are usually hypocritical.

3. In the context of the passage, the word "vigorous" most nearly signifies:

A) healthy.
B) vociferous.
C) diligent.
D) tolerant.

4. According the passage, the relationship of Franklin's writing style to his ideas is most analogous to which of the following?

A) A symphony which alternates between fast and slow sections.
B) An intricate painting composed entirely of basic geometric shapes.
C) A novel advocating virtues that the author does not uphold in his own personal life.
D) A movie showing the same events from different perspectives, each of which is equally valid.

5. The author probably quotes Franklin in paragraph 2 in order to:

A) illustrate his simple and unpretentious style.
B) contrast Franklin's and Lawrence's moral outlook.
C) deride the trite expressions common to his more popular writings.
D) emphasize his preference for action over speech.

6. Which of the following statements, if true, would most call into question the author's characterization of Benjamin Franklin's attitude towards religion?

A) Although Franklin often attended religious services, he did not claim formal membership in any religious institution.
B) Like D. H. Lawrence, Franklin was greatly intrigued by Eastern religions, helping to bring Buddhist and Hindu lecturers to Boston and Philadelphia.
C) Franklin was influential in removing "sacred and undeniable" from Thomas Jefferson's first draft of the Declaration of Independence and in replacing these words with "self-evident."
D) Active with the Freemasons, Franklin published pamphlets denouncing the beliefs of the Catholic Church.

7. It may be inferred from the passage that each of the following describes Benjamin Franklin's writings EXCEPT:

A) they attracted some readership outside the United States.
B) they at times addressed controversial religious topics.
C) they were notable for their somewhat commonplace style.
D) their style reflected in a certain fashion Franklin's attitude towards religion.

SOLUTIONS TO CHAPTER 10 PRACTICE PASSAGE 1

1. **B** This is an Inference question.
   - A: No. While the author does ask us to "remember that the Knicks, lifted high by his courage, went on to win game seven, bringing to New York basketball a new perspective", choice A goes too far by appending the idea of "physical injury" to that new perspective.
   - **B: Yes. The author says in paragraph 1 that "the Knicks, lifted high by his courage, went on to win game seven."**
   - C: No. This choice goes too far, since we do not know from the passage what Reed's motive was, or whether or not the coach was involved in his decision to play.
   - D: No. The word "necessary" makes this choice too strong. Remember that when dealing with inferences, it is best to stick with answers that do not stray too far from the passage. It is impossible to say with certainty that the Knicks would have lost had it not been for Reed's appearance. This makes B a better supported answer than choice D.

2. **D** This is a Vocabulary in Context question.
   - A: No. While "classical" as in classical music, or, as in traditional or elegant (which are other possible interpretations of the word "classical") may come to your mind when you think of opera, there is nothing in the passage to support this interpretation of the word.
   - B: No. As in choice A, this may fit your own interpretation of "operatic," but there isn't anything in this part of the passage to suggest a connection or relationship to music.
   - C: No. "Comedic" does not fit the author's description of the referees as respected, cool under pressure, and dramatic. It also doesn't fit the author's relatively serious tone in this passage.
   - **D: Yes. Be careful not to eliminate a word just because you don't know what it means. "Histrionic" is a synonym for "dramatic" and thus best fits the author's context.**

3. **A** This is a Weaken question.
   - A: **Yes. Koppett posits in paragraph 1 that "basketball, a game of constant movement and a thousand actions, is a difficult game to remember" and that "it is hardly ever...individual plays that one remembers." Because it is fast-paced and relies on action from multiple players, the author of the passage points out, fewer single plays stick out in our minds. In order to weaken Koppett's position, our credited response should describe a memorable singular moment. Choice A does this. While this choice doesn't destroy Koppett's argument, it is the only one of the four answers that is at all inconsistent with it.**
   - B: No. Choice B describes a memorable moment in a football game, in a way that is consistent with Koppett's claim about the difference between basketball and football.
   - C: No. This answer actually strengthens Koppett's position, since the passage points out that we remember the "style, movement and flair" of basketball players (paragraph 1).
   - D: No. As in choice C, this answer is consistent, not inconsistent. According to paragraph 5, "the versatility of each individual" is crucial, and "each individual is free to elaborate as the spirit moves him." Therefore, a discussion of an individual's strengths and weaknesses would fit with Koppett's position.

4. **B**   This is a Structure question.

A: No. This choice goes too far, since the author never tells us baseball and football are not challenging in their own way.

B: Yes. The author tells us that "basketball players must be improvisers. They have a score, a melody; each team has its own appropriate tempo, a style of game best suited to its talents; but within and around that general score, each individual is free to elaborate as the spirit moves him" (paragraph 4). This answer choice is the best paraphrase of this idea.

C: No. This option takes the metaphor too literally, and is too judgmental in tone towards football and baseball. Furthermore, nothing in the passage suggests that basketball is a newer sport.

D: No. While the author does mention speed in paragraph 4, this is not the primary purpose of the metaphor, but only one of many aspects within it. The main theme of the comparison is how basketball, like jazz, relies on individual action and creativity within the context of a group or team endeavor.

5. **A**   This is a Main Idea/Primary Purpose question.

A: Yes. This choice can include all of the author's major points, without going beyond the scope of the passage.

B: No. This option is too narrow; also, the author never makes mention of any critics of Koppett's ideas.

C: No. This answer might be tempting, since so much of the passage is devoted to comparing basketball and jazz. But since the answer frames it in terms of "comparing and contrasting basketball players and musicians," it misrepresents the focus of the passage, which is on the sport of basketball itself not just the players.

D: No. This choice is too narrow. Referees are only discussed in paragraph 2, and the rest of the passage isn't given in support of the author's claims about referees in that paragraph.

6. **C**   This is an Analogy question.

A: No. The soloist may be virtuosic, but not an equal member of a team. This choice also fails to capture the theme of constant interaction in the passage.

B: No. The director of a film is in charge of the other "players" rather than being on equal footing with the rest of the team.

C: Yes. Novak describes basketball players as all being virtuosic in their own way, but working together, all players being equally necessary to success. A member of a think tank involved in a brainstorming session would play a similar role, including the constant interaction and responsiveness to new scenarios that is described in the passage.

D: No. We don't have any indication in this choice that an average student would be virtuosic in his or her own way, and yet in constant interaction with the rest of the class, improvising as the class progressed in unpredictable ways.

7. **B**   This is a Structure/Except question.

A: No. This choice is supported by the passage. The coach's reaction demonstrates varied emotions in response to the unexpected twists and turns of the game.

B: Yes. This choice is not supported by the passage, and so is the correct answer to an EXCEPT question. This answer is too extreme; we don't know from the passage that the coach's role overall is limited, just that at times the coach's instructions are invalidated by rapid changes in the game as it plays out. Also, the there is no suggestion in the passage that the purpose of the reference is to contrast the role of the coach with that of the referee in terms of their relative importance.

C: No. This statement is supported by the passage. While we don't know that the coach plays a limited role overall, his or her role during the game is constrained, such that the command "Don't shoot" is invalidated by the rapidly changing nature of play on the court.

D: No. This statement is supported by the passage. The coach's scream of "Don't shoot" is contradicted by an unpredictable shift in the game which leads to a successful shot.

SOLUTIONS TO CHAPTER 10 PRACTICE PASSAGE 2

1.   **B**   This is a Main Idea/Primary Purpose question.

A: No. This choice may be eliminated because, although Franklin and Lawrence are contrasted, the passage makes no general claim that Franklin's writings were distinctive or much criticized. In fact, paragraph 1 suggests that his beliefs were shared by a wide range of other people.

B: **Yes. Both paragraphs 1 and 5 address the respect with which Franklin was viewed. Franklin's simple writing style also relates to the tolerance (paragraph 4) which the author describes as central to his character.**

C: No. The only reference to Franklin's success is in paragraph 1, which suggests that his worldly success derived from his beliefs. While tolerance may have been one of these beliefs, the passage as a whole is not about the reasons for his success in life, but about the beliefs themselves, and how they related to his style of writing.

D: No. This choice is attractive in appearing to draw on many components of the passage. However, the author does not claim that Franklin had deep insights into religious and moral questions. Complexity of thought (paragraph 3) is not necessarily the same as deep insight. Furthermore, this answer choice says nothing about Franklin's tolerance, which is a major theme in the passage. Finally, it was this complexity, not the deepness of his insight, which contrasted with Franklin's simple writing style.

2.   **A**   This is an Inference question.

A: **Yes. Paragraph 2 emphasizes that D. H. Lawrence was not outraged by Franklin's behavior but by the apparent hypocrisy of his publications, which the author describes as described as "priggish" and "commonplace" in paragraph 2.**

B: No. We know nothing of Lawrence's own family life.

C: No. Like choice B, this reaches beyond the available information since, although Lawrence was angered by success, there is nothing in the passage to indicate envy.

D: No. This answer may be attractive because it draws on language in paragraph 1. However, Lawrence believed Franklin was hypocritical in his success; we don't know how Lawrence felt about "successful religions" in general.

3.   **C**   This is a Vocabulary in Context question.

A: No. "Healthy" may be one literal definition of "vigorous," but it doesn't fit in the context of the passage, which is about Franklin's lack of will rather than his health.

B: No. "Vociferous" means outspoken. The issue in the passage is about Franklin's behavior, not his expressed opinions (which were at odds with his behavior).

C: **Yes. The author suggests that Franklin's lapses were somewhat common and that Franklin did not make any great effort to uphold family norms.**

D: No. Tolerance is not discussed until paragraph 5, and it is not directly relevant to this discussion of Franklin's failures to live up to his own standards of virtue in his private life.

4. **B**   This is an Analogy question.

    A: No. There is no alternation or back and forth (that is, first one, then the other, then back again to the first) between Franklin's style and ideas.

    B: Yes. The principle relationship (paragraph 3) is that Franklin's simple words, taken singly, may deceptively mask the complexity of his overall thought.

    C: No. This choice is attractive because it points to the charge of hypocrisy brought against him in paragraph 2. However, the question asks about the relationship between Franklin's style and his beliefs, not about a relationship between his beliefs and his private life.

    D: No. While this choice may reflect Franklin's tolerance towards other beliefs (paragraphs 4 and 5), it doesn't match the relationship between his writing style and his beliefs.

5. **A**   This is a Structure question.

    A: Yes. These words make Franklin's beliefs seem commonplace or simple.

    B: No. There is no reference to different moral positions in this paragraph.

    C: No. While the author does say that Franklin's maxims show a certain "priggishness" and commonplace nature, the passage goes on in paragraph 3 to show that the simple and commonplace nature of Franklin's individual statements hides to some extent the true complexity of his thought. Therefore, the author is not deriding or mocking his expressions, or calling them "trite" or trivial.

    D: No. Although this is a paraphrase of the second maxim, it does not relate to the author's purpose in including the quotation, which is to illustrate the simplicity of Franklin's sayings.

6. **D**   This is a Weaken question.

    A: No. The author makes no claim concerning Franklin's formal affiliation. The passage's characterization of Franklin's attitude toward religion, or of his self-professed "belief in God," doesn't rest on an assumption that Franklin was affiliated with a particular church.

    B: No. This choice would strengthen, not weaken, the author's claim that Franklin was tolerant towards other religious beliefs.

    C: No. This answer is consistent with the author's claim that Franklin denied any "sectarian monopoly of truth" and that he resisted dogma (paragraph 4).

    D: Yes. The author characterizes Franklin's attitude as tolerant of other beliefs. As part of this argument, the author states that Franklin, because of his tolerance, was respected by other diverse religious figures (paragraph 5). If Franklin denounced the beliefs of the Catholic Church, this would significantly undermine the author's characterization. Notice the difference between choice C and choice D. Choice C involves resistance to incorporating language that suggests religious dogma into the Declaration, but does not involve criticizing any particular beliefs themselves.

7. **B**   This is an Inference/Except question.

    A: No. Paragraph 1 demonstrates that Franklin's work was known internationally.

    B: Yes. Although Franklin spoke of God (paragraph 4), there is no evidence that his writings addressed religious topics, especially controversial religious topics. Also, the fact that D.H. Lawrence claimed that Franklin "found the rules which lead to success and turned them into a religion" (paragraph 1) can't be interpreted to mean that Franklin literally wrote about religion itself. Because you cannot infer this answer to be true based on the passage, it is the correct answer to an Except question.

    C: No. Their commonplace style is discussed in paragraphs 2 and 3. Note the more moderate wording of this choice as compared to choice B.

    D: No. This is a paraphrase of the first sentence of paragraph 4. Note the difference between choice B and choice D. Choice D says that the style of Franklin's writings reflected religious attitudes, but choice B states that his writings directly addressed religious topics.

Individual Passage Log

Passage # _____   Time spent on passage _____

Q#	Q type	Attractors	What did you do wrong?

Revised Strategy _____

Passage # _____   Time spent on passage _____

Q#	Q type	Attractors	What did you do wrong?

Revised Strategy _____

Chapter 11
Introduction to
the MCAT
Writing Sample

GOALS

1. To understand the format and scoring of the MCAT Writing Sample
2. To learn the topics and instructions of the MCAT Writing Sample

11.1 INTRODUCTION TO THE MCAT WRITING SAMPLE

Test Structure

- The Writing Sample section is the third section of the MCAT.
  It consists of two separate essays to be written on two different prompts. There is no choice of topic.
- You will have 30 minutes to complete each essay, for a section total of 60 minutes.
- If you finish the first essay before the 30 minutes is over, you can move on to the second essay. However, you can not save your leftover time. You will still have only 30 minutes for the second essay.

Purpose

The Writing Sample is designed to test your ability to analyze a topic in a non-technical field and to express your ideas clearly and consistently. This is not an application essay, and it is not a place to show off your science expertise. Therefore, don't discuss why you want to go to medical school, and don't throw in lots of scientific knowledge just to try to impress the reader. Your goal is to write a logical, analytical essay that directly addresses the question.

Scoring

The MCAT Writing Sample is scored on a letter scale of J through T, with O as the national median score. The average score for those matriculating is a P.

Here's how your MCAT essays are graded: Your first essay is read by two graders, one human and one computer grading program, who each assign it a numerical raw score of 1 to 6 (in increments of .5). Your second essay is read by two different graders, again one human and one computer, who each assign it a numerical raw score on the 1 to 6 scale. If there is a difference of more than a point between the scores for a single essay, it will go to a "supervisory reader" (human) to reconcile the difference. All of the resulting numerical scores are then averaged to give the total raw score.

This total raw score is then converted to a final letter grade on the J to T scale. (Since it's only the total raw score that matters, receiving a 2 and a 1 on one essay and a 5 and a 6 on the other is the same as receiving two 4's and two 3's. The total, 14, is the same. This would average out to a raw score of 3.5 and be converted to the same letter score, an "O.")

On your MCAT Score Report, you'll receive three numerical scaled scores, one for each of the three multiple-choice sections, a combined numerical score for those three sections, and one letter score for the Writing Sample. This total combined score might look like this, for example: "32 Q."

The Topics

The questions cover a wide range of subject matter, but the topics fall into predictable categories:

- Category 1: Government/Politics–Politicians–Elections
- Category 2: Wars/International Relations
- Category 3: The Nation/Citizenship/Democracy
- Category 4: Laws/Justice
- Category 5: Business Practices
- Category 6: Morality/Ethics
- Category 7: Science/Research
- Category 8: Education
- Category 9: Media/Advertising
- Category 10: Technology/Computers
- Category 11: History
- Category 12: Right to Privacy/Individual Rights

All of these topics are based on cultural or social issues that are, or should be, in the general experience of college students. One of your goals in your essay is to present yourself as someone who has thought about important concerns in our society and who can write a well-structured and well-reasoned analysis of those issues. You should develop a basic understanding of at least two examples in each of the above areas so that you can represent yourself in this way (or at least fake it!).

Your Essay

Mechanics

Basic editing functions are available on the test; you will be able to cut, paste and copy. However, at this time spell-check is not available.

A few spelling, grammar, or syntax mistakes will probably not affect your grade. However, an essay with many mistakes will be difficult to understand, and your score will suffer.

Length

The essays are graded not on length, but on a thorough treatment of the prompt tasks. However, all other things being equal, a longer essay is likely to score higher than a shorter essay. An essay that fully address-es all three tasks is typically around 500–700 words, about the equivalent of one and a half or two typed and double spaced pages (there are no page breaks or page limits on the test). Do not, however, write just to fill up space; an essay that is long but disorganized, repetitive, or incoherent will not get a high score.

Organization

All of the questions have the same three-part format (which we will discuss below) with three distinct tasks. The simplest and clearest way to organize your essay is in three paragraphs, each paragraph focus-ing, in order, on one of the three tasks. A formal introduction and conclusion are not required. Skip a line when you begin each new paragraph.

Focus

Many excellent writers find the MCAT essay structure confining, and feel that they can display their skills better by using the topic merely as a springboard to a discussion of other loftier, more interesting ideas. This is the road to ruin. No matter how witty or articulate you are, if you fail to address the prompt and the three tasks exactly as they are posed, your score will suffer drastically. (In fact, a response that is significantly off-topic may be assigned a "grade" of X, which means "not scorable.") This is not a license to be boring. However, use your creativity and insight within the boundaries of the topic as it is presented to you.

11.2   THE PROMPT AND THE TASKS

The format of the Writing Sample is entirely predictable. The instructions for each Writing Sample consist of a prompt (a statement of policy or principle, which is to be the topic of the essay) and three tasks (in-structions) that tell you how you are to respond to the prompt.

The prompt is a claim. That is, it's a sentence that either proposes an apparent absolute truth (for example, "A politician who tells the truth can never be re-elected") or states that one option is better than another (for example, "Politicians are more likely to succeed by lying than by telling the truth."). Whatever the exact wording or subject matter of the prompt, the most important thing to remember is:

> **The prompt appears to be a statement of fact, but in the context of the three tasks, it is never completely "true" or "false."**

Your natural inclination may be to agree or disagree with the prompt, and to attempt to prove your case that the prompt is either true or false. However, that is not your job! Your job is to see the validity in both sides, analyzing when and why the prompt would be true in some cases, and when and why it would be false in different circumstances.

The Three Tasks

The one-sentence prompt is followed by a paragraph setting out the three tasks.

1. The first task asks you to explain what the statement means; that is, when and why it would be valid.
2. The second task requires you to describe a case in which the prompt would not be true.
3. The third task asks you to explain the circumstances or factors that determine when the prompt is and is not true.

These three tasks will always be essentially the same, will always be presented to you in the same order, and should always be addressed in that order within the body of your essay.

Let's look at an example. Consider this statement:

The historical record is inherently subjective.

Write a unified essay in which you perform the following tasks. Explain what you think the above statement means. Describe a specific situation in which the historical record may not be subjective. Discuss what you think determines whether or not the historical record is subjective.

The prompt claims that in the recording of history, it is impossible to be objective, and you might be inclined to agree. However, you know that the second task requires you to discuss when the historical record may in fact be objective. Therefore, don't choose sides; instead, consider both sides of the issue.

The First Task

By asking you to "Explain what the above statement means," the first task for this prompt is asking you to explain why it might be impossible to be objective in the recording of history. It is fine to argue that it's *usually* impossible, but *do not* claim in the first section that it's *always* impossible, as this will contradict what you have to say in response to the second task. When confronted with an absolute or extreme statement in the prompt, put it into more moderate terms when you address the first task. That is, use language that allows for exceptions to the rule. Although you are not explicitly asked for an example in your response to the first task, a good essay will give one as an illustration of your claims.

The Second Task

The second task asks for an example of when the historical record might not be subjective; that is, when objectivity is possible. Here you will explain the circumstances and conditions that might make it possible to be objective when creating an historical record. Notice that the second task does not explicitly ask you to describe what it means to say that the historical record may not be subjective. However, a good essay will do so by explaining *why* it is possible to be objective in the example that you give.

The Third Task

The third task asks you to describe the conditions that determine when the historical record is inherently or necessarily subjective, and the **contrasting** conditions that determine when it is not. The goal of the third task is to provide the reader with a **rule or set of criteria** that could be applied to other cases as well, to decide whether or not objectivity will be possible in those circumstances. This rule should be based on the contrast you have already illustrated between your examples in the first and second tasks. However, don't just repeat your specific examples; *generalize* based on the contrast you have drawn between them.

The T-A-S Format

For simplicity's sake, we are going to rename the three tasks. They will henceforth be known as the **Thesis** (first task), the **Antithesis** (second task), and the **Synthesis** (third task). This is a highly structured essay format, generated by the structure of the question, that will help you to complete the tasks in an organized and thoughtful manner. The **Thesis–Antithesis–Synthesis (T-A-S) format** will be explained in more detail in the next chapter. These three tasks are not merely suggestions; *you must complete all of them*. No matter how brilliant your ideas or elegant your writing, you will get a low score if you fail to address all three tasks in your essay.

11.3   HOW TO PREPARE FOR THE ESSAY

Familiarize yourself with the AAMC list of Writing Sample items (prompts). They appear on the AAMC website at www.aamc.org/students/mcat/preparing/writingsampleitems.htm. The AAMC states that the prompts that will appear on the actual MCAT will be similar or identical to those on this list.

Think about the core ideas involved in the different questions and categories. What important social, political, or ethical concern is involved in each prompt?

Generate a list of examples from current events and history. Since the topics of the prompts fall into definable categories, it is easy to prepare a set of examples that you can use for many different prompts within the same category or in similar categories. Don't worry if you are not an expert in politics, history, etc. With an hour or two a week of brainstorming and simple research (on the web, from encyclopedias, and in newspapers and news magazines), you will be well prepared for any question you might get.

Make your examples strong and thoughtful. This is one of the main ways to make your essay shine. The best examples are:

- serious (they engage significant social, cultural, or moral concerns),
- real (not hypothetical),
- specific (times, places, people, detailed descriptions), and
- relevant (to the prompt, of course).

Because the topics are so predictable, the MCAT graders will see the same ideas over and over again. Catch the human reader's eye by using an example that he or she won't have already seen a thousand times. If the prompt asks whether a politician should be judged on the basis of personal morality, for example, you *could* write about former President Clinton and Monica Lewinsky. But so will most of the other test takers. If you can instead intelligently discuss, say, Thomas Jefferson and Sally Hemings, the human grader will be much more likely to wake up and pay attention to what you have to say.

Make your examples as specific as possible. If you can go beneath the surface and give a few relevant details (for example: What specific events occurred in the Civil Rights Movement? What was Gandhi really fighting for? What are some specific relevant provisions in the U. S. Constitution? Who was Sally Hemings?), it gives great power to your argument.

Practice, practice, practice. The format and tasks of the MCAT Writing Sample can seem strange and scary at first, but after you've written a dozen or so essays, and prepared ideas and examples that can apply to the different categories of prompts, it will all become familiar and comfortable.

At the end of each chapter in this book you will find a set of drills and exercises. These include:

1. Five Timed Essays. The questions appear in Chapters 13, 14, 16, 17, and 18. Write each of these essays on your computer within a strict 30-minute time limit. Each Timed Essay and some of the other exercises are followed by an analysis of the question and sample student essays. Note that many of these essays, even high-scoring ones, have typographical, grammatical, and/or spelling mistakes; these errors are reproduced from the original student response. Be sure to read through this material *after* you have written the timed essay.
2. Two Supplemental Prompts to be completed each week. It is best to write these within a 30-minute time limit. However, if you can't write both as full essays, at least create a T-A-S outline for each essay prompt.
3. Current Events Questions designed to get you thinking about good examples.
4. Additional drills and exercises.

11.4 WRITING SAMPLE EXERCISES

Exercise 1: Sample Prompt

Let's discuss a sample question in order to take a closer look at the T-A-S structure and to do some brainstorming. (On the next few pages you will find an analysis of the prompt and sample student essays; read through this material after you have done your own brainstorming and outlining on the following page.)

Consider this statement:

> **Education should focus on developing practical abilities rather than on ethical considerations.**

Write a unified essay in which you perform the following tasks. Explain what you think the above statement means. Describe a specific situation in which education should focus on ethical considerations. Discuss what you think determines when education should focus on developing practical abilities and when it should focus on ethical considerations.

Thesis: _____

_____

_____

_____

_____

_____

_____

_____

Antithesis: _____

_____

_____

_____

_____

_____

_____

_____

Synthesis: _____

_____

_____

_____

_____

_____

_____

_____

ANALYSIS OF THE PROMPT

This is a prompt on the topic of education. In a larger sense, it's also about ethics and society. We generally consider education to be a social institution, and the prompt asks you to think about the proper relationship between the social institution of education and ethics or values. Some key questions here are: What values do we share as a society? Who should teach them? What are the obligations of schools to the students and to society? In what types of education might ethics not be important?

The Thesis

In the Thesis, you need to explain why schools should teach practical skills and why ethics (values, morals, or principles) should not be taught in some circumstances. You might argue that schools have an obligation to prepare students for jobs. Or, you could base your argument on the idea that ethics are personal and thus should be taught at home; institutions (especially public ones) should not impose ethics on people. You also need to give an example that supports this point, and you should define both "ethics" and "practical abilities."

The Antithesis

In the Antithesis, you need to explain why it is important or necessary, at least in some cases, to teach ethics, and you need to explain and describe a specific case where ethical considerations should be taught. You might argue that certain ethical values are shared by all members of a community (respect for others, respect for the law, constitutional principles, etc.). Such ethics are not controversial and are necessary for social order, and thus they should be taught.

The Synthesis

For the Synthesis, you need to be a social policy-maker: When and why should the schools teach practical skills? When should the schools deal with ethical considerations? (or, What ethics should they teach?) Why? You might argue that the "determining factor" is the type of education (primary vs. secondary, public vs. private) or the type of ethical considerations (shared values vs. personal values).

Remember in each step to explain your reasons: Why should practical skills be taught in some cases but not in others? And why should ethics be taught in some cases, but not others?

Sample Student Response #1   A favorite professor once declared that the purpose of going to college was to learn how to learn. His idea relates to the belief that the object of education should be to teach practical skills, not ethics. Many employers would agree with such an argument; they hire college graduates, not because of what they have learned, but because of the skills they have mastered in the art of learning.

In a typical classroom setting, students are taught a variety of subjects from basic math to biology to history. For at least twelve years, an individual learns about the world, both near and far away, but does this include only skills? One needs only to sit in on a government history class to see when ethics are included in education. The Bill of Rights is explained throughout a child's school life more that once—he or she learns the meaning and importance of the concept of freedom inherent in the American constitution. Yet, who would argue that freedom is a skill, when in fact, it is an ethical idea we value? It seems quite clear to me that when one learns about American History, one is being taught to value the American way of life.

However, one could argue that ethics implies morality, and that our schools are not responsible for teaching our students right from wrong. I would argue with such a simple concept—parents are responsible for the moral education of their own children. Ethical values must and should be taught at home, but does this imply that education's only purpose is to teach practical skills? Once again, it seems obvious to me that education has a variety of goals which includes both developing practical abilities and learning ethical values.

To expand on this idea, one must consider the nature of education as well as its purpose. Is education limited to the classroom, or is the classroom of life included in an individual's education? Clearly, learning does not stop once we walk through the door of any school. As such, one could conclude that life is constantly educating us—our experience is teaching us new skills and new values every day.

In short, the idea that education's only object is to develop practical skills is an unrealistic concept. Education occurs in both formal and informal settings; every day we are faced with more things to learn, and just as one cannot limit education and learning to 6 hours a day, 5 days a week, one cannot separate the learning of skills and ethics. Regardless of the source of education, the object is to teach us as much about life as we can possibly learn, skills and values included.

Sample Student Response #1—Grader's Comments: This is a thoughtful response to the prompt, and it is well written. But notice that after reading it, it's hard to know what the author really thinks. No clear ideas or memorable examples stand out. Notice the short paragraphs, and the fact that the author keeps going back between practical skills as important and ethical values as important.

Occasionally, asking rhetorical questions can be a useful strategy in an MCAT essay, but the use of questions here contributes to larger problems: this essay is wishy-washy, unorganized, and too abstract. Throughout the essay, the author tries to argue both sides of the issue. This sounds indecisive. Remember to use the first paragraph (the Thesis) to support the truth in the prompt, and use the second paragraph for supporting the opposite of the prompt (the Antithesis). Also, the examples are very broad (the "Bill of Rights"). The use of specific, concrete examples would help to make this abstract topic more manageable. This essay would really benefit from using the T-A-S format. The format is set up so that each task is separated, and this makes your writing more organized and decisive.

Score: 3

Sample Student Response #2 Californians recently were asked to vote on a proposition that would fundamentally change the way education was administered in this state. Called "The School Voucher Initiative," the proposition would allow parents to use state money to send their children to any type of school — public or private, including religious schools. The measure was defeated, but many important questions were raised considering the nature of education.

The statement suggests that education should focus on empirical knowledge and the practical application of that knowledge. It contends that ethical judgments as to whether a particular idea or course of action is "Good" or "Bad" are best left out of the classroom. This view of education undoubtedly is grounded in the principle of the separation of Church and State, a principle our

11.4

country was founded on. California voters may have been concerned that the voucher system would encourage the use of state funds for value-based (religious) education. With such a system in place, a majority religion may trample on the religious freedoms of the minority.

But is the division between skill-based and ethics-based education so clear? After all, even the most liberal public school teaches students to obey the law, tolerate cultural differences, say "no" to drugs, and value human life. Even in a public institution, the base of all instruction is the value of education itself.

Maybe the way to examine this issue is to separate "societal" values and "group" values. The proper role of public education can be said to be the instruction of empirical knowledge and "societal" values — that is, fundamental ethical ideas that society as a whole generally agrees upon (for example, the value of human life). "Group" values—that is, values held by one segment of society only (such as the worship of a god)—are best left to private (elective) institutions so that minority views are not threatened.

Sample Student Response #2—Grader's Comments: This essay has a very strong example supporting the prompt: it is current and serious, and it conveys that the author is someone who pays attention to the important issues in his or her community. The essay uses two paragraphs to complete the first task (the Thesis). There are two very good things about the Thesis: the example, and the fact that the author explains the principle of the prompt (separation of church and state, an important democratic principle). It would be stronger if the essay linked the first two paragraphs, and if it made a clear claim (e.g., that school vouchers are wrong because they would allow the government to use funds for teaching religious values). In general, this is a very good Thesis response (in support of the prompt), but it comprises over half of the essay. Try to spend an equal amount of time on each task.

The Antithesis (paragraph 3 here) is much too abstract, and it is too short. A specific example (such as a program like D.A.R.E.) would be better than this "list" of general examples that are exceptions to the prompt.

The Synthesis (the last paragraph) is very good, as far as it goes. The distinction between "group" values (like keeping kids off of drugs) and "individual" values (like religion) is a thoughtful way to "divide up" the prompt. The distinction between public and private schools also works well here, but it's usually better to choose one clear way to distinguish the Thesis and the Antithesis sides, rather than listing a variety of different factors. The Synthesis would be even stronger if it dealt with the issue of developing practical abilities and when education should focus on these skills, rather than dealing only with the issues of ethics and values.

Score: 4

Exercise 2: Developing Examples

Obtain a copy of a recent newspaper, news magazine, or web news report. Read through it and choose at least four articles that discuss different ongoing national or world events, or that analyze serious social or political issues. Look through the list of AAMC prompts and find at least two prompts relevant to each one of your chosen articles.

Exercise 3: Current Events Question

In each chapter you'll be given a question to answer based on current events. You'll soon see how important an understanding of national and international events can be for the Writing Sample.

> Describe a recent event that illustrates the current and changing role of the United Nations in world peacekeeping. In your opinion, what is the function of the U.N.? When should the U.N. become involved in affairs within or between nations, and when should it not?

Exercise 4: Supplemental Prompts

In each chapter you will be given two supplemental MCAT-style essay prompts. For the first 4–6 prompts, it is fine to take a little extra time (5–10 minutes) to make sure that you are comfortable with the format before you start to work under strict time pressure. Starting with Chapter 14's Supplemental Prompts, however, time yourself strictly; allow 30 minutes per essay for planning *and* writing. To duplicate what your test experience will be, write the essays consecutively. If you don't have time to write both essays, at least make an outline for each prompt that describes the examples you'd use to illustrate your main points. Type your essays, but don't use spell-check, since you won't have that luxury on the real test.

Supplemental Prompt 1

Consider this statement:

> **Our understanding of human events is always influenced by personal bias.**

Write a unified essay in which you perform the following tasks. Explain what you think the above statement means. Describe a specific situation in which it might be possible for our understanding of human events not to be influenced by personal bias. Discuss what you think determines when our understanding of human events is influenced by personal bias and when it is not.

Supplemental Prompt 2

Consider this statement:

> **Any radical social transformation has long-term negative effects.**

Write a unified essay in which you perform the following tasks. Explain what you think the above statement means. Describe a specific situation in which a radical social transformation might not have long-term negative effects. Discuss what you think determines whether or not radical social transformations will have long-term negative effects.

Chapter 11 Summary

- Each set of essay instructions consists of a prompt and three tasks.

- Topics typically fall into the following categories:

  - Government/Politics–Politicians–Elections

  - Wars/International Relations

  - The Nation/Citizenship/Democracy

  - Laws/Justice

  - Business Practices

  - Morality/Ethics

  - Science/Research

  - Education

  - Media/Advertising

  - Technology/Computers

  - History

  - Right to Privacy/Individual Rights

- Addressing the three tasks is the foundation of your essay and of your Writing Sample Score.

- Be creative in your logical argument, but adhere to the standard format in your essay structure and writing style. Respond to the three tasks thoroughly, clearly, and in order.

Chapter 12
The T-A-S Structure

GOALS

1. To master a strong essay structure that can be applied to any prompt
2. To manage the essay's time limit effectively

12.1 OPTIONS AND IMPERATIVES PROMPTS

Prompts can be worded in two different ways: as Options or as Imperatives. Options present two choices, valuing one over the other. Here's an example of an Options prompt:

> **In any political negotiation, cooperation works better than threats of violence.**

To address an Options prompt, discuss in the Thesis when and why the first option (here, it's cooperation) would be preferable. The Antithesis should present a case that presents an exception to that rule (here, when a threat of violence may in fact be more effective). In the Synthesis, explain what determines when the first option or the second option would be more valid.

Imperative statements *appear* to offer only a single option or choice, as in the following:

> **It is impossible for a democratic system to function without a fully informed citizenry.**

However, the essential structure of the question as a whole will always be the same. To reply to this prompt, explain in the Thesis why in some or most cases, citizens must be well-informed. You must moderate the extreme language in the prompt to avoid setting up a contradiction with your Antithesis; for example, write, "In most cases, a democratic government should not withhold information from its citizens." In the Antithesis portion of your essay, discuss when the opposite would be true—when and why a democracy can function even if citizens do not have full information. In the Synthesis, discuss in what circumstances a fully informed citizenry would or would not be necessary for a democratic system to function.

Whatever the exact wording of the prompt, any argument is stronger when it takes account of the opposition. For the Options prompt above, explain in your Thesis not only why cooperation would be effective in your specific example, but why it would be more effective than threats. For the Imperatives prompt above, don't simply state in your Thesis case that full information is necessary; go on to explain why someone who defended withholding information in this instance would be incorrect or misguided.

12.2 THE T-A-S STRUCTURE

In the preceding chapter you learned about the three tasks that make up all MCAT Writing Sample items. The best strategy for completing these tasks is to use the Thesis–Antithesis–Synthesis (T-A-S) structure to organize your essay.

To illustrate each task, let's use the Options prompt above. The text of this item reads in full as follows:

Consider this statement:

In any political negotiation, cooperation works better than threats of violence.

Write a unified essay in which you perform the following tasks. Explain what you think the above statement means. Describe a specific situation in which a threat of violence might be more effective than a cooperation within a political negotiation. Discuss what you think determines whether cooperation or a threat of violence is more effective in political negotiations.

The Thesis

The Thesis is the first part of the essay, and it addresses the first task: Explain what you think the above statement means. Your response to this task should contain three basic parts.

Paraphrase and Explain the Prompt Statement

In this section, you'll be explaining when the prompt statement would be true. To introduce this discussion, put the prompt statement into your own words and begin to explore the core ideas it contains. For our sample prompt, the first sentences of your essay might read as follows:

Politics has often been called "the art of compromise." Any political system is made up of diverse elements with different interests and values who must find a way to coexist, and coexistence always requires some level of cooperation. On a larger scale, the international system constitutes a complex web of radically different political systems which must not only compete but also cooperate with each other to ensure their own well-being and even survival.

Define or Explain Any Key Terms that Appear in the Prompt Statement

In the prompt statement, "political negotiation" "cooperation" and "threat of violence" could each mean a variety of things. Make it clear how you will be defining and using those terms. Continuing our sample essay, we could write:

A successful political negotiation usually entails reaching some form of shared understanding and mutual agreement. This can lead to the establishment of a stable status quo that serves the interests of all involved. When those parties can find some common ground, threats to attack or destroy the other side are unnecessary and even counterproductive. Cooperation, which in a negotiation usually involves compromise, can be used to convince the other party of the validity of some basic idea or policy.

Give a Clear, Concrete, Specific, and Realistic Example of a Situation in Which the Prompt Statement Would in Fact be True, and Explain Why

The first task does not explicitly require a specific example, but the best essays will have one. For example:

It is in the international system that threats of violence are most dangerous, as the parties involved are in many cases powerful and heavily armed states. Violent threats against a state disrupt not only order within that state, but in the international arena as a whole. In most cases on this level, then, peaceful cooperation and accommodation presents the best chance for long-term stability. Take, for example, the formation of the European Union (EU). France and Germany fought each other in two World Wars, and a certain amount of tension still exists between them. However, they share with each other and other European nations a common interest in free trade and economic development. In the negotiations leading to the formation of the EU, each nation had to compromise, lowering trade barriers, eliminating tariffs, even giving up their own national currency. To achieve long-term economic cooperation, trust is essential. Threats to disrupt the economy of potential community members in order to gain some individual economic advantage would have been counterproductive for all involved. Thus in such cases when the negotiation involves economic relationships and alliances, and when trust is essential to maintaining those relationships, cooperation will always be more effective than violent threats.

Remember that your task is to explain when, not whether, the prompt is true. Don't argue in the Thesis that the prompt is always true. If you do, you will have to contradict yourself in the Antithesis when you discuss a situation in which the opposite is true.

The Antithesis

The Antithesis addresses the second task, and so should make up the second section of your essay. Here the question asks you to give a specific example in which the opposite of the prompt statement would be true. Your approach to this task should also contain three basic parts.

Write a Transitional Sentence

You don't need to get fancy here. In our sample essay, it is enough to say, for example:

However, in different circumstances, threats to the political, economic, or social order of another state may be necessary in order to reach a negotiated agreement and a stable status quo.

Explain the Antithesis Idea, as It Is Worded Within the Question

While the question explicitly only asks for an example, your example will be weak and unconvincing if you do not frame it with a more general discussion of the core ideas involved. In our sample essay:

When two nations do not share any common ground, attempted cooperation with the goal of convincing the other of the validity of a fundamental idea or policy may be ineffective. In such cases conflict may drag on for years, putting both parties at risk. This occurs most commonly in cases of ideological or territorial disputes, when many of the beliefs or interests of the two nations are mutually exclusive.

Give a Clear, Concrete, Specific, and Realistic Example of When the Antithesis Claim Would be True

Continuing our essay, we might write:

During the Cold War, for example, neither side came to accept the right of the other to exist. The U.S. and the U.S.S.R. managed to coexist not by finding common ground through cooperation, but by achieving Mutually Assured Destruction or MAD. That is, each side had the military capacity to destroy the other with nuclear weapons. Thus, both nations knew that a nuclear attack on the other could lead to disaster on a global scale. It was the credibility of the threat that underlied all negotiations between the superpowers and that maintained order by allowing the two mortal enemies to coexist in relative peace for many decades. It may only be when each side comes to believe that entering into open conflict will lead to the destruction of both sides that some kind of reluctant compromise and stable form of coexistence can be achieved.

The Synthesis

The Synthesis addresses the third task. This part of the question asks you to give a rule that can be used to determine when the prompt or Thesis statement is true, and conversely when the Antithesis statement is true. The Synthesis task is analytical. It is not enough to simply state that sometimes the Thesis is true and in other times it is false, or to just reiterate your examples. The Synthesis should explore what particular factors cause the prompt to be true or not.

It's a smart idea to plan your Synthesis in the outlining stage and to write toward it. Many students jump into the essay blindly, hoping that a bolt of inspiration will hit when it's time to write the Synthesis. It's better to begin knowing where you're going. A good test to see if your Synthesis is adequate is to think of another case or example that you have not discussed in your essay, and imagine the reader using your criteria to decide whether the Thesis or the Antithesis case would be true in that instance.

One way to start the paragraph is by comparing your two examples and analyzing what makes them qualitatively different. Then go on to generalize that difference into a rule or set of criteria that can be applied more broadly. What follows is one possible Synthesis to wrap up our sample essay:

A variety of factors determine whether attempts at cooperation or threats of violence and disruption provide the best road to successful negotiation, be it on an international, national or local level. When the parties come to the table with some common understanding of right and wrong, cooperation and compromise are possible. All countries agree that economic prosperity is good, and the economic and social systems of the various members of the EU were similar enough that they could be combined without the eradication of any single way of life. Economic competition within a cooperative system can leave all parties better off, when free flow of trade stimulates the economies of all who participate. However, when nations or other political actors hold or are structured around mutually exclusive ideologies, true cooperation may be impossible because there is no ideological common ground. Communism rules out the possibility of capitalism as a valid economic, social or political system, and vice versa. Thus, threats may be necessary to achieve some kind of negotiated settlement. In the final analysis, violence breeds violence, and the threat of violence is usually counterproductive in the long run. However, when no common ground exists, and when all parties involved can present a credible threat to the others, some form of tense and yet stable coexistence may be maintained through threats to disrupt the order of the other side or of the world as a whole.

12.3 HALLMARKS OF A GOOD ESSAY

The best essays will display the following characteristics:

Precision and Confidence

Don't use wishy-washy or vague wording in presenting your analysis. Project confidence in what you have to say.

Completeness

You must address all three tasks that accompany the prompt. No matter how brilliant your response, if it is does not address all three tasks, you cannot score above a 3 (out of 6). To cover the required aspects of the prompt in depth, you'll probably need the equivalent of at least one and a half to two double-spaced pages. While it's quality—not quantity—that matters, an essay that is too brief gives the impression that you don't have much to say.

Clarity

Think before you write. Convoluted wording and pointless repetition will not score you points. Two pages of clear and concise analysis are much better than three pages that continually repeat the same ideas or that are difficult for the reader to follow.

Consistency

All three sections of the essay must be consistent with each other. The Antithesis should not contradict what you have said in the Thesis. Your Synthesis criteria must be appropriate and applicable to both of your examples.

Comprehensibility

Pay attention to spelling, grammar, and sentence construction. Don't use big words if you are not absolutely sure that they mean what you think they mean. Use simple, direct language.

Concrete and Fully Explained Examples

Realistic, specific, and concrete examples work better than vague hypothetical examples. If you must use a hypothetical example, make it as specific and detailed as possible. Don't make the reader guess at why you chose the examples you cite; explain the relevance of your examples to the themes of the prompt.

Originality

Catch the reader's attention. Your central mission is to give a complete and logically consistent response. If you can add to that unique examples, thoughtful and insightful analysis that gets below the surface of the question, and a "hook" or catchy introduction to grab a reader's attention and draw her into the essay, your score will be higher.

12.4 NUMERICAL SCORING GUIDELINES

The chart below is one that the graders use as a guide for scoring your essays. Keep the criteria in mind as you write your practice essays at home. Note in particular how much you will hurt your score by neglecting even one of the tasks; no matter how good the rest of your essay is, if you don't address all three tasks, you won't score better than a 3.

Essay Score	Characteristics
6	• Fully addresses all three tasks • Substantial treatment of the topic • Superior depth and complexity of thought • Focused and coherent organization • Superior clarity and precision of expression
5	• Addresses all three tasks • Substantial treatment of the topic • Depth of thought • Coherent organization • Clarity and precision of expression
4	• Addresses all three tasks • Moderate treatment of the topic • Depth of thought • Generally coherent organization, but with some digressions • Idea expression generally shows clarity and precision
3	• Neglects or distorts one or more of the tasks • Minimal treatment of the topic • Some clarity of thought, but may be simplistic • May have some problems in organization • Basic fluency of expression
2	• Seriously neglects or distorts one or more of the tasks • Fails to analyze the topic in depth; problems with analysis • Thought is simplistic and underdeveloped • Problems with organization • Problems with mechanics/spelling make writing difficult to follow
1	• Neglects one or more of the tasks • Minimally addresses or fails to address the topic • Thought is simplistic and undeveloped • Marked problems with organization • Problems with mechanics/spelling/language make writing very difficult to follow

12.5 AN ESSAY-WRITING TIMETABLE

Thirty minutes is not a very long time. It's understandable that some students may be tempted to skip prewriting or proofreading in order to spend the maximum amount of time actually writing their essay. Prewriting and proofreading are essential, however, precisely because you have so little time to mess around. An essay created with the "plan as you go" approach betrays itself with sloppy logic and drifting organization. An essay that contains many mechanical errors because it wasn't proofread may be taken less seriously than its argument would merit. The following is a suggested timetable that will help you to pace yourself.

5–10 Minutes: Brainstorming and Outlining

Start writing notes on your scratch paper. Explore the definitions of key words; definitions will inspire your thesis and antithesis examples. Generate examples to illustrate your thesis and antithesis. Make an outline; jot down the key points you will address in your thesis, antithesis, and synthesis sections. Make sure that you have at least a rough version of your synthesis conditions.

15–20 Minutes: Writing

Write. Address all three tasks, using at least one separate paragraph for each. Skip a line in between each paragraph. Move toward a conclusion after 10 to 15 minutes of writing; that way, you'll ensure that you have sufficient time to develop your synthesis.

2–5 Minutes: Proofreading

Edit. Make sure you leave time to read your entire essay at least once, from the beginning. Imagine that you are the grader. Look for parts that don't make sense and do what you can to clarify them so that the reader won't have to struggle to understand your argument. Correct your spelling, grammar, and punctuation.

12.6 WRITING SAMPLE EXERCISES

12.6

Exercise 1: Sample Prompt

Let's discuss a sample question to take another look at the T-A-S structure and to do some brainstorming and outlining. On the next few pages you will find an analysis of the prompt and sample student essays. Read through this material after you have done your own brainstorming and outlining.

Consider this statement:

Most advertising encourages conformity to social norms.

Write a unified essay in which you perform the following tasks. Explain what you think the above statement means. Describe a specific situation in which advertising might not encourage conformity to social norms. Discuss what you think determines whether or not advertising encourages conformity to social norms.

Brainstorming (definitions, core ideas, possible examples, etc.): _____

_____

_____

_____

_____

_____

_____

_____

_____

_____

_____

_____

_____

_____

_____

Outline

Thesis: _____

_____

_____

_____

_____

_____

_____

_____

_____

_____

_____

Antithesis: _____

_____

_____

_____

_____

_____

_____

_____

_____

_____

_____

12.6

Synthesis: _____

_____

_____

_____

_____

_____

_____

_____

_____

_____

Analysis of the Prompt

This question asks you to think about how an advertisement may or may not encourage conformity to social norms. There are really three major factors involved in this topic: the motivation behind the ad, the appearance of the ad, and the actual effects of the ad.

In the course of explaining what the prompt statement means in the Thesis, you need to define and explain some key terms: What is conformity to social norms (looking and acting like everyone else? attempting to achieve a common ideal? accepting mainstream beliefs and values?)? What would qualify as not encouraging conformity (promoting self expression? a unique style? rejection of mainstream values?)? You can define terms however you like, as long as your definitions are reasonable and consistent with the rest of your essay. Choose a Thesis example that fits with the definition of terms you have chosen. That is, if you define conformity to social norms as accepting common values and beliefs, and use as an example clothing or cosmetics ads, you need to explain how what we use or wear reflects those common values.

In your Antithesis, you should choose an example that is comparable yet contrasting with your Thesis example. You might discuss a different kind of ad (e.g., public service announcements rather than ads selling products), ads promoting different kinds of products (e.g., educational services rather than consumer goods), different intended audiences (e.g., adults rather than children or teens), or different cultural or national contexts (e.g., advertising in Europe or Latin America rather than in the U.S.). Be careful not to contradict what you have already said in the Thesis. If you argue in the first section that ads selling products always promote conformity, don't choose an Antithesis example of ads that sell different kinds of products. Don't simply state your example. Be sure to describe its relevance to the terms of the prompt.

12.6

In the Synthesis, give a standard, rule, or set of criteria that we can use to decide if a particular advertisement is or is not likely to encourage conformity. The Synthesis should be based on the contrast you have drawn between your two examples, and should also return to the key issues you first introduced in the Thesis. Imagine, for example, that you had chosen clothing ads (e.g., The Gap or Old Navy commercials on television) as your Thesis example, and public service ads against drugs as your Antithesis case. In your Synthesis, you could argue for example that ads promoting products that relate to appearance (clothing, shoes, cosmetics, hair products etc.) always encourage conformity. To maximize profits, companies must create trends to keep consumers going back to the stores over and over, and must make everyone in the target audience believe that they need to fit in with the trend to be socially acceptable. Public service ads against drugs however, have no profit motive. To be successful, they don't require people to purchase a product, but may instead encourage people to stop purchasing or using certain products. A strong essay will recognize that these ads are in fact promoting a certain type of conformity (e.g., to not do drugs, to avoid cigarettes and alcohol, to read, to stay in school, etc.). The intended outcome, however, is that each person, free of chemical or educational impediments, can fully express his or her own self and live life to the fullest, whatever that means for that individual.

Student Response #1

Advertising runs the gamut of economics. In order to advertise on public television, one needs to have thousands of dollars. Companies that advertise on television must abide by certain regulations in order to have access to television. The rules are the same for each advertiser. For this reason, many T.V. commercials resemble each other. Advertisers conform to the system of selling products and attracting consumers through television ads.

A distinct form of advertising offers a variety of products in a variety of ways that promote the individual that is selling it. The world wide web does not put many restrictions on those who are using the internet for advertising. An individual may be as creative as he or she wants in order to sell a product. Individuality is expressed through these means. Therefore, these ads do not relate to social norms.

More individuals are using the internet to promote their own individuality by advertising their own creations. The determination of whether or not advertising promotes conformity is dictated by certain regulations. When rules and regulations are strict, as on television, the company will have to conform. On the contrary, when there is less regulation as in the internet, then no conformity is required.

Sample Student Response #1—Grader's Comments: This essay has a potentially valid idea; the medium through which an ad is communicated may affect the impact of that ad on its viewers. Unfortunately, the writer does not discuss how advertising may or may not promote conformity, but instead describes whether or not advertisers themselves are able to express their own individuality. The essay never makes a connection between being individualistic and promoting individualism, and so does not directly address the question. The essay is also difficult to follow, does not give concrete, detailed examples, and repeats its central idea (rules require conformity) without developing it further. Finally, it is too short to adequately cover the topic.

Score: 2

Student Response #2

Advertising in today's society plays a major role in introducing and cultivating new ideas, products, and merchandise. Advertising is an avenue to reach the general public with important information about the wealth of products being made to suit their every need. In some cases, advertising might be thought to serve individual needs but could really instead promote conformity through mass telecommunications. For example, when celebrities like Britney Spears or famous athletes endorse products like Pepsi or athletic shoes, it is a way for the advertising company to connect with the general public through the use of household names in the form of today's up-and-coming celebrities. With the public's rush to be more like famous people, they often assimilate and will tend to join the crowd without even thinking about what they are losing, their individuality.

Advertising also has other significant functions within society. In this sense, advertising promotes more individuality rather than conformity among its constituents. For example, when commercials (another form of advertising) advertise for political campaigns and agendas, the general public has the right to agree with certain politician's and their agendas or decide that they are not interested in anything political. For instance, with the 2000 presidential election between Gore and Bush, the general public had there choice to pick which ever candidate they saw as most fit to lead the country into the 21st century.

Advertising can quite possibly have similar roles when viewed to them trying to reach the general public. When advertising presents or depicts a picture of what a political figure and what he/she plans to do to solve certain issues, the general has the ultimate choice in the matter. They can make up their own mind independently of others. They can agree, disagree or remain impartial. On the other hand, when certain role models like celebrities indorse certain popular and common products, the public (especially teenagers) might assimilate to be more like others.

Sample Student Response #2—Grader's Comments: This writer chooses a good general example in the Thesis paragraph. However, the second paragraph illustrates a common mistake made on MCAT writing sample essays. It describes an example that is different, but not clearly contrasting with the Thesis case. Political ads sell a candidate while commercial ads sell a product. Both types of ads attempt to get the largest number of people to make the same choice. The essay does not explain how political choices, especially those encouraged by advertising, represent a lesser degree of conformity than consumer choices. Neither does it explain why consumer product ads render the viewer less free to agree or disagree with the message than do political ads. Finally, it doesn't specifically address the issue of social norms.

Without two clearly contrasting examples, the writer has nowhere to go in the Synthesis, beyond repeating what he has already said in the first two paragraphs. The Synthesis also raises a new issue (the special impact of advertising on teenagers) which is never explained. The point is a good one, but it should be introduced and explored in the Thesis paragraph.

In terms of style and clarity, the writer makes a few spelling and grammatical errors that do not seriously affect the reader's comprehension. A more serious problem lies in awkward phrasing and word choice, which gets worse in the final paragraph and makes it difficult to follow the writer's analysis. The essay is also overly repetitious and wordy. With clearer and more concise writing, the author would get more credit for the good ideas that he does have.

Score: 2.5

Student Response #3

Mass media plays a crucial role in our society, and therefore so does advertising. Anybody seeking to promote a product can do so most effectively through ads in newspapers, magazines, and most importantly, television, whose visual character makes it especially powerful. The images presented in ads not only try to convince us to buy a product or accept a belief, but may in fact change our own self-image by presenting an ideal to which we are supposed to aspire by buying their product. Because most ads seek to get as many people as possible to buy a particular product, most ads promote conformity to social norms by influencing the population to have the same preferences and to value the same objects. For example, advertising that promotes products to improve our appearance often have this effect. In ads geared largely towards women such as cosmetic ads, an image of beauty unattainable by most is presented to make women feel inadequate as they are, and induce them to buy an ever changing and "improved" array of products. Models in these ads present a uniform look of youth and of a certain kind of beauty. A few years ago the cosmetics company Lancome fired Isabella Rosellini not because she was no longer beautiful, but because they considered her to be too old to present an appropriate and attractive image. Ads geared largely towards men, such as Nike ads selling basketball shoes, present Michael Jordan as a similarly attractive yet unattainable ideal, and implores not to be better versions of ourselves but to "be like Mike." Ironically, these kinds of ads for both men and women are often themselves presented in a unique, witty, and creative way in order to catch the viewer's attention. Thus the ads themselves are individualistic, but their effect is to promote conformity to certain standards by inducing us to aspire to the same idealized image.

On the other hand, some advertising sells products that do the opposite by promoting individuality. Drugs that treat illnesses such as depression or anxiety may in fact appear to promote conformity, by getting everyone to feel or act the same. However, mental illnesses or disorders themselves make it difficult for an individual to fully express themselves as a unique person. These days, it is common to see television and magazine ads for drugs like Prozac that treat depression and social anxiety. Even drugs like Claritin, that treat allergies or other purely physical complaints help a person to live a fuller and freer life. The motivation of the drug companies may be purely selfish; they just want to sell as much of their product as they can. However, the images they use in their ads—people interacting easily and comfortably with others in a variety of social and professional situations, people who are now able to leave the house and function normally, or even people running through flowery fields and hiking in the woods when before their allergies would have kept them at home—are all images of people who are now more able to express themselves and live life as they wish to live it. Cynics may claim that the effect of widespread use of mood-altering drugs is to create a "Brave New World" as in Aldous Huxley's novel where the drug soma was used to keep everyone peaceful and "happy", and to wipe out any individualistic or rebellious urges that could disrupt the social order. However, the real effect is the opposite. People who are free of mental or physical impediments are more, not less able to go out into the world and to act and think freely. Whatever the motives of the advertisers may be, the effect of their product is to promote individuality and creativity rather than living up to some predetermined social standard.

Two main factors determine whether or not advertising promotes conformity to social norms. First, what is the nature of the ad, and does it promote a uniform ideal of beauty or attractiveness, or conversely an image of self-fulfillment and diversity of self-expression. Secondly, what is the actual effect of the product being sold. Does it help a person to more fully be themselves, or does it impose a foreign and unachievable ideal that is the same for all?

Sample Student Response #3—Grader's Comments: This essay presents two excellent examples that are appropriate to the question, comparable yet clearly contrasting, and fully described in terms of their relevance to the terms of the prompt. The writer gives a sophisticated response to the Thesis question, in particular by discussing how ads that are themselves individualistic or quirky may in fact promote conformity. She does tend to use run-on sentences and her train of thought in the second paragraph is a bit unorganized, but her ideas come through relatively clearly. The Synthesis treatment, however, is overly brief and sketchy, and out of keeping with the rest of the essay. All three tasks are equally important, and writers must manage their time appropriately.

Score: 5

Exercise 2: T-A-S Drill

For each of the following prompt statements, complete the following tasks:

1. Devise an example in which the prompt statement would be true.
2. Devise an example in which the opposite of the prompt statement would be true.
3. Describe the key difference between your two examples.

Prompt 1

In the business world, loyalty is based on self-interest rather than principle. _____

_____

_____

_____

_____

_____

_____

_____

_____

_____

_____

Prompt 2

Students cannot succeed without good teachers. _____

_____

_____

_____

_____

_____

_____

_____

_____

12.6

Prompt 3

True appreciation of art requires an understanding of the goals of the artist. _____

_____

_____

_____

_____

_____

_____

_____

_____

Prompt 4

The law offers greater protection to the wealthy than to the poor. _____

_____

_____

_____

_____

_____

_____

_____

_____

Exercise 3: Current Events Question

Describe a controversial event in the world of business or industry. Are there concerns about safety, the environment, or personal liberty? What are the needs of businesses? What are the needs of individuals and society? Do businesses have any social responsibilities beyond obeying the law? How should the needs of businesses, employees, consumers, and society as a whole be balanced?

Exercise 4: Supplemental Prompts

Here are two supplemental MCAT-style essay prompts. To duplicate your test experience, write the essays consecutively. If you don't have time to write both essays, at least make an outline for each prompt that describes your key ideas and the examples you'd use to illustrate your main points. And always type your essays, just as you will on the actual MCAT.

Supplemental Prompt 3

Consider this statement:

12.6

> A teacher's main goal should be to encourage a skeptical attitude among students.

Write a unified essay in which you perform the following tasks. Explain what you think the above statement means. Describe a specific situation in which a teacher's goal should not be to encourage a skeptical attitude among students. Discuss what you think determines when teachers should encourage skepticism and when they should not.

Supplemental Prompt 4

Consider this statement:

> Individual liberties cannot be maintained without open expression of ideas.

Write a unified essay in which you perform the following tasks. Explain what you think the above statement means. Describe a specific situation when individual liberties might be maintained without open expression of ideas. Discuss what you think determines when individual liberties can or cannot be maintained without open expression of ideas.

Chapter 12 Summary

- A strong essay should respond to all three of the tasks with the T-A-S structure.

- Use the T-A-S structure of the prompt to organize your essay.

- Plan your Synthesis in the prewriting stage.

- Focus on clarity in your organization and writing; make it easy for the grader to follow your logic and your ideas.

- Budget your time between outlining, writing, and proofreading.

Chapter 13
Prewriting

GOALS

1.   To approach the essay with a detailed and organized plan
2.   To identify and define and/or analyze key terms in the prompt
3.   To choose strong examples and explain their relevance to the prompt
4.   To center each essay on a core issue generated by the prompt

13.1   PREWRITING: A 4-STEP PROCESS

Some students, confident in their ability to come up with good ideas and to organize their thoughts as they write, forego prewriting altogether. Or, concerned about the time limits, they may jump into the first task without planning all three parts of the essay ahead of time. However, if you have ever been suddenly struck with the most profound and insightful approach to a topic hours after you have completed the essay, you need to refine your prewriting strategy. All students, in fact, will benefit from a brainstorming and outlining strategy. Good prewriting helps you figure out what you want to say when you still have time to say it, and ensures a well-organized, coherent, and consistent essay.

Brainstorming and outlining is particularly valuable on short, timed essays with a strictly defined topic, like the MCAT Writing Sample. You don't have time to backtrack if you forget a crucial point. If you get to the last five minutes and discover to your horror that you have gone off on a tangent, or that you have contradicted yourself within the essay, there's no time to fix the problem. Prewriting allows you to select and arrange the examples and analytical points that will make up the best possible essay.

Effective prewriting consists of the following four-step process. You don't have to perform these steps in one particular order. In fact, you'll probably find that your prewriting process is recursive; that is, you cycle through the steps a few times, with ideas from one step giving you new ideas for another step.

Outlining

- **STEP 1: BRAINSTORM EXAMPLES AND IDEAS**

- **STEP 2: IDENTIFY AND DEFINE AND/OR ANALYZE KEY TERMS**

- **STEP 3: DETERMINE THE STATEMENT'S CENTRAL QUESTION**

- **STEP 4: OUTLINE THE THREE TASKS**

STEP 1: BRAINSTORM EXAMPLES AND IDEAS

After reading the entire prompt statement carefully, use your scratch paper to jot down anything that comes to mind. Write down possible examples, potential Synthesis criteria, and issues that appear to be important to the topic. Focus from the beginning on the contrast at the heart of the question. This contrast must be illustrated by your Thesis and Antithesis examples, and will form the basis of your Synthesis.

It's crucial not to censor yourself at this stage. Much of what you write down will not be usable, but by letting your mind work freely, you'll uncover those great examples and ideas now, instead of leaving them to work their way to the surface hours later.

For example, let's consider the following MCAT Writing Sample item:

Consider this statement:

It is never justified for a citizen to break the law.

Write a unified essay in which you perform the following tasks. Explain what you think the above statement means. Describe a specific instance in which a citizen might justifiably break the law. Discuss what you think determines whether or not it is justified for citizens to break the law.

Here are some things that might come to mind for this prompt:

- What are the duties and rights of citizens?
- Do citizens have duties to other citizens, or to some ethical standard, that might conflict with their duty to obey the law?
- Can individual ethics be more important than social and/or economic stability?
- When should we obey the law even if it conflicts with our personal beliefs?
- When should we obey our own conscience, when that conscience conflicts with the law?
- By disobeying a law, are we undermining the legal system, or the nation as a whole?
- Are there times when the legal system or the nation should be undermined or transformed?

Possible sources of examples:

- Authoritarian or repressive regimes/situations: Iraq under Hussein, Cuba, Afghanistan under the Taliban, USSR, segregation in the United States
- Types of law: traffic, criminal, constitutional
- The student democracy movement in China, Gandhi and Indian independence, Waco/David Koresh (cults and antisocial movements), Thoreau and civil disobedience, Civil Rights Movement in the United States, laws protecting or abridging individual liberties

STEP 2: IDENTIFY AND DEFINE KEY TERMS

Identify the terms in the prompt that might be defined in several different ways. Abstract terms (e.g., "freedom," "duty," "justice") are the most likely candidates. Think of all possible definitions, and then narrow it down to the definition you want to use in your essay.

For example, in the prompt above, it seems pretty clear what breaking the law means. However, "the law" could be all written laws, federal but not state or local laws, or unwritten laws and social norms that make up our "national culture." Let's pick the most straightforward definition—all written laws. Secondly, what does it mean to discuss what citizens in particular should or should not do? Do citizens have responsibilities that non-citizen residents or visitors do not? Is that duty different in different times or places, or is there a basic responsibility that any citizen of any nation has? For our purposes here, let's define a citizen's duty in the specific context of a democratic state. We value democracy in large part because of the high value placed on protection of individual rights. Thus we could argue that a citizen's fundamental duty in a democracy is to help preserve those rights for all citizens and that this duty determines whether or not the breaking of a law is justified.

Choose reasonable, common-sense definitions. Keep your definitions consistent throughout the essay; don't base the contrast between your examples or your Synthesis criteria on defining key terms in two different ways.

STEP 3: DETERMINE THE STATEMENT'S CENTRAL QUESTION

These questions don't come out of nowhere (appearances sometimes to the contrary). Think about what important themes, debates, or political, social, or ethical controversies might have inspired the test writers to come up with this particular prompt. The prompt might ask you to think about democratic principles (equality, freedom of speech and religion, representative government etc.). Or, it may center on humanistic issues or social problems (How does technology affect people? How can our society improve? How do we address issues like crime, poverty, or illiteracy?). Finally, it may be generated by basic moral questions (when is it right or wrong to commit certain actions or hold particular beliefs?). Decide what core issues are involved in the prompt statement. Think about how these issues are embodied in the examples you choose and how they relate to the contrast between those examples. This step is the key to scoring a 4.5 or above.

In our sample prompt, our investigation of key terms, in particular "citizen," had led us to the central question embedded in the prompt. By asking about a citizen's duties toward the law, the question is really asking what responsibilities we have that involve obeying the law, and what other higher duties might compel us to break the law.

STEP 4: OUTLINE THE THREE TASKS

Organize your T-A-S argument with the central question or issue from Step 3 in mind. Good organization is one of the most important aspects of a high-scoring essay. The MCAT graders read and evaluate each essay in only a few minutes. A poorly organized essay is difficult to follow, and the human readers will not take extra time to piece together your ideas.

From your brainstorming session, select Thesis and Antithesis examples that are comparable yet clearly contrasting. Define your Synthesis criteria as closely as possible. This is the best way to ensure that your Synthesis is consistent with, and applicable, to your two examples.

Some people find it useful and time-effective to write quite detailed outlines, while others effectively use much briefer versions. Discover what works best for you.

What follows is one possible outline for our sample item. Keep in mind that this is an outline, not a full essay. Feel free to abbreviate words and sentences in your own outline, as long as your abbreviations are clear to you.

Thesis

Paraphrase the prompt: Citizenship confers certain privileges, and as well imposes certain responsibilities. One of those responsibilities in a democracy is to obey the law, whenever such obedience does not compromise some higher principle or greater duty.

Define and/or analyze key terms: "Citizens": Citizens in a democracy participate in the formation of the law through their elected representatives on the local, state, and national level. This gives them a duty to obey that law in most cases, so as to ensure the protection of every citizen's rights and well-being.

Central Thesis question: When and why must citizens obey the written law (even if they would prefer not to)?

Example: Need to allow freedom of speech, even when offensive to most or many: e.g., Ku Klux Klan march in Skokie, Illinois in the 1980s.

Relevance of example: Even though many disagreed passionately with the decision of the courts that the laws guaranteeing free speech applied to the KKK, those in disagreement still had a duty as citizens to tolerate the Klan's march through a largely Jewish neighborhood. To do otherwise would be to erode the protections afforded to all.

Antithesis

Transitional Antithesis Question When would some higher duty compel us to break the law?

Example: Civil Rights Movement and Rosa Parks

Relevance of example: The laws themselves (segregation, Jim Crow, voting tests) were antithetical to basic democratic ideals and practice. Thus, they undermined and weakened democracy from the inside, and it was a citizen's duty to work to eradicate them. Sometimes, civil disobedience was the only effective way (explain why).

Synthesis

General principle: When the laws reflect the founding ideals of the nation they must be obeyed, even if in the short run individuals are offended or harmed, to ensure the long-term health and strength of the nation. When laws are passed that violate those fundamental ideals (which happens most often at the state or local level), citizens not only have no duty to obey, but are ethically required to disobey those laws and work to create fairer laws.

13.2 WRITING SAMPLE EXERCISES

Exercise 1: Prewriting

Let's do some brainstorming and outlining on the following prompt. Once you have completed the four steps below, read through the sample analysis that follows.

The primary duty of a democracy is to fight oppression.

Write a unified essay in which you perform the following tasks. Explain what the above statement means. Describe a situation in which the primary duty of a democracy is to do something other than fight oppression. Discuss what you think determines when the primary duty of a democracy is to fight oppression.

1. Brainstorm examples and ideas: _____

_____

_____

2. Identify and define key terms: _____

_____

_____

3. Determine the statement's central question: _____

_____

_____

4. Outline the three tasks

   • Thesis: _____

_____

_____

• Antithesis: _____

_____

_____

_____

• Synthesis: _____

_____

_____

Exercise 1: Sample Prewriting Responses

Prompt: The primary duty of a democracy is to fight oppression.

1. **Brainstorm examples and ideas**
   Forms of oppression:
   • Domestic (in the United States) or in other parts of the world
   • Domestic torture; discrimination based on race, on gender, on sexual preference
   • International: genocide, discrimination based on ethnicity, gender, political affiliation, sexual preference, use of torture, totalitarian political systems

   Possible examples:
   • Guatemala: 1954 coup against Arbenz, and subsequent oppression of indigenous peoples
   • Kosovo: ethnic cleansing
   • Darfur: genocide
   • Saudi Arabia: treatment of women
   • Rwanda: genocide
   • Cuba: politics
   • China: politics

   Ways in which oppression may be fought:
   • Military intervention
   • Economic sanctions
   • Diplomacy

   Other duties of a democracy:
   • ensure own national security
   • respect sovereignty of other nations
   • respect cultural and ideological differences in our own and other societies

2. **Identify and define key terms**

"duty of a democracy": what a democracy is ethically required to do by the fact that it is representative political system based on certain political and social ideals. (A democracy is morally required to promote human rights around the world, and is also required to act in the best interests of citizens of that democracy and to respect cultural diversity.)

"oppression": use of power in an unjust way, by denial of basic human or political rights

"fighting oppression": active and direct intervention to end the activity

3. **Determine the statement's central question**

When does our duty to live up to democratic ideals by intervening to end what we perceive to be oppression conflict with another duty of a democracy, and when should one or the other take precedence?

4. **Outline the three tasks**

Thesis

> Primary duty of a democracy is to directly fight oppression in cases where basic internationally-recognized human rights are being violated through use of genocide.

Example: Darfur/Sudan (genocide arising from conflict beginning in 2003, continuing today — Janjaweed and Sudanese military genocide against non-Arab muslims including the Fur ethnic group): U.S. should intervene, ideally in concert with other nations and the U.N., to protect the population which is under severe and prolonged physical attack.

Antithesis

> Duty to respect cultural differences and sovereignty of other nations takes precedence when "oppression" may be culturally defined or relate to differing political ideologies; that is, "we" may see it as oppression but those in that or similar cultures may not.

Example: women in Saudi Arabia. Even though treatment of women (limitations on employment, education, access to legal system in not being allowed to testify in most cases, lack of mobility/not allowed to drive and dress) is seen by many in Western democracies as oppression, can argue that it is culturally defined.

Synthesis

> What determines whether or not the primary duty of a democracy is to fight oppression is the form of oppression itself. If it entails killing or widespread use of torture, have a duty to do what we can to stop it; no culture accepts these actions as justified. However, if what constitutes oppression may be culturally defined, such as role of women, or go back to a debate about legitimacy of different political systems (China, Cuba), while we may use our influence in the world to change those ideas, our duty as a democracy to respect cultural differences takes precedence over our desire to fight what we, but not others, may see as oppression.

Exercise 2: Current Events Question

Describe a current event in the world that involves the violation of human rights. Whose rights are being violated and why? What are the political issues involved? Are other nations involved in any way? Should other nations intervene?

Exercise 3: Supplemental Prompts

Here are two supplemental MCAT-style essay prompts. Write the essays consecutively. If you don't have time to write both essays during the week, at least make an outline for each prompt that describes the examples you'd use to illustrate your main points.

Supplemental Prompt 5

Consider this statement:

Inventions intended to liberate us usually imprison us instead.

Write a unified essay in which you perform the following tasks. Explain what you think the above statement means. Describe a specific situation in which inventions intended to liberate us might not imprison us. Discuss what you think determines whether or not inventions intended to liberate us will imprison us instead.

Supplemental Prompt 6

Consider this statement:

The most important duty of a government is to ensure the health and safety of its people.

Write a unified essay in which you perform the following tasks. Explain what you think the above statement means. Describe a specific situation in which the most important duty of a government might justifiably be something other than ensuring the health and safety of its people. Discuss what you think determines when the most important duty of a government is to ensure the health and safety of its people.

13.3 TIMED ESSAY #1

Give yourself 30 minutes to write this essay. Do it on your computer but do not use spell-check. After you write the essay, read through the analysis of the prompt and three student essays that follow.

Consider this statement:

> **People too often believe that liberty is maximized when obligations are minimized.**

Write a unified essay in which you perform the following tasks. Explain what you think the above statement means. Describe a specific situation in which we might think that liberty is maximized when obligations are not minimized. Discuss what you think determines whether or not we believe that liberty is maximized when obligations are minimized.

Analysis of the Prompt

When confronted with a vague and abstract prompt statement, don't panic. Do some brainstorming, jotting down everything that pops into your mind, and good ideas and examples will come to you. Your first step should always be to read the entire prompt carefully. Note the wording of the Thesis in this case: It is asking not only when we might believe that having fewer obligations increases our freedom. These words carry a negative connotation that must be addressed in your essay.

This prompt involves two central and related questions. First, what is liberty? Second, how should we measure our liberty? You might discuss political liberties, liberty in the workplace, or liberty in our relationships with friends and family. Be sure also to define or analyze "people" and "obligations." "People" could refer to a country in the international arena, and "liberty" could be a lack of obligation to involve ourselves in the concerns of other nations. Or, "people" could be defined as individual citizens of a particular country, and "liberty" could be the lack of obligation to involve ourselves as individuals in the concerns of other citizens. "People" could also refer to a particular age group, ethnic group, economic or social class, or community.

In both the Thesis and Synthesis, note and respond to the use of the phrase "too often." Do not choose examples of unfair or unjust obligations, as they will not be entirely appropriate to the wording of the question. In the Synthesis, avoid the cop-out "it depends on the individual" criterion. Yes, different people will have different ways of thinking about liberty, but what makes them different? Why are they different? What qualities can we discern in a person or group of people in order to decide if they are more likely to see obligations as limitations on their liberty?

In the student essays that follow, note that the writers use quite similar examples. What makes the difference between a low-scoring and a high-scoring essay is how clearly and fully those examples are explained (especially in terms of their relevance to the prompt statement) and how easy it is to follow the writer's logic and organization.

Student Response #1   In the United States, people too often believe that liberty is maximized when obligations are minimized. That is, they use a lack of obligation or duty as an example to the level of freedom that they have. An example of this is the freedom gained by people in the U.S. due to the lack of obligation to attend a religious institution. In some countries such as Iran, people are required to attend a mosque on holy days, and to attend religious schools as children. As a result, Americans use this example to measure the amount of liberty that they have. That is, a lack of obligation to attend leads to an increase in freedom because they are not forced to attend religious events if they do not wish to, and they will not be prosecuted for not doing so.

However, there are also situations in which Americans measure their liberty by the existence of obligations. For example, even though voting is not required by law, it is considered an obligation for a citizen to vote by both the people and by the government itself. Even though this leads to an increased duty to the citizens, it is still used to measure freedom. This is because the obligation to vote increases the amount if freedom an individual has. When they vote, they have the opportunity to choose who represents them, and what decisions are made concerning their community, city, state, and country. Whenever and individual has more input into the path of his or her life, they also have more freedom by definition.

What determines whether people they have more liberty when they have fewer obligations depends on if the obligation or lack thereof leads to an increase or decrease of freedom. People measure their freedom by whether the obligation or lack thereof leads to an increase in freedom. That is, whenever a lack of obligation leads to an increase in freedom, it is used to measure an individual's freedom, and the same is true for when an obligation is used as a measure of freedom. This is because citizens of the United States believe that they have more freedoms than people in other countries. Therefore, when they discuss the amount if freedom that they have, they employ an obligation or a lack thereof of citizens with more limited freedom.

Sample Student Response #1—Grader's Comments: This writer begins by reproducing the wording of the prompt statement, but fails to respond to it in the body of the essay. Why shouldn't we measure our liberty by the lack of obligation to practice a particular religion? By the description of her Thesis example, the author indicates that mandatory religious practice is a bad thing and that freedom of religion is preferable, leading to a logical inconsistency in the Thesis paragraph.

The Synthesis is quite difficult to follow—the writer clearly has not thought out her criteria ahead of time and has nowhere to go at this point. The author seems to be saying we measure our freedom by whether or not we are free. This is circular reasoning; that is, it states something that is true by definition.

The Antithesis is actually quite good, with a well-chosen example and a nice description of how the obligation to vote is seen by U.S. citizens as something that maximizes our freedom in a larger sense. However, the logical inconsistencies, unclear writing, and failure to address key issues in the prompt in the first and last paragraphs make it impossible for this essay to score a 3 or above.

Score: 2.5

Student Response #2   Because our nation is founded on the principles of freedom and democracy, the maximization of personal freedom is our goal, as long as one person's freedom does not infringe on another's rights. Freedom and the right to make personal decisions on one own forms the basis of the U.S. Constitution. In that context, we often measure our personal liberty or freedom by our lack of obligation to act in a certain way, or to fulfill another's needs and desires. In this way, we often define our freedom by what actions the state or government cannot force on us. In some other countries, citizens are required to vote, and are liable to prosecution if they cannot produce evidence that they did vote. In the U.S., however, we are not legally obligated to do so. The result, however, is that shockingly low numbers go to the polls, seeing electoral participation as a burden rather than a privilege that should be enjoyed. By defining our freedom by our lack of obligations, we undermine our democracy.

In other areas of life, however, we define our liberty by our obligation to act in a particular way, in terms of what we "should" do. For example, in the 1954 Brown vs. Board of Education decision, the Supreme Court ruled in favor of school desegregation. In this landmark case, the decision led to the increase of rights and personal freedom of the African American population. In this case, we measure our freedom by knowing what we should do or what is right, that is, our obligation to protect equal rights for all citizens. We are proud of the fact that in the U.S., no group can be legally discriminated against, and we see ourselves as more free because of it.

Liberty in many ways is an abstraction. We can clearly see when obligations that seem pointless infringe on our desires to pursue our own personal goals. It is difficult to see, sometimes, how giving up some of our time and energy in the short run actually maximizes our personal freedom. In this sense, what determines whether or not we see obligations as limiting our liberty depends on whether or not we think our actions have a direct impact on others or on society. One vote doesn't seem to make much of a difference. Because we cannot see directly how our personal decision not to vote affects others and ourselves, we think we are more free because we are not required to do so, when in reality the opposite is true. Because we can directly observe the impact discrimination has on other individuals, it seems more real, and by complying with the obligation to respect the rights of others, we feel ourselves and our society to be more free.

Sample Student Response #2—Grader's Comments: This writer chooses two excellent examples, and begins to address some core issues in the Thesis (the Constitution as a source for our ideas about liberty). He also does a good job of addressing the negative spin the wording places on the issue of measuring our freedom by our lack of responsibilities. However, the essay runs into some problems in showing a clear contrast in the two examples, beyond the fact that one represents negative behavior, and the other shows positive actions. Most people believe that we "should" vote, just as most would defend the principle of equality. Both the right to vote and the right to equal treatment before the law are principles embodied in the Constitution. At the end of the second paragraph, it is unclear why people see both the lack of obligation to vote and the existence of an obligation to respect the equality of others as indications that we are free.

It is in the Synthesis that this essay really shines. The Synthesis criterion (how visible the effects of our actions are) is insightful and unusual; it shows that the writer has put real thought into the issue instead of giving a prefabricated, superficial response. It seems as if the writer has figured out what he really wanted to say in the course of writing the first two paragraphs. If the writer had woven these ideas into the rest of the essay, this response could score in the 5–6 range.

Score: 4.5

Student Response #3   The American Revolutionary War was fought in part to free the colonists from the obligation to support Britain through their taxes and their labor. The colonists believed that they existed for themselves, not to serve another's interests. The nation that resulted was and still is characterized by a spirit of liberty and individual autonomy, principles that are enshrined in our founding documents, the Declaration of Independence and the Constitution. This spirit reverberates through all levels of our social and political system. On a national level, we can see it in our low level of taxation, and correspondingly low level of social services, compared to many European nations. On an individual level, we tend to believe that each person is fundamentally responsible only to him or herself and family, and tend to measure our personal liberty by the extent to which we can live life free of obligations put upon us by other individuals. People tend not to see themselves as members of a community; many do not even know their neighbors. In our modern and increasingly alienated society, people tend to avoid getting involved in the problems of others, feeling that it is not their responsibility to take action. In a famous case that occurred years ago in New York City, a woman named Kitty Genovese was stabbed to death on her front step. The attack and her death took almost a half hour, but none of the hundreds of people who could hear her screams intervened, or even took the trouble to call the police. When questioned later, most said that they "didn't want to get involved." When obligations entail entanglement in the lives and troubles of individuals outside our immediate circle of friends and family, we tend to believe that liberty is increased by the lack of obligation. As we can see in the example above, this sometimes has a tragic outcome.

However, we believe we have this freedom as citizens, and American citizens often accept the responsibilities of citizenship, that is, responsibilities to the nation, as a necessary part of maintaining our freedom. We have the privilege and the duty to vote, the right to be tried by a jury of our peers and so the responsibility to serve on a jury, the duty to defend our nation militarily when the country is attacked. Ironically, we often try to get out of fulfilling these duties (thus low voting rates and the difficulty courts have in filling jury panels with competent people). But at the same time we feel we should serve in these ways, and we feel guilty when we don't. No one who fails to vote brags about it, and many of those who do vote proudly wear a sticker proclaiming "I voted." Americans measure their freedom in part through the existence of these obligations, because these obligations define and ensure the function of a democratic system.

What determines whether or not we see obligations as minimizing our liberty depends on to whom we are or would be obliged. People often go out of their way to help strangers, but they bristle at the idea that they would be required to do so. Other countries have laws that make it illegal in some cases to stand by and watch a crime being committed, but no such laws exist in the U.S. We feel that we are not required to serve the interests or protect the well-being of other people. On the other hand, when the obligation is to an abstract ideal like democracy or justice or the nation, we see it as our duty as free citizens to serve, even if we don't actually do so. Many, however, do serve; some people who would not stop to buy a homeless person dinner will volunteer for the military in times of war, risking their very life. A democracy is government of the people, for the people and by the people. Thus the more private citizens are allowed or required to participate in different aspects of the government, the more free we perceive that system to be. Perhaps we see the nation and our democracy as extensions of ourselves; by serving the democratic nation, we are really serving ourselves.

Sample Student Response #3—Grader's Comments: This essay succeeds on a variety of levels. It defines key terms smoothly in the course of discussing central issues involved in the prompt, cites and explains valid examples in the Thesis and Antithesis, and provides Synthesis criteria that go beyond the specific examples and that could potentially be applied to evaluate other cases. It also does a nice job of providing a relevant historical context that introduces the Thesis and that is relevant to the Antithesis as well. The final sentence comes a bit abruptly, but it is an interesting and thoughtful close to the discussion. The essay is not perfect. It is at times overly wordy and repetitious. In the Antithesis, the author gives a series of general examples, when it would be better to choose one to explore in greater depth. The Synthesis is a bit unfocused and rambling. However, given the time constraints, it is an excellent response.

Score: 6

Chapter 13 Summary

- The 4-Step Prewriting Process will help you to produce a sophisticated interpretation of the prompt. These steps are: Brainstorming, Identifying and Defining and/or Analyzing the Key Terms, Determining the Statement's Central Question, and Outlining the Three Tasks.

- Define and clarify your ideas and examples (including your Synthesis rule) during prewriting; don't wait until after you've begun to write the essay itself.

- Focus on showing a clear contrast between your Thesis and Antithesis examples.

- Stick to the issue of the prompt; don't go off on a tangent.

- Be careful to budget your time so that you can fully address the Synthesis task, the most complicated (and in some ways, the most important) task of the essay.

Chapter 14
Focus on the Thesis

GOALS

1. To identify a Thesis principle
2. To use specific, sophisticated examples
3. To connect the Thesis example to the terms of the question

14.1 ARTICULATE THE THESIS PRINCIPLE

As you know by now, the Thesis is the part of the essay where you address when and why the prompt statement would be true. To accomplish this, you need to provide a strong Thesis example. However, the best essays will also address the core principle underlying the prompt statement.

- A good way to start is to ask yourself the following question at the prewriting stage:

When and why, *in principle*, should this statement be true?

When you pose the question in this way, you focus on the ideals expressed in the statement. This will help you to generate a complex, sophisticated response to the prompt that deals with important issues rather than simplistic cases.

Consider, for example, the following prompt:

A representative government should not withhold information from those it represents.

Write a unified essay in which you perform the following tasks. Explain what you think the above statement means. Describe a specific situation in which a representative government might be justified in withholding information from those it represents. Discuss what you think determines whether or not a representative government is justified in withholding information from those it represents.

Why, in principle, should this statement be true? One reason would be that a basic tenet of democratic representation is that citizens need information in order to make important decisions, including electoral decisions. They also need information in order to hold their elected representatives accountable for those representatives' actions. The ideal underlying this statement is that *people deserve to play an active role in their government*. The assertion of this ideal will be the crux of a Thesis written on this prompt, and will give context and meaning to your Thesis example.

14.2 A THESIS PARAGRAPH MODEL

Once you've decided on the principle underlying your Thesis, you can incorporate it into your Thesis paragraph. The model outlined below lists the important components of a strong Thesis, each of which must be relevant to the basic principle.

1. Start with a hook.
2. Paraphrase the prompt statement.
3. Define and/or analyze key terms.
4. Explain the core Thesis principle.
5. Give a concrete example demonstrating the truth of the prompt.
6. Explain the relevance of the example to the terms of the question.

The model is meant to be an outlining guide, not a pattern you must follow in all cases. There are several ways to organize a Thesis paragraph effectively. At first, it will be easier for you to write a strong Thesis if you follow these steps closely. Later on, as you become more comfortable with the format, you may find another effective way in which to organize your thoughts within the paragraph. Just make sure that you include all six of these components.

Start with a Hook

Hook is a term that journalists use to describe the first line of any piece of writing. Effective hooks are *specific*, *concrete*, and relatively *short*—all characteristics that make them engaging and easy to remember. A good hook will tantalize readers (at least the human ones) and encourage them to read on. Your score will be healthier if your essay is interesting from its very first line.

Prepare your hooks ahead of time. Don't spend 5 of your 30 minutes brainstorming hooks; instead, devise and memorize a series of hooks that would be appropriate for a variety of prompts within each category. If you use one, be sure that it's appropriate for that specific prompt, and that you follow it with a few sentences that show its relevance to the prompt.

The following are examples of different kinds of hooks. Each of them connects to the ideal that *people deserve to play an active role in their government.*

- **Narrative**
My friend Sonja often reflects on her life before and after immigrating from Moscow.

- **Question**
What are the rights and responsibilities of voters in a representative political system?

- **Description**
In times of war or political conflict abroad, governments have an especially high degree of control over information.

- **Definition**

For those of us lucky enough to live in a representative democracy, the act of voting is a kind of peaceful revolution.

- **Fact**

The framers of the United States Constitution had in mind a vision of democracy quite different from the present conception.

- **Statistic**

For a country that values political representation so much, the United States has an alarmingly low voter turnout rate.

- **Quotation**

Thomas Jefferson once said, "Reflection, with information, is all which our countrymen need to bring themselves and their affairs to right."

Paraphrase the Prompt Statement

Your Thesis should contain a paraphrase of the statement in your own words. This allows you to connect to the terms of the question, and to begin to set up your Thesis-Antithesis contrast. It's important to reflect the language of the prompt throughout your essay, but don't repeat it verbatim.

Furthermore, if the prompt is phrased in absolute terms and you reproduce that extreme wording in your Thesis, you will contradict yourself in the Antithesis task. Instead, rephrase the statement in a more moderate way; that is, phrase it so that you can propose exceptions to it in the Antithesis.

For example, you might rewrite the prompt *A representative government should not withhold information from those it represents* in one of the following ways:

A democratic system cannot function well without well-informed voters.

Representation without free access to certain information about the activities of the government is a contradiction in terms.

For the will of the people to be effectively expressed, a democratic representative must provide voters with a certain amount of information about its activities at home and abroad.

Define and/or Analyze Key Terms

In the preceding chapter, we worked on expanding definitions of important terms. There are two ways to define the important terms in the statement in the body of your essay: explicitly and implicitly. Implicit definitions tend to work more smoothly. However, a somewhat choppy or awkward explicit definition is better than no definition at all.

With the *explicit* method, you state your definition outright:

Withholding information means keeping secrets from or misrepresenting the facts to the public.

A term is *implicitly* defined when its meaning is suggested through context:

When governmental officials wish to carry out controversial or potentially unpopular policies, they may wish to misrepresent the true nature of those policies, or even keep the public completely in the dark.

Definitions are important for three reasons:

- First, abstract or vague terms like *skills, values, betrayal, soul, freedom, conformity,* or *justice* must be defined or explained in order for you to narrow your essay's parameters. In 30 minutes you just don't have the time to deal with every aspect of the idea of *justice*, for example.
- Second, your essay will also lack impact if you leave abstract terms undefined. Abstractions have many connotations; if you don't specify what *you* mean, you'll end up sounding as if you don't mean anything at all.
- Third, and most important, the contrast between your Thesis and Antithesis examples will depend in part on how you define and explain key terms.

Not every term in the prompt must be literally defined. The meaning of some terms is self-evident. For example, in this prompt "those it represents" does not require explicit definition. However, the meaning and relevance of representation should be analyzed in terms of how it relates to the core issue or principle of the prompt. Be careful to remain true to all terms in the prompt throughout the Thesis (and throughout the essay as a whole); don't change the meaning of key terms part-way through.

Explain the Core Thesis Principle

It is important to remember that paraphrasing the prompt and explaining it are two different tasks—and that *both* are crucial. Do not state something to be true without explaining *why* it is true. If you want to make a convincing argument, you need to explain yourself at each key step. By explaining and expanding on the core principle embodied in the Thesis statement, you are laying the foundation for a compelling Thesis example.

For example, you might have chosen to use the paraphrase,

A democratic system cannot function well without well-informed voters.

A sophisticated explanation of that paraphrase would expand on the reasons why representative democracy requires a relatively free flow of information. In doing so, it is likely to address the following questions: How is the role of a voter in a representative state different from that of a citizen in a totalitarian or authoritarian nation? How is the relationship between voter and government defined? How would a lack of information undermine a democratic state? What kinds of information are absolutely necessary? Who gets to decide what is and is not necessary information? In addressing these questions, you are explaining why people deserve to play an active role in a representative government.

Steps 3 and 4 can be interchanged; sometimes, an expanded definition will lead smoothly to an explanation of the prompt, and sometimes the reverse will be true.

Give a Concrete Example Demonstrating the Truth of the Prompt

For the great majority of questions, the best essay examples come from history or current events. Avoid using personal examples; they are usually too limiting and will rarely effectively communicate the core issue of the prompt. Strong examples have four characteristics:

1. They are relevant to the prompt (and this relevance is clearly explained).
2. They are specific.
3. They are real (rather than hypothetical).
4. They are serious (they engage a serious social, moral, or political problem).

In our example, you can take one of two approaches. You can discuss a case in which a representative government, such as the United States, did not keep secrets, and why the lack of secrecy in that case was valid or beneficial. Conversely, you can discuss an instance in which the government did withhold information, and why secrecy was in that case illegitimate or harmful.

One case of unjustified secrecy might be the actions of the United States in the case of East Timor, when the U.S. government acted, by some accounts, to withhold information from the public regarding the Indonesian government's repression of the East Timorese population in the 1970s. The U.S. government also misrepresented its relationship with the Indonesian state (see the sample Thesis paragraph in Section 4.4). Instead of only referring vaguely to "the role of the U.S. government in political crises abroad," this example of a particular case is specific, directly relevant, and interesting.

Explain the Relevance of the Example

Examples are crucial to your Thesis, and so is an explanation of those examples. Many promising Thesis paragraphs lose points because their writers stop after stating the example, leaving it up to readers to figure out how the example connects with the prompt. Do not omit this important step. Readers can be more clueless than you would imagine—and they are usually following your reasoning a lot less closely than you are. Always follow an example with at least two explanatory sentences.

For instance, you might expand upon and explain the East Timor example by explaining what happened in East Timor and how the U.S. government used its influence to limit press coverage of the repression. Discuss how the U.S. government underplayed its own connection to the Indonesian government so as to avoid demands for action that would endanger its own relationship with a repressive but politically useful ally. You would also need to explain why this contravened the interests or the rights (or both) of citizens of a representative democracy.

14.3 GENERATING STRONG EXAMPLES

Real and Hypothetical Examples

A **real** example is an actual case from current events or history. A **hypothetical** example is based on circumstances of the real world, but comes from the imagination of the writer. It presents itself not as something that actually happened in a specific instance, but as an illustration of the usual or common state of affairs. To the reader, a real example is more convincing and more interesting, and it suggests that you are "tuned in" to important events in the world around you. However, hypothetical examples are always better than no example at all. If you must use a hypothetical, make it as specific and detailed as possible.

Different Levels of Examples

Both real and hypothetical examples can be found on different levels. When you're stuck for an example, it's helpful to think how the statement might apply to these levels:

1. Community/city
2. Statewide
3. National
4. International

For most prompts, higher-level examples are more persuasive than are lower-level ones. You may feel more comfortable right now writing about your own personal experiences than about national or international events. The best way to lose that discomfort is to become well-informed about current events.

Current and Historical Events

In addition to writing skills, the Writing Sample section tests your familiarity with the events and issues that surround you in the world at large. This is one of the reasons we've included a current events question in each chapter in this book; your essay will be more impressive if it demonstrates a sophisticated understanding of current (or historical) events. Of course, no one can know everything that goes on in our complicated world, but it is possible to develop a basic understanding of important issues.

Many students illustrate their essays with "the Greatest Hits" of history: the American Civil War, World War II, the Civil Rights Movement, the war in Iraq, and so forth. There is nothing inherently wrong with using these examples; often, however, students betray their ignorance by discussing these events in the most superficial way. Don't just mention the Civil War; write about the Northern victory at the bloody battle of Gettysburg. Don't refer in a blanket way to World War II; discuss, for example, the internment of Japanese-Americans. Don't just drop the term "Civil Rights Movement" and expect to convey something real; discuss Rosa Parks and the Montgomery bus boycott.

Get a good working knowledge of four current events and four historical events on each of the four levels, and you'll be able to apply one of them to almost any prompt.

Some good sources of news:

1. Internet news sources (NYTimes.com, LATimes.com, BBC.com, Slate.com, Yahoonews.com, etc.). Also, Wikipedia.org is an easy way to do quick research on historical examples.
2. The front page of a major hardcopy newspaper (*The New York Times, The Los Angeles Times, The Washington Post*, etc.). On page 2 or 3 of the first section you'll usually find quick summaries of statewide, national, and international stories.
3. National Public Radio. Listen to *Morning Edition* on your car radio on the way to school and *All Things Considered* in the evening for entertaining and in-depth news and cultural reports.
4. If your understanding of business and economics is rocky, try listening to the afternoon news program *Marketplace* on many public radio stations. Put out by USC, *Marketplace* is interesting and accessible to even the least economically-minded.
5. *The News Hour with Jim Lehrer* is one of the best news programs on television. You'll find it on public television in the early evening. If cable, network, or local news shows seem too fluffy or superficial for you, try this intelligent alternative.
6. News magazines such as *Time* and *Newsweek* can give you a good perspective on national and international news.

Brainstorming for Examples

Here is a technique for anyone who gets stuck for examples. As we explained in the preceding chapter, one part of Prewriting is definition expansion. Once you have taken a key word and defined it, ask yourself questions about the ideas you came up with. Then try to answer each question, thinking of specific instances, on any level, that would illustrate your answer. Here is an example of the brainstorming process you might go through for our sample essay.

Definition Expansion

"withholding information"   Pretending information doesn't exist
Misleading the public or lying
Openly withholding information

Generate Questions About Your Definitions

Q1: Does the government ever tell the public it is withholding information for the nation's own good?

Q2: When would that claim be illegitimate?

Q3: When might the government not even tell the public that it is withholding information, or pretend the information doesn't exist?

Q4: When might the government try to suppress the action of a free press to limit what information is available?

Q5: When might the government or governmental leaders illegitimately try to mislead the public about its own policies or actions?

Answer Your Questions

A1: Yes, common and commonly accepted practice (e.g., in war, information about battle plans and tactics)

A2: When the public needs that information to evaluate the legitimacy of the overall policy (e.g., the war) itself

A3: When that information itself would endanger the public good or national security (e.g., the Manhattan Project—Antithesis example?)

A4: When they think the information might endanger national security (legitimate: Gulf War, interviews with Osama Bin Laden, Manhattan Project) or when they want to avoid public debate or controversy (illegitimate: East Timor, Nicaragua and the Contras, Vietnam War)

A5: When politicians want to protect their own political career (Monica Lewinsky and Clinton) or pursue immoral, ineffective, or potentially unpopular policies (Nicaragua, East Timor, Vietnam, Savings & Loan subsidies)

14.4 PUTTING IT ALL TOGETHER

Here is one possible Thesis paragraph in response to our sample prompt:

A representative government should not withhold information from those it represents.

Thomas Jefferson once said, "Reflection, with information, is all which our countrymen need to bring themselves and their affairs to right." Jefferson made this statement in the context of discussing the nature of a truly representative democracy, and the role to be played within it by an informed citizenry. He believed that a government exists to serve and express the will of the people, and that for that will to be both well-formed and effectively expressed, a democratic government must provide the voting public with a certain amount of information regarding its activities both at home and abroad. If a government acts in deep secrecy and withholds or misrepresents crucial facts about its activities, the citizenry cannot ensure that the government is acting in the people's best interests and in accordance with their beliefs and values. Furthermore, a central tenet of any representative democratic system is accountability. If the people cannot discover what their representatives are doing, they cannot hold them responsible for the outcome of those actions. One example of when the U.S. government illegitimately kept secrets from the population was in the case of East Timor. East Timor is an island, claimed by Indonesia, that had never been fully within the Indonesian state's sphere of influence. In 1975, however, Indonesia invaded the island to crush an independence movement. By some accounts, up to one tenth of the Timorese population was killed in the resulting slaughter. The U.S. government, which saw Indonesia as an important Cold War ally, claimed that it was suspending all military and economic support in protest; in fact, the level of support increased after the invasion. Perhaps even more disturbingly, certain Congressmen successfully pressured major U.S. media sources to limit their reporting of the situation. To this day, few people know of the massacre, or of the U.S. role in supporting or perpetuating the repression. In this case, the government not only failed to disclose its true role, but carried on a campaign of disinformation so that the American public was unable to discern the truth. Secrecy here made it impossible for the voting public to voice its opinion about the legitimacy or illegitimacy of the actions taken by their government in their name, or to hold those responsible accountable.

14.5

14.5 WRITING SAMPLE EXERCISES

Exercise 1: Defining the Thesis Principle

For each of the following prompts, define at least one ideal or principle at the core of the statement.

1. Only the wealthy are morally required to use their resources to help the less fortunate. _____

_____

2. Domestic policy is the most important determinant of a nation's strength. _____

_____

3. Workers are never justified in keeping secrets from their employers. _____

_____

4. The media portrays an unrealistic view of reality. _____

_____

5. The best education takes individual needs of students into account. _____

_____

6. Open debate about government policy only makes that government stronger. _____

_____

Exercise 2: Creating Strong Examples

Each of the following examples represents a "greatest hit"; that is, an example that is commonly used in MCAT essays. If you wish to use one of these examples, you need to make it specific and concrete enough to show that you know and understand the events involved and the importance of those events (see "Current and Historical Events" above). Even better, choose a different, less common example illustrating the same point. For instance, if you need an example of a repressive regime that carries out genocidal policies, you could, along with many thousands of other test takers, discuss Hitler and the Nazi regime. Or, instead, you could make your essay stand out by discussing Pol Pot and Cambodia after the end of the Vietnam War.

For each of the following examples, do three things.

1. Identify at least one core issue or principle involved in each case.
2. List at least three specific events, people, or ideas involved in that case.
3. List at least two alternative examples that could be used to illustrate the same theme or themes.

1. Hitler and Nazism: _____

_____

_____

2. The U.S. Revolutionary War: _____

_____

_____

3. The U.S. Constitution and Bill of Rights: _____

_____

_____

4. Slavery in the United States: _____

_____

_____

5. The U.S. Civil War: _____

_____

_____

6. World Wars I and II: _____

_____

_____

7. The Vietnam War: _____

_____

_____

8. The Civil Rights Movement: _____

_____

_____

9. Watergate: _____

_____

_____

10. The Clinton/Lewinsky scandal: _____

_____

_____

11. 9/11 and Al Qaeda: _____

_____

_____

12. The U.S. wars in Iraq and Afghanistan: _____

_____

_____

Exercise 3: Current Events Question

Discuss a current event that illustrates the situation of an oppressed minority group. What is the history behind this group's oppression? What is the group's greatest hope for change?

Exercise 4: Supplemental Prompts

Here are two supplemental MCAT-style essay prompts. Time yourself strictly; allow 30 minutes per essay for planning *and* writing. To duplicate your test experience, write the essays consecutively. If you don't have time to write both essays during the week, at least make an outline for each prompt that describes the examples you'd use to illustrate your main points.

Supplemental Prompt 7

Consider this statement:

> **Voters make electoral decisions based on personality rather than policy.**

Write a unified essay in which you perform the following tasks. Explain what you think the above statement means. Describe a specific situation in which voters might make electoral decisions based on policy rather than personality. Discuss what you think determines whether voters make electoral decisions based on personality or on policy.

Supplemental Prompt 8

Consider this statement:

> **Certain actions are always wrong, regardless of the intent of the actor.**

Write a unified essay in which you perform the following tasks. Explain what you think the above statement means. Describe a specific situation in which the validity of an action might be affected by the intent of the actor. Discuss what you think determines when intentions affect the validity of an action.

14.6   TIMED ESSAY #2

Give yourself 30 minutes to write this essay. Do it on your computer but do not use spell-check. After you write the essay, read through the analysis of the prompt and two student essays that follow.

Consider this statement:

> **Politicians should live by a stricter ethical code than other people.**

Write a unified essay in which you perform the following tasks. Explain what you think the above statement means. Describe a specific situation in which a politician might not live by a stricter ethical code than other people. Discuss what you think determines when politicians should live by a stricter ethical code than other people, and when they legitimately might not.

Analysis of the Prompt

This is a prompt that implicitly asks how the job of a politician is qualitatively different from other jobs or functions in society. To say that politicians should live by a stricter ethical code than other people is to say that there is something special about being a politician such that we might judge that person's actions by higher standards than we might use to evaluate the morality of, say, a CEO, a construction worker, a lawyer, a homemaker, etc. For the Thesis, then, you need to address this special role, and discuss in what instances we *should* use special standards to judge the ethical behavior of a politician. Note the word "should"; an essay that simply argues that we *do* hold them to different standards is incomplete if it does not explain why these special standards are legitimate or justified. Make it clear in the Thesis what you mean by "politician" (national leaders? any elected representative? well-known leaders? any person with a governmental function or role? etc.). You should also explain what you mean by "stricter ethical code."

The Antithesis must explain in what circumstances politicians legitimately might not live by a stricter ethical code than other people. Avoid an Antithesis example that discusses different as opposed to stricter standards (for example, politicians imposing their own personal moral beliefs on policymaking). You might discuss different kinds of politicians, different activities of similar politicians, or different roles played by politicians in different aspects of their lives. You could, for example, argue that behavior relating to their public role—that is, their job—should be judged more strictly, while in their private lives (e.g., within their families) they should be held to the same standards as anyone else. Be careful to fully explain the rationale behind your distinction. If you argue that a president should not be judged more harshly in his "private life" for acts of adultery or child abuse, for example, make sure to explain *why* his special role as a representative of the nation does not require exemplary behavior in all aspects of life.

Your Synthesis should apply consistently to both of your examples. Provide a rule that defines when a politician should and should not live by stricter ethical standards. Is it based on whether or not that person is seen as a role model? Whether or not their ethical or unethical behavior can affect their constituency? Perhaps it depends not on the person but the circumstances, e.g., whether or not we are in times of war or economic crisis, or in peacetime.

Student Response #1

Politicians serve as representatives of their constituents. The inherent nature of their job makes them, to a certain degree, into a celebrity. They are often well-known throughout their community as well as outside of their communities. Because of our system of democratic representation, it is believed that our politicians should, for the most part, act in an acceptable manner and uphold higher ethical standards than an average person.

The way of life is different for a politician in that he or she does need to keep up a positive image or else run the risk of not getting re-elected. As a result of this pressure to maintain this image, they can't be seen having a drink at a bar after a long day's work. They aren't supposed to be seen having a smoke when put under heavy pressure. Furthermore, they definitely shouldn't be caving in to infidelity. All of these things are seen in a negative light and all politicians linked to them won't be helping boost their careers any.

On the other hand, the normal citizen sometimes will allow for these standards to drop under the right circumstances. For instance, our Commander-in-Chief has the power to declare war and cause hundreds of casualties. They are expected to loosen their ethical standards to ironically "do what is right." That is, it is OK for our government to fight Iraq in defense of poor little Kuwait. Never mind all of the destruction that the war caused. Economic sanctions and embargoes also fall into this category, although they lead to starvation, unemployment, etc.

In the end, politicians should act in a proper way for the most part. They should *do* their best to represent their communities well. However, the exception to this is when you have to lower standards for the good of your constituents. Nixon and the Watergate affair was a play for personal gain of power so that was seen as not right. George Bush ordering air strikes over Tel Aviv in the 90's was seen in good light. As was the economic embargo against Vietnam in the 80's. Both of these tied into our nation's belief in liberty and democracy.

Sample Student Response #1—Grader's Comments: This writer makes a good start at defining the special nature of a politician's job. He does not, however, define what he means by "a stricter ethical code." It is not clear why smoking or drinking in a bar would be seen as unethical behavior. More importantly, the essay never addresses the core issue of why it *should* be seen as unethical. The author refers to behaving in an "unacceptable manner," but does not show that this behavior is more unacceptable for a politician than for other people. The issue of infidelity comes closer to clearly unethical behavior, but the fact that it would hurt the politician's chances of reelection doesn't in and of itself show that he or she <u>should</u> be judged more harshly than others for infidelity.

The Antithesis runs into some serious problems when it discusses the morality of war-making. The author indicates that declaring and prosecuting a war represents a lowering of ethical standards, but at the same time argues that in doing so the leader is doing "what's right." A politician then is required to go to war in order to protect the nation; how can that involve being held to looser ethical standards? This is instead a case of *different*, rather than equivalent or looser, ethical rules applying to a political leader.

The Synthesis makes an excellent distinction between actions taken to increase one's own political power, and those taken for the good of the nation. Unfortunately, this is not particularly applicable to the Thesis cases of personal "misbehavior" or unhealthy habits, and it is inconsistent with the claim in the Antithesis that actions taken for the good of the nation in war are unethical. Finally, the problem of "stricter" versus "different" standards still applies.

Score: 2.5

Student Response #2   A politician is primarily a public citizen and lives a public life. His or her moral decisions have a direct effect on their constituents. That puts the politician in a position of authority and power, and so that position must in many cases be accompanied by an increased ethical conscience. This may be seen specifically when a conflict of interest arises when a politician has the capacity to harm his or her constituents. Such a situation recently arose when the former Vice President of the US, Dick Cheney, was forced to relinquish his vast holdings and involvement in energy corporations after he took office. In becoming a politician and moving from the private to the public sector, a public figure with public authority, he had to understand and comply with the high ethical responsibility that came with that power. That power would allow him to manipulate the energy market to his financial advantage, robbing the people he represents of their tax dollars.

However, one cannot forget that a politician is also at the same time a private citizen, leading a private life. In their private lives, politicians deserve the privacy that is the basic right of all citizens. Thus, the ethics of a politician in the inner circle of his personal life does not need to comply with a stricter standard than other citizens. For he or she is a private citizens as well. This argument is explicitly shown by the Monica Lewinsky scandal in which President Clinton was impeached because his political adversaries took advantage of an unethical decision he made in his personal life. By any standards, Clinton's actions were unethical, but he committed them without harming the people he represents on a national level. If a private citizen commits adultery, we condemn them for harming their family and others in their private circle of friends, but we do not believe that they can no longer do their job, or that they should lose their job. Clinton should have been condemned as would any person for a personal ethical lapse, not held to a higher standard of ethical behavior and had his job put in jeopardy.

The public and private spheres of influence must be taken into account when deciding when politicians should maintain higher ethical standards than other citizens. Immoral decisions made in the public sphere of a politician's life may detrimentally affect many of the innocent people the politician is supposed to protect, as part of their sworn duty to the nation or the community. And yet immoral behavior in a politician's private life should be understood. For it is one's right to control the personal aspects of one's life. Without this right, humans are not truly free.

Sample Student Response #2—Grader's Comments:

This author does a nice job of indicating why a politician plays a special role, and gives an excellent specific and well detailed Thesis example. The Thesis would be even stronger if it more directly addressed the comparative theme implicit in the prompt. Other people in positions of power also have the capacity to manipulate the economy and harm large numbers of people through their actions (e.g., powerful people in the business world, such as Bill Gates). The author suggests, but does not explicitly discuss why political use of power is qualitatively different.

The Antithesis relies on an overused but appropriate example, and raises an excellent distinction between the public and private lives of politicians. It also goes on to explain why this is a relevant distinction (one's constituents are not harmed). This essay, unlike the first sample essay, sticks to the terms of the prompt, discussing why this kind of unethical behavior should be judged harshly, but not more harshly than for private citizens. The Antithesis would be even stronger with some discussion of why this kind of unethical behavior, especially when it becomes public and identified with the office of the Presidency, does not in fact cause some kind of "national" harm (e.g., by reducing people's faith and trust in the political system).

The Synthesis is the weakest section of the essay, in part because it is not entirely consistent with the Antithesis. In the Antithesis, the author argues that "private" unethical behavior by politicians should be judged equally harshly, while in the Synthesis he suggests that everyone has a right to certain kinds of unethical behavior. With a more fully developed and consistent Synthesis, this essay could have scored in the 5–6 range.

Score: 4.5

Chapter 14 Summary

- Articulate the core principle involved in the prompt statement.

- A Thesis Paragraph Model:

    - Start with a hook (and transitional sentences).

    - Paraphrase the prompt statement.

    - Define and analyze key terms (if they are abstract or vague).

    - Explain the core Thesis principle.

    - Give a strong example demonstrating the truth in the statement.

    - Explain the relevance of your example to the terms of the prompt.

- Defining abstract terms is key to writing a strong Thesis (and can provide the basis for a strong Antithesis as well).

- A strong example will be relevant to the statement, specific, and concrete.

- Examples may be real or hypothetical, but real-world examples are best.

- Examples may be on any of the following levels: community/city, state, national, or international.

- To have strong examples on hand, read, listen to, or watch a good source of news every day.

- Brainstorming for examples:

    - Definition expansion

    - Generate questions about your definitions

    - Answer your questions

Chapter 15
Focus on
the Antithesis

GOALS

1. To identify the Antithesis principle
2. To give a strong Antithesis example
3. To build a clear Thesis–Antithesis contrast

15.1   FOCUS ON THE ANTITHESIS

A sophisticated argument must consider more than one side of an issue. The three prompt tasks are set up to not just to encourage you, but to require you to do this in your essay. In the Thesis, you explain the principle guiding or underlying the prompt statement and discuss the conditions that would make it true. In the Antithesis you must discuss the principle or ideal embodied in the opposite of the prompt, and the conditions under which the opposite of the prompt statement would be true.

When formulating the Antithesis, ask yourself the following questions:

1. Where is the weakness in the prompt claim?
2. What would require an exception to the rule expressed in the Thesis?
3. What is valid or compelling about the Antithesis position?
4. Why, in fact and in principle, could the Antithesis argument be true?

Remember that by the wording of the Antithesis task there is always some truth in the opposing statement. An essay that invalidates or rejects one part of the question by arguing that the Antithesis (or the Thesis) is never true, or that one side of the question is always more compelling than the other, has broken the rules set out by the question. Even if you firmly believe that one side of the prompt statement is always true (e.g., that the government should never keep secrets from the voting population, regardless of the circumstances or the costs of disclosure), you cannot write your essay in order to prove that case. Incomplete or one-sided essays will be judged very harshly by the MCAT graders. You can use the questions listed above to find your way to a reasonable Antithesis response, regardless of your own personal position on the matter.

Let's look at some essay topics in this light. Each of the following questions includes only the prompt statement and the Antithesis task for that prompt.

1. **A stable society depends on citizens who follow the rules.** Describe a specific situation in which a stable society might not depend on citizens who follow the rules.
   - When wouldn't following the rules be necessary for stability? Might the two sometimes even be mutually exclusive? Why might stability require rule-breaking citizens (people who are creative, willing to take a risk and experiment, unwilling to follow norms or traditions, etc.) in order to function or evolve? Might there be a relevant distinction based on different forms of stable societies, or different phases of the development of a society?
2. **Inequality is inherently unfair.** Describe a specific situation in which fairness might coexist with inequality.
   - Why might fairness sometimes require treating people differently? Does achieving fairness ever depend on taking individual characteristics or circumstances into account? Could fair treatment of different classes or categories of people (adults and children, rich and poor, citizens and non-citizens, mentally or physically ill and healthy, etc.) be based on different ethical rules or principles?
3. **In modern society, there is no such thing as privacy.** Describe a specific situation in which privacy might exist in modern society.
   - What aspects of a modern society might not reduce privacy, but instead increase it? Do aspects of modern society, such as new modes of communication (e.g., e-mail, faxes, cell phones, internet cameras, etc.) or travel, or labor-saving technologies, necessarily involve increased exposure of our lives to others, or might it close us off or isolate us from others in new ways?

15.2   AN ANTITHESIS PARAGRAPH MODEL

There are two ways of approaching the Antithesis task. You can argue that the prompt statement is usually true in principle and in practice, but that there are exceptions to the rule. Or, you can argue that the Thesis and Antithesis principles are equally valid, but that they apply to different cases or situations. Either way, use the following model to organize your Antithesis response:

1. Make the transition.
2. Define key terms (if necessary).
3. Explain the Antithesis principle.
4. Give a strong example.
5. Explain the relevance of the example.

We'll illustrate how to construct an Antithesis paragraph using our sample prompt from Chapter 4:

A representative government should not withhold information from those it represents.

Write a unified essay in which you perform the following tasks. Explain what you think the above statement means. Describe a specific situation in which a representative government might be justified in withholding information from those it represents. Discuss what you think determines whether or not a representative government is justified in withholding information from those it represents.

Make the Transition

The transition between the Thesis and the Antithesis paragraph involves an about-face in the direction of the argument. To avoid confusion in the first sentence of the Antithesis, you need to alert the reader that you are moving on to the second task. Use a pivotal word or phrase (e.g., *however, but, although, on the other hand*, etc.) to signal this shift.

Transitional Question

When is a representative government justified in withholding information?

Possible Transition Sentences

Nevertheless, there are limited instances in which governmental secrecy would be justified.

However, a democratic government has the duty not only to represent and serve the will of the people, but to protect the sovereignty and security of the nation as well.

Not all state secrets, however, are illegitimate.

On the other hand, sometimes state secrecy, while not ideal, is necessary for the survival of the nation.

Define Key Terms (If Necessary)

In most cases you will have already defined key terms in the Thesis. If the wording of the Antithesis brings in new abstract vocabulary, however, you may need to explain those terms in this paragraph.

Sometimes your Antithesis example might involve a variation on terms you have already defined. For example, you might have defined *withholding information* in the Thesis as "keeping information from the public in such a way that the population is not even aware of the existence of that information." In the Antithesis, you might explain that another form of withholding information is an "open" secret. That is, the government makes it known that certain information exists, but that it is not willing or able to divulge it.

Explain the Antithesis Principle

This section of your Antithesis paragraph is similar to the section in your Thesis paragraph where you explain the meaning of the paraphrased prompt. Don't rely on your readers' understanding of the opposition; spell out the justification for the existence of exceptions to the Thesis rule.

You might, for example, have written the transitional sentence, "However, a democratic government has the duty not only to represent and serve the will of the people, but also to protect the sovereignty and security of the nation." Your transition will be stronger if you follow it with a generalization or explanation of its meaning before you start to describe the example. In our sample prompt, you could point out that sometimes people want access to information that, if granted, could destroy them. In other cases, people are aware of this risk and feel safer if the information is withheld. In times of war or national security crises, then, sometimes a certain level of state secrecy is not only allowable but obligatory.

This discussion has the added benefit of laying the groundwork for your Synthesis criteria, which are based on the conditions or circumstances that distinguish your Thesis case from your Antithesis case.

Give a Strong Example

A strong example is as important to your Antithesis as it is to your Thesis. It's wise to have an Antithesis example that serves as a good partner to your Thesis example. In general, examples on the same level (see Chapter 14) work well together. Prompts about the actions or responsibilities of governments in particular essentially force you to choose examples on similar (national or international) levels.

For example, in our prompt about inequality (see Prompt 2 in Section 15.1 above), your Thesis example might be about the Civil Rights Movement and Constitutional guarantees of equal treatment before the law. This is equality on a high level. If your Antithesis example were to discuss "inequality" on a very small scale or personal level, such as how parents treat their children, this is a form of inequality so different from your first example that the two are not really comparable. Furthermore, the real-world and serious nature of your Thesis example makes the Antithesis case look trivial. A better, more comparable Antithesis example would be the Americans with Disabilities Act as it relates to hiring practices. A courtroom and a workplace are similar enough to be clearly comparable.

Avoid Antithesis examples on any level that are trivial or non-debatable. Take for instance our prompt about modern society privacy (see Prompt 3 in Section 15.1 above). An example of modern technology that has no impact or bearing on the lives of most individuals (e.g., NASA's technology that allows it to communicate with and control spacecraft like the Mars Pathfinder) may in fact not lead to a loss of personal privacy, but only because it cannot do this, by its very nature. This leaves you with nothing much to say in the rest of the Antithesis regarding the relevance of the example, and it traps you into circular reasoning in the Synthesis (circular reasoning is discussed in Chapter 16).

In our sample essay, we might choose an example of secrecy in wartime, like the Manhattan Project during World War II. In this case, the government believed that they were racing with Germany to build a nuclear weapon, and that the first nation to achieve it would win the war. Here, one could argue that the government had both the right and the duty to keep their efforts secret.

Explain the Relevance of the Example

Everything you learned in the preceding chapter about generating and incorporating examples for Thesis paragraphs can be applied to the Antithesis paragraph as well. As with the Thesis example, the Antithesis example cannot stand on its own; you need to expand on its relevance to the principle you have advanced in the Antithesis transition.

15.3   PUTTING IT ALL TOGETHER

Here, then, is one possible Antithesis response to our sample prompt on withholding information within a representative system.

However, a representative democratic government has the duty not only to represent and serve the will of the people, but also to protect the sovereignty and security of the nation. When a nation is at war or under attack, the government may have a legitimate right, even an obligation, to keep secrets from the voting public in the name of national security. The population often recognizes that disclosure of sensitive information like battle plans and tactics in this situation would be antithetical to their interests, and implicitly consents to secrecy. If a democratic nation is conquered in war by a non-democratic state, all of its guarantees of individual rights and protections against governmental abuse of power will disappear. For example, in World War II the U.S. believed that it was in a race with Germany to invent and use the atomic bomb. It was firmly believed in the U.S. and Europe that if Hitler got the bomb first, he would win the war. The U.S. gathered together thousands of scientists in Los Alamos in the top secret Manhattan Project, whose goal was to invent the A-Bomb. Secrecy in this case was necessary, as any information given to the public would necessarily make its way to Germany, and put the whole world at risk. One can argue about whether the development and use of the Bomb against Japan in 1945 was really in the long-term best interests of the world (given the problem of nuclear proliferation that followed). However, the secrecy surrounding its development at the time, with the goal of both shortening and winning the war, was fully justified. The conventional bombing campaign against Japan of which the American public was fully aware and in support, took hundreds of thousands of lives. The use of the Bomb was not qualitatively or ethically different from conventional bombing, and many argue that it served its intended purpose of cutting short the war and saving millions of lives on both sides.

15.4   WRITING SAMPLE EXERCISES

Exercise 1: Brainstorming Examples

For each of the following questions, come up with at least one pair of Thesis-Antithesis examples. Make sure that your examples are comparable yet contrasting. Make your examples as concrete and specific as possible. For each question, only the prompt statement and the Antithesis task are given.

1. **T:** Voters support politicians with whom they can personally identify.
    A: Describe a situation in which voters might support politicians with whom they cannot personally identify.

    _____

    _____

    _____

2. **T:** States should base their policies on the beliefs and desires of the residents of that state.
    A: Describe a specific situation in which states should not base their policies on the beliefs and desires of the residents of that state.

    _____

    _____

    _____

3. **T:** History repeats itself.
    A: Describe a specific situation in which history might not repeat itself.

    _____

    _____

    _____

4. **T:** A healthy economy requires allowing troubled businesses to fail.
    A: Describe a specific situation in which a healthy economy might not require allowing troubled businesses to fail.

    _____

    _____

    _____

Exercise 1: Brainstorming Examples—Sample Responses

1. Voters support politicians with whom they can personally identify.
    Thesis
    -   Ronald Reagan: known as "The Great Communicator" and "Teflon President"—popularity based on friendly and humorous personality rather than on policies. People felt like he was their grandfather.
    -   George W. Bush: voters said "would like to have a beer with him," colloquial language, "guy next door" image.

    Antithesis
    -   Eisenhower: anti-communism and pledge to end Korean War made him, as a war hero, popular in post-WWII era. Support based on strong leadership rather than personal identification.
    -   Obama: symbol of change, elected in time of war and economic crisis. Support based on desire for change in military and economic policy rather than personal identification.

2. States should base their policies on the beliefs and desires of the residents of that state.
    Thesis
    -   Taxation: New Hampshire has no sales or personal income tax. Fits with belief in individual self-sufficiency and minimizing role of government (state motto— "Live Free or Die"). Legitimate because affects only residents.
    -   State as in nation: Sweden, high levels of taxation to support high level of social services (education and health care)—based on belief in state taking active role in society. Legitimate because no international impact.

    Antithesis
    -   Desegregation in Little Rock Arkansas: Pres. Eisenhower sent troops to enforce desegregation (following Brown v. Board of Education decision in 1954) against wishes of Gov. Faubus and of many white residents of Arkansas. State should not base policy on beliefs that entail denying constitutional rights.
    -   State as in nation, and international policy: U.S. support for the Contras in Nicaragua in 1980s. States should not intervene militarily to change political system of socialist or communist nations, even if majority of U.S. population believes in superiority of our own form of democratic politics.

3. History repeats itself
    Thesis
    -   War: intervention in other nations (Vietnam, Nicaragua, Iraq). Events caused by basic human desires for power and self-defense will repeat.
    -   Economics: cycles of recession and depression often track back to similar factors. Examples: Great Depression stemming from stock market crash in 1939, the Panic of 1839 caused by crash of real estate market, and current recession caused by decline in real estate market and fed by stock market decline.

Antithesis
- Technology: Advances in computer technology have transformed society in part by making us dependent on it. This is a new problem—for example, widespread fear of what would happen in transition to year 2000 (Y2K) if coding problems crashed computer systems around the world.
- Theoretical science: rather than repeating past ideas, seeks to transform our understanding of reality. Examples: quantum mechanics and string theory.

4. A healthy economy requires allowing troubled businesses to fail.
   Thesis
   - If economy as a whole does not depend on that business. Example: Circuit City products available elsewhere.
   - If it is due to malfeasance or mismanagement on part of the business. Example: Enron and Worldcom

   Antithesis
   - If economy or society as a whole would suffer if the businesses failed. Example: 2009 bank bailouts.
   - If problems are not due to business's own actions. Example: airlines after 9/11.

Exercise 2: Matching Thesis and Antithesis Examples

For each of the following prompt statements, come up with at least 3 separate pairs (Thesis and Antithesis) of examples. Make sure that within each pair, your examples are contrasting (qualitatively different) and comparable (on similar levels). For each question, only the prompt statement and the Antithesis task are given.

1. **Individual rights should take precedence over the needs of the community.** Describe a specific situation in which individual rights should not take precedence over the needs of the community.

Thesis Examples	Antithesis Examples
1)	
2)	
3)	

2. **The best music is that which pleases the listener.** Describe a specific situation in which the best music might not be that which pleases the listener.

Thesis Examples	Antithesis Examples
1)	
2)	
3)	

3. **Good citizenship requires conforming to social norms.** Describe a specific situation in which good citizenship might not require conforming to social norms.

Thesis Examples	Antithesis Examples
1)	
2)	
3)	

4. **The best way for a business to thrive is to destroy the competition.** Describe a specific situation in which the best way for a business to thrive might not be to destroy the competition.

Thesis Examples	Antithesis Examples
1)	
2)	
3)	

Exercise 3: Current Events Question

Describe a current event in the world of medical science. Is there a new treatment, therapy, or drug that has the potential to alter the practice of medicine? Is this treatment, therapy, or drug controversial in any way? What do you think doctors, patients, and the government should do, and why?

Exercise 4: Supplemental Prompts

Here are two supplemental MCAT-style essay prompts to work on at home. Time yourself strictly; allow 30 minutes per essay for planning *and* writing. To duplicate your test experience, write the essays consecutively. If you don't have time to write both essays during the week, at least make an outline for each prompt that describes the examples you'd use to illustrate your main points.

Supplemental Prompt 9

Consider this statement:

> **A news reporter should never express a personal opinion.**

Write a unified essay in which you perform the following tasks. Explain what you think the above statement means. Describe a specific situation in which a news reporter might legitimately express a personal opinion. Discuss what you think determines when a news reporter should or should not express a personal opinion.

Supplemental Prompt 10

Consider this statement:

> **In a democracy, what constitutes justice should be defined by majority will.**

Write a unified essay in which you perform the following tasks. Explain what you think the above statement means. Describe a specific situation in which justice in a democracy should not be defined by the majority will. Discuss what you think determines whether or not justice in a democracy should be defined by majority will.

Chapter 15 Summary

- Approach the Antithesis task by asking:

  - Where is the weakness in the prompt claim?

  - What exceptions must be made to the prompt statement?

  - What is valid or compelling about the Antithesis argument?

  - Why, in fact and in principle, should the Antithesis argument be true?

- Include the following components in your Antithesis paragraph:

  - A transitional sentence

  - A definition of key terms when necessary

  - An explanation of the Antithesis principle

  - A strong example that clearly contrasts with your Thesis example

  - An explanation of the relevance of that example to the terms of the prompt

Chapter 16
Focus on
the Synthesis

GOALS

1. To articulate a clear Synthesis rule
2. To base your Synthesis on the contrast between your examples
3. To avoid circular reasoning

16.1   THE SYNTHESIS RULE

At one time or another, everyone has had the problem of a top-heavy essay. By the time we reach the end, we've run out of gas; we just want the terrible experience to be over. Unfortunately, the graders give equal weight to each of the three essay tasks. You need to save some time and energy for your Synthesis.

The best way to ensure that you have a valid Synthesis is to include that task in your brainstorming and outlining. Many of the best essays begin in the outlining process with a clear idea of what the Synthesis criteria will be. This helps you to choose clearly relevant and contrasting examples, and guarantees that your essay will constitute a complete, coherent whole (rather than a series of disconnected or contradictory paragraphs). Don't wait for inspiration to strike in the last few minutes. If it doesn't, you are stuck with an incomplete (that is, low scoring) essay or a superficial Synthesis that leaves a bad last impression in the reader's mind.

The Synthesis has a simple structure. It must contain the conditions under which the statement would hold true, and the conditions under which the opposite of the statement would hold true. The Synthesis task, the most abstract part of the question, often seems particularly difficult at first. You may have questions like these:

What Does *Conditions* Mean, Anyway?

Imagine yourself as the judge in a courtroom setting legal precedent for the future. You have to provide a set of "laws" by which the rest of humanity can judge its actions. Think of conditions as laws, guidelines, or rules that could be used by other judges in the future to decide similar cases.

How Can I Decide What the *Conditions* Should Be? Who Am I to Decide??

You're the judge, remember? Don't worry about finding the "correct" conditions. You decide what is correct. The prompts are designed to allow for a number of equally valid interpretations. When you ask yourself whether education should teach practical skills or ethical values, imagine that it is *your* school district, in question, *your* children. When you ask yourself what kinds of speech society should tolerate, imagine the speeches that you might want to give and the ways in which you might be silenced and why. When you personalize the situation, it's easier to dig out the guidelines that already exist in your mind.

How Specific Do These *Conditions* Have to Be?

Nothing rankles an essay grader more than a vague, inconclusive Synthesis that reads something like, "Individuals are better at solving problems when they're effective," or "We shouldn't try to conquer Nature when doing so is harmful." If you're setting the guidelines of law, you must be as specific as possible. Vague terms like *effective, harmful, good, bad*, etc., can be interpreted in so many ways that no one could use your laws as guidelines for behavior without further explanation.

16.2   A SYNTHESIS PARAGRAPH MODEL

Every Synthesis paragraph must contain the conditions under which the statement would hold true, and the conditions under which the opposite of the statement would hold true. Use the following model to organize your Synthesis response:

1. Make the transition: paraphrase the Synthesis task
2. State a general principle
3. Show how the principle applies to your examples
4. Explain, define, and refine the principle
5. Conclude

Let's look again at the sample prompt we have been using to illustrate each task.

A representative government should not withhold information from those it represents.

Write a unified essay in which you perform the following tasks. Explain what you think the above statement means. Describe a specific situation in which a representative government might be justified in withholding information from those it represents. Discuss what you think determines whether or not a representative government is justified in withholding information from those it represents.

Make the Transition

Signal to the reader that you are moving on to the third task. A paraphrase of the Synthesis task that includes a reference to the core issue of your argument will do the job. For our sample prompt, you might write the following:

Therefore, both the nature of the secret and the motivation behind the secrecy determine whether or not a representative government is justified in keeping information from the public.

State a General Principle

One hallmark of a well-developed essay is its inclusion of a general rule, principle, or criterion that could be applied to cases other than the ones you describe in your examples. It is usually much easier, however, to think in specific than in general terms. If you're stuck for a general principle, follow these guidelines (ideally, during your outlining process, not in the last 2 minutes!).

- **Ask yourself *why* your Antithesis example is an exception to the prompt statement.**

Secrecy in the case of the Manhattan project is justified because it was necessary to win the war, and because the voters implicitly consent to (or even desire) secrecy regarding battle tactics and weaponry.

- **Broaden this criterion or set of criteria to a more global or inclusive statement.**

If divulging information threatens the survival of the nation, and if the citizenry knows of and accepts the type of secrecy involved, governmental secrecy in a representative democracy may be justified.

- **Rephrase the global condition as a general rule.**

A democratic government is only ethically justified in keeping information from the voting public when lack of secrecy would threaten the democratic system itself. Because it is a democratic government, secrecy must also involve some level of consent on the part of the governed, be it explicit or implicit.

Show How the Principle Applies to Your Examples

Compare your two examples and show how the principle explains why the prompt is true in one case (certain conditions were met) and not in the other (the conditions were not met or other conditions were met). By connecting your examples to each other and to the criteria, you will improve your essay's coherence.

At this stage, do not simply reiterate the details of each example. Instead, focus on the fundamental contrast between the two, and begin to show how that contrast can be generalized.

Explain, Define, and Refine the Principle

When you state a principle, you introduce new language to the essay. A strong Synthesis will explain the terms of the principle. Many low-scoring essays use very general criteria like "cause harm to others" or "infringe on another's rights." These phrases are ambiguous. How much harm must be caused? How many people must be affected? How do we decide whose rights take precedence when there is a conflict? What constitutes infringement? When does harm caused to others outweigh individual rights or vice versa? Remember to clearly define ambiguous words in your Synthesis, and to explain *why* your criteria are valid or compelling.

One way to expand upon your principle is to show how it applies to other cases. However, only do this if you have time to explain *how and why* it applies. Simply listing a series of cases without discussing them detracts from, rather than adds to, your argument. Also, any new examples must be consistent with the examples you have provided in the first two tasks; do not introduce entirely new issues or change your definitions of key terms at the end of the essay. When in doubt, decide against bringing in new examples.

Conclude

Even if you are running out of time, you want to end your essay on a clear note. Take at least one sentence to "wrap up" your essay.

16.3   PUTTING IT ALL TOGETHER

Let's wrap up our sample essay with the following sample Synthesis paragraph.

Therefore, both the nature of the secret and the motivation behind it determine the legitimacy of governmental secrecy. A representative government is ethically justified in keeping secrets from the voting public only when lack of secrecy would threaten the democratic system itself. In a democracy, secrecy must also involve some level of consent on the part of the governed, be it explicit or implicit. In the case of East Timor, the U.S. government was not threatened by the independence movement. FRETILIN, the political party at the head of the movement, did not express an anti-American ideology or platform. Even if they had, they would have had no capacity to significantly harm U.S. political or economic interests. Because the public was actively misled by a campaign of disinformation, the voters did not even know the situation existed, and so did not and could not consent. A similar instance occurred before the Vietnam War, when the government exaggerated or even fabricated an attack on a U.S. ship in the Gulf of Tonkin, in order to drum up public and Congressional support for U.S. involvement in the conflict. In this case as well, national security was not in jeopardy, and the voting public was given no opportunity to withhold its consent. Conversely, without the secrecy necessitated by the Manhattan Project, the U.S. and its allies were in danger of losing the war. The public was fully behind the war effort and implicitly consented to any means necessary to win. When public support for a war or other governmental undertaking is less unanimous (as in Vietnam) however, consent must be expressed much more explicitly in order to legitimate governmental secrecy. In conclusion, a democratic government is guided and constrained by special rules, and at times apparently contradictory duties. It must act openly enough to be held accountable to the voting public, but must not at the same time put the nation at risk by making it vulnerable to its enemies. It is only in times of great crisis, then, that governmental secrecy can be justified.

16.4   USING SYNTHESIS DICHOTOMIES

Many Syntheses can be based on a dichotomy. A dichotomy describes a pair of mutually exclusive or contradictory terms. Many students find that it helps to come up with a relevant dichotomy first, in the prewriting stage, and then to find examples that fall on either side of the contrast.

Here's a list of some possible dichotomies.

- public/private
- rights/benefits
- large scale/small scale
- independence/interdependence
- individual/collective
- voluntary/involuntary
- local/federal
- domestic/international
- long term/short term
- objective/subjective
- permanent/changing
- socioeconomic/political
- rights/privileges
- children/adults
- needs/wants
- traditional/innovative
- wartime/peacetime

Here are some examples of how these dichotomies can be used.

- In the "education and ethics" essay (Chapter 11), many students base their Synthesis criteria on the public/private dichotomy: public school can teach only practical abilities, while private education should instill certain ethical values.
- The long term/short term dichotomy works well for prompts that ask when the government can limit our individual rights or impose other restrictions on us. This would apply to the sample essay we have been writing in Chapters 14–16 about governmental secrecy.
- The children/adults dichotomy applies to our question in Chapter 15 about inequality and fairness (see 15.1). You might argue that fairness for adults, who are equal before the law and responsible for their own actions, requires equality. On the other hand, fairness for children, who are not yet fully formed or "responsible" people, does not (thus the procedural differences between juvenile and adult courts).
- Or, you could use the voluntary/involuntary contrast for this same prompt: Fairness requires equality when we do not voluntarily accept being treated as unequal. Therefore, it is unacceptable to discriminate in hiring or in the workplace on the basis of race. However, when we voluntarily accept inequality, as when we accept a low-level position in a hierarchical organization, unequal treatment may be ethically acceptable.

16.5 AVOIDING CIRCULAR REASONING

Vague and inconclusive Synthesis criteria can lead you into a common pitfall: circular reasoning. An argument based on circular reasoning states something that is true by definition, as opposed to showing *why* that thing is true. By claiming, for example, that "A democratic government should only keep secrets when secrecy is justified," you are essentially arguing: "Governments can keep secrets when they are allowed to keep secrets." True, but that doesn't really tell us anything. Imagine trying to use this as a criterion or guideline to judge another case of governmental secrecy. To decide in that instance whether or not secrecy is justified, you would have to already know whether or not secrecy was justified.

So, things that are harmful are, by definition, things that should be avoided whenever possible. Policies that are beneficial are policies that we always want to implement. To say that we should do what is right, or avoid doing bad things, is to say nothing at all. If for example you argue that "it is best to be cautious unless caution would be detrimental," you are in essence making the radical claim that "caution is good unless it's bad."

Let's look to some of the examples we used in the last chapter for illustrations of what circular reasoning looks like, and to see how to avoid it.

1. **A stable society depends on citizens who follow the rules.** Describe a specific situation in which a stable society might not depend on citizens who follow the rules. Discuss what you think determines whether or not a stable society depends on citizens who follow the rules.
    *   A Synthesis criterion for this prompt based on circular reasoning might read, "When following rules is not necessary for stability, stability will be based on other characteristics."
    *   To avoid making this mistake, discuss what particular qualities of a society, of a people, of a time, or of a place will make following rules either necessary or unimportant. For example,

Whether or not following rules is necessary for stability depends on the maturity or immaturity of the nation. Young nations, in order to develop into stable democracies, need freethinking, creative citizens who are not bound by rules defining acceptable behavior. "Undisciplined" citizens are able to experiment and innovate, to arrive at the best possible way of organizing a new society and its politcal system. Well-established and highly developed nations and societies, however, need self-disciplined citizens who will follow the established political and social rules and ensure the continued stability of the nation.

2. **Inequality is inherently unfair.** Describe a specific situation in which fairness might coexist with inequality. Discuss what you think determines whether or not inequality is inherently unfair.

- A Synthesis statement on this prompt which argues that "when fairness can coexist with a fundamental belief that some people are inherently less or more valuable than other people, fairness does not require equality" is just saying the same thing twice. Instead, you might argue the following:

16.5

Fairness in the courtroom requires that we see all people as equal; that is, that we act by the tenet that we all have an equal right to a fair trial. Fairness in the business world, however, allows for treating some people as more skilled, more productive; that is, more valuable than others. Applying the rule of law differently in different cases is clearly unjust. But treating different job applicants or employees differently based on their "inequality" may in fact be ethically defensible.

3. **In modern society, there is no such thing as privacy.** Describe a specific situation in which privacy might exist in modern society. Discuss what you think determines when privacy can exist in modern society and when it cannot.

- A test taker who hasn't really thought through this issue might write in his or her Synthesis that "modern technologies that have no effect on our personal lives do not lead to a loss of personal privacy. New technology that lets the world intrude into our private affairs, however, always results in a loss of personal privacy." These two sentences are just taking up space. A more substantive Synthesis criterion might argue the following:

Whether or not advances brought about by modern society lead to a loss of privacy depends on if we have a choice whether or not to use those technologies. Those who work in fields in which they are required to immediately respond to e-mails and to keep their cell phones turned on at all times have lost an essential "private space" that used to be defined by the distinction between work-time and personal time. However, those who can find productive, satisfying, and well-paying jobs that do not require that they be constantly "reachable," or who are able to exert control over when they do and do not have to use these technologies, are able to maintain a barrier between public and private space.

16.6   WRITING SAMPLE EXERCISES

Exercise 1: Start With a Dichotomy

For each of the following prompts (the tasks are provided in abbreviated form), come up with at least one relevant dichotomy. Express this dichotomy as a Synthesis rule. Then, find a Thesis example and an Antithesis example that would illustrate each side of the dichotomy. Feel free to come up with new dichotomies that are not already on our list.

1. **A responsible government should never take risks.** Describe a specific situation in which a responsible government should take risks. Discuss what you think determines whether or not a responsible government should take risks.

Dichotomy: _____

_____

_____

Synthesis rule: _____

_____

_____

Thesis example: _____

_____

_____

Antithesis example: _____

_____

_____

16.6

2. **Punishment should fit the crime.** Describe a specific situation in which punishment should not fit the crime. Discuss what you think determines whether or not punishment should fit the crime.

Dichotomy: _____

_____

_____

Synthesis rule: _____

_____

_____

Thesis example: _____

_____

_____

Antithesis example: _____

_____

_____

3. **Governments have a duty to impose social responsibilities on businesses.** Describe a specific situation in which a government should not impose social responsibility on a business. Discuss what you think determines when governments should impose social responsibilities on businesses and when they should not.

Dichotomy: _____

_____

_____

Synthesis rule: _____

_____

_____

Thesis example: _____

_____

_____

Antithesis example: _____

_____

_____

4. **We have a right to know about the personal lives of famous people.** Describe a specific situation in which we may not have a right to know about the personal lives of famous people. Discuss what you think determines whether or not we have a right to know about the personal lives of famous people.

Dichotomy: _____

_____

_____

Synthesis rule: _____

_____

_____

Thesis example: _____

_____

_____

Antithesis example: _____

_____

_____

Exercise 2: Using Synthesis Dichotomies

Using the dichotomies listed in Section 16.4, complete the following two tasks.

I. Choose five dichotomies from the list. For each one, find at least two prompts (using the AAMC list) that could be addressed using that dichotomy. Write down a Synthesis principle for each prompt, based on the dichotomy you have chosen. In the end, you should have ten different Synthesis principles.

1)

2)

3)

4)

5)

II. Choose five different prompts from the AAMC list. For each prompt, choose two dichotomies that are applicable, and write Synthesis principles for that prompt based on each of the two dichotomies. In the end, you should have an additional ten Synthesis principles.

1)

2)

3)

4)

5)

Exercise 3: Current Events Question

Describe a controversial current event that involves the media (television, journalism, advertising, communication). What is happening? Why is it controversial? What basic principles are in conflict? How would *you* resolve this issue?

Exercise 4: Supplemental Prompts

Here are two supplemental MCAT-style essay prompts to work on at home. Time yourself strictly; allow 30 minutes per essay for planning *and* writing. To duplicate your test experience, write the essays consecutively. If you don't have time to write both essays during the week, at least make an outline for each prompt that describes the examples you'd use to illustrate your main points.

Supplemental Prompt 11

Consider this statement:

> **Businesses are morally required to limit their environmental impact.**

Write a unified essay in which you perform the following tasks. Explain what you think the above statement means. Describe a specific situation in which a business might justifiably not be morally required to limit its environmental impact. Discuss what you think determines whether or not a business is morally required to limit its environmental impact.

Supplemental Prompt 12

Consider this statement:

> **Creativity flourishes most within a repressive system.**

Write a unified essay in which you perform the following tasks. Explain what you think the above statement means. Describe a specific situation in which creativity might not flourish within a repressive system. Discuss what you think determines whether or not creativity flourishes most within a repressive system.

16.7 TIMED ESSAY #3

Give yourself 30 minutes to write this essay. Do it on your computer but do not use spell-check. After you write the essay, read through the analysis of the prompt and two student essays that follow.

Consider this statement:

> **The main responsibility of a business should be to maximize the physical safety of its employees.**

Write a unified essay in which you perform the following tasks. Explain what you think the above statement means. Describe a specific situation in which the main responsibility of a business might not be maximizing the physical safety of its employees. Discuss what you think determines when the main responsibility of a business should be to maximize the physical safety of its employees and when it should not.

Analysis of the Prompt

This question asks you to think about the duties a business has towards those it employs. Implicit in that question is the issue of how employee safety might be inconsistent with other duties or goals of a business. For example, increasing safety might lead to a decrease in profits, or to an inability of the employees to perform functions necessary for their job.

Take the word *should* in the prompt statement and in the Synthesis task seriously. If you simply give examples of jobs where safety is or is not assured, without discussing whether or not it *should* be assured, you have not answered the question. This applies to the Antithesis task as well, even though the word *should* does not explicitly appear in the wording of that task.

Be careful to set up your Synthesis by choosing two comparable yet clearly contrasting examples. If your Synthesis criterion is that employees should never be asked or required to risk their lives, and yet you give two examples of inherently dangerous work in which the risk of death is always part of the job, your Synthesis will be inconsistent with, or not applicable to, at least one of your examples, and your essay will be incomplete. Note as well the word *main*. You do not have to argue in the Thesis that safety is the only consideration, only that it is the most important one. In the same way, you do not need an Antithesis example in which safety is unimportant or irrelevant, just one in which other considerations take precedence.

Finally, avoid the "non-debatable" Antithesis example. In this case, that might be an example of someone who works in a situation where there is never any real risk. You could argue that in white-collar office jobs, there are no safety risks (under normal conditions) and so safety should not be the main responsibility. But that is essentially true by definition. This kind of "obviously true" Antithesis case is not particularly serious or interesting, and it leaves you with little to talk about in your Synthesis.

Student Response #1   Assuring the physical safety of its employees should be the main responsibility of business in most cases. Many employees are put in vulnerable position where a lack of concern for the safety of the employee can lead to a decrease in customer service, as well as serious injury or death to the employee. A primary example of these are employees that work the graveyard shift at 24 hour businesses. This is especially true for gas stations and small convenience stores where the employee may be alone. In these cases, the business should make the employee's safety a primary concern by taking actions such as installing bullet proof glass or safety cages, or even hiring security guards. This is because if the employee is constantly afraid of the customers and what they might do, he or she will not be able to serve any customer well. Furthermore, putting an employee in such a situation could be dangerous due to late-night crimes such a burglaries, and employees have a right in most cases to be protected from special risks by their employers.

There are other instances however, in which the primary concern of business must be something other than employee safety. Suppose a level four virus is released in a lab at the Center for Disease Control and Prevention. It becomes the businesses responsibility to ensure that this virus does not spread to the general public. There is a risk that some employees may have been exposed, but it is the duty of the business to contain these employees and prevent further human contact, even if it means that they remain untreated.

To determine when the primary responsibility of a business should be to protect employees safety the only reasonable answer is if the action of the business towards its employees saves lives or improves the well-being of everyone. Any action by business to protect its employees should always be the primary concern if this protection results in a net saving of lives or overall protection of health. Employee safety should never be compromised by factors other than the lives and well being of others.

Sample Student Response #1—Grader's Comments: This writer chooses two appropriate examples. Where the essay is weak is in the explanation of those examples, which sets the essay up for a weak Synthesis as well. In the Antithesis, in particular, it is not clear why an employee exposed to a dangerous virus should be expected to sacrifice his or her life for the safety of others. In fact, it is not entirely clear why this case is so different from the Thesis case; both are described as inherently dangerous jobs. Yes, saving the life of the Center worker may put others at risk, unlike the safety measures for the convenience store worker, but most people accept the validity of a right to self-defense, even if saving your own life puts others at risk. The difference between the two jobs seems clear, but that difference is not explicitly addressed by the author; she leaves it up to the reader to fill it in.

The lack of a clearly drawn contrast between the examples causes problems for the Synthesis. In the end, it gives a reasonable criterion (weighing the well-being of some against the well-being of a greater number of others), but up to that point the author doesn't seem to be sure of what she wants to say. If she had defined her Synthesis criteria in the outlining stage of writing, she could have woven it into the explanation of her examples, and the Synthesis would be both more clear and more compelling. In the final analysis, this is an adequate essay that had the potential to be a great essay. When you read the next response, notice how that author addresses the same general themes more successfully.

Score: 4

Student Response #2

It was in the late 1800's and early 1900's that the U.S. began to develop into an advanced industrial nation. During this time, the mass production of goods skyrocketed due to new manufacturing techniques and increased consumer demand. This lead to an increased demand for labor, and increased greed among manufacturers who were actively competing for a top place in this new capitalist economy. This greed for profits caused employers to crowd work areas and to ignore many aspects of workplace safety. The "ShirtWaist" fire in New York in which many hundreds of women died was one of the first major incidents that brought the issue of employee safety to light. In this case the factory was vastly overcrowded, and the exits were locked or blocked to stop workers form leaving during their shifts. When a fire broke out, the women were trapped inside the burning building. In this case it was the responsibility of the employer to provide a safe workplace and adequate exits, even if this would have cut somewhat into their profits. These kind of employees have no control themselves over the safety of their building. Also, sewing or manufacturing of clothing is not supposed to be a job in which you risk your life, and none of the women took the job with the expectation that they might die there.

However, there are some professions in which the safety of employees not only should not but cannot be maximized, due to the inherent nature of the job. In these jobs or businesses, assuring employee safety would interfere with his or her duties and responsibilities. For example, companies such as Blackwater are in the business of providing security and carrying out quasi-military missions in war zones. If the safety of the employee is made to be the primary concern, it could jeopardize the service that the business provides. The main duty of such an employee is to be put into dangerous situations in order to protect the life of someone else or to protect our security as a nation. If the employees safety was the most important thing, that would put the client or the mission in danger. This would nullify the whole purpose of the business. People who take on these kind of jobs know that danger, even to their lives, is part of the job, and they voluntarily accept that as a term of employment and are compensated for it.

Two related conditions determine whether a business's main responsibility is to protect workers. First, would workers' safety put a client or the nation as a whole at risk, or in more general terms make it impossible to do their job. Secondly, does the employee know of this risk ahead of time and accept it voluntarily, with appropriate compensation, or is the risk just a side effect of the employer's desire to maximize profits beyond normal levels. There will always be certain professions in which danger is part of the job. A firefighter, a security officer, a scientific researcher working with dangerous disease causing bacteria or even a professional football player, etc. does and should expect to put him or herself at risk on a regular basis, in order to protect the lives of others or to just do the job. Factory workers, or white collar workers, or anyone who works in an office or plant on the other hand has no need, and no expectation of the need, to risk their lives. They are put at risk against their will, which is never justified.

Sample Student Response #2—Grader's Comments:

As noted in the comments above, this essay is more successful on a variety of levels. The Thesis example is concrete and specific rather than hypothetical. The author also clearly explains its relevance to the prompt, that is, why the business had a responsibility to put worker safety above profit. The Antithesis example is also concrete and is described in enough detail to be convincing, and it sets up a clear contrast on which the author can build a strong Synthesis. Finally, in the Synthesis she gives clearly defined criteria that apply to both of her examples, and she indicates how they might apply more generally to other cases as well. The writing is at times a bit repetitive and wordy, but not to the extent that it interferes with the author's argument.

Score: 6.0

16.7

Chapter 16 Summary

- Avoid circular reasoning or vague, inconclusive criteria by outlining your Synthesis principle before beginning to write.

- A Synthesis Paragraph Model:

    - Write a transitional sentence.

    - State a general principle. Derive your general principle—the basis of your Synthesis—from the contrast between your Thesis and Antithesis examples.

    - Show how the principle applies to your examples.

    - Explain, define, and refine the principle.

    - Write a concluding sentence. Don't leave the reader hanging.

Chapter 17
Writing Clearly:
Part 1

GOALS

1. To strengthen and clarify your writing by
    - focusing on one idea at a time
    - using fewer words to express an idea
    - limiting your use of qualifiers and adverbs

2. To continue generating examples and criteria applicable to a wide range of essay prompts

17.1 WRITING CLEARLY: STYLE

Simplifying—and thus clarifying—your writing will improve your Writing Sample score. In order for your readers to understand exactly what you want to say, your argument must not be hidden in ponderous sentence construction. You don't want readers to have to do hard labor just to figure out what you are trying to communicate. You want to strip every sentence to its cleanest components. Here are some suggestions that will help clarify your writing:

Address One Idea at a Time

Don't try to put too much information into one sentence. If you're ever uncertain whether a sentence needs three commas and two semicolons or two colons and a dash, just make it into two separate sentences. Two simple sentences are better than one long convoluted one. Which of the following examples seems clearer to you?

Example #1:

Many people, politicians for instance, act like they are thinking of the people they represent by the comments made in their speeches, while at the same time they are filling their pockets at the expense of the taxpayers.

Example #2:

Many people appear to be thinking of others, but are actually thinking of themselves. For example, many politicians claim to be thinking of their constituents, but are in fact filling their pockets at the taxpayers' expense.

Use Fewer Words to Express an Idea

In a 30-minute essay, you don't have time to mess around. In an attempt to sound important, many of us "pad" our writing. Always consider whether there's a shorter way to express your thoughts. We are all guilty of some of the following types of clutter:

Cluttered	Clear
due to the fact that	because
with the possible exception of	except
until such time as	until
for the purpose of	for
referred to as	called
at the present time	now
at all times	always

Use Fewer Qualifiers

A qualifier is a little phrase we use to cover ourselves. Instead of plainly stating that "Former President Reagan sold arms in exchange for hostages," we feel more comfortable stating *"It's quite possible* that former President Reagan *practically* sold arms in *a kind of* exchange for people who were *basically* hostages." Over-qualifying weakens your writing. Prune out these words and expressions wherever possible:

kind of   basically

a bit   practically

sort of   essentially

pretty much   in a way

rather   quite

Another type of qualifier is the *personal qualifier*, where instead of stating the truth, I state the truth "in my opinion." Face it: Everything you state (except perhaps for scientific or historical facts) is your opinion. Personal qualifiers like the following can often be pruned:

to me
in my opinion
in my experience
I think
it is my belief
it is my contention
the way I see it

Use Fewer Adverbs

If you choose the right verb or adjective to begin with, an adverb is often unnecessary. Use an adverb only if it does useful work in the sentence. It's fine to say "the politician's campaign ran smoothly up to the primaries," because the adverb "smoothly" tells us something important about the running of the campaign. The adverb could be eliminated, however, if the verb were more specific: "The politician's campaign sailed up to the primaries." The combination of the strong verb *and* the adverb, as in "the politician's campaign sailed smoothly up to the primaries," is unnecessary because the adverb does no work. Here are other examples of unnecessary adverbs:

> very unique
> instantly startled
> dejectedly slumped
> effortlessly easy
> absolutely perfect
> totally flabbergasted
> completely undeniable

Writing Clearly Exercise: Eliminating Wordiness 1

Another way in which unnecessary words may sneak into your writing is through the use of redundant phrases. Pare each phrase listed below down to a single word. Answers are provided at the end of the chapter.

cooperate together _____

resulting effect _____

large in size _____

absolutely unprecedented _____

disappear from sight _____

new innovation _____

repeat again _____

totally unique _____

necessary essentials _____

Answers to Writing Clearly Exercise: Eliminating Wordiness 1

cooperate together: cooperate

resulting effect: effect

large in size: large

absolutely unprecedented : unprecedented

disappear from sight: disappear

new innovation: innovation

repeat again: repeat

totally unique: unique

necessary essentials: essentials

Writing Clearly Exercise: Eliminating Wordiness 2
Rewrite these sentences to make them less wordy. You will find examples of cleaner versions of these sentences at the end of the chapter.

1. It can be no doubt argued that the availability of dangerous and lethal guns and firearms are in part, to

some extent, responsible for the undeniable explosion of violence in our society today. _____

_____

_____

2. Why is it always imperative and necessary for the teaching educational establishment to subdue and

suppress the natural spirits and energies of adolescents in scholarly settings? _____

_____

_____

3. It seems to me that I believe one must not ignore the fact that Hamlet was a heroic character as well as a tragic and doomed character fated to suffer. _____

_____

_____

4. No one would deny the strong and truthful fact that young teenage pregnancy is on the rise and is increasing at an unbelievable rate each and every single day of the year. _____

_____

_____

Answers to Writing Clearly Exercise: Eliminating Wordiness 2

1. The availability of lethal firearms is partially responsible for the explosion of violence in to-day's society.
2. Why must the teaching of adolescents include the stifling of their natural spirit?
3. Hamlet was a heroic as well as tragic character.
4. Teenage pregnancy is rising at an unbelievable rate.

Limit Your Use of Passive Voice

Consistently writing in the active voice and limiting your use of the passive voice will make your writing more forceful, authoritative, and interesting. Look at the sentences below. They convey essentially the same basic idea, but they have very different effects on the reader.

- The Tobacco Industry deliberately withheld data about the dangers of second-hand smoke.
- Data about the dangers of second-hand smoke were deliberately withheld by the Tobacco Industry.

The first sentence is in the active voice; the second, in the passive voice.

The active voice has a clear subject-verb relationship which illustrates that the subject is doing the action. A sentence is in the passive voice when the subject of the sentence, instead of acting, is acted upon. By distancing the subject from the verb, the passive voice makes it appear that the action is being done to the subject.

The passive voice uses a form of *be* (is, am, are, was, were, been) plus the main verb in past participle form. The "do-er" of a passive voice sentence is either absent or relegated to the end of the sentence in a "by" phrase.

Writing Clearly Exercise: Eliminating the Passive Voice

Put each of the following sentences into the active voice. You can find examples of reworded sentences at the end of the chapter.

1. The Constitution was created by the Founders to protect individual rights against the abuse of federal power. _____

_____

_____

2. Information about the Vietnam War was withheld by the government. _____

_____

_____

3. The right to privacy was called upon by the Supreme Court to form the foundation of the Roe v. Wade decision. _____

_____

_____

4. Teachers in many school districts are now often required by administrators to "teach to the test." ____

_____

_____

5. Residents of planned communities are mandated by Block Associations to limit the number of cars parked in their driveways. _____

_____

_____

6. Mistakes were made by the president. _____

_____

_____

7. The gaze of the tiny porcupine was captured by the headlights of the oncoming Range Rover. _____

_____

_____

Answers to Writing Clearly Exercise: Eliminating the Passive Voice

1. The Founding Fathers created the Constitution to protect individual rights from abuse by the federal government.

2. The government withheld information about the Vietnam War.

3. The Supreme Court called upon the right to privacy in its decision on Roe v. Wade.

4. School administrators often require teachers to "teach to the test."

5. The Block Association has mandated how many cars can be parked in the driveways of planned communities.

6. The president made mistakes.

7. The Range Rover's headlights captured the gaze of the tiny porcupine.

Avoid Clichés Like the Plague

Clichés are comfortable. When we're stuck for the next word, a cliché will suddenly strike us, and we'll feel lucky. We write something like "this *tried and true* method" or "he was one of the *best and brightest.*" A cliché may let the writer off the hook, but the reader will be turned off. The reason a cliché is a cliché is because it is overused. Try something original instead.

17.2   WRITING SAMPLE EXERCISES

Exercise 1: Brainstorming

For each of the following prompts, come up with at least one set of contrasting Thesis and Antithesis examples, and define a Synthesis rule. Once you have completed the exercise, take a look at some possible examples that are provided at the end of the chapter.

1. **Countries are most likely to cooperate with each other for economic gain.** Explain what the above statement means. Describe a situation in which countries might cooperate with each other based on something other than economic gain. Discuss what you think determines when countries are most likely to cooperate with each other for economic gain. _____

_____

_____

_____

_____

_____

2. **True leaders inspire us through their actions rather than by their words.** Explain what the above statement means. Describe a situation in which a true leader may inspire us through words rather than actions. Discuss what you think determines whether true leaders are more likely to inspire us through actions or with their words. _____

_____

_____

_____

_____

_____

3. Human history is characterized by continual progress. Explain what the above statement means. Describe a situation in which human history is not characterized by continual progress. Discuss what you think determines when human history is characterized by continual progress and when it is not. _____

_____

_____

_____

_____

_____

Exercise 2: Brainstorming and Outlining

Step 1
Choose a prompt from the AAMC list. Take 5 minutes to outline one possible response, including all three tasks. Then, take another few minutes to create a second outline, using different examples and criteria. Finally, take another few minutes for a third outline. From these three outlines, identify the strongest one. Or, pick and choose the best parts from each to create a new, even better outline.

Step 2
Now take 20 minutes to write an essay using the "best of all possible outlines."

Do this exercise as many times as possible over the next few weeks. Each time, pick a prompt from a different category, expanding the range of examples and criteria at your disposal.

Exercise 3: Current Events Question

Discuss a current event in the world of education and educational reform. What are some problems with our current educational system at the primary, secondary, college, or post-graduate level? What solutions to those problems have been proposed and by whom? What are some criticisms of those proposed solutions?

Exercise 4: Supplemental Prompts

Here are two supplemental MCAT-style essay prompts to work on at home. Time yourself strictly; allow 30 minutes per essay for planning *and* writing. To duplicate your test experience, write the essays consecutively. If you don't have time to write both essays during the week, at least make an outline for each prompt that describes the examples you'd use to illustrate your main points.

Supplemental Prompt 13

Consider this statement:

> **People usually resist new ideas.**

Write a unified essay in which you perform the following tasks. Explain what you think the above statement means. Describe a specific situation in which people might not resist new ideas. Discuss what you think determines whether or not people will resist new ideas.

Supplemental Prompt 14

Consider this statement:

> **In a democracy, it is necessary for a minority party to oppose the actions of the majority party.**

Write a unified essay in which you perform the following tasks. Explain what you think the above statement means. Describe a specific situation in which it might not be necessary for a minority party to oppose the actions of the majority party. Discuss what you think determines when it is necessary in a democracy for a minority party to oppose the actions of the majority party and when it is not.

17.3 TIMED ESSAY #4

Give yourself 30 minutes to write this essay. Do it on your computer but do not use spell check. After you write the essay, read through the analysis of the prompt and the student essay that follows.

Consider this statement:

People should be able to decide what to do with the land that belongs to them.

Write a unified essay in which you perform the following tasks. Explain what you think the above statement means. Describe a specific situation in which people should not be able to decide what to do with the land that belongs to them. Discuss what you think determines when people should be able to decide what to do with land that belongs to them and when they should not.

Analysis of the Prompt

The fundamental issue underlying this prompt is the question of how we weigh the rights or interests of different individuals against each other, or the rights of the individual against the good of society. In responding, be careful to avoid the "non-debatable" Thesis. You might decide to argue, for example, that people have the right to do whatever they like with their land as long as they don't offend or trample on the rights of anyone else (e.g., I can put a swimming pool in my yard as long as it doesn't bother the neighbors or encroach upon their property). Okay, but what more is there to say?

Another version of an overly simplistic and limiting Thesis argument would be the claim that you can do whatever you wish with your land as long as you don't break any laws. The real danger, beyond limiting the scope and interest of your Thesis and Antithesis discussion, is that this type of argument leads down a path to a Synthesis criterion that reads something like this, "You can use your land however you like as long as no one has a problem with it." That is, "No, you don't have the right to decide how to use your land." Without a Thesis example to which someone might conceivably object, the Thesis side of the argument essentially disappears, and you are left with an incomplete or internally inconsistent essay.

The best Synthesis will explain how the rights and interests of landowners weigh against the (at time conflicting) rights and interests of others. When can people do what they like with their land, even in the face of objections by others? Conversely, when would the rights of other individuals or the interest of society of a whole constrain what people can do with their own land?

Student Response   Social critics frequently debate whether or not individuals have the right to decide how to use the land that belongs to them. Within this context, individuals refer to any person or party that occupies a piece of land. When individuals in a group govern themselves, then they clearly have the right to decide how to use the land that they inhabit. Native Americans were given the right of self-government as a result of the United States government's accepting responsibility for the systematic genocide of the Indians. Part of the deal included the rights that the Native Americans have to use their land in any fashion that they wanted (including when the use contradicted federal and state laws). As a result, many gambling casinos opened their doors on the land of Indian reservations, even though gambling is illegal in surrounding areas.

However, some people say that individuals do not always have the right to decide how to use the land that belongs to them. Edith Martin, an elderly native of Atlanta, was arrested by federal agents for growing marijuana in her backyard. Ms. Martin was growing the illegal substance because it allegedly eased the physical suffering that her son was experiencing as a result of chemotherapy administered for lung cancer. Prosecutors argued that though the land belonged to Ms. Martin, she still had to abide by the laws of her surrounding community. Even though it is easy to have compassion for a mother easing the pain of her child, the truth remains that Ms. Martin used the land in a way that contradicted laws that dictated how land should be used in that area. These laws were written by representative elected by the people and are intended to be in the best interest of the community as a whole.

An individual has as certain rights to do what they want with their own land. However, by choosing to buy or rent a piece of land, one is also choosing a set of laws that govern that land. Native Americans are allowed to build casinos because they are not subject to all of the same laws as other land-owners. But individuals like Ms. Martin enter into a tacitly understood agreement to abide by the rules that govern their land. The same rules that prevent Ms. Martin from growing marijuana also prevent others from destroying her property or harassing her or her family. As individuals in society, we must agree to certain limitations in order to achieve social harmony.

Sample Student Response—Grader's Comments: The strength of this essay is in the Synthesis. The Synthesis provides a criterion (following the law) as well as an explanation for why that criterion is important (social harmony). It also addresses the key question here: when should a right be restricted? The Thesis and the Antithesis have potentially good examples but they are a bit weak because the writer's opinion is not completely clear. Many students try to use the approach of arguing that some people take one side and some take the other, and then leave it at that. It is better to argue that there is validity in each side, and then delineate what specific factors determine *when* one side or the other will take precedence. The Antithesis argument comes close to circular reasoning (one is never allowed to do illegal things), but the writer hints at why we should obey the law (good of the community), which gives more substance to the argument. The essay as a whole would be stronger if this idea of the principles underlying the law was further developed.

Finally, while the example of special rights granted to Native Americans works very nicely in the context of the Thesis, it limits the applicability of the Synthesis rule or criterion. Can you think of another case in which a group has been given a similar right to self-government, to the extent that they are exempt from the law? The example is also worded too strongly. Native Americans cannot do anything they like (build nuclear weapons, for example) on their land. The essay would be stronger with a more generalizable Thesis example, or with some explanation of how we can identify similar characteristics in other cases.

Score: 4

EXERCISE 1: BRAINSTORMING—SAMPLE RESPONSES

1. Countries are most likely to cooperate with each other for economic gain.
   Thesis Examples:
   - European Union (EU)—formed out of convenience due to proximity and economic similarities. All nations benefit from elimination of trade barriers.
   - North American Free Trade Alliance (NAFTA)—cooperation between Canada, the U.S., and Mexico to lessen tariffs and other trade barriers.

   Antithesis Examples:
   - WWII Allies—mutual military necessity and a common enemy, rather than economic motives, caused this alliance.
   - USSR and Iraq—in the Iran/Iraq war, the USSR armed Iraq because they feared an Iranian victory, rather than for economic reasons.

   Synthesis Rule:
   In times of relative peace and prosperity, alliances between countries will be formed on the basis of mutual economic benefit. However, in times of emergency, national security and ideology will trump other considerations in the formation of international alliances.

2. True leaders inspire us through their actions rather than by their words.
   Thesis Examples:
   - Rosa Parks—her action of refusing to move to the back of the bus inspired the Montgomery Bus Boycott in Alabama, 1955.
   - Gandhi—his actions in the fight for Indian independence, such as only wearing clothing made in India and leading the Salt March and other non-violent demonstrations, as well as being arrested himself, inspired both domestic and international support for independence.

   Antithesis Examples
   - Feminist authors such as Carol Gilligan and Audre Lord—write and speak to variations on traditional feminist themes, with the goal of providing intellectual leadership.
   - Clarence Darrow—lawyer in early 1900's who used speeches during Leopold and Loeb trial to fight against the death penalty and in the Scopes trial to defend constitutional protection of free speech.

   Synthesis Rule:
   If you are trying to start a movement (or are within the early stages), actions are more inspirational, as they provide a galvanizing image which can mobilize people. If a leader is part of an evolving and continuing movement, words are more effective for communicating the complexity of the issues involved and inspiring intellectual agreement.

3. Human history is characterized by continued progress.
   Thesis Examples:
   - Technology: communication continually made faster and easier, from telegraph to cell phones and Skype.
   - Medicine: continuous deepening of understanding of the human body leads to continual improvement in treatments. May soon have gene therapy for currently incurable conditions such as sickle-cell anemia and cystic fibrosis.

Antithesis Examples:
- War: The incidence of conflict has not lessened, and improved technology has only increased the human cost. Nations always fight with other nations, and this will always be the case.
- Art: different artistic movements, from Impressionism to Abstract Expressionism to Pop Art should not be thought of as progress but rather different, equally valid forms of inspiration.

Synthesis Rule:
In aspects of human behavior driven by essential human nature, be it our capacity for hate or love, our proclivity for violence or our drive for self-expression, human history is characterized by variations on a theme rather than progress. Human nature itself never changes. However, when our capacity to manipulate our surroundings through tool-making is at issue, our history is defined by continual progress in the complexity and effectiveness of those tools.

Chapter 17 Summary

- Clarity is a primary goal in your writing. You can improve the clarity of your writing by focusing on one idea at a time, using fewer words to express an idea, and limiting your use of qualifiers and adverbs.

- Continue to familiarize yourself with the different categories of prompts, and to generate a variety of examples and Synthesis criteria within each category.

Chapter 18
Writing Clearly:
Part 2

GOALS

1. To strengthen and clarify your writing by:
   - using correct punctuation and grammar
   - avoiding run-on sentences
   - using nonsexist language

2. To continue generating strong examples and Synthesis criteria.

18.1   USING PUNCTUATION WISELY

Commas (,)

Very few people understand every rule for proper comma use in the English language. This lack of understanding leads to two disturbing phenomena: essays without commas and essays with commas everywhere. Here is a quick summary of proper comma use:

Use Commas to Set Off Introductory Elements.

- Breezing through my MCAT essay, I wondered if everyone were as well-prepared as I.
- Incidentally, I got an "S" on the Writing Sample section.
- Before you jump to any conclusions, I was only taking a mote out of her eye.

Use Commas to Separate Items in a Series.

- She made hot chocolate, cinnamon toast, scrambled eggs with cheese, and coffee cake.

  [Note: There's always great debate as to whether the final serial comma (before the *and*) is necessary. In this case, the comma must be added; otherwise, there will be a question about the contents of the scrambled eggs. In cases where no such ambiguity exists, the extra comma seems superfluous. Use your best judgment. When in doubt, separate all the items in a series with commas.]

Use Commas Around a Phrase or Clause that Could Be Removed Logically from the Sentence.

- The Verbal Reasoning section, the second section of the MCAT, always makes my palms sweat.
- Xavier, the student whose test was interrupted by marching band practice, would have liked to have had ear plugs.

Use a Comma to Separate Coordinate (Equally Important) Adjectives.
Do Not Use a Comma to Separate Non-coordinate Adjectives.
- It was a dark, stormy night.
- It was a messy triple bypass.

Do Not Use a Comma to Separate a Subject and a Verb.
- Incorrect: My new MCAT study group, meets at the local café.
- Correct: My new MCAT study group meets at the local café.

Do Not Use a Comma to Separate Compound Subjects or Predicates.
(A compound subject means two "do-ers"; a compound predicate means two actions done.)

- Incorrect: My best friend Xavier, and his brother Lou always tell me the truth about my practice essays.
- Correct: My best friend Xavier and his brother Lou always tell me the truth about my practice essays.
- Incorrect: Because of the strange tickling in the back of my throat, I stayed in bed, and gave myself a break from studying.
- Correct: Because of the strange tickling in the back of my throat, I stayed in bed and gave myself a break from studying.

Colons (:)
Use a colon to introduce an explanation or a list.

- "I think you judge Truman too charitably when you call him a child: he is more like a sweetly vicious old lady." *Tennessee Williams*
- "When I am dead, I hope it may be said: 'His sins were scarlet, but his books were read.'" *Hilaire Belloc*
- "Everything goes by the board to get the book written: honor, pride, decency..." *William Faulkner*

Semicolons (;)
Use a semicolon to join related independent clauses in a single sentence (a clause is independent if it can logically stand alone).

- "An artist is born kneeling; he fights to stand." *Hortense Calisher*
- "Why had I become a writer in the first place? Because I wasn't fit for society; I didn't fit into the system." *Brian Aldiss*

Dashes (—)

Use a dash for an abrupt shift. Use a pair of dashes (one on either side) to frame a parenthetical statement that interrupts the sentence. Dashes are more informal than colons.

- "Like a lot of what happens in novels, inspiration is a sort of spontaneous combustion—the oily rags of the head and heart." *Stanley Elkin*
- "Writers should be read—but neither seen nor heard." *Daphne du Maurier*
- "Of all the cants which are canted in this canting world—though the cant of hypocrites may be the worst—the cant of criticism is the most tormenting." *Laurence Sterne*

Exclamation Points (!)

Use exclamation points sparingly. Try to express excitement, surprise, or rage in the words you choose. A good rule of thumb is *one* exclamation point per essay, at the most.

- "You don't know what it is to stay a whole day with your head in your hands trying to squeeze your unfortunate brain so as to find a word... Ah! I certainly know the agonies of style." *Gustave Flaubert*

Question Marks (?)

Use a question mark after a direct question. Don't forget to use a question mark after rhetorical questions (ones that you make in the course of argument that you answer yourself).

- "Why shouldn't we quarrel about a word? What is the good of words if they aren't important enough to quarrel over? Why do we choose one word over another if there isn't any difference between them?" *G. K. Chesterton*

Quotation Marks (" ")

Use quotation marks to indicate a writer's exact words. Use quotation marks for titles of songs, chapters, essays, articles, or stories—a piece that is part of a larger whole. Periods and commas always go inside the quotation mark. Exclamation points and question marks go inside the quotation mark when they belong to the quotation and not to the larger sentence. Colons, semicolons, and dashes go outside the quotation mark.

- "That's not writing, that's typing." Truman Capote on Jack Kerouac

18.2   ELIMINATING FRAGMENTS AND RUN-ONS

A **fragment** is an unfinished sentence. It may lack a subject or verb, or it may be a dependent clause. Use this test for sentence fragments: Can the fragment logically stand alone, without the previous or following sentences?

- Fragment: My pencil broke during the last five minutes of the test. Pieces rolling beneath my chair.
- Correct Sentence: My pencil broke during the last five minute of the test, and the pieces rolled beneath my chair.

A **run-on** is an instance where two sentences run together when they should be separate. Sometimes the author forgets the necessary conjunction or the proper punctuation. Sometimes the two sentences are simply too long to fit together well.

- Run-on: Regardless of the weather, I will go spear fishing in Bali the water is as clear as glass.
- Correct Sentences: Regardless of the weather, I will go spear fishing in Bali where the water is as clear as glass.
  or
- Regardless of the weather, I will go spear fishing in Bali. The water there is as clear as glass.

Just as you need to avoid the use of incomplete sentences, you should avoid the use of incomplete words. A formal essay is not like the notes you take in organic chemistry. "W/" is not an acceptable substitute for *with*, and neither is "b/c" for *because*. Symbols are also not acceptable substitutes for words (@ for *at*, & for *and*, etc.). (In fact, try to avoid the use of "etc."; it is not entirely acceptable in formal writing. Use "and so forth" or "among others" instead.) And please don't indulge in any "cute" spelling ("nite" for *night*, "tho" for *though*). This kind of writing conveys a message that you don't care about your essay. Show the graders how serious you are by eliminating these shortcuts.

18.3   BRINGING YOUR NOUNS AND PRONOUNS INTO AGREEMENT

During your proofreading, be sure your pronouns agree with the nouns they represent (their antecedents). The most common mistake is to follow a singular noun with a plural pronoun (or vice versa), as in the following:

- If a writer misuses words, they will not do well on the MCAT.
  > The problem with this sentence is that the noun ("writer") is singular, but the pronoun ("they") is plural. The sentence would be correctly written as follows:
- If a writer misuses words, he or she will not do well on the MCAT.
  or
- If writers misuse words, they will not do well on the MCAT.

18.4   USING NONSEXIST LANGUAGE

Pronoun agreement problems often arise because the writer is trying to avoid a sexist use of language. Because there is no gender-neutral singular pronoun in English, many people use *they*, as in the incorrect sentence above. But there are other, more grammatically correct ways of getting around this problem.

One common, albeit quite awkward, solution is to use *he/she* or *his/her* in place of *they* or *their*. For example, instead of writing, "If someone doesn't pay income tax, then they will go to jail," you can write, "If someone doesn't pay income tax, then he or she will go to jail." A more graceful (and shorter) alternative to *he/she* is to use the plural form of both noun and pronoun: "If people don't pay income tax, they will go to jail." Using nonsexist language also means finding alternatives for the word *man* when you are referring to humans in general. Instead of *mankind* you can write *humankind* or *humanity*; instead of *mailman*, you can use *mail carrier*; rather than stating that something is *man-made* you can call it *manufactured* or *artificial*.

There are a number of good reasons for you to use nonsexist language. For one thing, it is coming to be the accepted usage; that is, it is the language educated people use to communicate their ideas. Many publications now make it their editorial policy to use only nongendered language. In addition, nonsexist language is often more accurate. Some of the people who deliver mail, for example, are female, so you are not describing the real state of affairs by referring to all of the people who deliver your mail as *men* (since it is no longer universally accepted that *man* refers to all humans). Finally, there is a good chance that at least one of your graders will be female, and that she—or, indeed, many male graders—will consider your use of the generic "he" to be a sign that you either are not aware of current academic conventions or do not think that they matter. It is best not to give your graders that impression.

Use of non-sexist language can feel awkward at first. Practice until it comes to seem natural; you may soon find that it is the old way of doing things that seems strange.

18.5   PUTTING IT ALL TOGETHER

Edit this essay by the writer Redundancy Verbosa. Can you correct its significant punctuation and wordiness problems? A sample edited essay is provided at the end of the chapter.

At least in my opinion no modern contemporary comic strip, can match the amusing wit and significant profundity of Bill Waterson's Calvin and Hobbes. It is not merely coincidence that the two primary main characters have names of great sixteenth-century thinkers, John Calvin a French Theologian & Thomas Hobbes an English philosopher. Calvin and Hobbes manifest themselves in Waterson's strip as respectively a maliciously precocious six year-old boy and a stuffed tiger animated and brought to life by the power of the boy's imagination.

As in Peanuts one of the great predecessors of Waterson's strip the children represented kind of seem to practically have all the wisdom of adults, w/ the sophisticated vocabularies and observations to match. In fact, at least to me, many of Waterson's strips seem to be constructed as catechisms — principles of doctrine expressed in philosophical or moral questions and answers. Mostly often it is Hobbes who must, answer these questions. Due to the fact that he is pretty much outside the human race, Hobbes is essentially in a way able to rise above and transcend the simple passions (for power and money, primarily) that beset the protagonist Calvin.

A picture is worth a 1000 words, and it can be said that in Calvin, and Hobbes the illustrated depictions are stunningly magnificent. Tho a Sun. strip might be composed of a single watercolor scene of the forested woods around the proximity of Calvin's home, the effect is lush stylish and expressive. Calvin and Hobbes are likely to be found riding down a sharply steep slope in their red wagon discussing their own mortality, or sitting @ their treehouse (where no girl is ever allowed) pondering gender issues. Or they may just slosh around in a mud puddle for the sheer joy of it.

18.6   WRITING SAMPLE EXERCISES

Exercise 1: Brainstorming

Think of an MCAT Writing Sample question as a square, made up of the Thesis, Antithesis, Synthesis, and the major theme or category that encompasses all three.

Given one corner of the square, you should be able to generate the other three. For example, in the square provided here only the Thesis example is filled in:

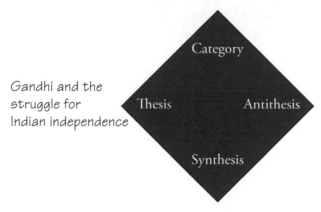

Gandhi and the struggle for Indian independence

You will then fill in the other three corners, in this case with a comparable yet contrasting Antithesis example, a Synthesis criterion and/or dichotomy that would apply to both, and a general theme or category that would include all three. There is no one correct answer, of course.

For this example, you might create the following square:

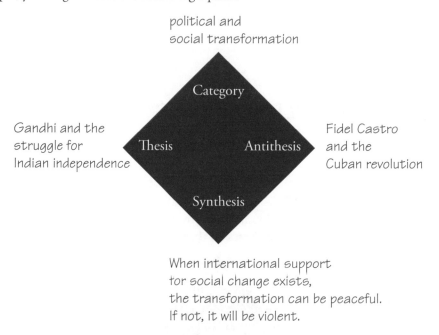

political and
social transformation

Category

Gandhi and the
struggle for
Indian independence

Thesis

Antithesis

Fidel Castro
and the
Cuban revolution

Synthesis

When international support
for social change exists,
the transformation can be peaceful.
If not, it will be violent.

Now do the same for the box below and those on the next page. Feel free to refer to a list of prompts or examples for inspiration. A list of sample responses is provided at the end of the chapter.

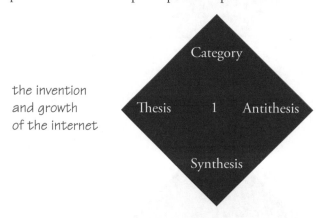

Category

the invention
and growth
of the internet

Thesis

1

Antithesis

Synthesis

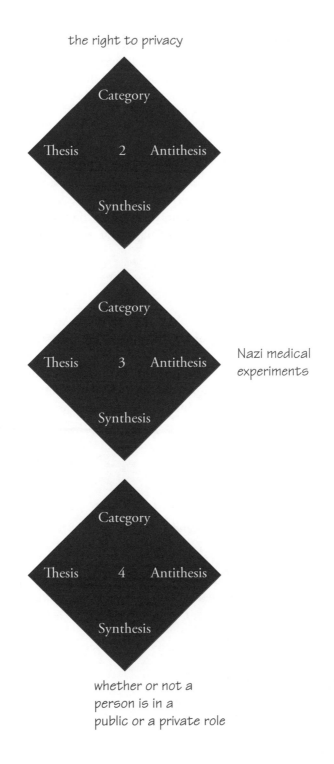

the right to privacy

Category

Thesis   2   Antithesis

Synthesis

Category

Thesis   3   Antithesis

Nazi medical
experiments

Synthesis

Category

Thesis   4   Antithesis

Synthesis

whether or not a
person is in a
public or a private role

Exercise 2: Current Events Question

Discuss a current event that illustrates one of the challenges faced by the American family. How does this challenge affect the day-to-day lives of ordinary families? What should the role of the government be and why?

Exercise 3: Supplemental Prompts

Here are two supplemental MCAT-style essay prompts to work on at home. Time yourself strictly; allow 30 minutes per essay for planning *and* writing. To duplicate your test experience, write the essays consecutively. If you don't have time to write both essays during the week, at least make an outline for each prompt that describes the examples you'd use to illustrate your main points.

Supplemental Prompt 15

Consider this statement:

> **Popularity is a valid measure of a politician's effectiveness.**

Write a unified essay in which you perform the following tasks. Explain what you think the above statement means. Describe a specific situation in which popularity might not be a valid measure of a politician's effectiveness. Discuss what you think determines whether or not popularity is a valid measure of a politician's effectiveness.

Supplemental Prompt 16

Consider this statement:

> **Speaking out is the best way to end social inequality.**

Write a unified essay in which you perform the following tasks. Explain what you think the above statement means. Describe a specific situation in which speaking out might not be the best way to end social inequality. Discuss what you think determines when speaking out is the best way to end social inequality.

18.7   TIMED ESSAY #5

Give yourself 30 minutes to write this essay. Write it on your computer but do not use spell-check. After you write the essay, read through the analysis of the prompt and the student essay that follows.

Consider this statement:

> **The law's essential role is to regulate society rather than to provide justice.**

Write a unified essay in which you perform the following tasks. Explain what you think the above statement means. Describe a specific situation in which the law's essential role might be to provide justice. Discuss what you think determines whether the law's essential role should be to regulate society or to provide justice.

Analysis of the Prompt

In outlining and addressing this question, your starting point should be the three abstract terms that are at the core of the prompt statement: *law, regulate society*, and *justice*. Those terms need to be defined in the first paragraph, either explicitly or implicitly. Make it clear in both your examples and in your explanations exactly what regulation of society and justice are, how they may come into conflict with each other (or why one might need to take precedence over the other), and what the relationship of both is to the law. Certain questions should be answered: What is the purpose of law? What roles does law play in society? When might there be a conflict between different roles?

The wording of the prompt implies that regulation of society and providing justice are to at least some extent distinct. It is fine to discuss how one might be necessary for the other (e.g., you can't ensure justice in a constant state of disorder). However, be careful not to argue that one is *only* important to the extent that it contributes to the other. For example, avoid arguing that providing justice should be the primary purpose of law when providing justice will contribute to the regulation of society. This implies that regulating society is *always* the essential role of law, and that justice exists simply to regulate society. The Antithesis should discuss when justice takes precedence over social regulation; that is, when ensuring justice is the true primary role of law. The Synthesis should define under what conditions regulating society is more important than justice, and conversely under what conditions justice is more important than regulating society.

Student Response   "Law and Order": these two notions of government's purpose have always been related. During times of trouble, either from foreign or domestic threats, a government may be forced to use law to regulate society and to maintain order, even at the expense of justice for its own citizens. The Alien and Sedition Acts of 1812 provide such an example. In a time of war, the U.S. government felt threatened by domestic opposition to the war and by foreign perpetrators against national security. Because the existence of the American nation and people was directly in great danger, the government had the right to use the law to regulate and control society, even though this order came at the expense of Americans' first Amendment rights.

And yet, when the state of the nation is not threatened in such an extreme manner, the essential role of law should be to provide justice. The basic rights of citizens cannot be manipulated or taken away at a time when the safety of that citizen's nation and so the citizen himself is not at risk. Such was the case during the U.S. involvement in the Vietnam War. Unlike the war of 1812, the existence of the government and nation was only indirectly and ideologically threatened. Therefore there was no dramatic need to curtail the freedom of student protesters to speak and assemble against U.S. involvement in the war. The government violated its purpose to ensure justice in a time when its people were relatively safe from danger, in order to advance its own hawkish policies.

Without the maintenance of a well-ordered society in the short run, justice may be threatened in the long run. A weak or conquered state can't protect the rights of its citizens. The primary purpose of government itself is placed between the significance and place of law with social order and justice. Only when a government's people are in danger of physical harm may such a body curtail their rights to ensure that they are not deprived of the basic and highest rights of their existence. One's life therefore is the one justice that law must ensure at the expense of order.

18.7

Sample Student Response—Grader's Comments: This writer clearly has a good knowledge of history, and it serves him well in his choice of examples. The Thesis and Antithesis cases are especially well-matched: they are both instances when the U.S. was at war, but under quite different circumstances. However, the essay raises more questions than it answers. First, the examples are not fully described. What did the Alien and Sedition Act do? How was free speech limited during both wars (huge protests were quite common during the Vietnam War). Second, it never defines what the core terms *law, justice,* and *regulation of society* mean. The reader is left to figure it out him or herself through the examples. In the examples, "justice" appears to be reducible to the rights of freedom of speech and assembly. This is a very narrow "definition," and it is never made clear what the relationship between rights and justice is. Social regulation appears to be the denial of these rights, and "law" is the tool the government uses to enforce this regulation, again very narrow uses of those terms. Because the author doesn't define or discuss those core terms, he keeps circling back to the same idea in all three sections—that is, that only a direct threat to the nation justifies limiting the right to free speech. That idea is a good one, but it is repeated rather than developed throughout the essay. Finally, the first two sentences of the Synthesis are excellent, and at that moment the author of the essay begins to get at some of the deeper issues involved. The rest of the paragraph is very difficult to follow, however. In sum, this essay does a lot of things wrong, which keeps it out of the 4.5 and above range, but it does some important things right as well, which raises the score to above average.

Score: 4

Putting It All Together: Sample Edited Essay

No contemporary comic strip can match the wit and profundity of Bill Waterson's Calvin and Hobbes. The title characters, named after the great sixteenth-century thinkers, John Calvin and Thomas Hobbes, manifest themselves as a precocious six-year-old boy and a stuffed tiger brought to life in the boy's imagination.

As in Peanuts, the children represented seem to have all the wisdom of adults with the vocabulary and power of observation to match. In fact, many of Waterson's strips are catechistic, exploring philosophical or moral questions. Most often, it is Hobbes who needs to work through these questions. Due to his non-human status, he is able to rise above the simple desires (power and money) that beset Calvin.

A picture is worth 1000 words, and the illustrated depictions are magnificent. Although a Sunday strip might consist of a single watercolor scene of the woods around Calvin's home, the effect is lush and expressive. Calvin and Hobbes are likely to be found tearing down a hill in their red wagon discussing their own mortality, or sitting in their tree house pondering gender issues. Or they may just be sloshing around in a mud puddle for the sheer joy of it.

18.7

WRITING SAMPLE EXERCISES: EXERCISE 1—SAMPLE RESPONSES

1. **Thesis: The invention and growth of the internet**

    - Category: Technology as redefining society

    - Antithesis: High-speed trains

    - Synthesis: Although the technology continues to redefine the way in which society communicates and interacts, the importance of face to face interaction will continue to be a draw.

2. **Category: The right to privacy**

    - Thesis: The 4th Amendment protects citizens from unreasonable search and seizure.

    - Antithesis: Airport searches and metal detectors encroach a little on an individual's privacy to protect society collectively.

    - Synthesis: Although the right to individual privacy from the government is fundamental, when the safety of others is at stake, there are legal exceptions to that right.

3. **Antithesis: Nazi medical experiments**

    - Category: Science as progress

    - Thesis: Space Program & Apollo 11

    - Synthesis: Scientific experimentation and development for its own good is admirable, except when it does harm (particularly non-consensual harm) to humans.

4. **Synthesis: Whether or not a person is in a public or private role**

    - Category: Appearance and perception

    - Thesis: Michelle Obama's wardrobe

    - Antithesis: The change in definitions of professional attire after the dotcom boom

18.7

Chapter 18 Summary

- You can enhance your MCAT Writing Sample score by adhering to a few rules for formal writing:

    - Learn the rules for comma usage and practice them until you gain proficiency. Skillful placement of commas will help to make your meaning clear.

    - Avoid fragmented and run-on sentences. They make it difficult for the reader to follow your line of thought.

    - Use nonsexist language.

    - Spell out all words in full. Avoid abbreviations, shortcut words, symbols, and "cute" spellings—they give the impression that you don't care about your writing.

- Continue to brainstorm examples and Synthesis criteria.

Chapter 19
Final Preparation

GOAL

1. To maintain your momentum (but not burn yourself out) up to the day of the MCAT

19.1 BEFORE THE EXAM

If the MCAT is in the next week or so, continue to brainstorm examples, generate Synthesis criteria, and familiarize yourself in general with the AAMC list of prompts. However, now is the time to begin tapering off your studying.

If the test is further away, however, here are some ways to maintain your focus and hone your skills over the next few weeks:

- Choose a prompt category, pick out three or four different prompts within that category, and come up with at least two paired Thesis-Antithesis examples and two Synthesis criteria for each question. Work on as many categories as possible until you have covered all of the major themes.
- Each time you come up with an example, review the list of prompts to find at least four more questions for which you could use that specific example. The more examples you have "in reserve," the better able you will be to write a clear and cogent essay in the small amount of time provided on the test.
- If you are studying with friends, exchange essays and critique each other's work.
- When you don't have the time (or the energy) to write a full essay, create a detailed outline instead.
- Rewrite one or more of your essays, addressing any weak points, improving your examples (or picking new ones) and further developing your explanations and Synthesis criteria.
- Reread the Numerical Scoring Guidelines in Chapter 12. Remind yourself of what the graders are looking for.
- Read a major newspaper, news magazine, or web news source for at least 20 minutes a day. Be on the lookout for examples you can use. Keep a list.
- Visualize walking into the MCAT with confidence, ready and able to do well!

19.2 WRITING SAMPLE EXERCISES

Exercise 1: Current Events Question

Discuss a recent technological innovation. How was it achieved? Did the government play a role? What are its expected benefits? What might be its drawbacks? What impact is it likely to have on society?

Exercise 2: Supplemental Prompts

Here are two supplemental MCAT-style essay prompts to work on at home. Time yourself strictly; allow 30 minutes per essay for planning *and* writing. To duplicate your test experience, write the essays consecutively. If you don't have time to write both essays during the week, at least make an outline for each prompt that describes the examples you'd use to illustrate your main points.

Supplemental Prompt 17

Consider this statement:

> **Ecological considerations are more important than a business's ability to make a profit.**

Write a unified essay in which you perform the following tasks. Explain what you think the above statement means. Describe a specific situation in which ecological considerations might not be more important than the business's ability to make a profit. Discuss what you think determines whether or not ecological considerations are more important than a business's ability to make a profit.

Supplemental Prompt 18

Consider this statement:

> **In government, the ability to compromise is more valuable than the ability to win a debate.**

Write a unified essay in which you perform the following tasks. Explain what you think the above statement means. Describe a specific situation in which in government the ability to compromise might not be more valuable than the ability to win a debate. Discuss what you think determines whether or not in government the ability to compromise is more valuable than the ability to win a debate.

Verbal Reasoning Appendix

APPLYING VERBAL REASONING TECHNIQUES TO THE SCIENCE PASSAGES

The challenges posed by the science sections of the MCAT differ in a number of important ways from those posed by the Verbal Reasoning section. Indeed, the differences must seem all too obvious. Most striking is the amount of information you need to bring with you to the test; even the brightest and most alert reader would be lost in Physics or Biology without an understanding of the basic scientific principles and a good grasp of the fundamental definitions and nomenclature. It's also the case that you must engage in a lot more problem-solving for the sciences than you do for Verbal Reasoning, where your primary task is to *find* answers rather than to calculate them. Verbal Reasoning passages tell you almost everything you need to know, while the science passages require you to know much more before you read them.

Nevertheless, there's a great deal of overlap in the skills required to do well on these apparently dissimilar sections. *You will not score very high in the sciences if you merely try to plug numbers into formulas or to spit back information that you've stuffed into your memory; you also need to be able to draw inferences from the passages, to extrapolate answers from the information provided to you.* You need to work quickly, wasting no time on calculating answers that can be taken directly from the text—or, conversely, on searching a passage for information that isn't there. Most important, you need to mobilize your scientific "common sense," your intuitive understanding of what is and isn't likely to be true for any described scenario involving the physical world. You also need to apply that common sense to the answer choices, eliminating those that are not likely ever to be true. For all of these tasks—looking for specific information, drawing inferences, evaluating the plausibility of answer choices—your Verbal Reasoning skills will be invaluable.

In short, to do well on the MCAT, you need to think both scientifically *and* strategically. Many people feel that they *must* work out the answer to every last question. There is something very noble in this endeavor, but it is not smart test-taking. Remember: You don't get extra points for the tougher questions. Use your knowledge of the test to help you find the correct answers.

For one thing, you should know when the passage information can help you, and when it cannot. There are, broadly speaking, three types of MCAT science questions:

1. **"Pure Science" (Memory) Questions**
   These are based entirely on information that you bring with you to the test; there is nothing in the passage that will help you solve them, or, there is no passage attached to the questions.
2. **Retrieval (Explicit) Questions**
   Less common than the other two question types, these require only that you *find* an answer in the passage.
3. **Application (Implicit) Questions**
   The most common question type, these require you to apply your scientific knowledge to the information in the passage.

Recognizing the question types will affect your solution strategy. You should answer all **Retrieval** questions. Their answers are right in the passage; just use the same techniques you would for Verbal Reasoning Retrieval questions, checking your final answer choice to make sure that it matches the information in the passage.

Application questions will vary in difficulty, depending on the amount and type of outside information involved. Some will require that you apply a quite basic principle; for example, that gases expand as they warm. Others call for more precise knowledge of, say, the function of a particular endocrine gland. Most questions will be Application, or Application/Retrieval (even Retrieval questions require some knowledge to recognize the answer). Your strategy here is to determine how much help the passage will give you, and to pass quickly over those questions for which you lack sufficient outside knowledge.

Finally, "Pure Science" questions are freestanding, or they deal with the passage *topic* but refer only nominally to the passage itself. You can skip a pure science question if you cannot work out the answer, coming back to it at the end of the section if you have time. Such a strategy doesn't work for Verbal Reasoning, because the questions are so closely based on the passages, and because once you've left a passage, you will most likely forget most of it. Pure Science questions, however, don't rely on context and can be solved at any point.

Solutions to Some Sample Passages

The following pages contain three passages from General Chemistry, Physics, and Biology and outline the ways in which you can use Verbal Reasoning strategies to tackles these types of passages. Note that these techniques are less useful for Organic Chemistry passages, which tend to have much less text, often consisting of little more than a few chemical equations. Solutions to all three passages can be found at the end of this Appendix.

MCAT G-CHEM DRILL: SOLUBILITY

Oxygen is transported from the lungs to the capillaries where it is released into the tissues. The oxygen in the circulatory system of mammals is bound to hemoglobin, a protein found in red blood cells.

Hemoglobin has a complex quaternary structure since it is composed of four separate polypeptide chains. Each polypeptide serves as a giant ligand for the single iron(II)-heme unit, the location of oxygen fixation. The oxygen-binding strength of the heme unit and transport efficiency are directly related to blood pH level.

Unlike oxygen, the carbon dioxide which is released into the capillaries by the surrounding tissue is transported by two different mechanisms. Foremost, carbon dioxide is rather soluble in water due to the following equilibria:

$$(1) \quad CO_2 + H_2O \rightleftharpoons H_2CO_3$$

$$(2) \quad H_2CO_3 \rightleftharpoons H^+ + HCO_3^-$$

Therefore, some carbon dioxide immediately dissolves into the blood plasma and is transported to the lungs as bicarbonate ion. Most mammals have an enzyme, carbonic anhydrase, to catalyze Reaction (1), because under normal conditions, CO_2 and carbonic acid cannot reach equilibrium fast enough for efficient transport.

In the second mechanism, CO_2 may react with the N-terminus of the protein chains of hemoglobin, forming a carbamate functional group:

$$(3) \ Hb{-}NH_2 = CO_2 \rightleftharpoons Hb{-}NHCOO^- + H^+$$

Once in the lungs, the Hb-carbamate decomposes to release CO_2, and Hb NH_2 is restored.

1. Carbon dioxide is much more soluble in water than is oxygen. Why?

A) Oxygen has a greater dipole moment.
B) Carbon dioxide has a greater dipole moment than oxygen.
C) Carbon dioxide is a polar molecule.
D) Carbon dioxide is reactive to nucleophilic attack.

2. The expiration of CO_2 from the bloodstream in the lungs:

A) increases blood pH.
B) decreases blood pH.
C) decreases the oxygen content of the blood.
D) None of the above

3. Acidosis—a condition characterized by a decrease in blood pH—rapidly develops after cardiac arrest because tissues continue to load the capillary plasma with more and more CO_2. If the blood pH is not buffered (reset to normal), the patient may die, even after cardiac revival. Why?

A) Too much CO_2 can cause a cell's lipid bilayer to decompose.
B) High concentrations of bicarbonate can cause insoluble salts to precipitate out of the plasma.
C) The nervous system can no longer function properly
D) Hemoglobin cannot effectively transport O_2.

4. If the enzyme carbonic anhydrase were added to a glass of soda pop which had been allowed to reach equilibrium with the atmosphere, it would:

A) produce a large number of carbon dioxide bubbles.
B) produce a large amount of oxygen.
C) form more carbonic acid.
D) have no effect on the equilibrium.

5. Which one of the following will decrease the solubility of CO_2 in water?

A) Increasing the external pressure of CO_2
B) Increasing the temperature of the water
C) Increasing the pH of the water
D) None of the above

6. What is the electron configuration of the iron(II) ion?

A) [Ar] $3d^6$
B) [Ar] $4s^2\ 3d^4$
C) [Ar] $4s^2\ 3d^6$
D) [Ar] $4s^2\ 3p^{10}$

VERBAL STRATEGIES FOR MCAT G-CHEM DRILL: SOLUBILITY

This passage deals with aspects of oxygen transport in the blood. It consists of four paragraphs, two of which include chemical reactions. Although it begins by referring to hemoglobin (paragraphs 1 and 2), the bulk of the questions have to do with plasma CO_2.

1. Oxygen/hemoglobin introduction
2. Structure and functionality of hemoglobin
3. Chemical reactions re: CO_2 solubility (especially re: carbonic acid)
4. CO_2 / hemoglobin reaction

1. Nominally, a **Pure Science** question—but you can make a good guess by treating this as a Retrieval question. See 3: "Foremost, carbon dioxide is rather soluble in water *because of* the following equilibrium reactions…" [emphasis added]. Since the passage states that the solubility of carbon dioxide is due to a chemical reaction, look for an answer choice that refers to a chemical reaction. This leads you to the correct answer, which is D.

2. An unusual example of a **Retrieval** question: The answer is really in the next question! You are asked what happens to the blood when CO_2 is expired by the lungs. Question 3 tells you that when plasma CO_2 goes up, blood pH goes down. Hence, when CO_2 goes down (via the lungs), blood pH must go up. This gives you A, the correct answer.

3. See paragraph 2: O_2 binding and transport is proportional to blood pH. Thus low pH = low oxygen transport = a dead person (answer choice D, in other words). This is mostly a **Retrieval** question.

4. See paragraph 3: **Apply** your knowledge of what "equilibrium" means to the information that carbonic anhydrase speeds up the reaction—until it reaches equilibrium.

5. **Pure Science**

6. **Pure Science**

MCAT PHYSICS DRILL: FORCE

Near the surface of the earth, the density of air is approximately 1.2 kg/m³. A hot-air balloon with total mass M (including passengers) and volume V will float motionless if there is no wind and the buoyant force (magnitude F_B) due to the air is equal to the weight of the balloon and passengers: $F_B = Mg$, where g is the magnitude of the acceleration due to gravity near the surface of the Earth.

The strength of the buoyant force may be altered by heating the air inside the balloon, thereby changing its volume. The total weight of the balloon may be decreased by equipping the balloon with sandbags that can be dropped to the ground.

Many hot-air balloons are equipped with propellers that drive air backward and allow the balloon to travel horizontally. All balloons have a maximum achievable volume which depends on the extent to which the air inside can be heated as well as on the elastic limits of the material used to construct the balloon.

1. A balloon, moving upward and eastward, casts a shadow that moves along the ground at a speed of 10 m/s. What is the balloon's total speed if its velocity vector makes an angle of 60° with the horizontal?

A) 5 m/s
B) 17 m/s
C) 20 m/s
D) 34 m/s

2. A balloon of total mass M sits motionless 40 m above the ground. A sandbag of mass m is dropped out of the balloon. What is then the net force on the balloon?

A) Mg
B) $(M - m)g$
C) mg
D) $(M + m)g$

3. Two unladen hot-air balloons are weighed and measured. Their masses and volumes are as follows:

Balloon I: Mass = 1200 kg; Volume = 1600 m³

Balloon II: Mass = 1100 kg; Volume = 1200 m³

Which of these balloons could be used to carry four people whose average mass is 100 kg each?

A) I only
B) II only
C) I and II
D) Neither balloon could carry such a load.

4. Which of the following best illustrates the flow of air inside a closed-top balloon as the air is heated by a flame directly beneath the opening at the base of the balloon?

A)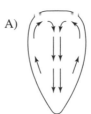

B)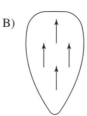

C)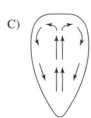

D)

5. A balloon is moving upward at constant velocity. Which one of the following equations involved the magnitudes of the gravitational force, F_G, the drag forces due to air resistance, F_D, and the buoyant force of the air, F_B, is correct?

A) $F_D + F_B > F_G$
B) $F_D + F_B = F_G$
C) $F_D + F_G < F_B$
D) $F_D + F_G = F_B$

6. A balloon for a county fair is designed to carry four 100-kg passengers when it is expanded to its maximum volume. The designers assumed the balloon would operate in ordinary spring temperatures. If, on the day of the fair, the temperature reaches a record-breaking maximum:

A) the balloon will not be able to achieve its maximum volume.
B) more sandbags will be needed for proper operation of the balloon.
C) the total weight the balloon is able to carry will be reduced.
D) once in flight, the balloon cannot be lowered until the ambient temperature drops.

7. A balloon has a mass of 1500 kg with no passengers. A typical passenger weighs 100 kg. A balloon with 5 passengers is floating motionless high above the ground when a 2 kg pelican lands on the balloon. Making which of the following adjustments would allow the balloon to remain floating motionless?

A) Increase the volume of the balloon by 0.1%
B) Slightly cool the air in the balloon
C) Drop a 4-kg sandbag from the balloon
D) None of the above

8. Four 100-kg people are holding a 1200-kg inflated balloon by means of four ropes. Three people let go and the balloon accelerates upward at 2 m/s^2. What is the tension in the rope that the last person is holding?

A) 200 N
B) 400 N
C) 800 N
D) 1200 N

VERBAL STRATEGIES FOR MCAT PHYSICS DRILL: FORCE

Three short paragraphs about hot-air balloons. Notice that almost all of the useful information is contained in paragraph 1.

1. Useful stuff: density of air, forces acting on the balloon, etc.
2. How to make a balloon go up (gee, Toto...)
3. Balloon propellers, elasticity

1. **Pure Science.** It doesn't matter if it's a balloon, a pelican, or the space shuttle that's moving upward and eastward; just mobilize your math here.

2. **Application.** Use your understanding of "net force" and apply it to paragraph 1: If it's motionless, there's no net force. If you dump a sandbag of mass m, what has changed?

3. **Application/Retrieval.** Be canny about this one. You're given the density of air. You aren't given any other information (e.g., the mass of air *inside* the balloon, the temperature of the air inside or outside of the balloon, etc.). Don't panic, thinking this is one of those questions where you need to remember some complicated Physics formula or something. With what you've been given, you must be able to answer this one by calculating the mass of air displaced by the balloon, and then seeing if it's more or less than the combined mass of the balloon and the passengers.

4. **Pure Science.** Or pure common sense: Where is the hot air going to go? And what is it going to do when it gets there? As for A, what would make the stream of hot air split into two? As for D, why would the air circulate counterclockwise as opposed to clockwise?

5. **Application.** See paragraph 1 and note that answer choices A and B can't be right because F_G and F_D have to go on the same side of the equation.

6. **Application.** Use your knowledge of what happens to air when it gets hot (it expands and its density decreases) to answer this one.

7. **Application**—but a little common sense would help, too. B makes no sense; you know what happens to balloons as they cool and shrink. C makes no sense because the pelican only weighs 2 kg. As often happens, you're left with two plausible answer choices—and, in a time crunch, you might want to abandon the calculations and figure that there *is* a way to adjust to one crummy bird landing on the balloon, so answer choice D is rather unlikely.

8. **Pure Science**

MCAT BIOLOGY DRILL: EMBRYOLOGY

The events that contribute to successful fertilization have been intensively studied in the soil nematode *Caenorhabditis elegans*. This organism has several advantages for developmental biology. First, at 1 mm in length, it is small enough to easily culture, and yet the embryos are large enough to see under a compound microscope. Second, its three-day life cycle makes it ideal for genetic studies. Third, *C. elegans* is a self-fertilizing hermaphroditic species — its two sexes are 1) male and 2) self-replicating hermaphrodite. Heterozygous mutations can easily be made homozygous by allowing the hermaphrodites to self-fertilize. Finally the males are missing an X chromosome, and can thus be crossed to normal XX hermaphrodites, facilitating genetic studies.

The entire developmental process from fertilization to adulthood can be observed under the compound microscope. Fertilization takes place in the hermaphrodites as the oocyte passes through the spermatheca, which is where the sperm are stored. If the embryos are collected at this point, the following events can be observed in the light microscope: After the entry of the sperm into the posterior end of the egg, the oocyte nucleus, having been suspended in diakinesis of meiotic prophase I, now completes the meiotic divisions. The excess genetic material is extruded as polar bodies, and the eggshell is secreted, forming an impermeable barrier that protects the developing embryo. The cytoplasmic rearrangements that follow begin with the female pronucleus migrating toward the male pronucleus. A pseudocleavage is observed, where a cleavage furrow appears but disappears without cell division. The pronuclei fuse in the posterior end of the cell, rotate, then move toward the center. At this point, the nucleus of the embryo is formed. Finally, the first division occurs, producing a smaller posterior (P) cell and a larger anterior cell (AB).

Another event that can be observed is the migration of granules from the cytoplasm of the fertilized embryo into the P cell — hence their name, P-granules. As the zygote develops by mitosis into a full organism, the P-granules become sequestered by the cells destined to become the germ line. The function of the P-granules is not known. Exposing the developing embryos to microtubule inhibitors (such as colcemid) blocks the migration of the pronuclei, but does not affect P-granule movement. The inhibitor of actin polymerization, cytochalasin B, has the opposite effect, preventing P-granule segregation, but allowing pronuclei to migrate. The entire process of fertilization, from entry of the sperm to the first cell division, takes about 35 minutes.

Material used in this test passage has been adapted from the following source:

Wood, W. B., *The Nematode, Caenorhabditis elegans,* Cold Spring Harbor monograph series #17; 1988.

1. Which of the following would be the least appropriate organism for studying developmental processes such as fertilization and the ensuing cell divisions?

A) The bacterium, *Escherichia coli*
B) The fruit fly, *Drosophila melanogaster*
C) The African clawed toad, *Xenopus laevis*
D) The human being, *Homo sapiens*

2. Since male nematodes arise as a result of nondisjunction in the XX hermaphrodite, what is their genotype?

A) XY
B) XXX
C) XO
D) XYY

3. What is the ploidy of the fertilized egg?

A) n
B) $2n$
C) $3n$
D) $4n$

4. The spermatheca is where:

A) the progenitor cells of the sperm enter meiosis.
B) sperm are stored in the hermaphrodite.
C) sperm received their protein coat.
D) sperm are stored in the males.

5. Which one of the following accurately describes pseudocleavage?

A) The embryo divides into two cells, which then fuse.
B) A cleavage furrow forms then disappears.
C) A cell membrane begins to form then disappears.
D) Polar bodies are formed.

6. When the pronuclei fuse, which of the following event(s) must occur for cell division to proceed?

    I.   Homologous chromosomes pair
    II. Recombination events occur
    III. Nuclear membranes are reorganized

A) I only
B) I and II only
C) III only
D) I, II, and III

7. The effects of colcemid and cytochalasin B on the embryo suggest that:

    I.   Microfilaments are involved in P-granule migration.
    II. Microfilaments are involved in pronuclear migrations.
    III. Microtubules are involved in pronuclear migrations.
    IV. Microtubules are involved in P-granules migration.

A) I and III only
B) I and IV only
C) II and III only
D) II and IV only

VERBAL STRATEGIES FOR MCAT BIOLOGY DRILL: EMBRYOLOGY

This passage is long and dense; let's map it. There are only three paragraphs here, but each is long and filled with detail. Annotate this passage so that you can find where important categories of information begin and end.

1: Nematode sex
   Research advantages:
   - size
   - 3-day life cycle
   - self-fertilizing hermaphrodite
   - males missing X chromosome
2: Development from fertilization to adulthood
   Map separate events after *oocyte* passes through *spermatheca*
3: Migration of P-granules
   (note: "P cell" is defined at the end of paragraph 2)

1. Pure Science. Don't sweat this one: how much fertilizing do bacteria do?

2. Retrieval. See paragraph 1: the hermaphrodite is XX, and the male is missing an X chromosome; $2 - 1 = ?$

3. Apply your knowledge of the meaning of "ploidy" and "diakinesis of meiotic prophase I" to the information in paragraph 2.

4. Retrieval. You can read the definition of "spermatheca" exactly from paragraph 2.

5. Retrieval: "pseudocleavage" is defined in paragraph 2.

6. Application

7. Retrieval/Application. See paragraph 3: Everything is spelled out for you except the role of microfilaments in pronuclear migration.

In general, using Verbal Reasoning techniques on the science passages will increase your speed and accuracy, and help you to make the most of your scientific knowledge. The MCAT does not demand an exhaustive understanding of biology, chemistry, and physics; rather, it requires you to have a sound basic knowledge of chemical and physical principles, and of the ways in which organisms function. Combine your scientific common sense with your critical reading skills to raise your science scores.

Use your understanding of the three types of science questions (Pure Science, Application, and Retrieval) to shape your solution strategies; make the information in the passages work for you. Don't waste your time working out a solution that the passage spells out for you; conversely, don't bother to search a passage for information that your map indicates isn't there.

SOLUTIONS TO MCAT G-CHEM DRILL: SOLUBILITY

1. **D**   The first three choices are false. O_2 and CO_2 are nonpolar (i.e., have no dipole). As a consequence of the electronegativity of the oxygen atoms, the carbon in carbon dioxide has a slight positive charge and is therefore attracted to any atom with a negative charge. Organic chemists use the term electrophile for an atom or molecule which has some positive charge and nucleophile for an atom or molecule with a negative charge. The oxygen in water is a mild nucleophile.

2. **A**   Based upon the first two equilibrium reactions in the passage, if the concentration of CO_2 were decreased, the first equilibrium would shift to the left. The subsequent reduction in the concentration of H_2CO_3 would cause the second equilibrium to also shift to the left, hence the concentration of H^+ would decrease and blood pH would increase.

3. **D**   The last sentence of paragraph two indicates that the transport efficiency of O_2 is directly related to the blood pH. Therefore, as blood pH decreases, so too does the ability of hemoglobin to transport oxygen. Choice A is incorrect because lipid bilayers are only unstable under extreme conditions. If this statement were true, drinking a glass of soda would be a painful experience. Bicarbonate is one of the most soluble anions, so choice B is not plausible. The passage does not provide any insight as to how the nervous system (choice C) would be impacted by acidosis.

4. **D**   A catalyst increases the rate at which a reaction reaches equilibrium. The addition of a catalyst to a system that is already at equilibrium, like this one, will have no effect.

5. **B**   The solubility of a gas in a liquid decreases with increasing temperature (as illustrated by the fact that CO_2 readily erupts from a bottle of warm soda). Choices A and C will increase the solubility of CO_2 gas in water.

6. **A**   Whenever dealing with electron configuration questions, first eliminate any choices that have the wrong number of electrons. A neutral Fe atom has twenty-six electrons, so Fe^{2+} must have twenty-four electrons. Choices C and D are eliminated because they account for twenty-six and thirty electrons, respectively. Choice A is the correct answer because transition metal elements always lose their valence s electrons (here the $4s$ electrons) before losing any d electrons (choice B is eliminated).

SOLUTIONS TO MCAT PHYSICS DRILL: FORCE

1. **C** The question says that the horizontal component of velocity, $v_x = v \cos \theta$, is 10 m/s. Since $\cos 60° = 1/2$, the total velocity v must be 20 m/s.

2. **C** As explained in the passage, dropping a sandbag does not change the buoyant force, but it does change the gravitational force. When the sandbag is dropped the gravitational force drops by mg while the buoyant force stays the same. Since the two forces originally balanced, the buoyant force is now bigger by mg. Note that the buoyant force is a constant Mg pointing up, while the gravitational force is originally Mg pointing down and then $(Mg - mg)$ pointing down after the sandbag is dropped.

3. **A** For a balloon to float, its density has to be less than that of air. So if the mass in kg divided by the volume in m^3 is less than 1.2 (the density of air), then the balloon floats. If you add the mass of the four people (total = 400 kg) to the mass of the balloon and divide by the volume, you get a value less than 1.2 for Balloon I only.

4. **C** The upward buoyant force (acting along the central axis of the balloon, directly above the flame) on the warmer, less dense air propels it upward. When it reaches the closed top of the balloon, it will be deflected downward. As the warmed air makes its journey, it cools, returns downward, and the cycle repeats.

5. **D** The buoyant force makes it go up; gravity and the drag force hold it back. The net force is zero since its velocity is constant ($a = 0$), so the upward forces are equal to the downward forces, as stated in choice D.

6. **C** Warmer air is less dense than cooler air. Less dense air will give a smaller buoyant force and the balloon will be able to carry less weight.

7. **A** The pelican is 2 kg added on to 2000 kg for the balloon and passengers. This is a 0.1% increase in mass and therefore a 0.1% increase in gravitational force. Increasing the volume by 0.1% will result in a compensating increase in the buoyant force (which is $\rho g V$, where ρ is the density of the air).

8. **D** The rope is pulling a 100-kg person at an acceleration of 2 m/s^2, so the tension (the force on the person exerted by the rope) is just $T = m(g + a) = 100(10 + 2) = 1200$ N.

SOLUTIONS TO MCAT BIOLOGY DRILL: EMBRYOLOGY

1. **A**   Since bacteria are unicellular and reproduce asexually through binary fission, they do not undergo fertilization, and would not be appropriate organisms to study that process. All the other organisms listed reproduce sexually; they can be (and have been!) used for developmental studies (choices B, C, and D can be eliminated).

2. **C**   The question states that the males are the result of nondisjunction in the hermaphrodite. Nondisjunction is the failure of the chromosomes to separate properly during cell division. Since the hermaphrodite has two X chromosomes and no Y chromosomes, and the male arises from the hermaphrodite, the males cannot contain Y chromosomes (choices A and D are wrong; do not always assume male organisms have Y chromosomes). Furthermore, the passage states that the males are missing an X chromosome, not that they have gained one (choice B is wrong).

3. **C**   The sperm nucleus is $1n$ (choice A is wrong), and because the oocyte has not yet completed meiosis I (it is suspended in prophase I), its nucleus is $2n$ (choice B is wrong). Therefore, the ploidy of the fertilized egg is $3n$ ($1n$ sperm + $2n$ oocyte, choice D is wrong).

4. **B**   The passage states that sperm are stored in the spermatheca (choices A and C are wrong) and that this is found in the hermaphrodite (choice D is wrong).

5. **B**   The passage describes pseudocleavage as an event where a cleavage furrow appears, then disappears without cell division (choice A is wrong). Formation of a cleavage furrow does not require the formation of a cell membrane (the existing membrane simply pinches inward, choice C is wrong), and polar bodies are formed during the meiotic division of the oocyte following fertilization (choice D is wrong).

6. **C**   The cell division that occurs after fusion of the pronuclei is mitosis. Pairing of homologous chromosomes (Item I) and recombination events (Item II) occur during meiosis, so these statements are false (choices A, B, and D can be eliminated). Only Item III is true; nuclear membranes must be reorganized both when the pronuclei fuse and when the (now) embryonic nucleus disintegrates during prophase.

7. **A**   The passage states cytochalasin B inhibits actin polymerization (actin filaments are also called microfilaments) and prevents P-granule movement, thus movement of the P-granules must depend on microfilaments; Item I is true (choices C and D can be eliminated). However, cytochalasin B does not affect migration of the pronuclei, so that process must not depend on microfilaments; Item II is false. The passage also states that colcemid inhibits microtubules and prevents migration of the pronuclei, thus migration must depend on microtubules; Item III is true (choice B can be eliminated). However, colcemid does not affect P-granules movement, so that process must not depend on microtubules; Item IV is false.

Writing Sample
Appendix

A.1 NATIONAL COUNCIL OF TEACHERS GUIDELINES FOR NONSEXIST LANGUAGE

Although *man* has carried the dual meaning of adult human and adult male, its meaning is now so closely identified with adult male that the generic use of *man* and other words with masculine markers should be avoided whenever possible.

Examples	Alternatives
mankind	humanity, human beings, people, humankind
the best man for the job	the best person for the job
the common man	the average person, ordinary people
man's achievements	human achievements
man-made	synthetic, manufactured, crafted, machine-made, artificial
manhandle	wrestle, mistreat

The use of *man* in occupational terms when persons holding the jobs could be either female or male should be avoided.

Examples	Alternatives
chairman	coordinator, moderator, director, head, chair
businessman	executive, manager
fireman	firefighter
mailman	mail carrier
policeman, policewoman	police officer

Because English has no generic singular—or common-sex—pronoun, we have used *he*, *his*, and *him* in such expressions as "the student...he." When we constantly personify *the judge, the critic, the executive*, and so forth as male by using the pronoun *he*, we are conditioning ourselves against the idea of a female judge, critic, executive, etc. There are several alternative approaches:

Recast into the Plural

Example	Alternative
Give each student his paper as soon as he is finished.	Give students their papers as soon as they are finished.

Reword to Eliminate Unnecessary Gender Problems

Example	Alternative
The average student is worried about his grades.	The average student is worried about grades.

Replace the Masculine Pronoun with One, You, or (Sparingly) He or She as Appropriate

Example	Alternative
A student who is satisfied with his performance on the pretest can take the post-test.	A student who is satisfied with his or her performance on the pretest can take the post-test.

Alternate Male and Female Examples and Expressions

Example	Alternative
Let each student participate. Has he had a chance to talk? Could he feel left out?	Let each student participate. Has he had a chance to talk? Could she feel left out?

A.2 INTERVIEW AND PERSONAL STATEMENT PREPARATION QUESTIONS

Although the MCAT Writing Sample will not involve prompts concerning medical school or your decision to go there, the work you've done over past months in preparation for this section of the MCAT has helped you to think about important issues. Certainly one of your most important personal issues is your goal of becoming a physician. The following list of questions will prepare you for your interviews and inspire your personal statements. Try to answer a few each week. Answers that are written out will be the most fully formed and the ones you are likely to remember.

1. Where did you grow up and go to school? What was your town/community like? How did this shape your views?
2. What was your family life like? What do your parents do?
3. How is your relationship with your parents and siblings now? How did your family life shape you as a person?
4. Was one particular person an inspiration to you in your life? Why?
5. Why did you choose your undergraduate major?
6. How have you tried to achieve breadth in your undergraduate education?
7. How has your undergraduate research experience, if any, better prepared you for a medical career?
8. If you get into medical school, you will be making a huge time commitment. What *won't* you give up in order to be successful in your medical career?
9. How have the jobs, volunteer opportunities, or extracurricular experiences that you have had made you better prepared for the responsibilities of being a physician?
10. How do you envision using your medical school education?
11. You have stated many humanistic and socially responsible ideals in your essays. What have you done so far to demonstrate those ideals in practice?
12. How would you describe yourself in terms of your greatest strengths and weaknesses?
13. In the broad sense, what travels have you taken, and what exposure to cultures other than your own have you had?
14. Thinking of examples from your recent past, how would you assess your empathy and compassion?
15. What excites you about medicine in general?
16. What do you know about the current trends in our nation's health care system?
17. Tell me what you believe to be the most pressing health issues today. Why?
18. What do you feel are the social responsibilities of a physician?
19. What is the most important social problem facing the United States today, and why?
20. How do you think national health insurance might affect physicians, patients, and society?
21. In what manner and to what degree do you stay in touch with current events?

22. What books, films, or other media come to mind as having been particularly important to your non-science education?
23. What is "success," in your opinion? After practicing medicine for 20 years, what kind of "successes" do you hope to have achieved?
24. What qualities do you look for in a physician? Can you provide an example of a physician who exemplifies these ideals? How does he or she do this?
25. What kind of experiences have you had working with sick people? What have you learned from these experiences?
26. If you could invite four people from the past to dinner, who would they be, and why? What would you talk to them about?
27. Do you have any "blemishes" on your academic record? If so, explain the circumstances.
28. If you are a minority candidate, how do you feel your background uniquely prepares you to be, and will influence you as, a physician?
29. If you are not a minority, how do you feel prepared to meet the diverse needs of a multiethnic, multicultural patient population?
30. To what extent do you feel that you owe a debt to humanity? To what extent do you owe a debt to those less fortunate than you?
31. Who has been influential in your decision to pursue a medical career?
32. What special qualities do you feel you possess that would set you apart from other medical school candidates? What makes you unique or different as a medical school candidate?
33. What sort of expectations will you hold for your classmates?
34. What are the three most important properties you think the ideal medical student should have?
35. What kind of medical schools are you applying to, and why?
36. Pick any specific medical school that you are applying to, and tell the interviewer about it. What goes on there, and what makes it particularly desirable to you?
37. What general and specific skills would you hope an "ideal" medical school experience would give you? How might your ideal school achieve that result?
38. When did you decide to become an MD, and why?
39. Why did you decide to choose medicine and not some other field where you can help others, such as nursing, physical therapy, pharmacology, psychology, education, or social work?
40. How have you tested your motivation to become an MD? Please explain.
41. Where do you see yourself in 5 years? In ten years?
42. Have you decided what to specialize in? How did you reach this decision?
43. What will you do if you are not accepted to medical school this year? Have you an alternative career plan?
44. Is there anything else we have not covered that you feel the interviewer should know about you or your interest in becoming a physician?

GOOD LUCK ON THE MCAT AND IN MEDICAL SCHOOL!

Passage Permissions Information

C.L.R. James, *Beyond A Boundary*. © 1983 Pantheon.

C. Steinwedel, "Making Social Groups, One Person at a Time: The Identification of Individuals by Estate, Religious Confession, and Ethnicity in Late Imperial Russia," *Documenting Individual Identity: The Development of State Practices in the Modern World*. © 2001 Princeton University Press.

Jane Caplan, *Documenting Individual Identity: The Development of State Practices in the Modern World*. © 2001 Princeton University Press.

Jacob Bronowski and Bruce Mazlish, *The Western Intellectual Tradition: From Leonardo to Hegel,* pgs. 350–362. © 1960 Jacob Bronowski and Bruce Mazlish. Reprinted with permission of HarperCollins Publishers.

M. Novak, *The Joy of Sports*. © 1976 Basic Books.

NOTES

NOTES

NOTES

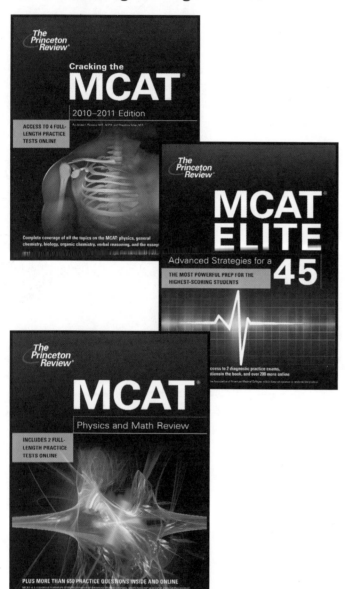